CAMBRIDGE

THE BRIDGE OF SIGHS, ST. JOHN'S
COLLEGE

This Bridge joins the Third Court with the Fourth
or New Court. The building on the right, seen
through the bridge, is the Library, and dates back
to 1624.

Readers are welcome to explore our other editions on our website:
www.vernon-library.com

First published 1907
This edition published by Vernon Library 2019

Publisher's notes and editing are © Vernon Library 2019
All rights reserved.

www.vernon-library.com
www.facebook.com/vernonlibraryuk

Vernon
L I B R A R Y

ISBN-13: 978-1092991742

Preface

"OF making many books there is no end." When I set about writing this book I was ready to believe that the University had not its fair share of the literary output. Cambridge indeed does not appear to suggest, does not lend itself to, the numberless little brochures or hymns of praise which accompany the honoured years of the sister university ; in weighty tomes and valuable *collectanea* of MSS., however, it possesse" works (such as Cooper's Annals, the Cole and Baker MSS., and Willis and Clark's Architectural History) not possessed by Oxford and unrivalled, perhaps, by any English town.

In the middle of last century the invaluable Fuller was the most readily accessible authority, but the last thirty years have seen the publication of the monumental work of Messieurs Willis and Clark, and of the History of the University by Mr. J. Bass Mullinger, while at the same time the slighter literature of the subject has not been neglected.

Cambridge

Nevertheless there is room, I hope, for a short book on the present lines.

It is, I believe, the first time that a chapter on the women's colleges has anywhere appeared, and certainly the first time that such a chapter forms part of an account of the University. I have taken pains to authenticate the description here given, for events which occurred thirty—even twenty—years back are now fading out of remembrance and some of those who took part in them are no longer with us.

A first and last chapter on the origin of universities and on the sister universities have been omitted for the purposes of this volume.

The pleasantest part of my task still remains to be performed—to thank all those, both in and out of Cambridge, who have kindly afforded me facilities, have obtained information on innumerable points, or lightened my labours by lending books. In addition to this welcome assistance my thanks are specially due to Mr. J. Willis Clark, late fellow of Trinity, and Registrary of the University, for sparing time to read the proof sheets of Chapters I. and II.—for sparing time and not sparing trouble ; to the Master of Peterhouse and to Dr. A. W. Verrall (fellow and late tutor of Trinity) for reading the proof sheets of portions of Chapter II. and portions of Chapter III. ; to Mr. C. W. Moule fellow and librarian of Corpus Christi, Mr.

Preface

Ellis H. Minns assistant-librarian, and late fellow, of Pembroke, to Miss M. G. Kennedy, and to the Mistress of Girton; to the Assistant Keeper of MSS. at the British Museum, and the Librarian at Lambeth; to Lord Francis Hervey and Sir Ernest Clarke who kindly supplied some annotated references to the school at Bury from the Curteys Register, and last but not least to the Rev. H. F. Stewart (chaplain of Trinity) and Mrs. Stewart, the former of whom has been good enough to read portions of the proof sheets of Chapter IV.

For any opinions expressed I am, of course, alone responsible.

M. A. R. T.

February 1907.

Contents

CHAPTER I

THE ORIGIN OF THE UNIVERSITY OF CAMBRIDGE

The northern schools—legends—the town—the river—the fen monasteries —the school of glomery—the religious orders—the jurisdiction of Ely—the clerk and the religious.

School and university—Stourbridge fair—the university in the xiii century—foundation of endowed scholars—hostels   .   1-51

CHAPTER II

THE COLLEGES

The university and the colleges—the collegiate system—eras of college building—Peterhouse—Michaelhouse—*collegium* and *aula*—Clare— college statutes—architectural scheme of a college — Pembroke— founders of colleges — Gonville — Trinity Hall — Corpus Christi— Cambridge in 1353—Chaucer at Cambridge—the schools, library, the university printers and the Pitt Press, the senate house—King's— King's College chapel—Cambridge college chapels—Queens'—English sovereigns at Cambridge — S. Catherine's — Jesus — Christ's — Lady Margaret and Bishop Fisher—S. John's—Magdalene—King's Hall and Trinity College—college libraries—gateways—Caius—monks in Cambridge—Emmanuel—Sidney Sussex—Downing—public hostels— nationality of founders and general scope of their foundations—university and college revenues   52-156

ix

Cambridge

CHAPTER III

THE UNIVERSITY AS A DEGREE-GIVING BODY

Meaning of a degree—the kinds of degrees—the bachelor—the ancient exercises of the schools called acts, opponencies, and responsions—the sophister — questionist — determiner—master — regent master — the degree of *M.A.*—introduction of written examinations—the tripos.

The subjects of study and examination : the *trivium* and *quadrivium* —grammar—Aristotle's logic—rhetoric—the three learned faculties— the doctorate—development in university studies—the development of the mathematical tripos—the senior wrangler—the classical tripos —Greek at Cambridge—the moral sciences tripos—philosophy at Cambridge—the natural sciences tripos—science at Cambridge—the language triposes—lists of the triposes—changing value of the examination tests—the double tripos—present conditions for the *B.A.* degree —modern changes in the examinations—standard of the ordinary and honour degree, examples.

Method of tuition at Cambridge—the lecture—the class—the weekly paper —the professorial chairs—readerships—lectureships—Lambeth degrees — degrees by royal mandate — honorary degrees — the "modern subjects"—and the idea of a university .   .   157-201

CHAPTER IV

COLLEGIATE AND SOCIAL LIFE AT THE UNIVERSITY

University and college officers :—chancellor and vice-chancellor—the senate —graces—proctors—bedells—the master of a college—the vice-master or president—the fellows—unmarried and married fellows—the combination room—dons' clubs—'Hobson's choice'—the dons of last century—classes of students :—scholar—pensioner—fellow-commoner —sizar—age of scholars—privileges of peers—position of the sizar— college quarters and expenses—'non-colls'—early discipline—jurisdiction of the university in the town—present discipline :—the proctors —fines—'halls'—'chapels'—town lodgings—expulsion—rustication —'gates'—the tutor—academical dress—cap and gown—the undergraduates' day—the gyp—the college kitchen—'hall'—'wines'—teas

Contents

—the May term—idleness—rioting—modern studies and tripos entries
—athletics—the Union Society—Sunday at Cambridge—scarlet days
—academic terms and the long vacation—multiplication of scholarships—class from which the academic population has been drawn and
careers of university men :—the Church—the rise of an opulent
middle class—the aristocratic era—English conception of the benefits
of a university—examples of the classes from which the men have
come—recruiting grounds of the university—popularity of colleges—
numbers in the colleges—religion at Cambridge—Cambridge politics—
— university settlement at Camberwell — married dons and future
changes   202-249

CHAPTER V

UNIVERSITY MEN AND NATIONAL MOVEMENTS

Men who owe nothing to a university—40 great Englishmen—Cambridge
    men : the scientists, the poets, the dramatists, other literary men, the
    philosophers, the churchmen, lawyers, and physicians, the statesmen.
        National movements : King John and the barons—the peasants'
    revolt — York and Lancaster — the new world — Charles and the
    Parliament—James II. and the University—the Declaration of In-
    dulgence — the Nonjurors — William and Mary and Cambridge
    whiggery—Jacobitism and Toryism at Cambridge in the reign of
    Anne—George I. and Cambridge—modern political movements.
        Religious movements : Lollards, the early reformers, the question
    of the divorce, Lutheranism at Cambridge, later reformers and the
    Reformation, the English bible, and service books, the Cambridge
    martyrs, the Puritans, the Presbyterians, the Independents, the
    Latitudinarians, the Deists, the evangelical movement, the Tractarian
    movement, anti-calvinism.
        Intellectual movements : the New Learning and the age of
    Elizabeth—the Royal Society—the Cambridge Platonists—modern
    science.
        Connexion of Cambridge founders and eminent men with the
    university—early Cambridge names—a group of great names in the
    xiii and xiv centuries—Cambridge men in the historical plays of
    Shakespeare—genealogical tables of founders—Cantabrigians from the
    xv century to the present day—Cambridge men who have taken no
    degree   250-309

Cambridge

CHAPTER VI

GIRTON AND NEWNHAM

Etheldreda of Ely and Hild of Whitby connect the school of York with the monastery of Ely—English women and education—the four "noble and devoute countesses" and two queens at Cambridge—the rise of the movement for university education—two separate movements—Girton—Newnham—rise of the university lecture movement—Anne Clough—the Newnham Halls and Newnham College—the first triposes—the "Graces" of 1881—social life at the women's colleges—character and choice of work among women—the degree—status of women's colleges at Cambridge and Oxford—and status elsewhere . . . 310-360

List of Illustrations

1. The Bridge of Sighs, S. John's College . . *Frontispiece*

FACING PAGE

2. Norman Church of the Holy Sepulchre . . . 4

3. Market Square 10

4. The Old Gateway of King's College 16

5. S. John's College Gateway and Tower from Trinity
Street 24

6. Oriel Window of the Hall, Trinity Great Court . . 34

7. The Old Castle Inn 50

8. Peterhouse from the Street. 56

9. Peterhouse—The First Court 58

10. Peterhouse from the Fellows' Garden 62

11. Clare College and Bridge from the Cam—Autumn
Evening 64

12. Clare College and Bridge from the Avenue . . . 66

13. The Hall of Clare College 68

14. The Old Court, Pembroke College 72

15. A Court and Cloisters in Pembroke College. . . 74

16. Trinity Hall 78

17. S. Botolph's Church and Corpus College from the
Steps of the Pitt Press, Trumpington Street . . 80

Cambridge

		FACING PAGE
18.	The Old Court, Corpus Christi College . . .	82
19.	S. Benedict's Church from Free School Lane . .	84
20.	King's College Gateway and Chapel—Twilight Effect .	90
21.	Gateway of King's College, King's Parade . . .	98
22.	King's College Chapel and the Entrance Court, from the Fellows' Buildings	100
23.	King's College Chapel and the Fellows' Buildings .	102
24.	King's College Chapel Interior from the Choir . .	104
25.	The Hall of King's College	106
26.	Entrance Gateway, Queens' College	108
27.	An Old Court in Queens' College	110
28.	Queens' College from the River Front . . .	112
29.	Gateway of S. Catherine's College	114
30.	Gateway of Jesus College	116
31.	The Gateway of Christ's College from S. Andrew's Street	118
32.	The Fellows' Building in Christ's College . . .	120
33.	Milton's Mulberry Tree in the Fellows' Garden, Christ's College	122
34.	The Gateway and Tower of S. John's College . .	124
35.	Entrance to S. John's College Chapel from the First Court	126
36.	The Second Court of S. John's College . . .	128
37.	The Combination Room, S. John's College . .	130
38.	The Library Window, S. John's College, from the Bridge of Sighs	132
39.	Old Gateway and Bridge	134
40.	Pepys' Library, Magdalene College	136
41.	The Gateway of Trinity College	138

List of Illustrations

FACING PAGE

42. The Great Court, Trinity College 140
43. The Hall of Trinity College from Nevile's Court . 142
44. Nevile's Gate, Trinity College 144
45. Trinity College Bridge and Avenue, with Gate leading into the New Court 146
46. Caius College and the Senate House from S. Mary's Passage. 148
47. The Gate of Virtue, Gonville and Caius College . . 150
48. The Gate of Honour, Caius College 152
49. The First Court of Emmanuel College . . . 154
50. The Old Court in Emmanuel College . . . 156
51. The Lake and New Buildings, Emmanuel College . 158
52. The Cloister Court, Sidney Sussex College . . . 160
53. Downing College from the Entrance in Regent Street . 162
54. Trumpington Street from Peterhouse 172
55. Peashill 180
56. Old Houses near S. Edward's Church and S. Edward's Passage 184
57. Market Street and Holy Trinity Church . . . 192
58. Great S. Mary's, from Trinity Street 196
59. The Lake in Botanic Gardens 210
60. Parker's Piece 216
61. Trinity Bridge, King's College Chapel in the Distance . 224
62. The Tower of S. John's College Chapel from the River 238
63. University Boat-houses on the Cam—Sunset . . 244
64. Ditton Corner, on the Cam 248
65. The Fitzwilliam Museum—Evening 256
66. University Church of Great S. Mary 270

Cambridge

		FACING PAGE
67. Addenbrooke's Hospital in Trumpington Street .	.	290
68. The Great Bridge—Bridge Street . . .	.	312
69. View of Cambridge from the Castle Hill .	.	316
70. Girton College—Evening	.	320
71. The Boathouse on Robinson Crusoe's Island	.	324
72. Queens' Lane—the Site of the old Mill Street .	.	326
73. Merton Hall	.	328
74. Newnham College, Gateway . . .	.	338
75. The Granary on the Cam	.	342
76. Grantchester Mill	.	346
77. Madingley Windmill	.	352

Map at end of Volume.

*The Illustrations in this volume have been engraved and printed in England
by the Hentschel Colourtype Process.*

A Bibliography

ACKERMANN.——History of the University of Cambridge. 2 vols. 1815.

ANSTEY, H.——Munimenta Academica. Rolls Series. London 1868.

ATKINSON, THOMAS DINHAM.——Cambridge Described & Illustrated, with an introduction by John Willis Clark, *M.A.* 1897.

BAKER MSS.
> 42 vols. collected & compiled by Thomas Baker fellow of S. John's College, 19 of which are preserved at the University, the others at the Brit. Mus.

BAKER—MAYOR.——History of the College of S. John the Evangelist.
Cambridge 1869.
> The Baker MSS. (Harl. MS. 1039) relating to S. John's edited by J. E. B. Mayor.

BALL, W. W. ROUSE.——Trinity College, Cambridge. London 1906.
> In the College Monograph series.

BARNWELL CHARTULARY.——Brit. Mus. Harl. MSS. No. 3601.

BENTHAM, JAMES.——History & Antiquities of Ely. Norwich 1812.

„ —STEVENSON.——A supplement to the 2nd ed. of Mr. Bentham's History & Antiquities of Ely. Norwich 1817.

CAIUS, JOHN.——De Antiquitate Cantebrigiensis Academiae.
Londini, in aedibus Johannis Day 1574.

CAMBRIDGE ANTIQUARIAN SOCIETY'S PUBLICATIONS.

CAMBRIDGE PORTFOLIO.——Edited by Rev. J. J. Smith, fellow & tutor of Gonville & Caius. 1840.

Cambridge

CARTER, EDMUND.——History of the University of Cambridge to 1753. 2 vols. London 1753.

> With MS. notes by Cole, in the Bodleian Library. (Containing the list of the chancellors.)

CLARK, JOHN WILLIS.——Cambridge. Brief historical & descriptive Notes. Illustrated. 1890.

„ ——The Observances in use at the Augustinian Priory of S. Giles & S. Andrew at Barnwell, Cambridgeshire. Edited with a translation & glossary. Cambridge 1897.

COLE MSS.——(Harleian MSS.)

> 60 vols., bequeathed by William Cole of King's College to the British Museum.

COOPER, CHARLES HENRY.——Annals of Cambridge. 4 vols. Cambridge 1843.

> An additional pamphlet gives the Statutes of Victoria.

„ ——Memorials of Cambridge. 3 vols. Cambridge 1860-66.

> The edition of 1880 is enlarged from the work of Le Keux.

„ ——Memoir of Margaret Countess of Richmond & Derby. Cambridge 1874.

„ & THOMPSON COOPER.——Athenae Cantabrigienses. Cambridge 1858-1861.

> Vol. i. 1500-1585. Vol. ii. 1586-1609.

DYER, GEORGE.——The Privileges of the University of Cambridge. 2 vols. London 1824.

> The Statutes of Elizabeth are printed in vol. i. 1559.

„ ——History of the University & Colleges of Cambridge. 2 vols. 1814.

EVERETT, WILLIAM.——On the Cam. London, S. O. Beeton, 1866.

FULLER, THOMAS, D.D.——The History of the University of Cambridge (to the year 1634). Edited by Marmaduke Prickett, chaplain of Trinity, & Thomas Wright, of Trinity. Cambridge 1840.

HARE, ROBERT, of Gonville & Caius.——Register of Charters, Liberties, & Privileges of the University & the Town.

> The nucleus of Dyer's *Privileges*. The original is in the public chest of the University, & there is a copy, made by Hare, in the Registry.

HOBHOUSE, EDMUND, Bishop of Nelson, N.Z.——Sketch of the Life of Walter de Merton. Oxford 1859.

Bibliography

HUMPHRY, G. M., *M.D., F.R.S.* (late Professor of Anatomy).——Guide to Cambridge, the Town, University, & Colleges.　　Cambridge 1883.

HUNDRED ROLLS (for Cambridge).——*Rotuli Hundredorum, temp. Hen. III. et Edw. I. in Turr. Lond. &c. asservati.* Record Commission. 1812-1818.

LOGGAN, DAVID, *S.P.D.*——Cantabrigia Illustrata.　　　　　　1690.
　　Containing the University costumes of the xvii century.

MASTERS—LAMB.——History of the College of Corpus Christi in the University of Cambridge. (With additional matter & a continuation to the present time, by John Lamb.)　　　　Cambridge 1831.

"MIND," a quarterly review of Psychology & Philosophy.　Vol. i.
　　　　　　　　　　　　　　　　Williams & Norgate 1876.

MULLINGER, J. BASS.——History of the University of Cambridge from the earliest times to the Royal Injunctions of 1535.　University Press 1874.

　　　　"　　——History of the University of Cambridge from the Royal Injunctions of 1535 to the Accession of Charles I. University Press 1884.

PARKER, MATTHEW.——Academiae Historia Cantabrigiensis.

　　　　"　　RICHARD, *B.D.*, fellow of Caius (1622).——History & Antiquities of the University of Cambridge.
　　　　　　　　　　　London, printed at the Hat & Star, 1721.

PEACOCK, GEORGE, *D.D.*, Dean of Ely, *V.P.R.S.*——Observations on the Statutes of the University of Cambridge. London & Cambridge 1841.

　　　　"　　——Appendix to Observations on the University Statutes.　1841.

SEARLE, W. G.——Ingulf & the Historia Croylandensis—an investigation attempted.　Camb. Ant. Soc. Pub. xxvii.　　　Cambridge 1894.

STOKYS, MATTHEW, & JOHN BUCK.——The Bedells' Books.
　　In Cole MSS. & in Peacock.

TAYLOR, RICHARD.——Index Monasticus. The Abbeys & other Monasteries formerly established in the diocese of Norwich & kingdom of East Anglia.　　　　　　　　　　　London 1821.

THOMPSON, ALEXANDER HAMILTON.——Cambridge & its Colleges. Illustrated by E. H. New.　(Little Library.)　　　　　　1898.

TULLOCH, PRINCIPAL.——Rational Theology in England in the xvii Century.　2 vols.　　　　　　　　　　　　　1872.

VENN, JOHN, *Sc.D., F.R.S.*——Biographical History of Gonville & Caius College (1349-1897).　3 vols.　　　　Cambridge 1897-1902.

Cambridge

WILLIS, ROBERT, and CLARK, J. W.——The Architectural History of the University of Cambridge & of the Colleges of Cambridge & Eton. 4 vols. University Press 1886

WORDSWORTH, CHRISTOPHER, fellow of Peterhouse.——Scholae Academicae. University Press 1877.

    „   ——Social Life at the English Universities in the xviii Century. Cambridge 1874.

To the above must be added the College Histories, published by F. E. Robinson, London.

Peterhouse (Walker) 1906.
Clare (Wardale) 1899.
Gonville and Caius (Venn) 1901.
Trinity Hall (Malden) 1902.
Corpus Christi (Stokes) 1898.
King's (Austen Leigh) 1899.
Queens' (J. H. Gray) 1899.

S. Catherine's (Bp. of Bristol) 1902.
Jesus (A. Gray) 1902.
Christ's (Peile) 1900.
S. John's (Mullinger) 1901.
Magdalene (Preston) 1904.
Emmanuel (Shuckburgh) 1904.
Sidney (Edwards) 1899.
Downing (Pettit Stevens) 1899.

No complete bibliography of the subject—of the MSS. or printed matter—has been attempted. The above is a list of some Cambridge documents and books most of which have been consulted personally by the writer of the present volume.

CAMBRIDGE

CHAPTER I

I. *pp.* 1-30.

The northern schools—legends—the town—the river—the fen
monasteries—the school of glomery—the religious orders—
the jurisdiction of Ely—the clerk and the religious.

In Saxon times our schools of learning were grouped
round York the Roman centre of Britain, which represented not only the Roman tradition but the vigorous
Christianity of the north. It is this auspicious combination which nourished for over a hundred years the
university spirit before universities, carried through
Alcuin this spirit to the Continent, and eventually
brought learning hand in hand with Christianity to
Germany. Whatever may be true as to the distribution
of talent in England later in its history, in the vii and
viii centuries our great school was to be found at
York, and England's learned men hailed from the
kingdom of Northumbria.

Cambridge

The School of York. York and Rome. The School of York originated in the school established by Hild for the Celtic clan community over which she presided ; and Caedmon the first English poet, John of Beverley, Wilfrid of York, Bede the father of English learning, and the scholar Alcuin who has been called " minister of Public Instruction to Charlemagne " were the noble fruit it put forth. Its history was determined at the Synod of Whitby where Hild appears as the link between the Celtic Aidan and the Roman Wilfrid, a representative figure of the genius of English religion. She had been baptized by Paulinus but her sympathies were with the Scottish Church. The victory of Wilfrid did not destroy that dual character of English Christianity which accompanied its mind and its liturgy to the last days of the religious domination of Rome in the realm ; but through this victory York again entered the hegemony of Latin civilisation, was bound afresh to the overshadowing tradition of Rome, and thenceforth sealed with an European character its schools of learning.

York and Canterbury. And through York Rome again takes possession of England. In the vii century Christianity in Kent had ceased to be the Christianity of Augustine ; with the fall of Edwin Northumbria forgot the Christianity of Paulinus ; but the immediate result of the Roman victory at York was the mission of Theodore to Canterbury, where the episcopal school he inaugurated shared the honours though it never rivalled the learning of the School of York.

Origin of Cambridge University

York and Cambridge. The legends which relate that Bede came to study at Cambridge in 682, that Alcuin was one of its first doctors in theology, and that Alfred of Beverley, "the Treasurer," studied there, legends already known in the time of Chaucer, symbolise the spiritual relationship between the School of York and Cambridge. Those large elements which had operated at York—that combination of the shaping power of Rome with the insular force of Angle, Celt, and Saxon—had in them the promise of the English genius and the English character ; and one seems to trace the same wide tradition, the operation of similarly large elements, in the future seat of learning at Cambridge. The university of Chaucer, Spenser, and Milton, of Fox, Fisher, and Langton, of Ascham, Bacon, Newton, Whewell, and Lightfoot, may well be regarded as the spiritual descendant of the School which first held the torch of English learning never again to be entirely extinguished in this country.[1]

Early legends of the origin of Cambridge. Further down, in the east of England, there in fact existed a still earlier school than the schools at York, established in 635 by Siegebert king of East Anglia. The site of this school was very probably Seaham or Dunwich ; but legend connects it with Cambridge, and the memory of King Siegebert is kept green in the annual commemorations of the university.[2] A legend referring

---

[1] Cf. iii. p. 172.

[2] Siegebert, who had been baptized in France, on returning to his own country and becoming king of East Anglia "desiring to imitate those

3

NORMAN CHURCH OF THE HOLY
SEPULCHRE

Believed to be the oldest of the four round Churches
in England, built about 1120-40.

Cambridge

to the same period connects Cambridge with Canterbury. According to this, Ethelbert of Kent by the command of Gregory the Great assigned a residence at Cambridge for some learned men from " the village of Canterbury " (598-604). Legend also relates that Edward the Elder founded the Cambridge schools when he was repairing the ravages of the Danes in East Anglia, and gave to them a charter of incorporation.

The fact not only that the neighbourhood of Cambridge, like Canterbury and York, was the site of an early Anglo-Saxon school, but that Cambridge was itself a Roman station, gave rise in its turn to another legend of the origin of the university. According to this it was founded by Cantaber the son-in-law of King Gurgentius and brother of Partholin the Spanish king of Ireland, who gave his name to it, a name, no doubt, formed from the *Cantabri*, the Spanish auxiliaries mentioned by Caesar. Lydgate's panegyric of the university shows us that a tradition of its antiquity made up of both Roman and School of York elements received credence in the xiv century ; nay, remembering that Cambridge had been a Roman town, men found no difficulty in supposing that Caesar had carried off a supply of Cambridge dons to the capital of the world.

things which he had seen well ordered in France, at once set up a school in which youths could be instructed in letters, and was helped herein by bishop Felix who came to him from Kent, and who supplied him with paedagogues and masters after the custom of the men of Kent."—Bede, cap. xviii.

4

Origin of Cambridge University

The town of Cambridge. The Roman fortress lay on the left bank of the river, at the hamlet of Grantchester (*Granta, castrum*); the town of Cambridge proper, on the same bank, being called *Grantabrigge*. Here it was that William the Conqueror's castle was built on the site of a British earthwork still known as Castle Mound, and here British as well as Roman coins and other Roman remains have been discovered. The British town of Cair-Graunth has been identified with both sites ; while the Roman station marked in Saxon maps as *Camboritum* or *Camboricum* has hitherto been confounded with the site of the Norman fortress. We do not know where Camboricum was, but we no longer identify it with Cambridge.[1]

In the time of Bede, and earlier, Grantchester was a desolate ruin,[2] but Grantabridge was a place of some importance at the time of the Domesday survey, and we find that nearly thirty of its four hundred houses were destroyed to make room for William's castle.[3] The town which is still called Grantabridge in the Anglo-Saxon Chronicle, in Domesday, and in Henry I.'s

[1] Cair-Graunt means the Castle on the Granta, and is changed in the A-S. Chronicle for *Grantacaester*.

[2] "*Civitatulam quandam desolatam . . . quae lingua anglorum Granta-caestir vocatur.*"—Bede, cap. xix.

[3] The castle, ruinous by the middle of the xv c., was quarried to supply stone for King's College and other university buildings in that and the next century. Edw. III. had quarried it for King's Hall, and Hen. IV. granted more of the stone for King's Hall chapel. Finally Mary gave the stone to Sir Robert Huddleston in 1557 for his new house at Sawston : "Hereby that stately structure, anciently the ornament of Cambridge, is at this day reduced next to nothing," writes Fuller.

5

Cambridge

charter, becomes Cantebruge before the middle of the xii century, and Cantebrigge in Chaucer.[1]

Roman roads. Two great Roman roads met near the Castle Mound, the one being the only way across the pathless fens, running from the coast of Norfolk through Ely to Cambridge and thence on to Cirencester and Bath ; the other—*via Devana*—was the great highway (along the site of the present Huntingdon road) which led from Cambridge out of the fen country, stretching from Chester[2] on the northwest to Colchester on the south-east. This road crossed the only high ground in the flat country round Cambridge—the low range of hills called the Gogmagogs and Castle Mound itself.

The river. The river Granta gave its name to the British and Roman towns (Cair-Graunth, Grantchester), to the university city, and to the whole shire. The Granta or Cam, for it is now called by both names, is made by the confluence of two small streams which meet beyond Grantchester ; the eastern branch, the

---

[1] A.-S. Chron., *Grantebrycge.* Domesday, *Grentebrige.* Henry I.'s charter (1118) *Grantebrugeshire* and borough of *Grantebruge.* In Matilda's grant of the earldom of Cambridge (before 1146) *Cantebruggescire.* Temp. John, *Cantebrige, Cantebrig.* Temp. Hen. III., *Cantebr.* (1218) *Cantabr.* (1231, 1261) *Cantabrigiense. Cauntebrigg.* and *Cantebrigg.* in the same deed relating to the Merton scholars (1269-70) Brit. Mus. Add. MSS. 5832. f. 74. Hundred Rolls (1276-9) *Cantebr.* In a document of Hugh de Balsham's, 1275, *Cantabr.* Barnwell Chartulary, circ. 1295, *Cantebrige, Cantebrigesire, burgum Cantebrigiae.* In the earliest college statutes (1324) *Cantebrigia.* In Chaucer, Cantebrigge, Cantebregge. In the first half of the next (xvth) century we have *Cambrugge* in a petition sent by King's Hall to the Franciscans. Cf. also note *infra* p. 7, on the name of the river.

[2] The Roman *Deva.*

6

Origin of Cambridge University

Granta, rising in Cambridgeshire, the western, the Rhee, in Hertfordshire. What other river in England can boast that it has been celebrated by our poets in every age ? For Milton it is *Camus*, for Byron *Granta*, both names serve the muse of Gray ; it is Wordsworth's *Cam*, but Spenser calls it *Guant*, and also *Ouse*, the name it takes before reaching Ely, although the waters of the " plenteous Ouse " join the Granta much lower down.[1]

The ford. The important thing about the river, which determined the history of the town on its banks, was that between Grantabridge and Grantchester it was fordable, and here only could it be traversed by those going to and from the east of England and the Midlands. Near Trumpington, indeed, a part of the Via

[1] Caius, writing in 1447, says that the town is divided into two parts by the Canta and the Rhee, called earlier le Ee ; and by Spenser the Cle. We have *Granta*, *Guant*, and *Cante* : the *r* dropped out, and *G* was replaced by *C* in the name of both town and river (see *supra*). Cante does not seem to have been the name of a river at all. The river bank by Castle Mound is spoken of in the xiv c. as " the common bank called Cante " : one arm at least of the Cambridge river was known simply as " the water " [Prof. Skeat has pointed out that Ee is the xii, xiii, and xiv c. form of the A-S. *éa*, cognate with *aqua*] and for centuries there would appear to have been no need for any other name. In Henry of Huntingdon's Chronicle (1130) the river is called the *Grenta* ; but Lydgate writes

> And of this noble vniuersitie
> Sett on this ryver which is called Cante.

In the same decade Spenser knows only the Guant (*Faery Queene, Book iv. Canto xi.* 1590) and Camden for the first time tells us that it was called both Granta and Cam (*alii Grantam, Camum alii.* 1586) the name used as we have seen by Milton. If there was no river Cante *à fortiori* there was no river Cam ; for the *m* in the name of the town is only another change in the original first syllable of Cambridge. See *footnote*, p. 6.

Cambridge

Devana had been carried by the Romans right through the water.[1]

In the ix century the province of Cambridge—the *Flavia Caesariensis* of the Romans—formed part of the Danelagh.[2] Throughout the middle ages, writes Mr. J. W. Clark, the town "was a frontier fortress on the edge of the great wild . . . which stretched as far as the Wash": and no place suffered more from invasion and fire. The Danes completely destroyed it in 870, after the capture of York ; and the fortunes of the two cities were again linked two hundred years later when William, fresh from the reduction of the northern capital, turned A.D. 1068-1070. his steps to Cambridge and made it the centre of his operations against the outstanding isle of Ely. A second destruction at the hands of the Danes occurred in 1010, and in 1088 Cambridge was again devastated with the rest of Cambridgeshire by Robert Curthose. This, however, led to a vigorous re-instatement of the city by Henry I. who showed it many marks of favour. A.D. 1102. In the second year of his reign he ordered the townsmen to pay their dues to the bedells, and about this

[1] Trumpington is 2 miles S., Grantchester 2 miles S.S.W. of the town.

[2] 878. It was from the town (Grantebrycge) that the Danes set forth, two years before, and surprised Alfred at Wareham. In the time of Ethelred, just before the Danish invasion, Cambridge was a royal mint ; it was so in the time of the Conqueror, and had a Danish 'moneyer,' and continued to be so under the Plantagenet kings : even Henry VI. coined money at Cambridge. In Domesday the town is described as a "Hundred," a description, says Stubbs, belonging to big towns with large surrounding common land—Norwich and Canterbury are similarly described. After the history of the town became merged in that of the university, two parliaments were summoned there ; in 1388, and in 1447 (afterwards held at Bury-St.-Edmund's). For the city, see also p. 36 and v. p. 260.

time the ferry which had hitherto been "a vagrant
. . . even anywhere where passengers could get waft-
age over," [1] was established at Cambridge, bringing
traffic in its train.   In 1106 the first signs of returning
prosperity were seen in the settlement of the Jews.
The Cambridge Jewry was near the market-place, and
the Cambridge Jews were noted for their "civil
carriage," none of the customary outrageous charges
being brought against them there. [2]   Twelve years later,   A.D. 1118.
the king gave a charter to the burgesses.

Cambridge was at no period of its history a great
or even a prosperous commercial centre.   East Anglia
has always been a corner of England to itself, not on
the direct line to anywhere, and offering very few points
of vantage to the statesman or the merchant.   The
course of a river determines the history of a town, as
it first determines its site.   This is well exemplified
in the histories of the Granta and the "Isis."   The
"Isis" is a reach of the Thames, [3] and this fact with its
moral political and commercial implications has coloured
the whole history of the town on its banks—everything
came to Oxford by the river from London, and dignified
alderman or humble bargeman shared with the lesser
centre the life of the greater.   The Granta and Ouse
have a history in every sense the opposite of this.
Through the centuries, long before Oxford was a town

---

[1] Fuller, p. 7.

[2] The edict expelling the Jews from England dates from 1290, and the
Jews left Cambridge the year following.

[3] The fancy appellations Cam and Isis appear to have both been due
to Camden.   They are not heard of before his work appeared in 1586.

MARKET SQUARE

This picture represents what is called Half Market, which takes place on Wednesday. Market day, properly speaking, is on Saturday, when the square is filled with stalls. The church is Great St. Mary's, and King's College Chapel is seen in the distance on the left.

Cambridge

at all,[1] the sounds we hear are the thud of the Ely barge as it strikes the bank of deserted Grantchester, and Sexberga's messengers borrow from the neighbourhood of the future university the sepulture for the founder of Ely—the gift of a civilisation still older than hers.[2] Or, three hundred and fifty years later, the chant of the Ely monks is wafted out upon the water as Canute bids his men rest a moment on their oars to listen

Merrily sang the monks of Ely when Canute the king rowed by.

The convent messenger, the Danish king, the Norman conqueror, may come up the water, but they make the stir they find, and the river leaves no trace behind them.

So the university town owes nothing to adventitious causes ; makes no bid for public favour, and has no tentacles to put forth to obtain it. But the river has, nevertheless, determined its activities as well as its reticences. It will give rise to a fair, and Stourbridge fair will become one of the greatest fairs in the kingdom. The fish market was another source of traffic. Ely and Cambridge fish were celebrated— Bede, indeed, derives "Ely" from the abundance of its eels, although *helyg* (the willow) seems the more

[1] Cambridge, writes Doctor Jessopp, existed as a town and fortress "a thousand years before Oxford was anything but a desolate swamp, or at most a trumpery village, where a handful of Britons speared eels, hunted for deer, and laboriously manufactured earthenware pots."

[2] They found a Roman stone coffin, sculptured ; one, apparently, of many known to have been left there, for portions of Roman sarcophagi are even now to be seen walled up in the church at Grantchester. Bede, cap. xix.

Origin of Cambridge University

probable original.[1] The kings of England patronised this market, Henry III. sending for his fish to Cambridge even when he was staying at Oxford ; and Chaucer is careful to note that the Cambridge miller was an angler, skilled in mending his nets.[2] The isle of Ely, so-called because cut off by river and mere from the rest of Cambridgeshire, was proverbial for the turbulence of its population, and the men of Ely drew the men of Cambridge into their quarrels, or harried them on their own account. Cambridge Castle was built as an outpost against the English earls who with Hereward resisted the Conqueror at Ely ; it was at Ely that another determined stand was made by Simon de Montfort's followers after Cambridge had been regained for John ; and Henry III. had to bring relief to the university town when its neighbours burnt and plundered it during the years 1266-1270. The two centres were inseparable for weal or woe, and the intellectual as well as the political life of Cambridge was coloured for centuries by the activities of its neighbour.

The fen monasteries. The proximity of the great fen monasteries must be reckoned as the chief factor in the earlier scholastic—the pre-university—history of Cambridge. Ely, Crowland, Bury-St.-Edmund's and

[1] The pollard willow is the chief denizen of the fens.
[2] The water runs flows and dances through the Cantabrigian's life. The king's and the bishop's mills, Newnham mill just beyond, the Mill street, and the hythes, all courted constant recognition. As at Ely, the *hythes* were the small trading ports along the river : there was Dame Nichol's hythe, Cornhythe, Flaxhythe, Salthythe, Clayhythe.

11

Cambridge

Peterborough were among the most important and the most ancient religious houses in the country. Crowland and Bury both had abbey schools influenced, as we shall see, in the early xii century by the famous school at Orléans; Ely had besides an episcopal school, and as monastery, school, and cathedral, was in constant domestic relations with her neighbour of Cambridge.[1]

Crowland. Among these famous houses, surrounded by undrained marshes, like islands, forbidding and yet inviting access, none was more isolated than Crowland which, reared as Venice upon piles and stakes driven into the marshy ground, shone like a beacon out of the mysterious silence and solitude. The story that abbot A.D. 1109. Joffred of Crowland sent four Orléans monks full of new learning to his Cambridge manor of Cottenham[2] early in the xii century, who held disputations in a large barn, has been shown to be entirely legendary. Yet the moment chosen by the self-styled continuator of

---

[1] For the vii c. foundation of *Ely* see chap. vi. p. 311. The see dates from 1107, when the minster became a cathedral. *Crowland*, in Lincolnshire on the borders of Cambridgeshire, was built over the tomb of Guthlac, a prince and a saint of the house of Mercia, in the vii c. *Bury* rose after the martyrdom of the East Anglian king Edmund (870) c. 903; it did not become a monastery till 1020. *Peterborough* was founded by Wulfhere, king of Mercia from 659 to 674: it formed part of the diocese of Lincoln till the xvi c. Ramsey and Thorney were other fen monasteries. Ramsey was on the borders, in Huntingdonshire, but Thorney was in Cambridgeshire. Peterborough and Thorney with Ely and Crowland were sacked by the Danes in 870. All these were 'black Benedictine' houses.

[2] Cottenham 7 miles north of Cambridge; the benefice became an advowson of Chatteris abbey in the isle of Ely, and was bestowed by the abbess on Warham in 1500.

Origin of Cambridge University

Ingulph is singularly felicitous.[1]   We know nothing of any sources of information which may have been open to a xiv century forger ; but it is certain that some such scholastic movements were fermenting in Cambridge in the xii century.   Joffred had been prior at Orléans which was a flourishing school, and we have evidence that this school actually influenced the university of Cambridge.   The abbey house of Crowland was burnt in 1091 and the rebuilding was not undertaken till 1113.   It was likely enough that the abbot should look out for something for his learned monks to do, and should make use of an outlying manor near to such a centre as Cambridge as a promising field for activities restricted through the disaster to his house. Moreover the energies of the lecturers, we are told, were directed against Jewish doctrines, and the Jews, as we have seen, had come to Cambridge three years before.   The town was rising in prosperity, and the charter of 1118 points to the conclusion that people and trade had been attracted to it since Henry's first rescript sixteen years earlier.[2]

Whether among those attracted to Cambridge we are to count the large influx of scholars who are said to have listened to the Crowland monks, or not, it is certain that Cambridge became once more in 1174 the A.D. 1174.

[1] Joffred was appointed abbot of Crowland in 1109 in succession to Ingulph : the xiv c. forgery the *Historia Croylandensis* pretends to be written by Ingulph (*nat.* 1030) and continued by Peter of Blois. It contains fables about the antiquity of Oxford. See *Ingulph and the Historia Croylandensis* by W. G. Searle, *M.A.*

[2] p. 8.

13

Cambridge

theatre of great disaster, and a destructive fire was only stayed when it could find no more fuel to feed it.[1]

The school of glomery. *Soi-disant* Peter of Blois declares that the monks when they set about teaching " took the university of Orléans for their pattern."[2] The earliest school we come across at Cambridge is a "school of glomery" under the patronage of the bishops of Ely. The archdeacon of Ely nominated the "master of the glomerels" and one of the chief acts of Hugh de Balsham was to limit the authority which the archdeaconry had thus come indirectly to exercise in university matters. From thenceforward the master of glomery is to have the same authority to compose disputes between glomerels as other regent masters had towards their scholars ; but in disputes with scholars or with townsmen as to lodgings or in grave matters affecting the jurisdiction of the university, the glomerels were to plead before the chancellor. There were thus two classes of students in the early days at Cambridge, 'glomerels' and 'scholars.' The former were subject to the *magister glomeriae* who in his turn was subject to the archdeacon of Ely ; the latter had grown up under the aegis of the regent masters and chancellor.

Now the school of glomery was nothing else than the time-honoured Cambridge school of grammar.[3] The

[1] Fuller.

[2] "The monk Odo, a singular grammarian and satirical poet, read grammar to the boys and those of the younger sort assigned to him " ; logic and rhetoric were imparted to the elder scholars. *Soi-disant Peter of Blois.*

[3] iii. p. 164. Their school was in the parish where the university schools

14

Origin of Cambridge University

word has been for centuries a local term known only
here, and it is therefore the more interesting to find
that the students of Orléans were called 'glomerel
clerks' (*clers glomeriaus*) and that they resisted the
invasion of their grammar schools by Aristotle's logic in
the xiii century.

> Paris et Orliens ce sont ij :
> C'est granz domages et granz deuls
> Que li uns à l'autre n'acorde.
> Savez por qui est la descorde ?
> Qu'il ne sont pas d'une science :
> Car Logique, qui toz jors tence,
> Claime les auctors autoriaus
> Et les clers d'Orliens glomeriaus.[1]

There were also 'glomerels' at Bury-St.-Edmund's
and Abbot Sampson's doings as regards the grammar
school there in the xii century bear a strong resemblance
to Balsham's doings at Cambridge in the xiiith.[2] The

rose later—under the shadow of Great S. Mary's ; and opposite was Le
Glomery Lane (the *Vicus Glomeriae*).

[1] *La Bataille des vii Ars.* Oeuvres Rutebeuf, Paris 1839, ii. 415.

[2] Abbot Sampson (*b.* 1135) had himself been "a poor clerke" at the
school of Bury, and William Diss, a Norfolk man, was the schoolmaster.
In 1160 Sampson became its *magister scholarum.* He proceeded to buy
certain stone houses—those solid structures which either as Jewish or
Norman building were sought for at Cambridge and at Oxford also—so
that the scholars might live rent free ; and in 1198 he endowed the
magister scolarum grammaticalium so that the tuition too became free.
(*The Chronicle of Jocelin of Brakelond*, newly edited by Sir Ernest
Clarke, *M.A., F.S.A.*) "School Hall Street" was just outside the abbey
precincts, and answered to the "School Street" and the *Vicus Glomeriae*
in Cambridge.   There was an ancient chapel in Cambridge dedicated to the
patron saint of Bury, and one of the chief possessions of that rich abbey was
the manor of Mildenhall, which provided the expenses of its sacrist and
cellarer : it is at least an interesting coincidence that Robert and Edmund

THE OLD GATEWAY OF KING'S COLLEGE

This gateway now forms the entrance to the Library
from Trinity Lane. The North door of King's
Chapel is seen in the distance.

persistence of the glomery school at Cambridge and the equally remarkable persistence of this school at Orléans goes far to justify the conjecture that it was Orléans which influenced Cambridge, not Paris : for Crowland had certainly been influenced by the same school, and Cambridge and Bury were both familiar with 'glomerels' ; the former under the jurisdiction of the diocesan the latter under that of the abbot.[1]

The religious orders. The canons. Cambridge presents us with an excellent example of the relations which secular and religious learning bore to one another in the foundation of universities. Ecclesiastically it was of no importance whatever ; it was not the seat of a bishop nor the fief of abbot or prior—the one monastic house was the nunnery of S. Rhadegund, founded before the middle of the xii century—and at no time in

of Mildenhall were original fellows of Michaelhouse ; the former was its second master, third master, according to Le Neve, of Peterhouse, and chancellor of the university in 1334. An abbot and a monk of Bury are two of those to be specially commemorated in every mass said by the scholars of the new foundation of Michaelhouse (1324) ; and Curteys the 24th abbot of Bury was one of the personages invited by Henry VI. to assist at the laying of the foundation stone of King's College. Walter Diss (a name well known in Bury) was a famous Carmelite friar at Cambridge in the xiv c. Fuller preserves the legend that Jocelyn, Abbot Sampson's Boswell, had studied in the Cambridge schools, the source of which is Bale who was a Carmelite of Norwich and Cambridge. Together these things perhaps suggest that the schools of Cambridge and Bury had some relation to each other as well as to Orléans.

Bury was reckoned among fen monasteries because of its Suffolk property (of which Mildenhall formed part) where the See of Ely possessed several manors.

[1] A Henry of Orléans was sub-bailiff of Cambridge in the 2nd year of Edw. I. (Hundred Rolls i. p. 49).

its history was the fate of the university determined by the learning of the cloister or its fortune raised by a doctrine of the schools. Ely, the outside influence which played the largest rôle, introduced no monastic elements, and within Cambridge itself the communities which had most part in its development were the canons, and canons always represented a half-way house between clerk and monk. If their contribution to European learning be altogether inferior to that of the Benedictine, they at no time showed any desire to impose a tradition or to stamp with their own hall mark the scholars who willingly attached themselves to canonical houses. The earliest community of canons in Cambridge was founded by a Norman, Hugolina wife to Picot Sheriff of the county, in 1092, in gratitude for her recovery from sickness. A.D. 1092. It was a foundation for six secular canons serving her church of S. Giles by the Castle, and the little community was transformed, twenty years later, by A.D. 1112. another Norman, Pain Peverel standard-bearer to the Duke of Normandy, into the Canons Regular of Barnwell under the rule of S. Augustine.[1] The six canons became thirty, and Barnwell Priory, on the other side of the river, became a house of considerable

[1] The transformation of houses of canons serving a church or cathedral into Regular Canons in the xii and xiii centuries was the effect of the rule indited by Yvo of Chartres which gave its final form and name to the "Canons Regular of S. Augustine" at the end of the xi c. The canons of S. Giles and Lanfranc's hospital of S. Gregory at Canterbury were among the earliest of these communities to be converted, in the reign of Henry I., into Regulars.

17   3

importance, and gave hospitality to Richard II. during the Cambridge parliament of 1388. It continued to exist till the Suppression. About 1135 a second canons' house was established on the present site of S. John's College. This was a hospital, or travellers' hospice, designed by a Cambridge burgess, Henry Frost, who gave the plot of land and endowed "a master and poor brethren of the rule of S. Austin" to dispense the charity of the house.[1] If the Barnwell canons of S. Giles were among the earliest friends of the scholars, the canons of the hospice of S. John were to play the most important part in their history.[2] S. John's and the other xii century foundation of S. Rhadegund were dissolved under similar circumstances within thirteen years of one another, the latter in 1497 the former in 1510.[3]

---

[1] In the xi and xii centuries a large number of hospitals of the order of S. Augustine were founded for the relief of poor and impotent persons, the type being that of the Whittington hospital in London. Sometimes their object was to succour the wayfarer, sometimes they were virtually almshouses where leprous and indigent "brethren" formed the larger part of the community with a few "healthful brethren" and the master to look after them. Such was the origin, in the xi c., of the Knights of Malta, or Order of the Hospital of S. John of Jerusalem. At Canterbury Lanfranc erected a hospital of S. Gregory; at Oxford the hospital of S. Bartholomew, founded in the reign of Hen. I., was bestowed by Edw. III. on Oriel College; and Magdalen, Oxford, was erected on the site of another S. John's hospital, which numbered brethren and sisters among its members. Amalfi merchants trading to the Holy Land endowed the first "master and brethren" of the Order of S. John of Jerusalem; a well-to-do burgess endowed the Cambridge hospice, and the nobles, the bishops, and the sovereign himself are to be numbered among the founders and benefactors of these first almshouses and hospitals. Cf. ii. p. 117 n.

[2] See chap. ii. Peterhouse and S. John's.

[3] See chap. ii. S. John's and Jesus Colleges.

Origin of Cambridge University

There was a third community of Canons Regular at Cambridge. The Lincolnshire community founded by S. Gilbert of Sempringham in the xii century settled near Peterhouse in 1291. Their hostel " S. Edmund's " took its name from the old chapel dedicated to the martyr-king enshrined at Bury-St.-Edmund's, and a licence of Edward III.'s permitting the canons to acquire houses and lands in the town styles them "the Prior and Canons of the chapel of S. Edmund." We hear of these possessions early in the xiv century when (in 1417) the Prior of S. Edmund's leases land ; and again in 1474 when the community sell land to William Bassett. Of the 26 houses of this Order—the only Order of English origin—there were two in the isle of Ely,[1] while a fourth was established near Hitchin. The Barnwell Memoranda announcing their arrival in Cambridge say : "The canons of Sempringham first came A.D. 1291. to dwell at the chapel of S. Edmund, and earnestly set about hearing lectures and attending disputations."

Friars.
Carmelites.
The four orders of friars were all represented in Cambridge, and all settled there in the course of the xiii century. The Carmelites or

[1] Fordham and Mirmaud-at-Welle. The Gilbertines of Chiksand in Bedfordshire had a house and garden in King's Childers' Lane by King's Hall, which they leased to the university for the schools quadrangle in 1433. The Gilbertines were a double Order of nuns and canons ; the former followed the Cistercian rule but were never affiliated to that Order. The canons followed the rule of S. Augustine, but the sympathies, like the dress, of the Gilbertines were Cistercian : "*militat sub instituto Cisterciensi.*" Only in this indirect way did Citeaux enter Cambridge : but see i. p. 25 and ii. p. 143.

Cambridge

Whitefriars were the first to arrive, settling in 1200 at Chesterton near the town, then at Newnham, and finally in Mill Street (1291). For nearly a hundred years the Carmelites took no part in the academic life of Cambridge. They refused to graduate, and showed no desire to display the insignia of a secular doctorate over the peculiarly sacred habit of their Order. It was, indeed, at Cambridge that S. Simon Stock had had, in 1251, his vision of the Blessed Virgin, and had received from her hands the celebrated "scapular of Our Lady of Mount Carmel"; and it was not till forty years after this that the Carmelite Humphrey Necton, at the urgent instance of the then chancellor of the university, consented to take the degree of Doctor in Theology.[1] In the reign of Richard II. this was the richest religious house in Cambridge, and Edmund Langley Earl of Cambridge and Courtney Archbishop of Canterbury lodged there during the parliament of 1388. The Cambridge Carmelites put forth several eminent men : Bale, the historian, had been a Carmelite at Norwich before proceeding to the university; Walter Diss, a zealous opponent of the Lollards, was confessor to that friend of Cambridge John of Gaunt; Nicholas Cantilupe (1441) wrote the *Historiola Cantabrigiae*,[2] and friar Nicholas Kenton was chancellor of

---

[1] The Carmelite Bale says : *ex omni factione sua primus tandem fuit qui theologicus doctor sit effectus.* Pits says the same in the *De illust. Angl. Script.* For Carmelite property in Cambridge see also vi. pp. 325-6.

[2] This was the treatise known in Cambridge as 'the black book,' in which Prior Cantilupe tells of Cantaber and his son Grantanus, and their foundation of Cambridge on the site of Caergrant.

the university as late as the middle of the xv century.

Franciscans. The Franciscans, or Greyfriars, came to Cambridge soon after their arrival in England, and during the lifetime of S. Francis. Among the nine friars who landed in 1224 there were three Englishmen, Richard Ingworth (the only friar in priest's orders), who was accompanied probably by another East Anglian, and by Richard of Devon. This East Anglian element among the first Franciscans is noteworthy, for the first Franciscan readers in divinity at both universities hailed from our Eastern counties. The Cambridge burgesses established the friars at the Jewish synagogue next to the prison.[1] These uncomfortable quarters were exchanged later for a site in the present Sidney Street, where Edward I. built them a friary. Here they took part and share in the life of the university : the novices and younger brethren studied and graduated, the elder taught ; while the church of the Franciscans, which was one of the finest buildings in the town, served the purposes of a university church before the rebuilding of Great S. Mary's.

Dominicans. The Dominicans, or Blackfriars, did not reach Cambridge till about the last quarter of the xiii century,[2] fifty years after the Franciscans. A strange

---

[1] The prison or tolbooth had been the house of Benjamin the Jew, which became university property in the reign of Elizabeth, but after a famous trial in the next reign reverted to the citizens. Like the Jewish houses elsewhere it was amongst the most solid structures in the town.

[2] Dugdale says "before 1275." Their priory was enlarged and perhaps refounded by Alice, wife of de Vere second Earl of Oxford.

destiny decreed that a house which had once been under the patronage of the seraphic Francis should nurture Oliver Cromwell and become the first Protestant college ; and that the house of "the Lord's Watchdogs" (*Dominicanes*) should become the front and centre of Puritanism in the university.[1]

Austinfriars. The last to arrive were the Austinfriars, who entered Cambridge in 1290, at the same time as the Sempringham canons, just as the first Carmelite took his university degree, and as the Jews were expelled from the town. The priory was behind the present college of Corpus Christi, occupying part of the site of the Botanical Gardens, where the new museums now stand. Here was nurtured Miles Coverdale whose reforming principles were imbibed from its prior Barnes afterwards burned as a heretic.[2] Like the other Cambridge friars, the Austinfriars were dissolved at the Reformation.[3]

Other friars at Cambridge. There were other friars in Cambridge. The friars of the Sack[4] or *De poenitentia Jesu*, were established in S. Mary's parish in 1291,

[1] Chap. ii., Sidney Sussex and Emmanuel Colleges.

[2] v. p. 275.

[3] All branches of the Augustinians were represented at Cambridge : the Augustinian canon at Barnwell, the hospitaller at S. John's, and the hermit-friar at the Austin friary. '*The friars heremites of the order of S. Austin*' were settled in Suffolk from the middle of the xiii c., probably by Richard de Clare Earl of Gloucester and Lord of the honour of Clare. One of their chief benefactors was Elizabeth de Burgh. See Clare College chap. ii. p. 64.

[4] Confraternities and friars "of the Sack," known as *Sacconi* in their birthplace, Italy, and so called because of the loose gown or 'sack' common to begging friars and confraternities, and also because of the large sacks

then in the parish of S. Peter. This was one of the spurious orders of Franciscans suppressed, as a result of the Council of Lyons, in 1307. The Barnwell Chartulary, however, has recorded for us that "these brethren of the Sack gathered together many scholars and good, and multiplied exceedingly until the time of the Council of Lyons."

Other religious houses at Cambridge. The Bethlemite friars came over here in 1257, and appear to have had only one house in England, that in Trumpington Street.[1] Our-Lady-friars (*Fratres de Domina*) are first heard of about thirty years later (1288). They were settled near the castle (and are hence called in the Barnwell Chartulary: *Fratres beatae Mariae ad Castrum*) and are only heard of at Cambridge and at Norwich where they arrived before 1290 and were there established at the time of the plague.[2] The Cambridge burgesses had an ancient leper hospital at Stourbridge, under the dedication of " S. Mary Magdalene for lepers." In the closing years of the xiv century Henry Tangmer, alderman of the Guild of Corpus Christi, founded the Hermitage of S. Anne and Hospital of Lazars. About the same time (1395) the Benedictine nuns of S. Leonard of Stratford-le-Bowe granted a curtilage

which they sometimes carried when begging for the poor, were associations due to the preaching of S. Francis and especially of S. Antony of Padua in the first quarter of the xiii c. So that the Cambridge friars, dispersed after the Council of Lyons in 1307, were one of the earliest of these communities ; and it is interesting to find them addicted to scholarship.

[1] Matthew Paris, anno 1257. *Concessa est mansio fratribus Bethleemitis in Cantabrigia, silicet in vico qui ducit versus Trumpintonam.*

[2] They were begging friars following the rule of S. Austin.

ST. JOHN'S COLLEGE GATEWAY AND
TOWER FROM TRINITY STREET

Trinity Chapel is seen on the left behind the trees.

Cambridge

in Scholars' Lane to the university.[1] The Priories of
Anglesey S. John of Jerusalem and Tyltey and the
abbeys of Crowland (p. 12) and Denney all held land
in Cambridge.

The prior and convent of Anglesey, a Cambridgeshire house of Regular Canons, owned land here as
early as 1278-9, and were of some importance in the
town in the xiv century.[2] The land held by the knights
of S. John was not part of the confiscated Templar
property, all of which escheated to the Order, but
was purchased by them early in the reign of Edward I.[3]
It lay in the university centre between Mill Street and
School Street ("Milnestrete alias Seynt Johnstrete")
and was a parcel of open land on which was their
patronal church of S. John Baptist, and Crouched or
S. Crosse's Hostel.[4] In 1432 William Hulle, pre-
ceptor of Swenefeld, Templecombe, and Quenyngton,
and prior of the English Langue, sold this ground
to the university for the schools quadrangle, and the
New Schools of Canon Law were built upon it.[5] The

---

[1] They had held land in Cambridge for over 100 years " of the gift of
the earl of Mandeville." At the Suppression they were seized of land in
Haslyngfeld, co. Cambridge. Cf. ii. p. 96.

[2] The property was situated "in Henney,' a well-known part of Mill
Street in the parish of S. John Baptist, and included the stone house on
the high street by S. Michael's rectory house which passed to the family of
Sir John Cambridge in 1311 was by him bequeathed to Corpus Christi
College, and became the nucleus of Gonville Hall. The prior of Anglesey
is found leasing this land in the reign of Edward III., and selling it to
Henry VI. in 1447. The priory lay between Cambridge and Newmarket.

[3] *Rot. Hund.* ii. 360. Cf. also *ibid.* p. 370.

[4] pp. 25 *n.*, 49 and ii. p. 90.

[5] Another piece of this ground was conveyed by Henry VI. (who

24

knights' property was on the west of the schools quadrangle, the property of the nuns of Stratford-le-Bowe on the east. Denney and Tyltey both owned land on the site of Christ's Pieces and elsewhere in the xv century. The former was a Franciscan nunnery founded by Marie de Chatillon Countess of Pembroke (p. 69) on land which was claimed from her by the knights of S. John as part of the sequestrated Templar property. It lay on the borders of the fen between Cambridge and Ely. The latter was a Cistercian house in Essex.[1]

The rôle reserved for these houses and congregations in the earlier history of the university was subordinate. By the time that every Benedictine house was required by the Constitution of Honorius III.

bought it of the university in the same year) to Trinity Hall in 1440 (and became the college garden). It is there described as "a void ground" *pertinent' priori et confratribus sancti Johannis in Anglia.* Crouched hostel had already been pulled down for the schools. Like other hostels in Mill Street—God's house, S. Nicholas, and Austin's (see King's and Christ's Colleges) it stood, as we see, on open ground : "a certain garden of the hostel of the Holy Cross" we hear of in 1421.

[1] It is supposed that monks from Denney and Tyltey came here to study. The former was in fact a cell to Ely abbey before Marie de Chatillon transferred the Franciscans of Waterbeach thither. The two 'nuns of the Order of S. Clare' who were friends of Erasmus at Cambridge were probably inmates of Denney. In *Rot. Hund.* two other communities are recorded : the *moniales de Pato,* of whom we know nothing—there is a *Paston* in Norfolk and another in Northants.; and 'the monks of the Holy Trinity at Cambridge' who are mentioned in the Oxford Hundred Rolls of the 7th year of Edw. I. : the name affords another instance of the antiquity and popularity of this dedication to the Trinity, which we find at Michaelhouse, Trinity Hall, Trinity church, and in the guild of the Trinity at Cambridge.

Cambridge

(1216-1227) to send some of its students to the universities, learning had already passed from the monastery to the university, and the monks' hostel at Cambridge[1] signalised the change. The part taken by the friars is not less instructive. The refusal of the Carmelites (throughout the xiii century) to pursue the academic course is valuable evidence of the conflict between secular and religious studies at the rise of the university. The Franciscans were the most important of the mendicants in England, and as such took a paramount place at both Cambridge and Oxford; but at the former their action was inconspicuous, and there is nothing to indicate that they were at any time or in any sense "nursing fathers" to Cambridge university whatever they may have been elsewhere.

The moment when they made their appearance was at least as propitious historically as it had been at Oxford, and the independent growth of Cambridge, its escape from the intellectual thraldom of that scholasticism of which the Franciscans were the chief exponents, are hence doubly significant. The quarrels which arose in the early xiv century between the officials of the university and the friars prove that the religious societies which shared its academic life did by no means act in permanent harmony with it. Thus in 1303 the chancellor quarrelled with the Franciscans and Dominicans and excommunicated two of the friars, and later in the century the university had to prohibit

[1] p. 127.

26

novices in the Cambridge friaries from proceeding to their degrees under eighteen years of age. Then, as now, the Franciscans were accustomed to recruit very little lads for the noviciate, all of whom probably received their education at the public Cambridge schools of grammar and theology, and might be seen strutting about as full-fledged "masters of arts before they were masters of themselves."[1]

Before the xiii century closed—from the date of Hugh de Balsham's death—the university ceased to receive any help from monastic learning, for the monks avoided Cambridge, and even Norwich priory sent its students to Oxford.[2] Less than a hundred years elapsed, and we find Gaunt, Pembroke, and Scrope— the court party—opposing the pretensions and the temporalities of the clergy in the company of Cambridge men. .Pembroke—the representative of the house of Valence[3]—is their spokesman, and it is Scrope and Sir Robert Thorpe, Master of a Cambridge college, who take the Purse and the Seals from the hands of their episcopal holders Brantingham and William of Wykeham. This movement, as Stubbs points out, was independent of Wyclif's; and it is remarkable that while William of Wykeham was influencing Oxford the theories for which he stood were being repulsed at Cambridge.

A.D. 1371.

[1] Fuller.

[2] For later monastic influences in Cambridge, see ii. pp. 127-9, Magdalene College.

[3] Pembroke College p. 69. For Scrope see ii. 94, v. 295 ; for Thorpe ii. 75, 96, v. 295.

Cambridge

There remains the relation of the university to the see of Ely. The episcopal jurisdiction of Ely in the university did not long survive the building of colleges. The scholars refused to plead in the archdeacon's court, and Balsham upheld them—their statutes already provided as much.[1] Bishop Montacute also set limits to diocesan authority.[2] In 1317 John XXII. withdrew the university from the spiritual jurisdiction not only of the diocesan but of the provincial archbishop ; but it was the friction arising from the failure of some of the bishops of Ely to recognise the spiritual independence of the chancellor which resulted in the celebrated court held at Barnwell priory at the instance of Martin V., in 1430, under the presidency of its prior. Two forged bulls of Honorius and Sergius[3] were cited as vii century evidence of the spiritual liberties of Cam-

[1] . . . *in statutis universitatis ejusdem . . . familia scholarium . . . immunitate et libertate gaudeant qua et scholares, ut coram archidiacono non respondeant* . . . (Balsham's Judgment A.D. 127⅘). The *Statuta Antiqua*, the old body of statutes of the university, have for the most part no chronological arrangement, and the date cannot in some cases be determined to within a century. The earliest 'grace' to which a date is attached belongs to the year 1359, but there is another referable to the year 127⅘. The latest, reduced to chronological order, is of the year 1506. The *Statuta Antiqua* were replaced in the 12th year of Elizabeth by a fresh body of statutes, and these again by the statutes of Victoria, 1882. The former are printed in Dyer's *Privileges of the University*.

[2] Simon Montacute (1337-1345) ceded the right of the bishops of Ely to the presentation of fellowships in their own college of Peterhouse. Cf. also iv. pp. 203-4.

[3] Dated February 20, 624 ; and 689. Martin's bull recognises their authority. Copies exist in the Cambridge Registry, Nos. 107 and 114 in the catalogue.

bridge, and the Pope in a third bull set the question for ever at rest in favour of the university. The solemn visitation of the colleges which had taken place under the auspices of Archbishop Arundel in 1401 was probably the result of the temporary victory obtained by the Primate when the chancellor refused to take an oath of obedience to him.

The early college statutes were as eager to repel the religious as the rule of Benedict, the father of western monasticism, was to repel the clergyman.[1] The statutes of Michaelhouse (1334), the earliest which have reached us intact, provide that neither monk nor friar should obtain admittance to the college. The statutes of Peterhouse enact that no one deciding to enter a religious order can remain on the foundation. It must at the same time be clearly realised that some of the earliest colleges were little more than clerical seminaries.[2] What is peculiar to Cambridge is that there a monk made the earliest attempt to endow learning for the secular clergy—a monk who was also a bishop, the ever-memorable Hugh Balsham. The non-monastic direction taken was by no means as yet an anti-monastic one ; but at the rise of both universities, as soon as scholars were endowed and endowed houses began to be built for them, the monastic and the academic careers were regarded as incompatible vocations. It was the separation of the *clerk* from the

---

[1] "*Si quis de ordine sacerdotium in monasterio suscipi rogaverit, non quidem citius ei assentiatur.*"—*Regula S. P. Benedicti, caput lx.*

[2] See, chap. ii., Michaelhouse, Corpus, Gonville, and Trinity Hall.

Cambridge

religious, the recognition by Balsham of the secular scholar and of an endowed foundation for such scholars which was neither a religious house nor an *episcopia,* that transformed a more or less fortuitous concourse of students and teachers—a mere amplification, as at Oxford, of the school system of other great centres— into a chartered corporation of scholars—a university.[1]

II

School and university—Stourbridge fair—the university in the xiii century—Foundation of endowed scholars—hostels.

Both our universities doubtless count a school life of eight centuries at least : but a school life, the activity of teachers and scholars, is not the same thing as a university life. We have already said that Oxford owed its history to the constant communication between it and London, to its accessibility from the capital which made it the frequent resort not only of our kings but, what is more to our purpose, of scholars European and English.[2] The ferment created by their lectures no doubt kept alive the desire for knowledge and the spirit of enquiry among the motley population

[1] A chartered corporation and a university in the sense of a *studium generale* possessing European privileges. Cambridge was a *universitas* many years before this, and was so familiarly styled by Henry III. in 1231.

[2] It has been pointed out that our knowledge of Oxford's intellectual activity during the xii c. is confined to the visits of three or four celebrated teachers who lectured to its changing population and in its schools, among which the priory school of S. Frideswide was the most important. We must not of course confuse the activities of monastic and episcopal schools with those of a university.

of the town ; a moral atmosphere which in its turn attracted students. At Cambridge everything was the opposite of this. S. Frideswide's at Oxford was a poor religious house, but it was in the heart of the town ; the monastery at Ely was a great religious house, but its school was many miles from the university. Cambridge, as we have seen, was accessible to no great centre, there was nothing to attract the traveller who if he visited it almost certainly went out of his way to do so. Nevertheless some influences were at work in the xii century which determined the transformation of Cambridge into a *studium generale*, a university. The river near the town, as I have already said, gave rise to one of the greatest fairs in England, and Mr. J. W. Clark is disposed to see in the concourse of people brought together by Stourbridge fair the determining factor in our university history. The fair was called after the Stour a stream lower down the river, and was held in a large cornfield near Barnwell. It began on the feast of S. Bartholomew, August 24, and lasted till the fourteenth day after the feast of the Exaltation of the Cross (September 14). These five weeks of revelry proved more disturbing to Cambridge studies than the May term of to-day ; xiii century scholars spent their money at Stourbridge fair as Isaac Newton spent his in the xviith ; there he acquired his prism in August 1661 and a book on " Judicial Astrology " the geometry and trigonometry of which were then as ' Greek ' to him. Sea-borne goods which had probably always been brought inland up the river to this point, formed the nucleus of the fair at Stourbridge. It is generally agreed that three other English fairs exceeded the Cambridge fair in importance, those at Bristol, Bartholomew's in London, and Lynton. Defoe however describes it as the largest in Europe, greater than that at Nuremberg or than the Frankfort mart. It A.D. 1211. was already highly prosperous when King John made over its dues to the leper hospice of S. Mary Magdalene; and it has been suggested that this was the ancient fair to which Irish merchants brought their cloth in the time of Athelstan.

Why so uncommercial a district became the site of one of the greatest fairs in Europe, and why a *studium generale* became established there, are problems both of which we cannot resolve. There always remains at the bottom some virtue in the apparently unpropitious city on the banks of the Granta which as an Italian would say *fece da sè*. But Mr. J. W. Clark's suggestion has at least placed the two problems in juxtaposition : the growing importance of the schools and the growing importance of the fair both meet us in the opening lustres of the xiii century ; the fair, that is, has its roots in the preceding century when the fate of the embryo seat of learning lay in the balance. How should a fair, how should an extraordinary concourse of people, help to consolidate a university ? Simply because this was the age of peripatetic teaching, because it was the custom all through the middle ages for wandering scholars to find themselves where men gathered together, and to claim for a theorem of Roscellinus or a doctrine

Origin of Cambridge University

from Araby brought by the crusaders the ear of a crowd which had just been entertained by the Norman jongleur.

Earliest references to Cambridge university. Our first glimpse of the Cambridge schools shows us an immigration of the scholars of one university to the other. In 1209, A.D. 1209 10th of John. in consequence of an unjust retaliation upon the students, Oxford was depleted and its scholars found their way to Cambridge.[1] Nine years later we have a rescript of Henry III.'s (1218) ordering all those clerks A.D. 1218 2nd of Henry III. who had adhered to Louis to depart the realm. In the eleven years which elapsed between this and 1229 the Franciscans had established themselves at Cambridge, and in that year as a result of Henry's invitation to A.D. 1229 13th of Henry III. Paris students to settle in England there was a considerable influx of foreigners to the university, the echo of which may be traced in two interesting rescripts of the year 1231. In one of these the king charges the mayor A.D. 1231 15th of Henry III. and bailiffs of the town to deal fairly with members of the university in the matter of lodgings, and enjoins them to establish according to "university custom" two masters and two liegemen of the town to act as "taxors."[2] Dating the rescript from Oxford on the third day of May the king writes: "It is already sufficiently known to you that a multitude of scholars has gathered to our town of Cambridge, for the sake of study, both from the regions near home and from beyond the seas; the which is most grateful and accept-

---

[1] Matthew Paris, *in anno* 1209: *Ita quod nec unus ex omni universitate remansit.*   [2] p. 47.

ORIEL WINDOW OF THE HALL, TRINITY
GREAT COURT

In the nearer part of the picture is the Master's
Lodge, and in the far distance two turrets of King's
Chapel stand up against the evening sky.

Cambridge

able to us, because it gives an example of no small convenience to our whole realm, and our honour is thereby increased ; and you especially, among whom these students are loyally dwelling should feel it matter of no little gratulation and rejoicing." [1] In the second rescript, dated from Oxford on the same day, the king enjoins that no clerk shall live in the town (*quod nullus clericus moretur in villa*) who is not under a *magister scholarum*.[2]

Charters and Bulls. These letters patent addressed to the mayor
Charter of and burgesses of the town by Henry III.
Hen.III.A.D. 1231.
Bull of in 1231 are the earliest existing document
John XXII. which can be regarded in the light of a
A.D. 1317. university charter.[3] At the same time it
appears by no means certain that royal letters had not been addressed earlier to Cambridge in which the

---

[1] *Satis constat vobis quod apud villam nostram Cantebr' studendi causa e diversis partibus tam cismarinis quam transmarinis confluit multitudo, quod valde gratum habemus et acceptamus, cum exemplum toti regno nostro commodum non modicum, et honor nobis accrescat, et vos specialiter inter quos fideliter conversantur studentes non mediocriter gaudere debetis et laetari.*

[2] *Clerk* and *scholar* were used interchangeably in the xiii c. as they are in these two rescripts, *clericus* being employed in the rescript of 1218 and in that addressed to the sheriff (*vicecomes*) of the county cited above : *Quoniam ut audivimus plures nominantur* clerici *apud Cantabr. qui sub nullius magistri scholarum sunt disciplina et tuitione, sed potius mentiuntur se esse* scholares *cum non sint* . . . In a further rescript of the king's the meaning is no less clear : *Ita tamen quod ad suspensionem vel mutilationem clericorum non procedatis, sed eos alio modo per consilium universitatis Cantabr. castigetis.* (Referring to "insults recently offered to certain northern scholars of the university of Cambridge," 1261.) In the Hundred Rolls, at the same period, we have *clerici de Merton* and *scholares de Merton* ; and *clerici in scholis degentes* is W. de Merton's own description of his scholars.

[3] The charter of Oxford university belongs to the same reign.

34

Origin of Cambridge University

academic society there was treated as a moral entity. In the following reign the jury of Cambridge made oath to the effect that " the Chancellor and Masters of the university had appropriated to themselves more ample liberties than were warranted in the charters granted them by the king's predecessors " ;[1] and in the same way when, at the request of Edward II., John XXII. erects Cambridge into a *studium generale* in the second year of his pontificate, he reaffirms and confirms the privileges with which his predecessors in the apostolic chair and the English kings had adorned the university : *omnia privilegia et indulta praedicto studio . . . a pontificibus et regibus praedictis concessa.*[2] In this instrument he refers to Cambridge university as *studium ab olim ibi ordinatum,* " the university from old time there established." Cambridge and Oxford, however, like the earliest centres of learning in Italy and France—Bologna and Paris—*grew into universities* ; papal authorisations follow instead of preceding their institution. In other cases universities were definite creations which make their first appearance with a bull of institution and inauguration attached to them.[3]

Henry III.'s writs in behalf of Cambridge begin in the second and cover the fifty years of his reign. In the 45th and again in the 50th year he repeats and confirms his previous rescripts. The scholastic

[1] *Rot. Hund.* 7th Edw. I.

[2] The Pope no doubt refers to the forged bulls (p. 28) but his reference to previous royal rescripts is likely to be more correct, and to have been supplied by Edward himself.

[3] See *studium generale* pp. 30 *n.*, 31.

35

Cambridge

prosperity of Cambridge dates from this reign as its
civil prosperity dates from that of Henry I. ; and the
traditions that Cambridge was Beauclerk's *alma mater*
and that Henry V. was a student at Oxford probably
both derive from the signal favours shown to the two
by these monarchs respectively.[1] Cambridge however
was greatly reduced in the reign of John, especially
about the year 1214 in spite of the recent immigration
from Oxford.

The Henrys and But from the accession of Henry III.
the Edwards. onwards the university city became the
special care of the Henrys and the Edwards. Edward I.,
while still Prince of Wales, visited the town in 1254

[1] The importance of Cambridge was steadily growing in the reigns of
Henry I. and Stephen. The isle of Ely supported Matilda ; and the earldom of Cambridge was conferred both by her and by Stephen for the
first time. The former by her letters, issued before the year 1146, bestowed
it on her favourite Aubrey de Vere, " if the King of Scotland hath it not,"
as prior in dignity to the counties of " Oxfordshire, Berkshire, Wiltshire,
or Dorsetshire " one of which he was to take if Stephen's gift of the earldom of Cambridge to Saint David of Scotland held good. De Vere had to
accept the county of Oxford which has since remained in that family—the
earldom of Cambridge passing to royal hands and becoming in time a royal
dukedom. David of Scotland held Cambridge in his own and Huntingdon
in right of his wife. Malcolm of Scotland held both earldoms together in
exchange for the northern counties of Northumberland and Cumberland.
The union of these earldoms is still represented by the union of Huntingdon and Cambridge under one *vicecomes* or sheriff. Edward III. created his
wife's brother (the Count of Hainault) and after him his son Edmund
Langley, earls of Cambridge. Edmund's son Richard held the earldom
until his attainder, and his son Richard Duke of York was again created
Earl of Cambridge by Henry V. (p. 295). This was Edward IV.'s father in
whom the earldom became merged in the crown. The arms of Edmund
Langley, Duke of York and Earl of Cambridge, are on the first of the 6
shields of·arms of Edward's sons over the entrance gate of Trinity ; beneath
is inscribed : EDMONDUS D. EBOR. C. CANTABRUGIE.

Origin of Cambridge University

and undertook the pacification of the quarrels in which scholars and townsmen were engaged.[1] A document sealed with his own seal and those of the university and the borough ordained that henceforth 13 scholars and 10 burgesses should be chosen to represent the interests of both parties. Five of the former were to be Englishmen, 3 Scotchmen, 3 Irishmen, and 2 from Wales. The proportions are interesting.[2] It was soon after Edward's accession that the refusal of Cambridge students to obey summonses to the archidiaconal courts led to Balsham's judicious settlement of the point.[3]

4th Edw. I. A.D. 1276.

Edward II. continued the interest shown in Cambridge by his father and grandfather ; not only obtaining for it the status of a *studium generale* but maintaining a group of scholars there at his own charges—"king's scholars" who were to rank with Ely and Merton scholars in historical importance. The favour shown to the university by the magnificent king his son was perhaps the one instance in which he took pains to fulfil the intentions of his murdered father.[4]

A.D. 1317.

[1] See "Town and Gown" chap. iv. p. 233 *n.*

[2] Cf. "the students from regions near home" (*e partibus diversis tam cismarinis . . .*) of his father's rescript p. 33.

[3] For other references to this important document see *ante* pp. 14, 28 ; chap. iii. p. 165 *n*, iv. p. 203.

[4] Henry VI., VII., VIII., and Edward VI. continued the favour shown by the Henrys and Edwards to Cambridge ; the exceptions were Henry V. and Edward IV. See ii. p. 101, v. p. 262. For the relation of the English queens to the university see Queens' College pp. 109, 112, and p. 114.

Edward III. allowed the university to appropriate any church of the yearly value of £40 ; to receive (through its chancellor) the oaths of the mayor and aldermen and the bailiffs ; to take cognizance of all causes in

Cambridge

In the long reign of Henry III., in the year 1257, Hugh de Balsham,[1] subprior of Ely, was made tenth bishop of the diocese ; and it was then that he placed and endowed at S. John's hospital a group of secular students known as "Ely scholars," who were the object of his anxious care until his death in 1286. His scheme and its results are described in the next chapter.[2] At this time there were no endowed houses at Cambridge, no school buildings, no endowed scholars.[3] It was some thirty years after the arrival of the Franciscans, the Carmelites had as yet taken no part in the academic life, and many years were to elapse before the Dominicans made their appearance. It was fifty years since the Oxford immigration, and thirty since the king had invited over the students from Paris. The distinction that was now made between the clerk-canon, or the clerk-friar, and the scholar in arts or theology who would remain a secular, converted, as we have said, the university corporation into something more—a *studium generale*, and led, as we shall see, to the building of the first endowed colleges.

Walter de Merton. Contemporaneously with Balsham there lived and toiled another college legislator, Walter de Merton, Chancellor of England and after-

which the scholars were concerned, "maim and felony" excepted ; and required that the chancellor should not be disquieted if he imprisoned offenders ; that masters of arts should not be cited out of the university ; and that the mayor should make assay of the weight of bread as often as the chancellor demanded it.

[1] pp. 29, 54.
[2] Peterhouse p. 55, S. John's pp. 122-3.
[3] Except Kilkenny's exhibitioners, *infra* p. 40.

wards Bishop of Rochester. His prime importance
in developing the collegiate conception will be seen in
the next chapter ; here we are concerned with him as
a founder of endowed scholars. Merton had eight
nephews to educate, and he set about designing an
academic scheme the far-reaching effects of which
endure to this day, although the steps of the scheme
are involved in an obscurity which responds to his own
hesitations. He first assigned his manor of Malden, A.D. 1264
adjoining Merton in Surrey, as a chef-lieu and endowment for " poor scholars in the schools " who are living
under a code of rules prescribed by himself. During
the next five years he acquired lands both in Cambridge and Oxford ; his chief acquisition at the former
being in 1269, when he purchased an estate lying under
the shadow of the Conqueror's castle which included
the Norman manor house known as the School of
Pythagoras. This property had been in the possession
of the Dunnings since the Conquest, and was afterwards known as the Merton estate. In the same year
William de Manfield, who held a mortgage on this
property, states that he had given his lands in Cambridge to the house, scholars, and brethren of Merton
—*domui et scholaribus et fratribus de Merton.*[1] Mean-

---

[1] " I have given to God, the Blessed Virgin, blessed John Baptist, and
to the House of the Scholars of Merton " : these words occur in the same
deed with those in the text. *Harl. Add. MSS.* 5832. *ff.* 74, 75. The gift
includes a stone house in the town: *Dedi etiam et concessi prefatae domui
. . . domum illam lapideam in Cauntebrigg. cum gardino et curia adjacente . . .*
Three deeds relating to the same transaction are dated *mense Martii* 54th of
Hen. III. In *Rot. Hund.* 7th Edw. I. p. 366, a certain John gives a quit
rent to the scholars of Merton for 18 acres of this property.

Cambridge

while Walter de Merton had been buying land at Oxford,[1] and in 1274 he definitely moved the hall at Malden and refounded it as Merton College in the sister university ; the formula hitherto maintained in his charters and statutes (see ii. p. 68) being now changed, and "poor scholars who are studying at Oxford or elsewhere where a *studium generale* exists" (*Oxoniae, aut alibi, ubi studium viget generale*) becomes "who are studying at Oxford where there is a university" (*Oxoniae ubi universitas viget studentium*).

The scheme thus crowned in 1274 had had its birth twelve years before when in 1262 Gilbert de Clare Earl of Gloucester allowed the manor of Malden to be assigned to the Austin priory of Merton or to some other religious house for the sustenance of *clerici in scholis degentes* (poor clerks in the schools) who were living according to Merton's prescriptions.[2] This vesting of endowments in a religious house was already familiar at both universities. The Bishop of Ely (Kilkenny) had vested his exhibitions for divinity students in the prior of Barnwell in 1256, and it appears that this was Merton's first intention. Two years later, however, we find him assigning Malden and other manors to his nephews, the beneficiaries being still described as "poor scholars in the schools."

Any scholars maintained at either university by these endowments were "Merton scholars." This is

---

[1] The priory of S. Frideswide granted him land in 1265, and he obtained much more two years later.

[2] The wording provides for the existing or any other *ordinatio* Merton may formulate.

again made perfectly clear when the charter (and statutes) of 1270 were issued, in which Walter de Merton settles the Cambridge estates as part of the Malden endowments for " scholars studying in Oxford or elsewhere." It was part of his plan to acquire local endowments at both universities, and also that vast clerical patronage in the different shires which was obviously destined to ensure the future of his scholars. This was the scheme eventually concentrated in the foundation of Merton, Oxford : and when Bishop Hobhouse is inclined to anticipate the date at which Merton scholars were established there, we may entirely agree with him, only adding that if there were certainly Merton scholars at Oxford before 1274, there were no less certainly Merton scholars at Cambridge also before that date. Merton's scholars had their chef-lieu at Malden, but were studying at these two universities, and possessed endowments at both during the decade 1264-1274.

The Hundred Rolls furnish us with ample references to the Cambridge scholars. In the Rolls for the borough and town of Cambridge, the 2nd year of Edward I., they are accused of poaching on the A.D. 1274. fishing rights of the townsmen. "A servant of the House of the Merton scholars[1] had appropriated to his masters' use a certain foss common to the whole town." In the later inquisitions of the 7th of Edward I. A.D. 1278-9. we find them figuring among the most considerable Cambridge landlords, one entry showing them to us

[1] "*Domus scolarium de Merton.*" *Burg. Cantebr. Rot. Hund.* i. 55.

Cambridge

as purchasers of land from Manfield : *Item scolares de Merton tenent unum mesuagium cum quadraginta et quinque acris terre . . . quas emerunt de Willelmo de Manefeld.*[1]

A.D. 1278-9. Three of these entries point to tenure of no very recent date. Thus Eustace Dunning sold to Walter Howe a messuage with a croft which Eustace had inherited from his father Hervey Dunning, and for which the Howes, in accordance with an assignment made by Eustace Dunning, gave twelve pence a year to the clerks of Merton (*per assignationem praedicti Eustachi clericis de Merton xii*[d]).[2] The declaration is made by John son and heir of Walter Howe, so that Eustace Dunning's appointment in favour of the

A.D. 1278-9. Merton clerks refers to some time back. Again, Agnes daughter of the tailor Philip inherited a messuage in the parish of S. Peter which her father "had held of the Merton scholars." In the last place the Cambridge jurymen affirm that two annual attendances should have been made at the court of Chesterton for a holding of Eustace Dunning's, but that the scholars of Merton had failed to put in an appearance *for the past six years.*[3]

These transactions cannot be held to relate to an

---

[1] *Rot. Hund.* ii. 360.

[2] The "Merton clerks," *clerici de Merton,* are mentioned again in the next paragraph. At the same date a certain Johanna declares that she had as a marriage portion from her father a messuage given him by Cecil at the Castle, for which is paid a quit rent of twelve pence a year to "the scholars of Merton." *Rot. Hund.* ii. 379. In the Hundred of Chesterton (p. 402) we find that "the scholars of Merton hold of the fee of Hervey Dunning" such and such properties. They also paid a quit rent to Edmund Crouchback for lands he held (on the death of de Montfort) as earl of Leicester.

[3] *Rot. Hund.* ii. 364, 407.

Origin of Cambridge University

estate managed for the Oxford college founded in 1274, and to a period covering not more than four or five years. From 1274, which is also the date of the earliest Hundred Rolls, the Merton scholars were definitely and finally established at Oxford ; and when John Howe and Agnes Taylor gave their evidence it is probable that there were no longer Merton scholars in Cambridge : what their depositions seem to indicate is a concurrent antiquity for Merton scholars at both universities. If these scholars had not been settled among them when these land transactions occurred the references would certainly have been to scholares de Merton *Oxoniae*,[1] and it is well worthy of notice that the only two instances in the Cambridge Hundred Rolls where " the Merton scholars at Oxford " are referred to are two instances where Walter de Merton is said to have " alienated " land in Cambridge for the use of the scholars in Oxford.[2]

No doubt it had always been part of Merton's design to found a residential college for his scholars at one of the universities ; and he had perhaps strong reasons for establishing this at Cambridge. His great patron

[1] The general rule in these Rolls is to add no qualification of origin in cases where the owner, or religious house, has another habitation in the locality to which the transaction refers. Hence we find " the prior of Anglesey," " the prioress of Stratford," side by side with " the scholars of Merton " in the Cambridge Hundred Rolls (cf. *Rot. Hund.* ii. 364).

[2] Grantchester (7th Edw. I. p. 565) : *et tota dicta pars alienata est scolaribus Oxon' per dominum Walter' de Merton', nescit quo warranto.* Gamlingay : " William of Leicester sold the whole of that holding to *dominus* Walter de Merton and the said Walter *gave it all to the scholars* of the *domus de Merton Oxonie*."

Cambridge

was Chief-Justice Bassett, and the Bassetts were Cambridge landowners. His patron in the original assignment of Malden manor was Gilbert de Clare whose family gave its name in the next century to the eponymous college at the same university. Was the *domus de Merton* of "the scholars and brethren" (p. 39) in fact at one time such a residence? where poor scholars, some of them perchance from Merton priory school itself, lived under the auspices of the Merton brethren? Certain it is that a prior of Merton intrudes himself and his affairs into the Cambridge Hundred Rolls.[1] It is also certain that the House of Scholars of Merton is first heard of not at Oxford but at Cambridge. Mr. J. W. Clark has pointed out in another connexion that the words *domus* and *aula* were employed when a building was "appropriated by endowment as a fixed residence for a body of scholars." Our *domus scholarium de Merton* on which Cambridge

---

[1] "Villani ejusd' Gunnor' dicunt quod *prior de Mertone*" held the advowson of the church of Barton. (*Rot. Hund.* ii. 564.)

The Bishop of Nelson points out that the scholars were called not after Walter de Merton, but after the place—Merton priory. Merton himself had no surname ; he was born at Basingstoke, and was perhaps educated at the priory from which he also took his name. Beket was certainly educated at this well-known Merton, which gave its name to the "Statute of Merton" devised there in 1236, and was also the theatre of a council held by the archbishop 22 years later. At the evaluation of 1291, the priory held property in Norfolk (*Index Monasticus*). The Cambridge estates settled on the scholars of the *domus apud Meandon* (Malden) in 1270 were in Gamlingay, *Merton, Over-Merton*, Chesterton, etc. It is worth notice that among a number of scholars who received the king's pardon in 1261 for the part they had taken in a riot, there is a *William de Merton*, servant to two of the East Anglian scholars implicated.

44

Origin of Cambridge University

lands were bestowed—to which Cambridge lands were confirmed—in 1269, could not have been either in Surrey or at Oxford.

Whether there was a house of Merton scholars at Cambridge before there was a house of Merton scholars at Oxford, or not, it would appear that a like antiquity must be claimed for the scholars themselves at both universities.[1]

Universities in other towns. The licence to found a university at Northampton. One of the odd things about Merton's movements is that though he began buying land in Oxford the year after the Malden foundation (1265), he made his chief acquisition in Cambridge as late as 1269, and that a year later when he issued a revised set of statutes (1270) he still makes no allusion to any change of locality. It is possible that in 1265 when he wrote " at Oxford or at, any other university " he had in mind the tentatives then being made to found an English university in some other town. It was in fact in 1262, the 45th year of the reign of Henry III., that Cambridge students had migrated to Northampton with the king's licence to found a university. The traditional bickerings between southerners and northerners three years previously had been the cause of the exodus, and the Cambridge scholars found many Oxonians already there

---

[1] For the " Ely scholars " see ii. pp. 122-3. The first *to leave an endowment* for scholars was William of Durham in 1249 ; but several years elapsed before the fund was utilised, scholars maintained, or University College Oxford founded. University College was thus the outcome of an earlier *intention* to endow, and Balliol College was an earlier foundation in embryo, than either Peterhouse or Merton.

Cambridge

who had migrated from Oxford after their quarrel with the papal legate in 1238 but had obtained no licence to institute a university. The licence accorded to the masters and scholars of Cambridge university was withdrawn four years later on a representation being made to Henry III. that a university at Northampton must prove prejudicial to Oxford.[1] Migrations of students to other towns took place throughout the xiii century. They begin in 1209 when there was a general exodus from Oxford not only to Cambridge but to the town of Reading. Thirty years later the Oxonians migrated to Northampton and Salisbury, being followed to the former in 1262 as we have just seen by many Cambridge " masters and scholars." These migrations certainly indicate that Oxford and Cambridge were not yet regarded as such permanent homes of English scholarship that other sites could not be substituted. The event which most impressed the popular imagination occurred when both universities had attained to European fame—the exodus in the reign of Edward III. from Oxford to Stamford which caused the king in 1333 to issue his royal letters forbidding any one to teach there. It had been prophesied that the studies pursued at Oxford would be transferred to Stamford,

[1] The preamble of these letters addressed to the civic authorities at Northampton is as follows : *Occasione cuiusdam magnae contentionis in villa Cantabrigiensi triennio jam elapso subortae nonnulli clericorum tunc ibidem studentium unanimiter ab ipsa villa recessissent, se usque ad villam nostram praedictam Northam. transferentes et ibidem (studiis inherendo) novam construere universitatem cupientes.* The letters are dated from Westminster 1 Feb. in the 49th year of his reign (1265). *Rot. Claus.* 49, *Hen. III. membr.* 10. *d.* [1 Feb. 1264-5].

and the Cambridge floods gave rise to another prophecy, recorded by Spenser, which showed that the Stamford incident still occupied men's minds. The flat Lincolnshire country would, it was said, become completely flooded, and Stamford then would

> ——shine in learning more than ever did
> Cambridge or Oxford England's goodly beames.

No migration took place from Cambridge after the foundation of its first college. But before we enter upon this period of its history, and find ourselves in the brilliant epoch which was so soon to overtake the university in the xiv century, let us see what arrangements were made for the accommodation of the scholar population previous to the existence of colleges.

At first—in the xii and the early part of the xiii centuries—scholars lived each at his own charges; perhaps groups of three and four would club together, but every scholar was then, as Fuller expressively has it, "his own founder and his own benefactor." [1] The rescript of the early years of Henry III., already cited, introduces us to the town hostels—*hospitia locanda* ; and establishes the taxing of lodging house charges by the *taxatores*, a usage probably rendered the more necessary owing to the great influx of students two years before, when the demand for lodgings must have been very much in excess of the supply.[2] These town hostels, the result of town enterprise, were subject to

A.D. 1231
15th of
Henry III.

[1] Chaucer shows us that the system of private lodgings continued in vogue at Oxford even in the late xiv c. His "pore scholer" lodges in the house of a well-to-do carpenter. [2] p. 33.

47

the four "taxors" only, and were under no other academic supervision.[1] It seems highly probable, however, that the king's rescript gave rise to the university hostels, some thirty of which were in existence fifty years later. In any case the rescript leads us to conclude that the town hostels were in existence in the previous century, and supplies us with a date before which we cannot suppose that any university hostel existed.

The university hostel. The university hostelries or inns for the accommodation of scholars who lived there at their own charges were intermediate between the town lodging house and the college, which they both anticipate and supplement. A number of scholars joined together, elected their own principal, and paid him at a fixed rate for board and lodging. At first, therefore, the university like the town hostel was a private enterprise, scholars undertook the charge of them in their private capacity. The head of the hostel was called the Principal. Later on these institutions changed their democratic character. The government passed entirely into the hands of the principal, certain oaths were exacted of him, and he kept a list of the scholars in his house.[2] The principal collected a rent from the inmates, though in some hostels the accommodation appears to have been free. All these changes, we may imagine, belong to the time when

[1] Cf. the regulations for lodgings at the present day, iv. pp. 224, 225.

[2] Caius speaks of "two principals" overseeing respectively the studies and the economics of Physwick hostel.

Origin of Cambridge University

some of the hostels were affiliated to colleges, becoming thenceforward subject in all respects to the customs and discipline of the endowed foundation. Thus S. Mary's hostel, where Matthew Parker studied, was affiliated to Corpus, Borden's belonged to S. John's hospital, then to Ely, and in 1448 was affiliated to Clare ; S. Bernard's belonged first to Queens' then to Corpus ; S. Austin's to King's. The hostels took their name sometimes from the neighbouring church or chapel, or other saintly patron, and sometimes from their proprietor. "Newmarket" and "Harleston" hostels must have served for students from these neighbouring towns. The monks who first came to study in Cambridge lived in lodgings ; but these were soon exchanged for the monastic hostel, hence "Ely hostel" and "Monks' hostel."[1] Those zealous learners the friars of the Sack had Jesu hostel, dismantled in 1307, the Sempringham canons had S. Edmund's hostel, the Barnwell canons had a hostel in the town called S. Augustine's, and the hospitaller knights of S. John owned Crouched and S. John's hostels in School Lane and Mill Street.[2] Rud's offers a good example of a xiii century Cambridge hostel, and Physwick of one of the xivth. The former is mentioned in 1283 and was part of the compensation allowed in that year to S. John's for the alienated hostels at Peterhouse,[3] it still exists, almost unaltered,

[1] Cf. ii. Trinity Hall p. 79, Magdalene pp. 127, 128.

[2] Crouched, Crutched, for *Crossed*. So the Trinitarians who also wore a conspicuous cross on their habit were known in England as Crutched friars.   [3] p. 56.

THE OLD CASTLE INN

Now styled "Ye Olde Castel Hotel." The Baptist
Church and the Police Courts are seen just beyond,
and the Roman Catholic Church in the distance.
The near trees are in the grounds of Emmanuel
College.

Cambridge

and forms part of the Castle inn in S. Andrew's Street.
Physwick was the private residence of an esquire bedell
of that name who bequeathed it for the purposes of a
hostel in 1393. It was affiliated to Gonville and was
in use until absorbed in the buildings of Trinity
College in the xvi century.

Cambridge hostels were highly important foundations. The 8 jurists' hostels housed eighty and a
hundred students apiece, and the large hostels of
S. Bernard, S. Thomas, S. Mary, and S. Augustine sometimes housed twenty and thirty regents without counting the non-regents and students.[1] A large proportion
of men whose names are not to be found on the books
of any college received their education in these houses.
The Inns, of which there were three at Cambridge
—Oving's, S. Zachary's, and S. Paul's—were smaller
and less important hostels and appear to have been
frequented by the richer students. Hostel and hall or
college existed side by side through the xiii, xiv, and
xv centuries. Indeed until the college system was
well established the hostels greatly exceeded the endowed halls in number, and they continued to supplement the latter until the completion of the large colleges
at the renascence. Some twenty were erected as late
as the xv and the opening years of the xvi centuries.
During the xiv and xv centuries many hostels were
destroyed to make room for the colleges ; and in the
xvith those which remained were abandoned, Trinity

[1] S. Austin's or Augustine's hostel had a length of 220 feet with 80 of
breadth.

Origin of Cambridge University

hostel, as Fuller testifies, being the only one remaining in use till 1540.[1]

[1] See *pensioners*, iv. p. 217 *n*.

Mr. J. Bass Mullinger has published (*Hist. Univ. Camb.* pp. 218-220) a highly interesting statute relating to hostels which dates in all probability from the end of the xiii c., and shows how rapidly university rights in these *hospitia locanda* were extended as a consequence of Henry's rescript (p. 47). Any scholar who "desired to be principal of a hostel" offered his "caution" —with sureties or pledges—to the landlord and became *ipso facto* its head, and could be instituted by the chancellor against the will of the landlord. The scholar, who has become principal, may not abdicate in favour of a fellow scholar but only give up possession to the said landlord. The next candidate could also appeal to the chancellor should the landlord refuse his request to succeed when a vacancy in the principalship occurred. An interesting clause provides that though the landlord should agree with the scholar-principal that "mine hostel" should not be taxed, the scholars who come to live there may, in spite of both of them, have the house taxed by the taxors, "inasmuch as agreements between private persons cannot have effect to the prejudice of public rights."

CHAPTER II

THE COLLEGES

The university and the colleges—the collegiate system—eras of
college building—Peterhouse—Michaelhouse—*collegium* and
aula—Clare—college statutes—architectural scheme of a college
—Pembroke — founders of colleges—Gonville—Trinity Hall
—Corpus Christi—Cambridge in 1353—Chaucer at Cambridge
— the schools, library, the university printers and the Pitt
Press, the senate house — King's — King's College chapel—
Cambridge college chapels — Queens' — English sovereigns at
Cambridge—S. Catherine's—Jesus—Christ's—Lady Margaret
and Bishop Fisher—S. John's—Magdalene—King's Hall and
Trinity College—college libraries—gateways—Caius—monks
in Cambridge—Emmanuel—Sidney Sussex—Downing—public
hostels — nationality of founders and general scope of their
foundations—university and college revenues.

THE college is an endowed foundation providing for
the residence and maintenance of teachers—masters or
graduates, and for the free education of a certain number
of poor scholars, to whose company are added, according to the capacity of the building, other students who
are able to live at their own charges.

Relation of the Much has been said about the relation of
college to the the college to the university. By some it
university.
is supposed that the latter is nothing but
the aggregate of the former ; that somewhere in the

52

The Colleges

time of the Georges "the university" arrogated to itself a separate existence, and that since that time university offices have taken precedence of collegiate offices.[1] The *universitas*, the corporation of scholars, must and did precede any college foundation : at the same time we cannot distinguish the development of either of our universities from the rise of these foundations, whose history has, ever since, been the history of the academic society. Each college is independent and autonomous, and though the aggregate of colleges does not constitute the university, each collegiate foundation forms part and parcel of it in virtue of its union with the incorporated society of Chancellor Masters and Scholars which formed at first and still forms "the university."

The college the distinguishing characteristic of Cambridge and Oxford. It is the collegiate system which distinguishes the English universities from all others. Everywhere else in Europe students live in their own private lodgings and have complete control of their lives, subject to no supervision whatever ; the university has no rights over them and no means of ensuring their good behaviour during the period in which they choose to attend its lectures. In many parts of Europe the student passes from a school curriculum in which he has been treated as a complete dependent, on whose sense of common fairplay and honour, even, no reliance can be placed, to a curriculum in which he at once becomes his own absolute master. English instinct is against this— against abandoning a young man at a critical moment

[1] For university and collegiate officials, see iv. pp. 203-10.

53

of his life to his own devices, his own unsupported endeavours, as it is against ruling him by a system of espionage in his school days. It is in favour in both cases of the moral support to be found in an external guarantee for order, orderliness—and of a tacit assistance to good instincts, a tacit resistance to bad ; and the result is the university college.

The origin of the The result, as we say, is an English result,
college system. and is the development of a scheme to which shape was first given by Walter de Merton, Chancellor of England and afterwards Bishop of Rochester, and Hugh de Balsham Bishop and formerly subprior of Ely, in the reign of Henry III.[1] An endowed house and college statutes formed part of this fine academic scheme, which, in all its amplitude and completeness, sprang Athena-like from the brain of Walter de Merton, and was destined from the first to be realised in a university. It must, nevertheless, be clearly borne in mind that the original college dwellings—and the college statutes—were designed for adult scholars, they were, in fact, the earliest training colleges for teachers, and it is only later that their advantages were extended in equal measure to the taught.[2]

The era of College building began in the xiii century
college building. and ended with the xvith. The first great period of building, however, belongs to the second quarter of the xiv century, and no less than seven colleges and halls were founded between the years 1324 and 1352. Ninety years elapsed before the

[1] i. 29, 38, ii. 55-6.   [2] See iv. 217 n., and early college discipline pp. 221-2.

The Colleges

second period, which began with the foundation of King's College in 1441 and ended with the foundation of S. John's in 1509. The third and last period opened a hundred years after the foundation of King's and closed with the foundation of the first Protestant colleges fifty years later (1595) :

First period.	Second period.	Third period.
Peterhouse 1284		
(28 years)	(68 years)	(50 years)
Michaelhouse 1324	King's College 1441	Magdalene 1542
Clare 1326-38	Queens' 1448	Trinity 1546
King's Hall 1337	S. Catherine's 1473	(Caius 1557)
Pembroke 1347	Jesus 1495	Emmanuel 1584
Gonville Hall 1348	Christ's 1505	Sidney Sussex 1595
Trinity Hall 1350	S. John's 1509	
Corpus Christi 1352		

There were therefore 8 colleges in Cambridge by the middle of the xiv century ; when the xvi century opened there were 14, and at its close 12 of the previous buildings remained and 4 new had been added. Downing College (built 1805) must be added to these, making at the present day a total of 17 colleges.

Peterhouse. Peterhouse was founded by Hugh de Balsham[1] for his Ely scholars whom he had in vain attempted to unite, with a separate endowment of their

[1] Balsham (a village 9½ miles S.E. of Cambridge) was one of the 10 manorhouses, palaces, and castles of the bishops of Ely in the xiv c. Montacute resided here in 1341. In 1401 a controversy regarding archidiaconal jurisdiction in the university was held here : a similar dispute occurred in Balsham's time (p. 28). On the alienation of this manor from the see of Ely it was purchased by the founder of the Charterhouse, and now forms part of the endowment of that college. There is a mention of Hugh de Balsham (Hugo de Belesale) in Matthew Paris.

PETERHOUSE FROM THE STREET

The Tower of the Congregational Church in the
distance.

Cambridge

own, under the same roof as the canons of S. John's Hospital.[1] In 1284 he removed the Ely clerks to two hostels by S. Peter's church at the other end of the town, and at his death two years later left three hundred marks for the erection of a hall. This was built in 1290 on the south-west and formed with the scholars' chambers the only collegiate building at Peterhouse till the close of the xiv century. Here then were the primitive elements of a college ; the hostel or scholars' lodging house to which was added a common meeting and dining room, or hall. The little parish church of S. Peter served for prayers and gave its name to the college. College chapels were not built till considerably later : the example first given by Pembroke College in the next century not being followed for another hundred years. The quadrangle was not begun till 1424. A combination room[2] opening out from the hall, and a library, were added along the south side. Over the former was the master's room, over the latter the students' quarters ; and all looked upon the ancient lawn, the meadow with its elms beyond and, stretching to the right, with its water gate, Coe fen.

Ye brown, o'er-arching groves,
That contemplation loves,
Where willowy Camus lingers with delight !
Oft at the blush of dawn
I trod your level lawn

With Freedom by my side, and soft-eyed Melancholy.[3]

[1] S. John's College, pp. 122-3.   [2] iv. p. 214.
[3] Gray, *Installation Ode*. There has been little water in Coe fen for the

The Colleges

Hostels and church, facing the Trumpington road, were just without Trumpington gate. In 1309 the college area was extended southwards, over the ground occupied by Jesu hostel.[1] The property of the Gilbertine canons was added in the XVI century. The college area covers the space between Trumpington Street and Coe fen, and Little S. Mary's church and Scroope Terrace; two-thirds of the site of the Fitzwilliam Museum being ground purchased from Peterhouse. The new Gisborne building (1825) is built on the west beyond the hall. The frontage of Peterhouse on Trumpington Street is unpromising; nothing suggests the charm of the buildings on the south side or the open country beyond, stored with historical memories. From the hall, a site unrivalled in the university, opens the panelled combination room,[2] the "Good Women" of Chaucer limned, in one of its bays, recalling

> The chambres and parlers of a sorte
> With bay windowes

described by the poet's contemporary.

last hundred years. The wall and water gate were made during the mastership of Warkworth and the episcopacy of Alcock (1486-1500) and ornamented with the arms of the latter, who was probably a Peterhouse man.

[1] i. p. 22. Their house was on a messuage purchased by them "opposite the chapel of S. Edmund": it lay on the south of the two hostels, and reached "as far as the marsh "—*i.e.* Coe fen.

[2] The rebuilding of the hall and combination room took place in 1866-70. Gilbert Scott, William Morris, Burne-Jones and Ford Madox Brown were called in, and an excellent piece of work accomplished, the fellows' old "Stone parlour" and "inner parlour" being thrown into one to make the present picturesque combination room.

PETERHOUSE—THE FIRST COURT

The entrance to the chapel faces the spectator. On
the right is seen the Combination Room (1460) and
the Hall. Through the Cloisters we get a view into
the street. This is the oldest college in Cambridge.

Cambridge

Above the xvi century library (of which Balsham's own books were the nucleus, enriched by Whittlesey, Bottlesham, Arundel, Warkworth, Gray, Perne, and Cosin)[1] a charming corner room in the students' quarters has been set apart by the present Master for evening study, a veritable *solarium* where the readers are surrounded by the portraits of the great sons of Peterhouse.

The chapel A.D. 1628. Old S. Peter's church was perhaps burnt down in 1338-1340 by a fire which is supposed to have also destroyed the chapel of S. Edmund. On its site rose the present church of Little S. Mary.[2] But in the early xvii century a movement was set afoot at Peterhouse which resulted in the erection of a college chapel. It now stands in the midst of the college buildings, and one of the two ancient hostels, "the little ostle," was demolished to provide a site. Matthew Wren, uncle of Sir Christopher and then Master of the college, afterwards Bishop of Ely, was the builder. The desire of the fellows of Peterhouse for a chapel of their own coincided with the movement in the English Church for an elaborate ritual. As it stands it is a perfect specimen of a xvii century chapel, with its dark oak stalls, and its east window spared from Commonwealth marauders by the expedient of removing the glass piece by piece and hiding it till the

[1] College libraries, p. 138 *n.* The two Beauforts, the Cardinal and the Duke of Exeter, and two of Henry VI.'s physicians Roger Marshall and John Somerset (p. 106), all enriched this library.

[2] *Beata Maria de Gratia.* For S. Peter's church and Peterhouse chapel, see *Willis and Clark, i. p. 40.*

The Colleges

iconoclastic fever had spent itself. But still we have only the shell of the original chapel, the roof of which was adorned with figures of a hundred and fifty angels the statue of S. Peter presiding from the west. Nine years later all this was pulled down by the Commonwealth men and the ritualist movement it embodied came to an end.[1]

Hall portraits. Peterhouse hall, in common with the halls of all other colleges, contains the portraits of its great men : here, however, they look down upon us not only from the wall above the high table but from the stained glass of the windows. Holbroke Master of the college, chancellor of the university during the Barnwell process, and an early student of science ; Cardinal Beaufort scholar of the house who represented Henry V. at the Council of Constance, and was himself, perhaps, *papabile* ; Warkworth writing his Lancastrian Chronicle—are in their doctor's scarlet : here also are Whitgift, Cosin, and Crashaw, who is depicted as a canon of Loreto ; the poet Gray, the third duke of Grafton chancellor of the university and Prime Minister, and Henry Cavendish the physicist. The panel portraits were removed here from the Stone parlour. The painting of Bishop Law by Romney (?) reminds us that many of the Laws were at Peterhouse, including the first Lord Ellenborough. Over the high table is Lord Kelvin the latest famous son of the house. Among these must also be noted Thomas Heywood "a prose Shakspeare," Hutchinson " the regicide "

[1] v. p. 280.

59

one of the first Puritan gentlemen and one of the best, Peter Baro, Markland the classical critic, and Sherlock who measured himself against Bossuet.

Peterhouse owes nothing to royal endowments but it has not lived outside the stir of national movements either political or religious. There were fervent Lancastrians within its walls in the xv century, fervent partisans of the Stuarts in the xviith. It was, second to none in England, the anti-Puritan college, numbering among its masters Wren and Cosin, and that Doctor Andrew Perne who was among its most munificent benefactors.[1] Perne was a Petrean first and a theologian afterwards, and, as vice-chancellor, was to be found burning the remains of Martin Bucer and Paul Fagius[2] in order to ingratiate the university with Mary, and signing the Thirty-nine Articles on the accession of Elizabeth. The letters AP AP on the weather cock of his college are said to mean : Andrew Perne, " a Papist " or " a Protestant," as you will ; and in Cantabrigian language a coat that has been turned is a coat that has been *perned*, and *pernare* signifies to change your opinions with frequency.

Since the xvii century Peterhouse has been connected with no great movements. In the xv century and again in the early xixth it produced eminent physical

---

[1] v. pp. 263-4. Isaac Barrow uncle of his great namesake was one of the fellows ejected by the Puritan commissioners, before his nephew who had been entered for the college could come into residence. Crashaw was another; and Whitgift was a third fellow whose name stands for anti-Puritanism.

[2] Both sent by Edward VI. to inculcate Protestant doctrine in Cambridge.

The Colleges

and mathematical students; and in the xviii century Sir William Browne, President of the College of Physicians, learnt here his science. Scotchmen have a predilection for the college; and a nucleus of history men is being formed under the present Master's guidance.

Little S. Mary's. The patronage of the historical church which was for three or four centuries the chapel of Peterhouse remains in the hands of the college. It is indeed an integral part of Peterhouse for every Petrean. But its interest does not end here; it reaches across the Atlantic and binds the new continent to the home-hearth of learning in England. A monument in the chapel to Godfrey Washington who died in 1729 bears the arms *argent two bars gules, in chief three estoiles*—the origin of the Stars and Stripes. The Washington crest is an eagle issuant from a crown—affirming sovereignty or escaping from a monarchy?[1]

Cherry Hinton. The Rectory of Cherry Hinton two and a half miles south-east of Cambridge, on the way to the village of Balsham, is no less important in the history of the Ely scholars. In the xiv century the endowment of the college was not sufficient for their maintenance all the year round: the college nevertheless had made rapid progress since its separate existence at Peterhouse began, and Fordham Bishop of Ely (1388-1426) decided to confirm to them the greater tithes of Cherry Hinton of which the college is to this day

[1] See v. p. 278.

PETERHOUSE FROM THE FELLOWS'
GARDEN

On the right is the Combination Room (1460), while
farther back in the picture is the Hall, a continuation
of this range of most ancient and picturesque buildings.

rector ; but which had indeed been first assigned them by Bishop Simon Langham as early as 1362.[1]

A visit to this interesting church completes our picture of the college which "his affection for learning and the state of the poor scholars who were much put to it for conveniency of lodging " persuaded Balsham to endow.

Peterhouse lodge. The lodge of Peterhouse is on the opposite side of Trumpington Street, and is the only example of a lodge outside the college precincts in the university. The house belonged to Charles Beaumont, nephew of the metaphysical poet Joseph Beaumont who was Master of Peterhouse, and was bequeathed by him for the college lodge in 1727.

Peterhouse has always been one of the small colleges. Balsham founded it for a master, 14 fellows, and a few Bible clerks.[2] In the time of Charles I. (1634) it maintained 19 fellows, 29 Bible clerks, and 8 scholars, making with the college officers and other students a total of 106. Sixty years earlier, when Caius wrote, there were 96 inmates, and in the middle of the xviii century, 90. To-day there are 11 fellowships, and 23 scholarships varying from £20 to £80 a year in value.

[1] In the reign of Richard II. the merits of the Peterhouse scholars were as celebrated as their "indigence" was "notorious"; they continued in unceasing exercise of discipline and study, and the tithes of Cherry Hinton appear to have been bestowed in the hope of providing through them a bulwark against lollardry.

[2] The Bible-clerks (*bibliotistae*) were so called because it was their duty to read the Scriptures in hall at meal time : they were a sort of poorer scholar or 'sizar,' see iv. p. 219.

The Colleges

The bishops of Ely have never ceased to be the visitors of the college.

Michaelhouse. Nearly forty years elapsed before a second college was projected. On September 27 1324 Hervey de Stanton, who like other founders in both universities — like Merton, Alcock, Wykeham, and Wolsey—was a notable pluralist,[1] opened Michaelhouse on the present site of Trinity. His purchases for the site had been made in 1323-4, and as was the case with the foundations preceding and succeeding it, Michaelhouse was an adaptation of edifices already existing. It remained one of the principal collegiate buildings until the xvi century and was successively enlarged by absorbing both Crouched and Gregory's as students' hostels.

Domus aula collegium. As Peterhouse was called "the House-of-Scholars of S. Peter," so was Michaelhouse called "the House-of-Scholars of S. Michael." It will be seen that *domus* and *aula* were the earliest appellations. As *hospitia* or *diversoria literarum* signified the unendowed house, so *domus* or *aula scholarium* signified the endowed house. Such compound titles as "house of S. Peter or hall-of-scholars of the Bishop of Ely" precede, as they explain, the later title *college*. A college denotes not a dwelling but a community : precisely the same distinction is to

---

[1] He was Chancellor of the Exchequer to Edward II. ; Canon of York and Wells, and Rector of East Dereham and of North Creake in Norfolk. For Michaelhouse, see also Statutes p. 67 and Trinity College p. 133.

CLARE COLLEGE AND BRIDGE FROM
THE CAM—AUTUMN EVENING

Cambridge

be drawn between *domus* and *collegium* as between *monasterium* and *conventus*. Every university *domus* was intended for a college of scholars, as every religious house was intended for a convent of religious ; the transition was easy, though not logical, from "college of the hall of Valense-Marie" to Valence-Marie College, and to-day the word is used indiscriminately to mean both the building and the community.[1]

Clare Hall 1326-1338. Clare Hall was erected on the site of University Hall, a house for scholars founded during the chancellorship of Richard de Badew who obtained the king's licence for it on February 20 1326, when he was lodged at Barnwell.[2] In the next reign (1344, 18th of Edward III.) it is referred to as "the hospice belonging to Cambridge university." This hall, like Peterhouse, originated in two hostels purchased for the university in the street running parallel to the High Street, from the present site of Queen's to the back gate of Trinity.[3] Twelve years later Elizabeth de Burgh[4] sister and co-heiress of

[1] Elizabeth de Burgh speaks of "the college" of her "aforesaid house." Cf. the words used by the founder of Trinity Hall as regards his own foundation : University Calendar *sub rubrica* Trinity Hall.

[2] See royal visits, p. 113.   [3] See Mill Street, pp. 96-7 *n.*

[4] She was daughter of Gilbert de Clare, Earl of Gloucester and Hertford by Joan daughter of Edward I. Her brother and co-heir fell at Bannockburn 1314. Like Lady Margaret she was three times married, first to John de Burgh son and heir of Richard Earl of Ulster, her third husband also being an Irishman.

Chancellor Badew was a member of the Chelmsford knightly family of that name.

The Colleges

Gilbert Earl of Clare founded her college and in 1340 she obtained possession of University Hall,[1] and decreed in 1359 that it should thenceforth be known as the " House of Clare."[2]

The scheme of building of Clare Hall was quadrangular ; but no college was longer in the building. A hall, combination room, and Master's room were on the west, while the chapel at the north-east angle was not built till 1535.[3] The scholars had till then kept their prayers in the parish church of S. Zachary and in the south chancel aisle of S. Edward's. The present chapel was not begun till 1764. As we see it now Clare is a homogeneous piece of work of the time of Charles I., and in its classical beauty is one of the finest in Cambridge. This complete rebuilding occupied twenty-six years—from 1635 to 1661. There is no record of the architect, though an unsupported tradition points to Inigo Jones.

When one pictures Clare Hall it is to recall " the Backs," the characteristic feature of Cambridge scenery which rivals the beauty of " the gardens " in the sister university. The grounds of the succession of collegiate

---

[1] April 5 1340. Grant by the university of the *domus universitatis* to Elizabeth de Burgh Lady de Clare, in consideration of her gift of the advowson of Litlyngton. See Caius p. 144 *n.*

[2] Peterhouse, Michaelhouse, Clare House—the earliest name for a Cambridge college ; Corpus was also incorporated as the *Domus Scholarium Corporis Christi*, etc. King's Hall is the first to be so styled and is followed by Pembroke Hall. In 1440 we have King's College. Peterhouse and Trinity Hall are now the only colleges which retain the older style, although Clare itself was called Clare Hall until 1856.

[3] Cf. p. 109 *n.*

9

CLARE COLLEGE AND BRIDGE FROM
THE AVENUE

King's College Chapel is seen through the trees.

buildings fronting the ancient High Street, with sloping lawns, bowling green, and fellows' garden, extend along the backs of the colleges beyond the narrow river over which each college throws its bridge, and beyond again runs the well known road and the college playgrounds.

Clare is supposed to have been the "Soler hall" of Chaucer's Tale.[1] It has enjoyed the reputation of a fashionable college, and indeed of a "sporting college." It no doubt enjoyed the former reputation from the first, as a foundation under the patronage of the great house of Clare, and furnished some of the overdressed dandies who flocked to Cambridge in Chaucer's time, as well as his "pore" Yorkshire "scolers" or others like them. Ralph Cudworth was Master of the college; Tillotson Archbishop of Canterbury, the martyr bishop Latimer, and Whiston the successor of Newton were its fellows; and Nicholas Heath primate of York, Sir George Downing, Cole the antiquary, Townshend, Chancellor of the Exchequer, the first Marquis Cornwallis, Brodrick Archbishop of Cashel, and Whitehead the laureate were its *alumni*. It was founded for 20 fellows or scholars, 6 of whom were to be in priests' orders. In 1634 there were 15 fellows and 32 scholars, in all 106 inmates. In the time of Caius there had been 129, and in the middle of the xviii century there were about 100. There are

[1] "Soler," apparently used for a loggia or balcony. East Anglian belfries were called bell-solers. Cf. *solarium* for an upper chamber, and *nei solai* (Ital.) for "in the garrets." In early Cambridge college nomenclature *solar* was an upstairs, *celar* (cellar) a downstairs room.

The Colleges

now 18 fellowships and 31 scholarships ranging in value from £20 to £60.

College statutes. The statutes of Clare Hall were written by the founder in 1359, a year before her death. The statutes of Peterhouse[1] and of Pembroke do not exist in their original form—and those of Hervey de Stanton for Michaelhouse and of Elizabeth de Burgh for Clare must be held to be the two types of Cambridge college statutes. Of these the latter rank as the most enlightened original code framed for a Cambridge college. Stanton's contain little more than directions for the conduct of a clerical seminary, and this type was followed by the framers of the statutes of Corpus Christi and in their general intention by Gonville in statutes afterwards modified by Bateman. The statutes of King's Hall framed for Richard II. reverted to the Merton type ; Henry VI.'s statutes for King's follow, as we shall see, the type already laid down by William of Wykeham, while Lady Margaret Countess of Richmond, and John Fisher Bishop of Rochester framed statutes which contain some original elements.

Elizabeth de Burgh's originality consists in her realisation of the value of learning and of general knowledge for all kinds of men and for its own sake. " In every degree, whether ecclesiastical or temporal, skill in learning is of no mean advantage ; which although sought for by many persons in many ways is

---

[1] Simon Montacute, 17th Bishop of Ely, re-wrote the statutes of Peterhouse, 1338-44.

THE HALL OF CLARE COLLEGE

The notable features of this interior are the plaster
ceiling and the large oak figures over the fireplace,
the latter designed by Sir M. Digby Wyatt 1870-72.

Cambridge

to be found most fully in the university where a *studium generale* is known to flourish."[1] Thence it sends forth its "disciples," "who have tasted its sweetness," skilled and fitted, to fill their place in the world. She wishes to promote, with the advancement of religious worship and the welfare of the state, "the extension of these sciences"; her object being that "the pearl of knowledge" "once discovered and acquired by study and learning" "should not lie hid," but be diffused more and more widely, and when so diffused give light to them that walk in the darkness of the shadow of ignorance.[2]

The statutes of Marie Valence were written twelve years earlier and even in the form in which they have come down to us have a character of their own and conform to none of the three types of Merton, Michaelhouse, or Clare.[3]

Merton's statutes were issued in 1264, 1270, and 1274, and the 1274 statutes exist in the university library in a register of the Bishops of Lincoln. Mr. J. Bass Mullinger has printed Hervey de Stanton's in Appendix D. to his "History of the University of Cambridge"; they are contained in the Michaelhouse book in the muniment room of Trinity.

For King's Hall, founded in 1337, see page 131.

[1] Cf. Merton's "Oxoniae, vel alibi ubi *studium vigere* contigerit" (1264), and the words in Alan Bassett's bequest for monastic scholars at Oxford or elsewhere *ubi studium fuerit universitatis* (1233).

[2] See also p. 86 footnote.

[3] The proportion of priests among the fellows (*i.e.* scholars on the foundation) was to be 6 in 30, 4 in 20, 2 in 12. See also pp. 152 and 153.

The Colleges

Pembroke Hall was founded in 1347 by Marie daughter of Guy de Chatillon comte de Saint-Paul and of Mary grand-daughter of Henry III. She was of the blood of that Walter de Chatillon who in the retreat from Damietta during the 7th crusade, held a village alone against successive assaults of the Saracen ; and having drawn forth their missiles from his body after each sally, charged afresh to the cry of *Chatillon! Chevaliers!*—and the widow of Aymer de Valence Earl of Pembroke the inexorable enemy of Robert Bruce in Edward's wars against the Scottish king. Pembroke stands opposite Peterhouse and several hostels were destroyed to make room for it. It was called by the founder the hall of Valencemarie, and in Latin documents *aula Pembrochiana.*

Architectural scheme of a college. With Pembroke the first college foundation stone was laid in Cambridge. Here for the first time we have a homogeneous collegiate house and not a mere adaptation of preexisting buildings, and may therefore enquire what was the architectural plan of a college. The principle of the quadrangle, although it underwent considerable architectural development, was recognised with the first attempt at college architecture.[1] The special collegiate buildings at first occupied one side of the court only. Here, facing the gateway, were to be found the hall with its buttery and kitchen, above the hall the Master's lodging, with perhaps a garret bedroom above it—the *solarium.* The combination room attiguous

[1] Cf. King's Hall, p. 132.

69

Cambridge

to the hall makes its appearance in the next century, and at right angles or parallel to this main block stretch the students' chambers and studies. A muniment room or treasury is over the gate ; the library, occupying a third side,[1] and the chapel, come later ; and last of all the architectural gateway is added.[2] Meadows and fields and the Master's plot of ground are soon developed into the Master's garden, the fellows' garden, the bowling green, and tennis court. By the xv century the buildings round a courtyard easily assume the plan of the new domestic dwelling of that epoch, of which the type is Haddon Hall Derbyshire and, in Cambridge, Queens' College : the college *domus* of the xiv century becomes the quadrangular manor-house of the xvth and xvith. In such a scheme of public buildings only a few scholars could be lodged in the main court, and smaller quadrangles for their accommodation were therefore added. University Hostel formed one side of such a second court in Pembroke ; Clare and Queens' had also second courts, and their example was followed at Christ's and S. John's.

Here then we have a scheme of building which is neither monastic nor feudal. It may with propriety be called scholastic but it is also essentially domestic architecture. The college quadrangle as we see it evolved in Cambridge is the earliest attempt at devising

[1] The xv c. library at Pembroke was over the hall ; the older library of the same date at Peterhouse was next the hall.

[2] The earliest of these features appears at Pembroke, which had a treasury. For the combination room see p. 135 and iv. p. 214. For the gateway, p. 140. For students' studies, iv. p. 232 n.

The Colleges

a dwelling which should resemble neither the cloister nor the castle, should suggest neither enclosure nor self-defence—a scholastic dwelling. The college is the outcome of that moment in our history when feudalism had played its part and monasticism was losing its power ; it represents what the rise of the universities themselves represents and its architectural interest is unique. No monastic terms are retained ; the hall is not a refectory, the one constant monastic and canonical feature, the church, has no part at all in the scheme—the scholars were men not separated from their fellows and they used the parish church.

The first collegiate dwelling houses, like the English manor-house, consciously or unconsciously followed one of the oldest house-plans known to civilisation—the scheme of dwelling-rooms round a court was that of the Roman house.* The *aula seu domus scholarium* had moreover as its starting point—like the earliest *domus ecclesiae*—a hall in a house ; the hall is the nucleus of the college.[1]

The site of Pembroke. Marie de Saint-Paul, like her predecessor Elizabeth de Burgh, purchased university property for the site of her college. "University hostel" which stood here formed one side of the narrow quadrangle the building of which was at once begun, and a messuage of Hervey de Stanton's formed the

[1] Cf. Peterhouse p. 56. The Christian church evolved in Rome no doubt originated in the domestic *aula*, the basilica, of a great private house, and was surrounded by those dwelling-rooms which constituted the first *titulus* or *domus ecclesiae*. So at Cambridge we have a *domus collegii*, and *domus vel aula scholarium* sancti Michaelis or Clarae.

THE OLD COURT, PEMBROKE COLLEGE

The Dining Hall is seen on the right of the picture.

Cambridge

other. Within five years the complete area had been acquired, and it is probable that the south side was also partly built before the founder's death in 1377. On the west were the hall and kitchen, on the east, abutting on the street, was the gate with students' chambers on either side of it. With the hostel the founder bought an acre of meadowland which she converted into an orchard—" the orchard against Pembroke Hall " it is called in her lifetime. She also obtained permission from two of the Avignon popes—Innocent VI. and Urban V.—to erect a chapel and bell tower, and these were built, after the middle of the xiv century, at the north west corner of the closed quadrangle. This interesting site was used later as a library and is still a reference library and lecture room. Traces of fresco remain under the panelling, and the chaplain's room with its hagioscope for the altar is on the east. The lower part of the bell tower also still exists.

In 1389 the college acquired Cosyn's Place, and later Bolton's, and in 1451 a perpetual lease of S. Thomas's hostel. University hostel retained its name till the last quarter of the xvi century, and it was only pulled down in 1659 to make room for the Hitcham building which now forms the south side of the second court. There is nothing left of the xiv and xv century structures. The present lodge, hall, and library and the other new buildings in stone and red brick have all been erected since 1870. The chapel occupies part of the site of S. Thomas's hostel, and was built by Matthew Wren, Bishop of Ely and Master of Peter-

72

The Colleges

house, at his own charges; the architect being his nephew Christopher Wren. The bishop had already built Peterhouse chapel and this new work was undertaken in fulfilment of his intention to make some pious offering if he were ever liberated from the Tower, where the Parliament kept him between the years 1642 and 1658. The fine combination room is panelled with the oak from the xvii century hall. The portrait of Marie de Saint-Paul presides in the present hall with that of Henry VI. flanked by busts of Pitt, Gray, and Stokes.

Two spiritual relationships were bequeathed by the founder to the college. One with the Franciscan friars, the other with the Minoresses of Denney. The former connexion ceased almost as soon as it was devised, for the existing edition of the statutes (made after the founder's death) omits all mention of it.[1]

No college but Trinity outshines Pembroke for the fame of its scholars and none for the antiquity of its fame. Henry VI. in a charter granting lands speaks of it as "this eminent and most precious college, which is and ever hath been resplendent among all places in the university."[2] The king so favoured it that it was called his "adopted daughter"; and when Elizabeth

[1] After the founder's death two rectors were to exercise complete jurisdiction, one of these was to be a secular graduate but the other is to be a Franciscan. Moreover the fellows of the college were "to give their best counsel and aid" to the abbess and sisters of Denney abbey who had from the founder "a common origin with them." For Denney, see i. p. 25, 25 n.

[2] *Notabile et insigne et quam pretiosum collegium quod inter omnia loca universitatis . . mirabiliter splendet et semper resplenduit.*

73   10

A COURT AND CLOISTERS IN PEMBROKE COLLEGE

This represents the First or Entrance Court of the
College.   Beyond the Cloisters is the Chapel designed
by Sir Christopher Wren and completed in 1664.

Cambridge

rode past it on her way to her lodging at King's she saluted it with one of those happy phrases characteristic of the Tudors : " *O domus antiqua et religiosa !* " words which sum its significance in university history.

Pembroke is the *alma mater* of Edmund Spenser,[1] of Gray,[2] of the younger Pitt,[3] of Thixtil, fellow in 1519, whose extraordinary erudition is praised by Caius, of Wharton the anatomist, Sydenham the xvii century physician, Gabriel Harvey the "Hobbinoll" of the *Shepherd's Calendar*,[4] Sir George Stokes the mathematician, and Sir Henry Maine.[5] *Grindal and *Whitgift [6] of Canterbury, *Rotherham and *Booth of York, *Richard Fox Master of the college, Bishop of Winchester, and founder of Corpus Christi Oxford, the two Langtons Bishops of *S. David's and Winchester, *Ridley the martyr Bishop of London, *Lancelot Andrewes Bishop of Ely, then of Winchester, with

[1] Spenser entered as a sizar.

[2] Gray left Peterhouse on account of some horseplay on the part of its students who raised a cry of fire which brought him out of bed and down from his window overlooking Little S. Mary's church in an escape which his dread of fire had induced him to contrive. Of his treatment at Pembroke he writes that it was such as might have been extended to " Mary de Valence in person."

[3] Pitt in introducing his son to the college writes : " Such as he is, I am happy to place him at Pembroke ; and I need not say how much of his parents' hearts goes along with him." (Letter to the Senior tutor of the college, 1767.)

[4] He was afterwards fellow of Trinity Hall, and Spenser dedicates one of the Eclogues to him there.

[5] See Trinity Hall, p. 80.

[6] The asterisks denote Masters of the College. Whitgift migrated from Queens' to Pembroke, and was subsequently fellow of Peterhouse and Master of Pembroke. Langton of Winchester was a fellow.

The Colleges

*Felton and *Wren of Ely, are on its honour roll. The second Master was Robert Thorpe of Thorpe-next-Norwich, knighted by Edward III. and afterwards Lord Chancellor.[1] The old college garden, loved by Ridley, is much despoiled, but "Ridley's walk" remains. Pembroke gave two other martyrs for their religious opinions, Rogers and Bradford.[2] Two fellows of the college[3] in the reign of Edward III. died in Rome where they had gone to obtain from Innocent VI. possession of part of the original endowment of the college; a statute prescribes that mass shall be said for them each July.

In the library are Gower's *Confessio Amantis* and the *Golden Legend*, printed by Caxton. It is this last book which brought him the promise of "a buck in summer and a doe in winter" from the Earl of Arundel, for its great length had made him "half desperate to have accomplished it." There, too, is Gray's MS. of the "Elegy." The college also possesses Bishop Andrewes' library. Matthew Wren is buried in the chapel, and his staff and mitre are preserved in the college, the latter being a solitary specimen of a post-reformation mitre; it was worn over a crimson silk cap.

The college was founded for 30 scholars, if the revenues permitted.[4] In the time of Caius it housed 87 members; in Fuller's time 100 (including 20 fellows and 33 scholars); in the middle of the xviii century the number of students averaged 50 or 60.

---

[1] pp. 27 and 96. [2] v. p. 275.
[3] Reyner D'Aubeney and Robert Stanton. [4] p. 68 *n.*

Cambridge

There are now 13 fellowships and 34 scholarships of the value of £20 to £80.

Founders of Cambridge colleges. The Cambridge colleges are remarkable for the large proportion of them founded and endowed by women. Of the 16 colleges built between the xiii and xvi centuries, now in existence, 6 are due to the munificence of women—Clare, Pembroke, Queens', Christ's, S. John's, and Sidney Sussex. Next as college builders come the chancellors of England, the bishops, and the kings who have each endowed the university with three colleges. Hervey de Stanton, Chancellor of the Exchequer in the reign of Edward II., Thomas Lord Audley chancellor to Henry VIII., and Sir Walter Mildmay Chancellor of the Exchequer to Elizabeth, all founded colleges, two of which still remain—Magdalene and Emmanuel.[1] Hugh Balsham of Ely, Bateman of Norwich, and Alcock of Ely founded three existing colleges—Peterhouse, Trinity Hall, and Jesus.[1] The kings of England account for some of the finest work in the university, King's Hall, King's College, and Trinity College.[2]

---

[1] Alcock himself, by a unique arrangement made with Rotherham, held the Seals conjointly with that prelate, then Bishop of Lincoln, from April to September 1474 ; and he had acted in parliament in the same capacity for Stillington in 1472. Merton whose Cambridge operations were described in the last chapter was Lord Chancellor ; so was Sir Walter Thorpe who began the Schools, and so were Booth and Rotherham who completed the Schools quadrangle and built the old library. John Somerset, who was chiefly instrumental in the founding of King's College, was Chancellor of the Exchequer to Henry VI.

[2] Cf. nationality of founders of colleges p. 150.

The Colleges

The early series In the series of Cambridge colleges the 3 of colleges. foundations of the early xiv century which followed Peterhouse were all merged in other colleges. Pembroke which was the sixth foundation was the first piece of collegiate building to be carried through in Cambridge, and Corpus Christi must rank as the second.

The colleges from Peterhouse to Pembroke :—

Peterhouse 1284
Michaelhouse 1324
{University Hall 1326
{Clare 1338
King's Hall 1337
Pembroke Hall 1347

(Gonville 1348
(Trinity Hall 1350)

Corpus 1352

Michaelhouse and King's Hall went to swell the greatness of Trinity ; University Hall became the foundation stone of Clare : and all of them, with Gonville and Trinity Hall, were incomplete adaptations of earlier buildings at the time when Pembroke and Corpus were finished.

We now come to two colleges which formed an East Anglian corner in the university.

Gonville Hall Within a month of the licence granted to 1348. Marie de Saint-Paul, Edmund Gonville obtained his for the erection of the hall which is called after him. Gonville was an East Anglian parson, rector of two Norfolk parishes and sometime vicar-general of the diocese of Ely. In one of these parishes his elder brother Sir Nicholas Gonville of Rushworth had already established a college of canons, and

TRINITY HALL

The nearer building seen in the picture is the old
Library, and beyond it are the Latham Buildings.

Cambridge

Edmund Gonville himself was a great favourer of the Dominicans. Edward III.'s licence enabled him to found a hall for 20 scholars in Lurteburgh (now Freeschool) Lane, between S. Benet's and great S. Mary's, in 1348. In 1352 this site was exchanged with Benet College for another on the other side of the High Street,[1] the present site of Gonville and Caius. The Hall was dedicated in honour of the Annunciation of the Blessed Virgin Mary, and enjoyed a great reputation among East Anglians and various proofs of papal favour up to the eve of the Reformation.[2] Like Corpus its object was the education of the clergy and theology was to be their study. Alexander VI. (1492-1503) licensed annually two of its students to preach in any part of England, apparently a unique permission.[3] Humphrey de la Pole—who resided for many years— and his brother Edward, sons of the second Duke of Suffolk, were students here ; so was Sir Thomas Gresham. Gonville was refounded as Gonville and Caius by Doctor Keys (Caius) two hundred years later.[4]

Trinity Hall   Edmund Gonville left William Bateman
A.D. 1350.   Bishop of Norwich his executor in the interests of his new foundation. Bateman, a notable

---

[1] The stone house (p. 24 *n.*) and John Goldcorn's property—all opposite Michaelhouse—were then fashioned by Bateman, after the founder's demise, as Gonville Hall.

[2] See Gonville and Caius, pp. 143-4.

[3] Twelve preachers from each university were annually licensed for any diocese in England. Gonville was now allowed two such licences on its own account.

[4] p. 141.

The Colleges

figure in the xiv century, set forth as Edward's ambassador to the King of France in the month that the Black Death made its appearance in East Anglia (March 1350), and died at Avignon on an embassy from the king to the Pope. In 1350 on his return from France,[1] he founded Trinity Hall, near Gonville, on the site of the hostel of the monks of Ely [2] which he obtained for that purpose.[3]

If Gonville's foundation was intended for the country parson, Bateman's was intended for the *prete di carriera*. Both were designed to repair the ravages in the ranks of the clergy left by the plague, but while Gonville's clerks were to devote their time to the study of theology Bateman's were to study exclusively civil and canon law. The college was built round a quadrangle,[4] and the religious services were kept in the church of S. John the Baptist (or Zachary) and afterwards in the north aisle of S. Edward's church ; these two churches being shared with the students of Clare. Indeed it was owing to Gardiner's policy and Ridley's advice that Trinity Hall escaped incorporation with Clare College in the reign of Edward VI. The library remains as it was in the early years of

[1] He landed at Yarmouth in June, and the charter of foundation is dated November 20.

[2] Magdalene, p. 127.

[3] The style "the keeper and scholars of the college of the Holy Trinity of Norwich," reminds us that the original dedication of this and Gonville corresponds to that of two of the ancient Cambridge guilds—the Holy Trinity and the Annunciation.

[4] The N.E. corner was obtained four years after the foundation by the purchase of a house at the corner of Henney Lane.

ST. BOTOLPH'S CHURCH AND CORPUS
COLLEGE FROM THE STEPS OF THE
PITT PRESS, TRUMPINGTON STREET

King's College is seen in the distance.

Cambridge

Elizabeth's reign, and was founded by Bateman with the gift of his own collection. The Norfolk men were famous litigants. Doctor Jessopp has shown that neither the Black Death nor any lesser tragedy could hold them from an appeal to the law on every trivial pretext. That the first college of jurists should have been founded by a native of Norwich is certainly therefore a fitting circumstance.

Stephen Gardiner Bishop of Winchester and Chancellor of England was Master of Trinity Hall in the reign of Edward VI. and again in the first year of Mary. He used to say "if all his palaces were blown down by iniquity, he would creep honestly into that shell"—the mastership of Trinity Hall. Other distinguished Masters were Haddon,[1] Master of the Requests to Elizabeth, and Sir Henry Maine who had been fellow and tutor. Bishop Sampson, a pupil of Erasmus, Thirlby, Glisson,[2] Bilney, one of the early reformers, Lord Chesterfield, Bulwer Lytton, and Leslie Stephen were all members of Trinity Hall, which is still the college of the larger number of Cambridge law students. There are 13 fellowships, and about 12 scholarships varying in value from £80 to £21 a year, besides exhibitions of the same value.

In the middle of the xiv century there were two important guilds in Cambridge, the one under the invocation of *Corpus Christi* "keeping their prayers in S. Benet's church," the other dedicated to the

[1] See also King's.   [2] See also Caius.

The Colleges

Blessed Virgin "observing their offices in S. Mary's church." These guilds or confraternities—which existed all through the middle ages as they had existed in classical Rome with precisely similar features— were to be found, as we know, especially among the artisan class, and took the place of our modern trades unions and mutual insurance societies. Like every enterprise of the ages of faith they had a semi-religious character, were usually attached as its "sisters and brethren" to some church, and owed their members not only material assistance but spiritual, paying for masses to be offered for the repose of the souls of all deceased brethren.

Corpus Christi It was two such guilds which forgetting
A.D. 1352. their differences and laying aside all emulations, joined together in the middle of the xiv century in order to found and endow a college in their town. The brethren of the guilds had been planning this enterprise since 1342, and in the following years those who possessed contiguous tenements in the parishes of S. Benet and S. Botolph pulled them down "and with one accord set about the task of establishing a college there." [1] "By this means *they cleared a site for their college square in form*." [2] Here then, as in the case of King's Hall and Pembroke, the earliest collegiate buildings designed as such, the plan was

[1] Account given of the building of Corpus by Archbishop Parker's Latin secretary, John Jocelyn, fellow of Queens'. It is supposed that the hall of the guild of Corpus Christi was near the old court ; S. Mary's guild met at the hostel of that name near the present Senate House. See also p. 83. [2] *Ibid.*

11

THE OLD COURT, CORPUS CHRISTI
COLLEGE

This is the oldest court in Cambridge.   The Tower
of the old Saxon Church of St. Benedict is seen in
the background.

quadrangular. Sometimes, as in the case of Trinity Hall, the adjacent buildings for completing the court could not be at once obtained, in others, as at Corpus itself and Clare, the courts are irregular, owing. to the same difficulty of getting the foursquare space. Corpus Christi college presents us, indeed, with the unique and perfect example in Cambridge of the ancient college court. By March 1352 a clear space, 220 feet long by 140 wide, had been cleared, and the guilds worked with so much good will that they had nearly finished the exterior wall of their college in the same year. "The building of the college as it appears at the present day," writes John Jocelyn, "with walls of enclosure, chambers arranged about a quadrangle, hall, kitchen, and Master's habitation, was fully finished in the days of Thomas Eltisley, the first Master [1352-1376] and of his successor" [1376-1377]. This original court is what we see also to-day: the buildings are in two floors, the garrets were added later. The hall range contains the Master's lodging with a *solarium* above it, a door and passage leading thence to the hall. The three other sides were devoted to scholars' chambers. S. Benet's served as the scholars' church, and the gate was on this side of the court.

Before the reign of Henry VIII. there was but little glass or panelling in either story of the building. But in Jocelyn's time the Master's and fellows' rooms were "skilfully decorated" with both. The fellows and scholars together panelled, paved, decorated, plastered, and glazed the public rooms of the college, in one case

The Colleges

" the college paying for the material and the scholars for the labour." Thus was this college born of the democratic spirit and the sentiment of union nurtured in the same spirit. The college was called " of Corpus Christi and the Blessed Virgin " but was familiarly known from the close of the xiv century to modern times as Benet College. It lay in the heart of the Saxon town, between the Saxon church of S. Benet and the church of the Saxon Botolph which also served the scholars for their prayers. The former was used until the year 1500, when a small chapel communicating with the south chancel of the church was built. In 1579 Sir Nicholas Bacon gave the college a chapel ; and the modern chapel is on its site. Sir Francis Drake was the largest contributor next to Bacon. The queen gave timber, and the scholars of the college again toiled side by side with the workmen.

On March 21, 1353 the guilds made over to their college Gonville's house in Lurteburgh Lane which they had exchanged with his executor Bateman. More ground was purchased facing the street and in time two large neighbouring hostels S. Mary's and S. Bernard's were acquired for students. The second court has all been built since 1823, and contains the modern hall, lodge, library and chapel, and muniment room, and the Lewes collection. The ancient hall serves as the present kitchen.

In the Library is one of the most valuable collections of MSS. in the country, the spoils of the dissolved monasteries gathered together by Archbishop

ST. BENEDICT'S CHURCH FROM FREE
SCHOOL LANE

Its Saxon tower is the oldest building left in Cambridge, and close by is the oldest piece of College
building, the wall of Corpus Christi.

Cambridge

Parker.   Here is the oldest or "Winchester" Anglo-Saxon Chronicle (to A.D. 892), and Jerome's version of the four gospels sent by Gregory to Augustin—"the most interesting MS. in England."   Here is the splendid Peterborough psalter and "bestiary"; a *penitentiale* of Archbishop Egbert's (A-S. translation); a Pontifical, probably written before 1407; a xv century MS. Homer rescued by Parker from the whilom baker of S. Augustine's Abbey; Matthew Paris' own copy of his history; the Sarum missal of 1506, and a copy of the great English bible of 1568. Here also is the first draft (1562) of the Articles of Religion, 42 in number, scored over by Matthew Parker's red chalk; the 3 articles which were finally omitted (dealing with the state of the departed, the last containing the statement "That all shall not be saved") are here struck out by Parker. The clause concerning the transubstantiation of the eucharist he has similarly overscored.

Corpus also houses some of the most interesting plate in the university.

Candle rents. The college was the chief sufferer in the Corpus Christi peasant revolt of 1381 principally on procession. College arms. account of the wealth which accrued to it from "candle rents," a tax chargeable on the tenants of all houses which had been guild property.[1]   On the festival of Corpus Christi—the

[1] The brethren and sisters of the two guilds presumably thus taxed all house property bequeathed by them to their college, to defray the expenses of the wax lights so freely used in funeral and other liturgical rites. It has been pointed out that the riots occurred two days after the feast of

The Colleges

Thursday in the Octave of Trinity—a great procession which included the officers of the united guild, the civic dignitaries, and the university authorities, perambulated the town from Benet Church to the bridge, the Master bearing the pyx under a rich canopy. Even after the dissolution of the guild the Master of Corpus continued the procession until it was abolished by Henry VIII. in the 27th year of his reign (153⅝). The ancient arms of the college consisted of the shields of the two guilds—the emblems of the Passion for Corpus Christi ; the triangle symbol of the Trinity for the guild of the Blessed Virgin, above, Christ crowning the Madonna and below, the guilds dedicating their college. Exception was taken to them in Parker's time as too papistical, and he got the heralds to change them. The new arms still however recorded the two guilds : quarterly, gules and azure, in the first and fourth a pelican, with her young, vulning herself ; in the second and third three lilies proper

> *Signat avis Christum, qui sanguine pascit alumnos ;*
> *Lilia, virgo parens, intemerata refert.*

Among its great names Corpus counts Sir Nicholas Bacon the father of Francis Lord Bacon, Matthew Parker who was Master of the college and its great benefactor in later times, Christopher Marlowe and Fletcher, Archbishop Tenison, Sir William Paston and a group of xvii century antiquaries, and Boyle ' the great

Corpus Christi, a comparatively new festival in England, and the contribution of wax tapers for this may have greatly aggravated the grievance. The feast is of xiii c. origin, the outdoor procession dates from the early xvth.

Cambridge

earl' of Cork. Roger Manners was a considerable benefactor. In the time of Henry VII. Elizabeth Duchess of Norfolk founded a bible clerkship and a fellowship, and placed the buttresses of the college.[1]

The college soon maintained 8 fellows, 6 scholars, and 3 bible clerks. All the inmates were destined by the founders for priests' orders, this being one of the four foundations in Cambridge due in whole or in part to the dearth of clerks consequent on the black death.[2] In the time of Caius Corpus held 93 persons and in Fuller's time 126. In the xviii century about 60. There are to-day 12 fellowships, about 15 scholarships varying from £80 to £30 in value, 3 sizarships worth £25 each, and 6 exhibitions for students from S. Paul's school, Canterbury, and the Norwich Grammar school varying from £18 to double this sum.[3]

The building of Corpus Christi marks an historical and closes an architectural epoch at Cambridge. The

[1] She was heiress to her sister Eleanor who had been betrothed to Edward IV. They were the daughters of John Talbot Earl of Shrewsbury, and Elizabeth's only child Ann was wife to Richard of York murdered in the Tower.

[2] The dearth of clerks or clergy and the failure of learning : the former engaged the attention of the founders of Gonville, Trinity Hall, and Corpus, the latter of the founder of Clare who writes : "to promote . . . the extension of these sciences, which by reason of the pestilence having swept away a multitude of men, are now beginning to fail rapidly."

[3] The fact that we have a guild college built in Cambridge is especially interesting, for, as Dr. Stubbs has shown, Cambridge ranks highest among English towns for its guild history. Even the Exeter statutes do not rival those of one of its ancient guilds which united the craft or religious guild with the frith-guild—the guild instituted for the religious interests of its

The Colleges

university had indeed two golden ages—the reign of
Edward III. and the reign of the Tudors. It has
not been sufficiently realised that Cambridge had no
European rival in scholastic activity in either period.
In Edward's reign six colleges were built there—King's
Hall, Clare, Pembroke, Gonville, Trinity Hall, and
Corpus ; only one college—Queens'—was founded at
Oxford during the same time. Three of these six
foundations signalise local enterprise, but the three
earlier are a record of the affection of Edward's house
for the university ; and it is their preference for
Cambridge in the xiv century and the preference of
the Tudors for it in the xvth and xvith which marks
its two great epochs.

members or to protect craftsmen and their craft, and the guild which was
an attempt "on the part of the public authorities to supplement the defective
execution of the law, by measures for mutual defence." The Cambridge
statutes, in fact, show us the guild as an element in the development of the
township or burgh, one of those communities within a community which
was the earliest expedient of civilisation, the earliest essay in organisation,
everywhere. The guild which combined these two institutions was a
thanes guild. It made and enforced legal enactments ; it paid the blood-
money if a member slew a man with righteous cause, and exacted eight
pounds from any one who robbed a member. "It is improbable" writes
Dr. Stubbs "that any institution on so large a scale existed in any other
town than London." In Athelstan's reign we have a complete code of such
a London frith-guild. (*Constitutional History of England*, vol. i. p. 414.)

It is against this historic background that we find the guilds of
Corpus Christi and the Blessed Virgin uniting to add a common scholastic
interest to interests civil and religious, by founding a college. The
guilds were lay institutions ; in two of the best known Cambridge guilds
priests were either excluded, or, if admitted, denied a share in the
government ; and a chaplain for the guild of the Blessed Virgin was
only to be maintained if the necessary assistance to the poorer members
permitted of it.

Cambridge

Cambridge in 1353. Let us look at the university as it was in the middle of the xiv century, and let it be the year 1353. It is 250 years since Henry I. began to reign ; 150 before Erasmus lived here, and 550 before our own time. It is the eve of that great change in the mental and moral *venue* of humanity which ushered in the modern world. The Oxford friar Occam, and with him scholasticism, had died four years before, Petrarch was mourning Laura, and Chaucer was walking the streets of Cambridge the man who was to be our link with the early Italian renascence and to clasp hands across the century with Erasmus. Lastly, it was at this moment in our history that the final adjustment of Norman and Saxon elements went hand in hand with the creation of an English language—a period of which Chaucer is our national representative. The town and university were just emerging from the havoc wrought by the " black death," but the royal and noble foundations which had sprung up on all sides before the appearance of the scourge had already attracted the youth round Edward's court to Cambridge ; necessitating in 1342 Archbishop Stratford's injunction against the curls and rings of the young coxcombs studying there.

Cambridge had in fact the reputation of the fashionable university, while its fame is extolled by Lydgate— a younger contemporary of Chaucer who had himself studied at Oxford—in words which show that at this date it was believed also to be the older university.[1]

[1] " Thus of Cambridge the name gan first shyne
As chieffe schoole and vniuersitie
Vnto this tyme fro the daye it began."

88

The Colleges

Let us suppose that Chaucer is returning from his first walk to Grantchester, along the Trumpington road, past the scene he describes in the *Reeve's Tale*, and let us follow him up the Saxon High street. He skirts Coe fen and reaches Peterhouse, its greater and its "little ostle" on the street, with Balsham's hall behind; and as he proceeds he sees on either hand conspicuous signs of the love of the Edwards for Cambridge—to the right the narrow quadrangle of Pembroke, beyond it, off the high road, past S. Botolph's and two hostels, lay the limestone walls of Corpus which had just passed under the protection of Henry of Lancaster;[1] its old court, then the newest of new courts at Cambridge, nestling against the Saxon church of S. Benet. Behind lay the Austinfriars, and across the road the Whitefriars from which Austin's Lane led to Austin's hostel, occupying with Mill street the site of the future King's College and King's College chapel. To the north of S. Benet's he sees the university church of Great S. Mary's, just rebuilt after the fire, and opposite are the schools begun a few years previously, with University, Clare, and Trinity Halls behind, and "le Stone house" of Gonville. Then still to his left, where now we see the buildings of Trinity, he beholds the "gret colledge" King's Hall which Edward III. has just built, Michaelhouse with

[1] The "good duke of Lancaster" was Alderman of the Guild of Corpus Christi. John of Gaunt greatly befriended the college. It was *anno 1356* that the "translation of the college of Corpus Christi out of lay hand to the patronage of the duke of Lancaster," took place; a document so entitled once formed part of the Registry MSS.

KING'S COLLEGE GATEWAY AND
CHAPEL—TWILIGHT EFFECT

The Gateway and Screen on the left hand, and be-
yond it the Chapel. In the distance the Senate
House, Caius College, and the Tower of St. John's
College Chapel.

Cambridge

Crouched hostel which passed into its possession in the February of this year, and its satellite hostels Ovyng's and Garret's.

Just beyond King's Hall is the building which forms the nucleus of the university in the Norman town —the hospital of S. John, bordering on Bridge street. As soon as this road is reached, which leads to the Great Bridge, we see the crusaders' round church of S. Sepulchre, and following the road to the right we come to the Greyfriars, to the site of the future God's House, and past Preachers' street to the Friars Preachers or Blackfriars. On our left, across in the Greencroft, we have left the Benedictine nunnery of S. Rhadegund. Returning past S. Sepulchre's we cross the river and come to the heart of the Norman town—the Conqueror's castle with the Norman manor house bought by Merton in its shadow, and the churches of S. Giles and S. Peter.

Many of the hostels had recently disappeared to make room for the colleges, but they were still as regards these latter nearly in the proportion of three to one—and these latter, with the sole exception of Peterhouse, had all arisen in the previous thirty years.

The sights and sounds in the streets suggested a new epoch—something already achieved and something about to be achieved. Something of stir before an awakening. The English language which was to prove in the hands of its masters one of the finest vehicles of literary expression began everywhere to be heard in place of the French of Norfolk and Stratford-atte-Bowe. The softer southern speech prevailed over

The Colleges

the northern, but the dialects of East Anglia and the Ridings of Yorks were perhaps most frequently heard. The canons of S. John and S. Giles, from the Norman side of the town, might be met in their black cloaks, the Gilbertine canons, from the Saxon side, all in white with the homely sheepskin cape. The Carmelites had already exchanged their striped brown and white cloak—representing Elijah's mantle singed with fire as it fell from the fiery chariot—for the white cloak to which they owe their name of Whitefriars. The Romites of S. Austin wore a hermit's dress.[1] Benedictine monks from Ely and Norwich could certainly be seen in the streets of Cambridge,[2] and the Benedictine nuns of S. Rhadegund rode and walked abroad in the black habit as it was the universal custom in that great order for nuns to do. The Dominicans looked like canons in their black *cappa*, the Franciscans like peasants in their coarse grey tunic roughly tied with cord.

Besides the Carmelites and Austinfriars there were the Bethlemite friars in Trumpington street and Our-Lady friars by the Castle ; the former could be distinguished at a distance by the red star of five rays on their cloaks with a sky blue circle in its centre— the star of Bethlehem ; but both these communities

---

[1] Augustinians never enjoyed their habit in comfort ; in the xiii c. they were obliged to make their leather girdle long and their tunic short because they were suspected of a desire to pass as corded and sandalled Franciscans, and to cover over their white tunic with black in the streets lest they should be taken for friars preachers.

[2] pp. 127, 128 *n.*, and p. 143, 143 *n.*

Cambridge

wore the habit—black over white—of the Dominicans. Scholars poor and rich jostled each other in the schools and in the public ways, wearing the long and short gowns of the day, the *cote* which had just come into fashion, or the habit of their order. There were doctors in the three faculties wearing scarlet gowns and the doctor's bonnet or *camaurum*, and there was a sprinkling of doctors and of students from Orléans, Padua, Pavia, and Paris.

A large number of the inmates of the colleges round, and of the scholars walking the streets, wear the clerical tonsure, many scores have the coronal tonsure of the friar—yet the feeling in the air is secular. Cambridge has always suggested a certain detachment ; neither zeal—perfervid or sour—nor the pressure of tradition upon living thought has had its proper home there. It has not represented monastic seclusion nor hieratic exclusion, and it did so at this moment of its history less than ever. The dawn of the coming renascence shone upon the walls at which we have been looking. The modern world has been born of the birth-pangs which have since convulsed Europe, and the walls which were then big with the future are now big with the past. But it is the greatness of Cambridge that amidst the multiple suggestiveness of its ancient halls of learning, tyranny of the past has no place. About it the dawn of the renascence still lingers ; and the early morning light which presided at its birth still defines the shadows and seems to temper the noon-day heat, as light and shade alternate in its history.

The Colleges

Chaucer at Cambridge. We have taken it for granted that Chaucer was walking the streets of Cambridge with us. We have no direct evidence as to where Chaucer studied ; but our indirect evidence is sufficient. In the " Canterbury Tales " Chaucer introduces us to two Cambridge scholars and to a clerk of Oxenforde ; and if one considers what would nowadays be called the internal evidence of the *Reeve's Tale* it is difficult to resist the conclusion that Chaucer was at Cambridge. How else should he know Trumpington so well ? Its brook, its bridge, its mill, its fen ? He knows about the " gret colledge " which had risen a few years previously ; he knows that its Master is called " the warden," that its scholars are also its " fellaws." He has learnt there the dialect of Yorkshiremen, and reproduces not only their turns of speech but characteristic terms—as *bete, kime, jossa*—in the East Anglian dialect. If we turn to the *Miller's Tale* all this local colouring is to seek. A " clerke of Oxenforde," indeed, was no unfamiliar figure in the xiv century, especially to a Londoner. Familiarity with the aspect of Cambridge and its neighbourhood was a very different matter.

Chaucer was probably himself of East Anglian origin. His grandfather Robert and John his father were both of Ipswich and London, and when he was kidnapped by his mother's family " Thomas Stace of Ipswich " is the kidnapper. There are two events of his young life known to us, and both suggest that he was at Cambridge. One of these we hear about from his evidence in the famous Scrope and Grosvenor suit

93

Cambridge

in 1386. An upstart knight—Sir Robert Grosvenor —whose name Chaucer had never heard before, had displayed the arms of the Scropes, and Chaucer testifies in the Court 'of Chivalry action which ensues that he had often seen Henry le Scrope use the proud armorials "azure, a bend or " in the French wars where they had been companions in arms twenty seven years before (1359). Now this great Yorkshire family were connected with Cambridge from Chaucer's time : Richard le Scrope, the son of his old comrade, was chancellor of the university in 1378.[1] Two members of the same family were chancellors in the next century, and the intermarriage of the Scropes with the Gonvilles is recorded there to this day in Scrope or " Scroope Terrace."[2] Is it not probable that Geoffrey Chaucer knew Henry Scrope at Cambridge and formed there the friendship which moved him to testify in his behalf thirty years later ?

This conjecture does not become less probable when we turn to the other incident in his early life, which came to light in 1866 with a fragment of the household accounts of the wife of Lionel Duke of Clarence. Here the name of Geoffrey Chaucer is mentioned (in 1357) as that of a junior member of her household. His early connexion with the house of Edward is therefore an historical fact like his later friendship with

[1] *Recorda et placita coram cancellario Ric. le Scrope in le Tollebouth. 2 Ric. II. 1378-9.*   MS. No. 49 in the Cambridge Registry.

[2] Stephen le Scrope was chancellor in 1400 and 1414, Richard Scroop (who had been Master of King's Hall) in 1461, and Lady Anne Scroope was one of the early benefactors of Gonville's hall ; see vi. p. 325, 325 *n.*

94

The Colleges

John of Gaunt. Now in 1352 Lionel Plantagenet had married Elizabeth de Burgh the grand-daughter and namesake of the founder of Clare Hall Cambridge. The "gret colledge" about which Chaucer tells us in the *Reeve's Tale* is called "Soler Hall" and "Soler Hall," so Caius records, was the ancient name for Clare. Remembering, however, the incomplete condition of Clare and of other foundations at this date the present writer supposes the "gret colledge" to have been King's Hall, the first imposing architectural undertaking in the university and the building which must *par excellence* have attracted attention in the middle of the xiv century.[1] It may also have been Chaucer's own college, and in this connexion it is worthy of notice that with the exception of the half-dozen "minor scholars" at Pembroke, King's Hall was at this time the only college which educated lads in their teens.

Assuming the year of the poet's birth to have been 1340 he would have been going to the university, according to the custom of those days, about the year 1353, and his place in Elizabeth de Burgh's household was probably already assured him when he went to Cambridge.[2] He was back in her service in his

---

[1] Edward himself speaks of it as "so important a college" in 1342. See p. 132. Since going to press I see that Mr. Rouse Ball identifies King's Hall as 'Solar Hall' in his monograph on Trinity College, published in March 1906. Prof. Willis conjectured that 'Solar Hall' = Garrett Hostel.

[2] King's Hall statutes name 14 as the age.

It will be remembered that Pembroke, Clare, Corpus, and King's Hall were all directly or indirectly connected with the reigning house. For the group of great names connected with Edward's household and with Cambridge at this time cf. v. pp. 291-295.

seventeenth year and therefore could not have had time to study at both universities : and we may add to this that although his general knowledge, which he had no time to acquire in later life, suggests that he received a university education, there is not a tittle of evidence to support the idea that Chaucer went to Oxford.

One more conjecture : had he got his information about prioress's French from the religious of the convent of S. Leonard of Stratford-atte-Bowe whom we find owning land in Cambridge from the days of Edward I. ?

The Schools. It is to this period of the history of The High Street Cambridge that the first university build- and School Street. ings as distinguished from collegiate buildings belong. During the chancellorship of Robert Thorpe, Knight, Master of Pembroke (1347-64) and Lord Chief Justice of the Common Pleas, afterwards Chancellor of England, the " schools quadrangle " was projected in that street of colleges, unrivalled in Europe, which prolonging the Trumpington Road as King's Parade or Trinity Street or S. John's Street was anciently known as the " School street " of the university. It was also the high street of the Saxon town of which S. Benet's tower was the nucleus, but whether the original Saxon town lay on this side of the river, or whether, as frequently happened in the xi century, the Saxon population retreated here leaving the Castle district to their Norman conquerors, we have no means of determining.[1]

[1] The main artery of the xiv and xv century university was not, as now,

The Colleges

There were, then, no public buildings up to the xiv century. The Greyfriars or the Austinfriars gave hospitality to the university on public occasions, and the only brick and mortar evidence of a university lay in the hostels and colleges. The "Schools" now erected were halls for lecturing and scholastic disputations; the north, west, and east sides were completed by the middle of the next century, the south side being added in accordance with a decision taken in 1457 to build "a *new* school of philosophy and civil law, or a library."[1] This was erected on university ground (on the south) next to the school of canon law (west). Over this last was the original library room (the "west room" 1457) and "a chapel of exceeding great beauty." The quadrangle contained the Divinity school (north) with the Regent and non-regent houses; opposite was the Sophisters' school with the *libraria communis* or *magna*; on the entrance side were the Chancellor's (Rotherham's) Library, Consistory court and Court of the Proctors and

the High street, but the Mill street (Milne street). It lay in a direct line between Clare Hall and Queens' Lane, and 7 colleges had their entrances on it: Michaelhouse, Trinity Hall, Clare, old King's College, S. Catherine's, and Queens'. Gonville was approached from the north end, and King's Hall lay on the same side. The church and property of the Knights of S. John and Garret's and Ovyng's hostels were in the same street. Mill street began at Queens' Lane, and led northwards from the King's and the Bishop's Mills, which gave it its name. The larger part was alienated in 1445 to build the second King's College.

Another characteristic feature of old Cambridge was the *King's Ditch* made by Henry III. in 1267, which starting from Castle Mound, with a walk beside it, formed the western boundary of King's Hall, Michaelhouse, and Trinity Hall, and polluted the water supply of Peterhouse even in Andrew Perne's time. [1] Temp. Laurence Booth, chancellor.

GATEWAY OF KING'S COLLEGE, KING'S PARADE

This is one of the most picturesque views in Cambridge. On the right are the Gateway and Screen and other portions of King's College; on the left are some ancient houses.

Cambridge

Taxors ; and facing this the Bachelors' school and the school of Medicine and Law ; the old "west room" having been converted into a school, by grace of the Senate, in 1547.[1]

The university library. The schools remained untouched till the opening years of the xviii century when the Regent House was pulled down to build the present university library. This is the oldest of the three great English libraries, and stands on ground which has always been university property. The early xv century library which was lodged in the Schools quadrangle originated in gifts of single volumes by private donors until 52 had been collected ; and books which were bequeathed in 1424 are still preserved. Fifty years later (1473) the proctors Ralph Sanger and Richard Tokerham made a catalogue of 330 books.[2] Rotherham Archbishop of York next presented 200 tomes, and Tunstall Bishop of Durham was another donor : many of these last gifts

[1] See Loggan's print, 1688. The great schools in the School street are first mentioned 1346-7. The divinity schools were the first to be completed, by Sir *William* Thorpe's executors, in 1398. The quadrangle was completed *c.* 1475. The eastern front was rebuilt in 1755. The buildings lie under the present library and are now used for the keeping of "acts" and for discussions, but not for lectures in the various faculties. The new Divinity schools are in S. John's street, and were erected by friends as a memorial of Bishop Selwyn. The Science schools, school of Human Anatomy, chemical laboratories, etc. are on the site of the university botanical garden which was once Austinfriars' property.

[2] The room where these were treasured was the *libraria communis* or *magna* (in the time of Caius the "old" or "public" library), which still exists on the south side, with Chancellor Rotherham's library on the east. The ancient two-storeyed building on the west which existed as early as 1438 still contains the old Canon Law (now the Arts) school, with the original library and the university chapel (disused for centuries) above (p. 97).

The Colleges

were " embezzled " by " pilferers " before the middle of the xvi century,[1] and the libraries of three successive Cambridge archbishops of Canterbury, Parker, Grindal, and Bancroft, formed the chief treasure of the university until 1715 when George I. purchased and presented the library of Moore Bishop of Ely which is the nucleus of the modern collection.[2]

There are 400,000 volumes on open shelves among which the student can wander at will and get his own books without applying to the library officials; a convenience which Lord Acton, the late Professor of Modern History, used to say made this the only serviceable library in Europe. Another privilege, which is possessed by all masters of arts, is that books may be taken home. Undergraduates, if in academic dress, have also free access. The university library is one of the three copyright libraries in England.[3]

The Pitt Press. A printing press was set up at Cambridge, early in the xvi century, by Siberch who said of himself that he was the first in England to print Greek—7 small volumes in the Greek character were printed by him at the university. Carter, however, tells us that an Italian Franciscan, William of Savona, printed a book at Cambridge in 1478, four years after Caxton had

[1] Fuller and Caius both record this fact.

[2] It consists of 700 MSS. and 30,000 volumes. Other and earlier benefactors to the library were Perne (1574), Fulke Greville, Stephen Perse of Caius, and George Villiers Duke of Buckingham.

There is a library "Chest" and endowments, amounting to about £2000, plus the income of £4500 from the common university Fund.

[3] A copy of every book and pamphlet published in England is sent here, to the British Museum, and to the Bodleian.

99

KING'S COLLEGE CHAPEL AND THE
ENTRANCE COURT, FROM THE
FELLOWS' BUILDINGS

A portion of the Chapel is seen on the left of the
picture with Great St. Mary's tower in the distance.
The Screen and Gate are on the right.

printed the first book in England. Lord Coke pointed out that this university enjoyed before Oxford the privilege of printing *omnes et omnigenas libros*, "all and every kind of book" (1534). This included the right to appoint 3 stationers or printers.

Siberch's printing place was on the present site of Caius. In 1655 the university obtained from Queens' College a lease of the ground at the corner of Silver street and Queens' lane — the historic Mill street district—now the site of the lodge and garden of S. Catherine's. In 1804 the present site was obtained for the university press, with a further "messuage fronting upon Trumpington street and Mill lane"; the remaining properties in Trumpington street, between Silver street and Mill street, being bought in 1831-3. The Pitt Press, a church-like structure, stands opposite to Pembroke (Pitt's) College, and owes its name to the fact that the surplus funds of the Pitt monument in Westminster abbey were a donation to the university towards defraying the cost. The building also contains the offices of the university Registrary.[1]

The Senate House was not founded till 1722, and lies on the north of the library.[2]

King's College.
A.D. 1441.
Ninety years passed after the building of Corpus before Henry VI. founded King's College, and Margaret of Anjou, his consort, founded

---

[1] The printing of bibles and of the Book of Common Prayer is still confined to the king's printer and the 2 universities. Until 1779 the printing of almanacks was also restricted to the universities and the Stationers' Company.   [2] See iii. p. 183, and iv. p. 205.

The Colleges

Queens'. It was in 1443 that the charter of the double foundation of Eton at Windsor and King's College at Cambridge was signed—the one " our royal college of S. Mary of Eton," the other " our royal college of S. Mary and S. Nicholas " ; for Henry dedicated his college to his patron saint Nicholas " of Bari " the patron of scholars. The king laid the foundation stone himself (p. 112) in the presence of John Langton chancellor of the university, the keeper of the Privy Seal, the chancellor of the Exchequer, and the bishops of Lincoln and Salisbury.[1] The king's father had intended to build a college at Oxford ; Henry VI. carried out his intention in endowing a college but decided that the university should be Cambridge. A small college called God's House which had just been founded,[2] together with Mill Street (acquired in 1445) and Augustine's hostel (in 1449) and the church of S. John Zachary, were pulled down to clear a space : but the original plan for the college was never carried out, and the buildings we now see were erected in the first quarter of the xviiith and in the xixth centuries.[3]

[1] Cf. the laying of the foundation stone of the Norman church of S. Giles in 1092, when Anselm of Canterbury and the Bishop of Lincoln (then the diocesan) were present.

[2] In 1439. Its site was the present ante-chapel, see Christ's College p. 117.

[3] The king's design did not at first include the connexion of Eton and King's. The foundations of a college and chapel for a rector and 12 scholars were first laid opposite Clare, between Mill Street and the Schools, on April 2, 1441. Within three years this foundation was changed into a society which, like Eton, is under a Provost and which was bound to provide the free education of poor Etonians. Here Henry imitated William of Wykeham, and the statutes which he drew up follow the lines laid

KING'S COLLEGE CHAPEL AND THE
FELLOWS' BUILDINGS '

The South door of the Chapel is seen to the right in the picture, and the Fellows' Buildings, constructed in 1723, are on the left. The Fountain with a statue of the founder, Henry the Sixth, was designed by H. A. Armstead, R.A.

Cambridge

The chapel. The only portion of the original plan executed was the chapel. The importance of King's College chapel is not only architectural ; is due not only to the fact that it was begun before the Italian classical revival as a monument of English Gothic, and completed in the full blaze of the renascence, but that it marks a chapter in the history of English religion. The church built for the old worship was consecrated for the new ; the first stone was laid by Henry VI. in the presence of great catholic prelates, the oaken screen—perhaps the finest woodwork in the country—bears the monogram of Henry VIII. and Anne Boleyn [1] twined with true lovers' knots. In the third place " this immense and down by the founder of Winchester and New College. The original "mean quadrant" was used till 1828 when it was sold to the university for the library extension on that side. The chapel fell down in 1536. A wall and gateway on the west, remain. The new design had the original court and Clare on the north, Austin's hostel and Whitefriars on the south : the chapel was to form the north side of a quadrangle measuring 230 × 238 feet (cf. the measurements of Corpus) ; and, as in previous colleges, the west side was to contain the hall and provost's lodging, a library and lecture rooms. The south and east sides were to be for the chambers and the latter was to have a gateway and tower. The present Queens' College is on the site of the Whitefriars' house ; and the old gate of King's which led from the chapel yard to Queens' Lane used to be known as "Friars' gate." (For a full account of this most interesting design the reader is referred to Messrs. Willis and Clark's book.)

For the modern buildings four *separate* ranges were designed, the first to be erected being the Gibbs' building on the west : the southern side and the screen have been built since 1824, Wilkins being the architect ; on this side are the hall, combination room, and library, and the Provost's lodge. Sir Gilbert Scott erected the building on the south east, which was projected after 1870.

[1] The Norfolk name of Boleyn is found at the university in the xv c. Henry Boleyn was proctor in 1454-5, and Anne's uncle was churchwarden of S. Clement's.

The Colleges

glorious work of fine intelligence," as Wordsworth calls
it, remains one of the very finest monuments of Perpendicular architecture ; and that beautiful English
feature the fan-vaulting, which is to be seen in the
Tudor chapel at the Guildhall, in Henry VII.'s chapel
at Westminster, and at S. David's (now ruinous), is
here carried out over a larger area than anywhere else.[1]

> That branching roof
> Self-poised, and scooped into ten thousand cells
> Where light and shade repose, where music dwells
> Lingering, and wandering on as loth to die—
> Like thoughts whose very sweetness yieldeth proof
> That they were born for immortality.

So writes Wordsworth ; and the stained glass windows,

[1] It has been suggested that Tudor architecture might be styled
Heraldic architecture, so freely does heraldry and blazonry enter into its
plan and the scheme of decoration. England's two great specimens of
the Perpendicular—King's College chapel and Henry VII.'s chapel at
Westminster—are pervaded by a "gorgeous display of heraldry." The
west and south entrances of King's are decorated with bold carvings of the
badges of Henry VII.—the crowned rose and portcullis. "No person ever
glanced his eye over the wonders around and above him, without being
awestruck at the daring of the architect that could plan, and the builders
that could erect such a structure. The whole of the lower part of the
Chapel beneath the windows is divided into panels, and every panel is
filled with the arms of the king who erected the building." "The
immense pendants hanging from the gorgeous roof are ornamented
with the rose, the royal badge of both the king and queen at this
period." (Clark's *Introduction to Heraldry*, edited by J. R. Planché, Rouge
Croix.) The arms and supporters of Eton, Henry VI. and VIII., Richard
II., Edward IV. and VIth, Mary and Elizabeth, appear also. The gateway
towers of Christ's and John's afford other examples of heraldic display as
the exclusive scheme of decoration—they bear the arms, supporters, and
badges of their founder, the mother of Henry VII. Finally the Entrance
Gateway tower of Trinity exhibits the arms of Edward III. and his six sons

103

KING'S COLLEGE CHAPEL INTERIOR
FROM THE CHOIR

Cambridge

the most 'complete and magnificent series' in the country says Carter, probably inspired Milton's

> —storied windows richly dight,
> Casting a dim religious light.
> There let the pealing organ blow,
> To the full voic'd quire below,
> In service high, and anthems clear,
> As may with sweetness through mine ear,
> Dissolve me into ecstasies,
> And bring all Heav'n before mine eyes.

On the death of the Lancastrian monarch, Edward IV. sequestrated the building funds, but returned a thousand pounds later, and Richard III. contributed £700 ; but it is Henry VII. who brought the work to completion.

King's is the only college in the university which receives only those students who intend to read for honours, and until 1857 its members could claim the *B.A.* degree without presenting themselves for examination.[1] The college was, almost immediately upon its foundation, exempted not only from archiepiscopal and episcopal control but also from the general jurisdiction

(William of Hatfield being represented by a blank shield) ; above is a statue of Henry VIII. No street—no town—in England presents anything like this "boast of heraldry" which Gray had always under his eyes in Cambridge. It is a permanent record of the two royal groups in England who preferred this university ; the gateway at Trinity being the *trait d'union* between them.

[1] "The scholars of King's enjoyed the questionable privilege of drifting into their degrees without examination. Lectures and rare compositions in Latin were the only demands upon their time," writes Lord Stratford de Redcliffe. The same arrangements obtained at New College Oxford until 50 years ago.

The Colleges

of the university. It was endowed for the accommodation of a Provost, 70 poor scholars, 10 secular priests,
16 choristers, and 6 clerks—a total of 103. Eton was
designed for 132 inmates.[1] 24 of the 48 scholarships
of King's are now open. Each of these scholarships is
of the annual value of £80. There are also 46 fellowships. The most celebrated Etonians have not however been educated at King's, among whose eminent
sons have been Croke, Cheke (of S. John's) Provost,
Woodlark the founder of S. Catherine's, third Provost
of the college and also its benefactor, Sir John
Harrington, Robert and Horace Walpole, Sir Francis
Walsingham, Lord Stratford de Redcliffe, Conisby,
Haddon, Giles Fletcher, Waller, Fleetwood, Oughtred
an Etonian on the first foundation, Whichcote (of
Emmanuel) Provost, Upton, Cole, and Charles Simeon
who was a life fellow. Nicholas Close (1551) and
Aldrich (1537) both bishops of Carlisle, the former
one of the original six fellows, the latter the intimate
of Erasmus, Rotherham of York (1467) a fellow and
a donor to the chapel fund, Fox of Hereford (1535),
William and George Day bishops of Winchester and
Chichester, one provost of Eton the other of King's,
Wickham of Lincoln and Winchester,[2] Nicholas West
(Bishop of Ely 1515) the friend of Fisher and More
and Richard Cox (1559) both scholars of the college,
Oliver King of Exeter, then of Bath and Wells (1492),

[1] The "13 poor men" who are to form part of the foundation at Eton
are an addition of Henry's own ; they do not appear on Wykeham's
foundation.

[2] For the Days, see v. p. 273 n. Wickham was vice-provost of Eton.

THE HALL OF KING'S COLLEGE

This was built by Wilkins 1824-28. On the walls
are several portraits by Hubert Herkomer, R.A.

Cambridge

Alley of Exeter, Guest of Rochester and Salisbury (1559), Goodrich of Ely (1534), Pearson, and Sumner, are among its prelates. Henry and Charles Brandon, heirs of their father the Duke of Suffolk, and nephews of Henry VIII. and both proficient scholars, died of the sweating sickness while in residence here in the reign of Edward VI. Cardinal Beaufort was a princely benefactor to the college, and John Somerset, physician to Henry VI., who came to Cambridge as an Oxford sophister and here graduated, was one of the chief instruments in its foundation, and drew up its statutes.[1]

The college has produced several great schoolmasters, and is now gradually acquiring a reputation for historical studies, about one third of the students being history men. The dedication to S. Nicholas is only retained in formal descriptions : *King's College* has been by common consent regarded as the fitting title for this truly royal foundation, and it recalls that still older King's Hall which is now merged in Trinity.[2]

---

[1] Somerset returned to Cambridge in later life, after he had fallen into disgrace and poverty, and met, like Metcalfe of John's, with small gratitude. Dr. Philip Baker, though a Catholic, retained the provostship under Elizabeth till 1570. For King's men see also pp. 174-5, 272-3-4 *n.*, 283.

[2] Eton is the only public school joined from its foundation with a Cambridge college. Merchant Taylors' used however to be related to Pembroke (which owes Spenser's presence there to this circumstance) and the ancient school of Bury used, it is said, to send its *alumni* to Gonville. S. Paul's school has tied scholarships and exhibitions at Corpus Christi and Trinity : Corpus was connected with Norwich school and Norfolk by Bacon, Parker, and other Norfolk benefactors, and has tied scholarships with King's School, Canterbury, and Westminster ; the last being also closely connected with Trinity College. Harrow has two tied scholarships at Caius ; Magdalene holds the Latimer Neville scholarships

The Colleges

The Cambridge College chapels. The importance of King's College chapel in university history since the xv century leads us to consider the rôle played in Cambridge by collegiate chapels. Every college chapel, and every church which has an historical connexion with the university, has served—as all early Christian edifices have served—other purposes than those of religious worship. What we have to remark in Cambridge is that this ancient custom continued there longer than elsewhere. The "Commencements" which took place later in the Senate House used to be held, as we have seen, in the famous church of the Greyfriars or in that of the Austinfriars. The University church—Great S. Mary's—was used by the university for its assemblies in the xiii century and was the scene of all great civic functions ; disputations were held in it on Elizabeth's visit in 1564. The college chapels were everywhere used for the transaction of important business ; the Provost of King's and other Masters are still elected in the chapel, documents are still sealed in the chapel of King's and Trinity, and the Thurston speech is still pronounced in the chapel of Caius. The choir of King's was used for degree examinations as late as 1851, and declamations are even now held in the chapel at Trinity. Indeed the "exercises of learning" "used" in the chapels was the reason given by the Corpus men to Lord Bacon's father when asking for a church to them-

for Shrewsbury, Marlborough, Uppingham, and Fettes schools, and tied exhibitions from Wisbech school. Uppingham is similarly connected with Emmanuel ; Peterhouse with Huntingdon Free Grammar School, and S. John's with 18 schools all over England and with several towns as well.

ENTRANCE GATEWAY, QUEENS'
COLLEGE

This old gateway forms the principal entrance to the
College from Queens' Lane.

Cambridge

selves; and Queen Elizabeth witnessed the *Aulularia* of Plautus in King's chapel on Sunday August 6th 1564, as the abbess and her nuns had assembled for Hrostwitha's play in the abbey church of Gandersheim six hundred years earlier. The building of colleges adjoining a parish church is a feature peculiar to Cambridge. Merton is the one exception at Oxford, and Pembroke is, as we have seen, the only early exception to this rule at Cambridge.[1]

List of pre-reformation colleges built with chapels :—
1. Pembroke 1355-63 (the existing chapel is xvii c.)
2. King's 1446-1536 (the existing chapel).
3. Queens' 1448 (defaced at the reformation and restored. But a xix c. chapel is now used).
4. Jesus 1495 (The then existing xii c. monastic chapel was rebuilt by the founder.)
5. S. Catherine's 1475 (the existing chapel is xvii c.)
6. Magdalene 1483 (completely restored in the middle of the xix c.)

Colleges built without chapels and with (generally) post-reformation chapels :—
1. Peterhouse (xvii c.)[1]
2. Michaelhouse (none).
3. King's Hall (chapel built temp. Edw. IV., and Ric. III. The site of the present chapel of Trinity College).
4. Clare (1535. The existing chapel is 1764).[1]
5. Gonville.[1]
6. Trinity Hall 1474.
7. Corpus 1500, and 1579 (the existing chapel is on the site of the latter, and was erected 1823).

Existing pre-reformation chapels :—
King's xv c.
Queens' xv c. (restored).
Jesus xv c.
Trinity Hall xv c.
Magdalene (restored) xv c.

Existing xvi c. chapels :—
Christ's 1505 (the original chapel, but defaced); Trinity, completed 1564-7.

At Caius, the present chapel is on the site of the xvi c. chapel; and at S. John's a xix c. structure replaces the xvi c. one, near the same site.

[1] A chapel of S. Lucy (erected 1245) came into the possession of Peter-

The Colleges

The oldest ecclesiastical site and building incorporated with a Cambridge college is therefore the chapel of Jesus (but cf. S. John's p. 126); the site of the earliest college chapel is at Pembroke—but it is a site merely; the oldest existing college chapel is King's.

Queens' College. The charter for the foundation of Queens' A.D. 1448. College is dated 15 April 1448, but by this date its north and east ranges were already built. Queen Margaret of Anjou had been so impressed with the beauty and majesty of the plans for King's College that she could find no rest till she had projected her own foundation—Queens'; to endow and perfect which she set to work with holy emulation; dedicating it in her turn to her patron saint, Margaret the legendary Virgin and Martyr whose body is shown at Montefiascone, and to Bernard of Citeaux. Two years previously the principal of S. Bernard's hostel had founded a college of S. Bernard, the site of which he changed in 1447 to the present site of Queens'. This formed the moral nucleus of the queens' college; but she obtained the larger part of the ground, near King's, from the Carmelites.

This is one of the three colleges in Cambridge built

house with the property of the friars of the Sack (1309) and was used by the fellows towards the end of that century. The licences obtained by Bateman (1352 and 1353) for chapels in Trinity Hall and Gonville were never acted upon. Gonville however had a house chapel in 1393. At this date Clare also had a chapel, which was used at the primate's visitation in 1401. The Clare Statutes (1359) direct that S. John Baptist's church be used. For ritual in the college chapels, see pp. 59, 145. Organs were placed in most of the chapels in the reign of Charles I., at a time when the courts, gates, and frontage of colleges underwent repair and decoration.

AN OLD COURT IN QUEENS' COLLEGE

This is the Cloister Court. In the quaint sixteenth-century buildings on the left is the Gallery, and facing the spectator is the doorway into the First Court. The Hall is seen on the right of this doorway.

Cambridge

of red brick, S. John's and S. Catherine's being the
others. The Queens' quadrangle is, as Messieurs
Willis and Clark tell us, the earliest now remaining
which claims attention for its architectural beauty. It
is 99 feet east and west by 84 north and south.[1] The
plan is not only a very perfect example of college
architecture, but is a model of the xv century English
manor-house, of the type of Haddon Hall ;[2] so that
Queens' College is as homogeneous a structure as
King's is heterogeneous. The hall is on the west,
adjoining it is the combination room, above, the
President's lodging with a bedchamber over it. The
north side is kept for the chapel and for the library
which is on the first floor. The chambers are on the
east and south sides, the gateway being in the former.
As in other colleges the passage to the grounds (or, as
in this case, to the second court) is between the hall
and the butteries. The west side of the quadrangle
which was gradually cloistered forms the east side of
the second court, and is washed by the Cam. The
beautiful gallery on the north has formed part of the
lodge since the xvi century,[3] and connects the old

[1] Cf. with the dimensions of Corpus old court which was considerably
larger (220 by 140), of the proposed quadrangle at King's p. 102 n., and with
the frontage of some of the hostels p. 50.

[2] Haddon Hall in Derbyshire ; the first owners of which were those
Peverels ("of the Peak ") who figure in Cambridge history at the time of the
Conquest (i. p. 17). The house passed to the Bassetts, a name which
was also well known in the university ; and from there—so the old story
runs—Dorothy Vernon, a daughter of the last owners of the manor, ran
away with Sir John the first Lord Manners.

[3] For the marriage of a xvi c. President of Queens', see iv. pp. 209, 212.

The Colleges

president's lodging with a set of rooms on the west side, among which is the audit room now used as a dining room.

Queens', like King's, was originally built with a chapel, and in both instances the foundation stone of the chapel was that of the college. A new chapel and buildings now lie beyond the President's garden on the north. There is a small court on the south of the cloister court which contains the rooms occupied by Erasmus, overhanging the college kitchen. Besides Erasmus, who lived here for at least four years, Fisher was there as President of the college until 1508, and Old Fuller was another of its worthies. Henry Bullock, the opposer of Protestantism and friend of Erasmus, was a fellow, so was Sir T. Smith; Bishop Pearson [1] and Ockley *alumni*. Henry Hastings Earl of Huntingdon, whose portrait hangs in the audit room, Manners Earl of Rutland, George Duke of Clarence, Cecilia Duchess of York, and Maud Countess of Oxford, were among its benefactors. But its chief benefactor was Andrew Doket, a friar (of what order is not known) and its first President, who saved the fortunes of the college after the fall of the House of Lancaster.[2] The picture of principal interest is also to be found in the lodge—Holbein's portrait of Erasmus which was painted during a visit made at the scholar's request to England.

[1] Pearson was educated here, then at King's of which he became fellow, and was Master of Jesus and, in 1662, of Trinity.

[2] See Bernard's hostel p. 109.

QUEENS' COLLEGE FROM THE
RIVER FRONT

On the left is seen the garden front of the President's
Lodge. The wooden bridge designed by Etheridge
(1749) is known as the Mathematical Bridge. In
the distance are the two old mills—the King's Mill
and the Bishop's Mill.

Cambridge

The college was originally endowed for a president and 4 fellows, and their principal study was to be theology. There are now 11 fellowships, and about 18 scholarships which vary in value from £30 to £60.

Queens' College is a monument of peace. The Yorkist queen Elizabeth Woodville continued Margaret of Anjou's work, and the two queens are the co-founders of the college. It is Elizabeth Woodville whose portrait looks down upon us in the hall, and it was she who changed Queen Margaret's dedication and called their joint work Queens' College.[1] It is also a monument to the unambitious but well-defined revival of learning that marked the reign of Edward IV., of which Woodville Earl Rivers, the queen's brother, Tiptoft Earl of Worcester, and Caxton himself are the representatives.

Kingly visitors to the university. Both King's and Queens' Colleges have offered hospitality on several occasions to English sovereigns. Henry VI. came to lay the foundation stone of King's in 1441 and was at King's Hall in 1445-6 (when he laid the foundation stone of his second college?), in 1448-9 and in 1452-3.[2] Edward IV. visited the university in 1463 and 1476.

---

[1] Margaret had however called it "the quenes collage of sainte Margarete and S. Bernard." In her petition for a charter she tells the king : "in the whiche vniuersitie is no college founded by eny quene of Englond hidertoward." The statutes were drawn up by Millington first Provost of King's, and others.

[2] Accounts of King's Hall. Here, too, the king was to have been lodged for the parliament of 1447.

The Colleges

Henry VII. paid five visits to Cambridge and stayed at Queens' in 1498 and again in 1506 when he occupied a chamber near the audit room. It was on this occasion that he attended the service for the eve of S. George's day in King's College chapel clad in the robes of the Garter. Henry VIII. was by his father's side during this visit, and came again in 1522. Mary came as far as Sir Robert Huddleston's when Jane Grey was proclaimed. Elizabeth was entertained in the Provost's lodge of King's, and it was when repairing to her rooms there after the solemn service in the chapel that she thanked God " that had sent her to this university where she was so received as she thought she could not be better." James I. visited Cambridge twice in 1615 and was again at Trinity College in 1623 and 1624 ; Charles I. (who had been Nevile's guest in 1613) was entertained there in 1632 and 1642 ; and Charles II. in the long gallery at S. John's in 1681. Anne was there in 1705, George I. in 1717, and George II. in 1728. Queen Victoria came in 1843 and again in 1847 when the Prince Consort was installed as Chancellor ; and Edward VII. visited the university in February 1904.

John had been in Cambridge the month before his death, September 1216 ; Henry III. was there in the second year of his reign (1218) ; Edward I. was there as Prince of Wales in 1270, and lodged again in the castle in 1294. Edward II. was the guest of Barnwell priory in 1326. Edward III. was there in September 1328. Richard II. was also lodged at Barnwell in 1388.

GATEWAY OF ST. CATHERINE'S COLLEGE

This is a view of the old Renaissance Gateway (1679), being the entrance to the College from Queens' Lane.

Cambridge

The Conqueror had been at Cambridge in 1070.

Matilda is the first queen-consort whom we can picture visiting the university town; Eleanor of Castile was frequently at Walsingham with Edward,[1] and she gave as we shall see a "chest" to the university. Margaret of Anjou was never there, but Elizabeth Woodville came in 1468. The mother of Henry VII. also came to see her college in 1505 and again with the king in 1506. Elizabeth of York accompanied Henry VII. in 1498; Catherine of Aragon slept at Queens' in 1519; and Henrietta Maria was with the king in 1631-2.

The erection of King's and Queens' Colleges opened a period of college building which lasted sixty years, and closed with the foundation of S. John's (in 1509).

S. Catherine's College, 1473. In 1473 Robert Woodlark chancellor of the university and third provost of King's, and one of the original scholars of that foundation, built a small college dedicated to the Glorious Virgin Martyr S. Catherine of Alexandria, with the object of extending "the usefulness of Church preaching, and the study of theology, philosophy, and other arts within the Church of England." The present red brick structure was erected two hundred years later, this being the only college except Clare which has been entirely rebuilt since its foundation. S. Catherine's, or "Cat's" as the under-

[1] Henry VII. was on his way to the same celebrated shrine when he came to Cambridge in 1506.

114

The Colleges

graduate familiarly calls it, is remarkable for the number of bishops it has educated, among whom were Archbishop Sandys, May of Carlisle, Brownrigg of Exeter, all of whom were Masters of the college, as was Overall of Norwich who migrated from S. John's : John Lightfoot, the orientalist, was its 16th Master, and Strype (who came here from Jesus), James Shirley the last of the dramatists,[1] Ray the naturalist, and Addenbrooke the founder of the well known hospital of that name at Cambridge, were also educated here.

The hall[2] was founded for a master and 3 fellows, and now maintains 6 fellows and 26 scholars.

Jesus College 1495. The next college is a solitary instance of the adaptation of monastic architecture to collegiate purposes in Cambridge. Alcock Bishop of Ely and joint lord chancellor with Rotherham obtained from Alexander VI. (149$\frac{6}{7}$) the dissolution of the ancient Benedictine nunnery of S. Rhadegund, and founded there a college which he dedicated to the *Blessed Virgin Mary, S. John Evangelist, and the glorious Virgin S. Rhadegund.* Its name of Jesus College records the growing cult of the name of Jesus, and the substitution was approved by the founder himself.[3]

If at Queens' we are in a xv century manor-house, at Jesus we are in a monastery ; and might well imagine ourselves for a moment back in one of the busiest centres

[1] He was at S. John's Oxford, which he left without his degree.
[2] "Hall of S. Katerine," the only foundation since King's College founded as a *hall* not a *college*.
[3] Willis and Clark.

GATEWAY OF JESUS COLLEGE

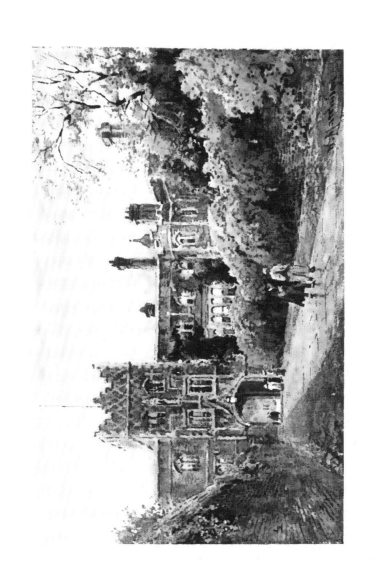

Cambridge

of old Cambridge if we pace the cloisters just before hall time when the stir is suggestive of the life of a great monastery. Even the legend " Song Room " over a doorway falls in with the illusion. James I. said that if he lived in the university he would pray at King's, eat at Trinity, and study and sleep at Jesus.

The chapel is the original conventual church[1] as rebuilt by Alcock. It contains xii century work, and represents the transition from Norman to Early English. The character of the college has been consistently evangelical in spite of the fact that Bancroft the Laudian archbishop before Laud, was here, and that he migrated here from Christ's on account of the latter's reputation for Puritanism. Cranmer was scholar, and fellow until his marriage, and was readmitted fellow when his wife died a year later. Archbishops Bancroft and Sterne, Laurence Sterne, Bale Bishop of Ossory, Strype, Fulke Greville, Fenton, Fawkes (the poet), Hartley, and S. T. Coleridge were members. The college which was founded for 6 fellows and 6 scholars, now maintains 16 fellows and some 20 scholars. The statutes

---

[1] It was the gift of Malcolm " the Maiden " of Scotland. The monastery was much enlarged and enriched by him *circa* 1160. Dugdale dates the house to the middle of Stephen's reign or perhaps as early as 1130. In the xiii c. Constantia wife to Earl Eustace granted to the nuns all the fisheries and water belonging to the town of Cambridge; and the convent at that time shared with the canons of S. John's and the Merton scholars the fame of being the greatest landlords in the town. See i. pp. 16, 18 and 36 *n.*, vi. p. 311 and ii. p. 109. On a stone by the south-eastern corner of the south transept in the church there is this inscription (A.D. 1261):

Moribus ornata
Jacet hic bona Berta Rosata.

The Colleges

were indited by James Stanley Bishop of Ely, stepson of Lady Margaret, and modified by his successor Nicholas West. Jesus College scholars were commended by the founder to the perpetual tutelage of the bishops of Ely, who when they lie there are said to lie in their own house.[1]

Christ's College A.D. 1505. Ten years later a most interesting foundation was made. A college called God's House had, as we have seen, been founded in the reign of Henry VI. and was appropriated by that monarch as part of the site of King's College. The foundation was a far-off echo of the plague in the previous century, and when the king took possession of the site he appears to have intended to endow a considerable college in its place in the parish of S. Andrew where he erected another God's House.[2] It was this design,

---

[1] Fuller.

[2] See iii. p. 165 n. Dyer points out that William Byngham is called "proctor and Master of God's House," but not founder : he considers that Hen. VI. was the founder, Byngham being its procurator as Doket was procurator of Queens' and Somerset of King's colleges. The facts recorded here and in chap. iii. appear to support this conclusion. At the same time Byngham in his letter to the king in 1439 distinctly claims to have built the house : "Goddeshous the which he hath made and edified in your towne of Cambridge." In the case of every Cambridge college the founder is the man who endows it. A college may owe its existence (as certainly in Byngham's case) to the energies of some one else, but its founder remains the man by whom it was built and endowed. A God's House at Ewelme in Oxfordshire was founded about the same time by William de la Pole and Alice his wife, Earl and Countess of Suffolk. "It is still in being," writes Tanner, "but the Mastership is annexed to the King's professor of Physic in the university of Oxford." A God's house was an almshouse for some object of mercy. Thirteen poor men were maintained at Ewelme.

THE GATEWAY OF CHRIST'S COLLEGE
FROM ST. ANDREW'S STREET

The Gateway is coeval with the founding of the
College, and dates from the first decade of the six-
teenth century.

left unfulfilled (for the house only supported four of the sixty scholars whom Henry VI. had himself proposed to maintain there) that John Fisher, chancellor of the university and Bishop of Rochester, brought to the notice of Lady Margaret Beaufort, daughter of the first Duke of Somerset, Countess of Richmond and Derby, the wife of Edmund Tudor and mother of Henry VII. ; and on the site of God's House she erected her own Christ's College, and made John Sickling its Proctor first Master. The quadrangle was encased in stone in the xviii century, but the gateway with its statue and armorials of the founder, and the oriel over the entrance to the Master's lodge recall the founder's time. Facing the gateway are the hall, the old combination room, and the lodge, and above were a set of rooms reserved for the founder's own use ; a turret staircase led therefrom to both hall and garden, as was the custom in a master's lodge. On the east of this "Tree court" is a building in the renascence style, thought to be one of the finest examples in England, and to have been the work of Inigo Jones (1642). The gold plate of the college was a bequest of Lady Margaret's and there is none finer in the university. Christ's is also noted for its gardens.

No college has been richer in great men. Milton was here for seven years, Henry More the Platonist, Latimer the scholar-bishop and martyr, Leland the antiquary, Nicholas Saunderson, Paley of the "Evidences," Archbishops Grindal and Bancroft, Bishop Porteous,

The Colleges

Sir Walter Mildmay,[1] Charles Darwin, and Sir John Seeley. Lightfoot the great Hebraist of his century, and Cudworth, were both Masters in the xvii century ; and in the previous century Exmew the Carthusian martyr (1535) and Richard Hall (afterwards Canon of Cambray), Fisher's biographer, were inmates. Here Milton wrote his hymn on the Nativity, and here he formed his friendship with Edward King—fellow of the college—in whose memory *Lycidas* was written.

The college was endowed for 12 fellows at least, half of whom were to hail from those northern counties in which both Lady Margaret and Fisher were interested ; the total endowment was for 60 persons. There are now 15 fellowships, 30 scholarships (£30 to £70) and some 4 sizarships of the value of £50 a year.[2]

Grammar, the original study of God's House,[3] and arts were to be studied in addition to theology, but excluding law and medicine ; and for the first time in college statutes lectures on the classical orators and poets are provided for, an attention to polite letters for their own sake which is supposed to have been due to the influence of Erasmus.

The Lady Margaret. The Lady Margaret, for with this title alone her memory is preserved at both universities, has, perhaps, no rival in Cambridge as both an interesting and an important figure in its history. She appears to have been one of the first in that age

---

[1] Founder of Emmanuel College. Fuller says he was "a serious student in" and benefactor of this college.

[2] Refer to iv. p. 217 *n*.   [3] p. 153, iii. p. 165 *n*.

THE FELLOWS' BUILDING IN CHRIST'S
COLLEGE

This building is in the Second Court. The design is
attributed to Inigo Jones. Through it we pass into
the Fellows' Garden, where we shall find the famous
mulberry tree sacred to Milton.

Cambridge

to understand that the university was to replace the monastery as the channel of English learning, and to endow colleges rather than religious houses. The two splendid foundations which owe their existence to her bear upon them a stronger personal impress than others. Alone of non-resident founders she retained for her own use a lodge in the college she founded. An anecdote when she was staying at Christ's, preserved for us by Fuller, comes across the centuries vivid with her personality. There is no episode in any university to compare with the scholastic partnership of Lady Margaret and Bishop Fisher, her chaplain, perpetual chancellor of the university, and Master of Michaelhouse. Both were in their measure " reformers before the reformation," both joined to the spirit of piety an abounding appreciation of the spirit of knowledge. At Cambridge and Oxford she founded those readerships in theology known as the Lady Margaret Professorships, and at Cambridge she instituted the Lady Margaret preachership. She died on 29 June 1509, and Erasmus wrote her epitaph in Westminster Abbey.[1]

Cardinal Fisher, Bishop of Rochester, and perpetual chancellor of the university. Fisher lived many years after her, and completed the foundation of S. John's. He pronounced 'that discourse at her obsequies which is our chief source of information about her.[2] Fisher was imprisoned, like Thomas More, for refusing to admit the

[1] She diverted some of her gifts to Henry VII.'s chapel at Westminster, with the king's consent, in favour of S. John's College Cambridge.
[2] " Fryvelous things, that were lytell to be regarded, she wold let pass

royal supremacy in things ecclesiastical ; covered with rags, and worn with neglect and ill-treatment, but consoled by a filial and courageous letter from his sons at S. John's, he was led out to die on June 22, 1534, the New Testament in his hand open at the words : "This is eternal life, to know Thee the only true God." He stands alone among the bishops of England to give his life for the principle for which the layman Thomas More laid down his. Pole in a letter to Charles V. narrates that Henry VIII. had said he supposed "that I" (Pole) "had never in all my travels met one who in letters and virtue could be compared to the Bishop of Rochester."

S. John's College, We next come to the most splendid
A.D. 1509. foundation hitherto realised at Cambridge.
The site chosen for a college which held its place through

by, but the other that were of weyght and substance, wherein she might proufyte, she wolde not let for any payne or labour, to take upon hande. All Englonde for her dethe had cause of wepynge . . . the students of both the unyversytees, to whom she was as a moder ; all the learned men of Englonde, to whom she was a veray patroness . . . all the noblemen and women to whom she was a myrroure and exampler of honoure ; all the comyn people of this realme, for whom she was in their cause a comyn medyatryce, and toke right grete displeasure for them."

Fisher was created cardinal priest of S. Vitalis, in the modern Via Nazionale (the ancient *titulus Vestinae*) by Paul III. When Henry VIII. heard that the Hat had been conferred, he exclaimed that he would not leave the bishop a head to wear it on. The following prayer appears in the Roman breviary for the feast day of Blessed John Fisher (June 22) :—
Deus, qui beato pontifici tuo Joanni pro veritate et justitia magno animo vitam profundere tribuisti ; da nobis ejus intercessione et exemplo ; vitam nostram pro Christo in hoc mundo perdere, ut eam in coelo invenire valeamus.

"The most inflexibly honest churchman who held a high station in that age."—Hallam. Fisher was confessor to Catherine of Aragon and to Lady Margaret.

MILTON'S MULBERRY TREE IN THE FELLOWS' GARDEN, CHRIST'S COLLEGE

King James I. is said to have introduced the culture of the mulberry tree, and it is probable that the one in this garden is the last survivor of a number bought in 1609. Milton was admitted to this College in 1625.

the xvi century as the first and most brilliant society in the university, could not have been more appropriate. It was that of S. John's Hospital, the first home of Cambridge students, the nucleus of the university, erected soon after the Conquest in the heart of the Norman town, and whence the first endowed scholars in christendom set forth to found a college.[1]

The whole history of the university is epitomised in the street which has S. John's at one end of it and Peterhouse at the other : the bishops of Ely have firm hold of either end, and lying against S. John's is that Pythagoras House which Merton bought from the Dunnings when he was planning his famous foundation in the xiii century. We have seen that it was at S. John's Hospital that Balsham introduced secular scholars in the same century, who should become *unum corpus et unum collegium* with the canons. The experiment did not succeed, and the canons saw the scholars depart with great relief to the other end of what was to prove the great street of colleges, whose limits were determined by this early conflict between seculars and religious.

In what year the Ely scholars were settled at S. John's remains uncertain, although there is no more important date in Cambridge history. Simon Montacute, Bishop of Ely, "who knew very well" as the historian of S. John's observes, says that the scholars had continued there *per longa tempora*, and Baker

[1] See i. 38 ; ii. 55-6. An old Ely Chartulary says : "Henry Frost ought never to be forgot, who gave birth to so noted a seat of religion, and afterwards to one of the most renowned seats of learning in Europe."

The Colleges

considers that in no construction of words can this be understood otherwise than as referring to the beginning of Hugh Balsham's prelacy at Ely.[1] The licence permitting the seculars to be engrafted on the old stock with their own endowment, is dated the ninth year of Edward I. (1280)[2] and the transference to Peterhouse took place three years after; but the date of the royal licence is no proof that the work to which it refers was initiated rather than completed and crowned in that year; Margaret of Anjou, for example, obtained her licence when three sides of the quadrangle at Queens' were nearing completion.[3] In any case the few months intervening between December 23, 1280 and the decision to remove to Peterhouse could not be described as a "long time," and as Balsham had become bishop of the diocese in 1257 it is most probable that he at once set about what it must certainly be supposed he had at heart while still subprior of Ely.

With S. John's we have the first of the large colleges. Henceforth Trinity and John's are "the big colleges" the others are "the 14 small colleges." It now consists of four large courts, three of which are of brickwork. The first court was erected between 1509-1616 on the pattern of the quadrangle at Christ's. The founder's grandson Henry VIII., whose coronation she lived to witness, not only sequestrated a large part of the funds she had destined for the building, but

[1] *History of the College of S. John the Evangelist*, Baker-Mayor, pp. 22-3.
[2] *Lit. Pat.* 9 *Edw. I. membr.* 28 (23 Dec. 1280). Printed in Commission Documents vol. ii. p. 1.
[3] Willis and Clark.

THE GATEWAY AND TOWER OF
ST. JOHN'S COLLEGE

The Kirke White memorial is seen in the foreground,
and behind it are the Divinity Schools ; to the left
is the Gateway of St. John's, with the Tower behind
it.   The enclosed space in the foreground was formerly
the site of All Saints' Church, pulled down in 1865.

fifteen years later beheaded Fisher her executor. The latter himself subscribed to the fund and was able before he died to erect a college for a Master and 21 fellows—the original design being for 50 fellows. But what thus fell short of the spirit of the earlier design has since been amply repaired, and a series of benefactors have made the college one of the most useful in England, with that large influence on the nation and large power of helping poorer students which its founders had so greatly at heart.

The Second Court was built chiefly at the expense of Mary Countess of Shrewsbury in 1595-1620. The Third Court was begun in 1623, with funds provided by Williams then Bishop of Lincoln, and finished by benefactors some of whom remained anonymous. The last Court was built in 1826 and is joined to the college by the " Bridge of Sighs." Beyond this is the beautiful "wilderness" commemorated by Wordsworth.

> ——Scarcely Spenser's self
> Could have more tranquil visions in his youth

he tells us, than he had had loitering in Cambridge nights under a " fairy work of earth," a certain lovely ash, wreathed in ivy. This is the site of the infirmary of the canons, the only portion of whose Hospital to be preserved was adapted as a college infirmary and was at the north side of the First Court : it was destroyed in 1863 when the present large chapel was built, which is the work of Gilbert Scott, and is 193 feet long. The large hall

The Colleges

measures 108 feet, and the portrait of Lady Margaret presides over the high table. The new combination room, which is now entered from the second court, was built in 1864, and is 93 feet long. The west side of the Third Court is cloistered, and from here leads the covered bridge, called from its resemblance to the bridge at Venice " the Bridge of Sighs." The stone bridge near it supplanted the old timber bridge in 1696. As at Queens', there is a long gallery on the first floor of the Second Court. Nowhere has the original modest " master's lodging " undergone more change than here. The lodging—two rooms over the old combination room, with an oriel, on the first court— was gradually extended, again as at Queens', along the gallery, and ran along part of the next court. Finally Scott built the present lodge, outside the courts altogether.

Christ's and S. John's are both profusely ornamented with the Tudor and Beaufort badges of the founder, and with her name-device the *marguerite*.[1] The ancient gateway has a canopied statue of the Evangelist. To the north and south of the new chapel porch are statues of Lady Margaret and of Fisher, and 16 statues of the benefactors and great members of the college : *Mary Cavendish Countess of Shrewsbury, *Sarah Alston Duchess of Somerset, *Williams Archbishop of York, and *Linacre who founded the Physics lecture here and at Merton Oxford, appear among the former. Among the latter are

[1] See p. 103 *n.*

ENTRANCE TO ST. JOHN'S COLLEGE
CHAPEL FROM THE FIRST COURT

In the corner on the right is seen the Doorway of the
Chapel, with the tower rising above it. On the left
is part of the Hall with a fine oriel window.

Cambridge

*Roger Ascham (fellow) (those asterisked are effigied) ; Sir John Cheke (fellow) ; *Bentley ; *Cecil Lord Burleigh ; *Lucius Lord Falkland[1] ; Fairfax, the parliamentary general ; *Wentworth Lord Strafford ; *Stillingfleet, *Overall,[2] *Gunning, and Selwyn, prelates ; *William Gilbert ; *Brook Taylor the naturalist ; *Clarkson the opponent of the slave trade ; Cave the ecclesiastical historian ; Metcalfe the most brilliant of its masters[3] ; Matthew Prior, Grindal the classic, Cecil Lord Salisbury, Ben Jonson, Wordsworth, Kirke White, Rowland Hill, Henry Martyn the missionary, Horne Tooke, Castlereagh, Palmerston, Wilberforce, Erasmus Darwin, Colenso, Herschell, Liveing, Adams the discoverer of Neptune, Benjamin Hall Kennedy, and *Baker the historian of the college. Fisher arranged a small chapel leading from the college chapel for his own resting place.[4] The site of S. John's chapel is as old an ecclesiastical site as Jesus chapel : the xvi century edifice was constructed close to the xii century canons' church, and the fine modern chapel is on the same site.

The licence for the college dates from 1511 ; the building was opened in 1516 ; and the statutes were drawn up by Fisher.

[1] v. p. 278.

[2] Overall had been a scholar at Trinity, and was Master of S. Catherine's.

[3] Metcalfe was the Catholic Master who made the great reputation of S. John's, but whom "the young fry of fellows" combined to oust in 1534. "Did not all the bricks of the college that day double their dye of redness to blush at the ingratitude of those that dwelt therein ?" (Fuller.)

[4] He was buried by the side of Sir Thomas More in the chapel of S. Peter ad Vincula in the Tower.

The Colleges

There are now 56 fellowships, 60 foundation scholars each receiving £50 annually, and 9 sizars £35 annually.

The next college which claims our attention must rank among the more interesting foundations on account of its origin rather than of its subsequent history.

Magdalene College, Near S. John's Hospital there was a site
A.D. 1542. traditionally connected with the lectures of Abbot Joffred's monks in 1109, and which in fact was afterwards Crowland Abbey property. When a monastic order possessed no convent in a university town, the monks were obliged to reside in lodgings, and this led, as we have already seen (i. p. 49) to the foundation of monastic hostels for their reception. There were two such hostels at Cambridge—Ely hostel and Monks' hostel. Ely hostel was the direct outcome of Benedict XII.'s Constitution in 1337[1] which reconfirmed an earlier injunction of Honorius III. 1216-27 requiring the Benedictines and Augustinians to send students in rotation from the monastery to the university, and provided that monks should live at the universities under a prior of Benedictines. It was purchased in 1340 (or earlier) by John de Crawden prior of Ely for the Ely monks and was made over to Bateman Bishop of Norwich seven years later for his foundation of Trinity Hall.

Ely then had been the pioneer in providing this accom-

---

[1] Constitutions for the reform of the Black Benedictine, Cistercian, and Augustinian Orders, issued in 1335, 1337, 1339.

THE SECOND COURT OF ST. JOHN'S
COLLEGE

The doorway on the right leads into the First Court.
The Dining Hall is in the building on the right and
the Combination Room on the left of the picture.   In
the background is the Chapel Tower with the sunset
light upon it.

Cambridge

modation, which served for Ely monks alone, and which, as we see, was speedily abolished. Those few Houses which still elected to send their monks to Cambridge[1] maintained them there thenceforth under the care of "the prior of students"; and it was owing to the energy of one of these Cambridge priors that Monks' hostel was projected in 1428, at a time when, as is then stated, no house existed for Crowland or other Benedictine monks, and the religious either shared the hostels with seculars or lived in lodgings in the town. The site for Monks' hostel consisted of two messuages granted in that year to the abbot of Crowland by the Cambridge burgesses. Crowland, Ely, Ramsey, and Walden each built portions for their own students.[2] Nearly a hundred years later, on the eve of the Reformation, Edward Stafford Duke of Buckingham refounded this hostel as Buckingham College. It was not com-

[1] i. p. 27. The university for English and Irish monks provided by papal authority and by the Cistercian Constitutions was Oxford. The licence for Monks' hostel Cambridge stipulates that all monks of the order of S. Benedict in England or in other the king's dominions shall henceforth dwell there together during the university course. There was a small recrudescence of monastic studies in Cambridge in the xiv c. when Ely hostel was built, and from this time forward 3 or 4 Ely monks were regularly to be found pursuing the university course there (Testimony of John of Sudbury, prior of students, at the Northampton chapter in 1426). But there was no prior of students at Cambridge till towards the end of that century; Ely hostel itself was dismantled before the middle of the century; the black monks of Norwich however came to Cambridge under Bateman's influence with what the bull of Sixtus IV. 150 years later shows to have been considerable constancy. See Caius pp. 143-4, 144 n.

[2] Chambers for Crowland were built by its abbot John of Wisbeach in 1476. John de Bardenay had preceded John of Sudbury as prior of Benedictines in 1423, and both were probably Crowland monks.

128

The Colleges

pleted at the time of his attainder two years afterwards (1521) and the property escheated in due course as a cell of Crowland Abbey to the crown.[1]

How soon Monks' hostel became " the monks' hostel of Buckingham " is by no means clear. That the Dukes of Buckingham were early patrons must be admitted on the evidence ; for even if the house was not known as Buckingham College in 1465, it was known as "the hostel called Bokyngham college " in 1483 while it was still Crowland property, and both hall and chapel were probably the gift of "deep revolving, witty Buckingham " the second Duke Henry.

"I have in this world sustained great damage and injury in serving the king's highness, which this grant shall recompense." So wrote Lord Chancellor Audley in a letter begging for a share of the plunder when Henry had determined on the suppression of the monasteries. The share he wanted and got was Walden Abbey in Essex on the borders of Cambridgeshire, and here he established himself on the site which his son was to transform into the mansion of Audley-End. He did more ; he proposed to himself, apparently, some sort of expiation to balance the "recompense," and in 1542 changed Buckingham into Magdalene College which he re-endowed. We have seen that Walden Abbey was itself one of the builders of Monks' hostel.

The mastership of the college is in the gift of the

[1] Dugdale. When Charles V. heard that Stafford Duke of Buckingham had been beheaded through the machinations of the butcher's son Wolsey, he exclaimed : " A butcher's dog has killed the fairest buck in England ! "

THE COMBINATION ROOM, ST. JOHN'S
COLLEGE

This Gallery is used by the Fellows and is 93 feet
long. It contains portraits of many College worthies.
The approach to it is by a Turret Staircase in the
Second Court. Its panelled walls and rich plaster-
work ceiling make it one of the finest specimens of
its kind left in England.

Cambridge

owner of Audley-End (now Lord Braybrooke). Nothing
of the xv century building remains. A window of
Pugin's adorns the chapel[1] replacing the old altar-piece
which is now in the library. The combination room leads
from the musicians' gallery of the pleasant hall, the only
instance of this arrangement in Cambridge.[2] In the time
of Fuller, Magdalene was a college of reading men :
" The scholars of this college, though farthest from the
schools, were in my time the first to be observed there,
and to as good purpose as any." [3] Twenty years ago it
was the fashionable college, and its members lived in
private lodgings, attending neither hall nor chapel.
Magdalene is in the parish of S. Giles, and it has been
conjectured that it occupies the site of the house of
the canons of S. Giles before they removed to Barnwell.
There is however no evidence for this, and there are no
documents at Magdalene earlier than Stafford's time.[4]

Archbishop Grindal,[5] Robert Rede chief justice
in 1509, Cumberland Bishop of Peterborough, and
Kingsley were educated here. So was Pepys, the diarist,
who bequeathed to the college his extraordinary collection

[1] It is clear from the masonry of the chapel that this was anterior to
the college of 1519. See Willis and Clark ii. 362, 364.

[2] Corpus hall is the only one in Cambridge not provided with a musicians'
gallery.

[3] The retired position of the earlier college had been, he held, a salutary
assistance to study : it "stood on the transcantine side, an anchoret in itself,
severed by the river from the rest of the university."

[4] Fuller and Carter say the college site was purchased by the convents of
Ely, Ramsey, and Walden. Cf. p. 128.

[5] Grindal is a good instance of a migrating student : he entered at
Magdalene, and subsequently migrated to Christ's and Pembroke, where
he became fellow and Master.

The Colleges

of books, engravings, maps, and plans. The Pepysian library is now preserved in a separate hall, in the donor's own bookshelves constructed after a plan of his own. It is by far the most interesting thing in the college, and would be unique anywhere. It is to be hoped we may soon have an official catalogue of its contents.

Magdalene is a small college, it has about 40 inmates, of whom 5 are fellows. In Fuller's time it held 140 persons, 11 being fellows and 22 scholars, the rest being as usual the college officers, domestics, and students.

Trinity College A.D. 1546. With Trinity College are joined together in indissoluble matrimony the two great periods of college building, and the culminating point of the renascence is reached : so that Trinity, alone, re-presents Cambridge architecturally and morally in its historical character of a university of the rebirth from its dawn to its meridian.

King's Hall A.D. 1337. When Henry VIII., whose effigy adorns the great gate, proposed to make a vast college on this site, he was proposing to expand the "great college" built by Edward III. whose effigy graces the older gateway within the court. Edward II. had maintained thirteen students at Cambridge as early as 1317 and the number was increased later to thirty-two : it was however left to his son to carry out the design of a "House-of-Scholars of the King."[1] We have already had frequently to refer to

[1] The university statute providing for the commemoration of benefactors and others, directs that mass be said every 5th of May for Edward II. as founder of King's Hall.

THE LIBRARY WINDOW, ST. JOHN'S
COLLEGE, FROM THE BRIDGE OF SIGHS

From this spot beautiful views are obtained up and
down the river.

this building, in which new interest has been awakened since the restoration (in 1904-6) of part of the old Hall lying behind King Edward's gateway towards the bowling green, and presenting architectural features fully justifying its xiv century fame as the most considerable collegiate enterprise thitherto undertaken. The Hall lay to the north west of the present quadrangle, covering the space now occupied by the ante-chapel,[1] Edward's gate, and the Master's lodge. The acquisition of the site affords a most interesting glimpse into contemporary Cambridge history : for no site represented such various interests and recalled so many of the great local names. The first plot of ground obtained was a messuage of Robert de Croyland's in 1336. Eight years later Edmund Walsyngham's house was purchased ; the house of Sir John de Cambridge who was knight of the shire and alderman of the guild of S. Mary was sold to the college in 1350 by his son Thomas ; and the next year saw the purchase from Thomas son of Sir Constantine de Mortimer, of a waste parcel of land next the river and S. John's Hospital, called the Cornhythe, which abutted on the last named property. Croyland's and Walsyngham's houses were first adapted, and formed a small irregular quadrangle. Later in the xiv century a new (irregular) court was constructed on the north of the present chapel. The original entrance was situated where the sundial now is ; here stood the Great Gate, the present

[1] Which is on the site of the hall, pulled down in 1557 to make room for the chapel.

The Colleges

Entrance Gate being built as late as 1535 to give King's Hall a frontage on the High Street. The Hall rebuilt in the later xiv century and added to in the xvth was however only the nucleus of Henry VIII.'s college. To the south west stood Michaelhouse ; this too was absorbed in the new building, and its second dedication to the holy and undivided Trinity was retained in Henry's college. Seven other buildings—all university hostels — were also absorbed — Gregory's, Crouched, Physwick, S. Margaret's, Tyled, Gerard's, and Oving's. The present kitchen occupies part of the site of Michaelhouse ; Physwick stood between the Queen's Gate and Trinity Street ; and the other hostels were grouped round these in S. Michael's and King's Hall Lanes.[1]

The work which had been begun by Lady Margaret at Christ's and S. John's—the final substitution of the college for the monastery school—was now completed by her grandson, the great despoiler of the monasteries, who appears to have designed Trinity College as a splendid atonement for the destruction of so many homes of learning. It was largely endowed with abbey lands, and Henry's undeniable interest in erudition seems to have found its ultimate satisfaction in a foundation into which there entered every element of that "new learning" which was humanistic before it was Protestant. That provision was here to be made for a wider field of knowledge than any hitherto contemplated in or out of a university, seems amply

[1] For changes made in the Mill Street district in the xv c. when the Schools Quadrangle and King's College were built, cf. pp. 24, 24 *n.*, 25 *n.*, 97 *n.*, 101 *n.*

OLD GATEWAY AND BRIDGE

These buildings form part of St. John's College, and
look on to the river. The Tower of the College
Chapel is seen in the background.

proved by the words of the founder ; who, after declaring that the college is intended for the " development and perpetuation of religion " (a well-chosen form of words ?), continues thus : *"for the cultivation of wholesome study in all departments of learning, knowledge of languages,* the education of youth in piety, virtue, self-restraint, and knowledge ; charity towards the poor, and the relief of the afflicted and distressed." The programme was so liberal that Mary herself endowed the college with monastic property, and Elizabeth completed the chapel which her sister had begun.

No building, indeed, in either university suggests in the same way and in the same degree that delightful mental combination of form and space which is the mark of the " Cambridge mind " in science if it is not so in literature. As we pass into the great court the buildings we see neither shut out the light nor hem in the thoughts. The enclosure they suggest is that formal enclosure of point and line which enables us to make propositions about infinity. Of all scholastic buildings in the world the great court of Trinity is that which best suggests the majesty and spaciousness of learning. Here one receives an impression of adequacy, balance, clearness, spaciousness, elevation, serenity, a certain high power of the imagination—the mathematical qualities, the qualities of the seeker after truth : an impression of the simple force of what is simply clear, the simple grandeur of that which can dispense with the mysterious ; of the dignity which accompanies those who have looked upon things as

The Colleges

they are in themselves, and have nothing adventitious to offer, yet what they offer holds a curious power of satisfying.

Does a man see all this as he walks into Trinity and learn from it the lesson which Cambridge spreads before him, or does he take it with him under the gateway and let Trinity Great Court represent for him what he already knows of Cambridge? What does it matter whether it suggests so much or is allowed to represent so much?

Trinity Great Court covers more than 90,000 square feet—an area of over 2 acres—and is the largest in any college. The building, carried out under Edward VI., received considerable modification during the mastership of Nevile (1593-1615) dean of Canterbury, who arranged the court on its present plan, erected the "Queen's gateway" and the fine renascence fountain, enlarged the original lodge, and built the hall and kitchen. On the west side, facing us as we enter, is the hall (1604) which was modelled on that of the Middle Temple. Next it are two combination rooms—the centre for generations of Cambridge fellows who first had their assembling room in King's Hall hard by[1]—but the façade here was spoiled in the xviii century when the oriel and frontage of the old hall of Michaelhouse were removed. A Jacobean porch leads us into the lodge, which occupies the site of King's Hall lodge. The great scholar Bentley, Master from 1700 to 1742, built the staircase and otherwise left his mark here. His

---

[1] There was a fellows' "parloure" in King's Hall as early as 1423-4.

PEPYS' LIBRARY, MAGDALENE COLLEGE

This range of old buildings houses the Pepysian
Library. The style is seventeenth century.

excursions into the classical were, however, curtailed during the mastership of Whewell (1840) when Alexander Beresford Hope subscribed to restore the Gothic character of the front and built the picturesque oriel.[1] The inscription stating that he had restored its ancient aspect to the house during the mastership of Whewell gave rise to the following amusing paraphrase :—

> This is the House that Hope built.
> This is the Master, rude and rough,
> Who lives in the House that Hope built.
> These are the seniors, greedy and gruff,
> Who toady the Master, rude and rough,
> Who lives in the House that Hope built.[2]

A.D. 1555–1564.

The chapel, on the north, was built by Mary, and

[1] There is a fine series of most valuable portraits in the Lodge ; among them one of Mary, and the standing portrait of the young Henry VIII. which Wordsworth made the subject of a poem. A careful list of university portraits appears at the end of Atkinson's volume, but such a list—useful and valuable as it is—tucked away somewhere in a book on Cambridge is not an adequate homage to so important a source of university history as these portraits. The loan exhibition at the Fitzwilliam Museum in 1884-5 was the first attempt to collect the Cambridge pictures : the example was followed by Oxford in 1904-6, and the Catalogue of portraits then published is a model of what can and should be done.

No complete list of the portraits of either university, however, at present exists. Many canvasses remain unidentified or misidentified ; some are doubtless perishing for want of care, and the artist's name has long disappeared from many more. The work therefore that remains to be done is a big one, but is eminently worth the doing.

[2] A sedan coach is preserved in the entrance hall of Trinity Lodge, and is used to transport visitors from the Gateway to the Lodge when the Master entertains. It is the college tradition that the coach was presented by Mrs. Worsley, wife of the then Master of Downing, to Christopher Wordsworth Master of Trinity, and brother of the poet (1820-41).

is one of the few churches erected in her reign, as Trinity College is itself one of the few places where her name is held in affection. Though it has none of the greatness of King's chapel, it yields to none in interest. The site is that of the chapel of King's Hall built for the scholars by Edward IV., the materials of which, with stone from the Greyfriars' house, the fen abbey of Ramsey, and Peterhouse, and lead from the Greyfriars and Mildenhall, were used in the construction. Elizabeth completed it nine years later (1564). The ante-chapel contains the statue of Newton,

> ————with his prism and silent face,
> The marble index of a mind for ever
> Voyaging through strange seas of Thought, alone

a work of Roubiliac's considered by Chantrey to be the noblest of English statues. Bacon, Barrow, Macaulay, and Whewell have also statues here, while Richard Porson is commemorated by a bust. Along the wall which faces us as we enter are sixteen memorial brasses chiefly to remarkable fellows of the college who have died within the last twenty years.

The great court leads in the usual way, by hall and butteries, to Nevile's court, another work of Dr. Nevile's, and here the library—to the building of which Newton contributed—was erected by subscription, the foundation stone being laid on February 26, 1676. The architect was Wren who also designed the bookcases of the "stately library" as those who had determined on its foundation had called it in anticipa-

THE GATEWAY OF TRINITY COLLEGE

The Great Entrance Gate, constructed about 1518-
35. The panels over the arch commemorate King
Edward the Third and his six sons. The Master's
lodge is seen in the distance through the gateway.

Cambridge

tion. The wood of the cases is Norway oak which
has been stained to imitate cedar. The building
is very rich with decoration inside and out ; the length
is 194 feet as compared with the chapel 210 feet and
the hall 100 feet. The staircase and pavement are
of marble. Pedestals with busts of members of the
college line the room on either side. The library
contains 90,000 volumes, with 1900 MSS. including a
Sarum missal on vellum of 1500, Milton's rough
draft notes of "Paradise Lost," the *Codex Augiensis* of
Paul's Epistles, four MSS. of Wyclif's bible, and the
Canterbury psalter.[1]

A New Court, to which George IV. contributed, was
erected in the first quarter of the xix century and Dr.
Whewell built, at his own expense, the Master's Court.
Upon the site of Garret's hostel, the then bishop of
Lichfield erected in 1670 a small building known as
"Bishop's hostel" which is used as students' quarters,
and the proceeds of letting it are spent according to
the founder's direction in the purchase of books for
the library. Macaulay "kept" here when he first went
up to Cambridge.

[1] This is the largest college library but it is not the most ancient. Peterhouse led the way in the xiii century with divinity and medicine books of
Balsham's. In 1418, 380 volumes were catalogued, containing "from six
to seven hundred distinct treatises." Here were to be found books on
law, medicine, astrology, and natural philosophy, as well as the pre-
ponderating theological tomes. Trinity Hall was another famous xiv century
library, and Pembroke has a catalogue of books in that and the next
century amounting to 140 volumes. In the xv century Queens' had 224,
and S. Catherine's 137 (in 1472 and 1475). In 1571 the French ambassador to
this country deemed the library at Peterhouse "the worthiest in all England."
Cf. the university library, p. 98.

The Colleges

The Mastership of Trinity has been, ever since the Reformation, one of the most important offices in the university ; but it is rendered still more distinguished by the great men who have successively filled it. The last Master of King's Hall became the first Master of Trinity and has had among his successors Isaac Barrow, William Bill, Whitgift, Wilkins, Bentley, and Whewell. Its chief benefactor Nevile was eighth Master.

Trinity has been equally great in literature and science, and has effected more for both in the three hundred and fifty years of its existence than any other centre of learning. Among its fellows it counts Newton, Adam Sedgwick, Ray, Barrow, Porson, Roger Cotes, Macaulay, Whewell, Westcott, Airy, Clerk Maxwell, Cayley, Hort, Thirlwall, Jebb. Among lawyers Bacon, Coke, and Lyndhurst ; among prelates Tunstall,[1] Whitgift, Lightfoot. Among other famous *alumni* are Robert Devereux, Cotton, Spelman, Thackeray, Granville (*M.A.* 1679), Peacock, Kinglake, Trench, De Morgan, F. D. Maurice, and the late Duke of Rutland (Lord John Manners). Among poets, Byron, Dryden, Andrew Marvell, Tennyson, Donne, Cowley, George Herbert, Monckton-Milnes. Another historic friendship like that between Spenser and Kirke at Pembroke, Milton and King at Christ's, and Gray and Walpole, grew up in the shadow of Trinity—the friendship of Tennyson and Arthur Hallam commemorated in *In Memoriam*.

[1] His name appears in the House List of King's Hall.

THE GREAT COURT, TRINITY COLLEGE

The largest at either University or in Europe. We
see the Great Gate in the picture on the right, facing
us—the Chapel. To the left of the Chapel is seen
King Edward's Gate, fourteenth century. The beautiful
Fountain in the middle of the picture is in the Renaissance style, and was built by Nevile in 1602, and
rebuilt in 1716.

Cambridge

There are 60 fellowships, 74 scholarships worth each £100 a year, and 16 sizarships of the value of £80 each. The students of Trinity number one-fourth of the undergraduate population. The college is not only the largest but the most important scholastic institution in the world : "being at this day" writes Fuller, "the stateliest and most uniform college in Christendom, out of which may be carved three Dutch universities." Among the college livings are the university church of S. Mary's, S. Michael's (the old church attached to Michaelhouse) Chesterton Vicarage, and several rectories and vicarages in the dioceses of Ely, York, Lincoln, Lichfield, London, Peterborough, and Carlisle, which include most of those belonging to King's Hall and Michaelhouse, with the exception of the Norwich benefices.[1]

Gateways. The gateway of Trinity with its four towers, the two interior being the larger and furnished with staircases, reminds us that the ornamental gateway was the last architectural addition to the college quadrangle. The first ornamental archway was the great gate built for King's Hall in 1426.[2] It was copied in the turreted gateway of Queens' College, and afterwards in the old gateway of King's,[3] and in the present gateways of

[1] The tithes of Great S. Mary's and Chesterton both belonged to King's Hall, on which the advowson of S. Peter's Northampton was bestowed, as Cherry Hinton had been bestowed on Peterhouse. The rectory of Chesterton, which had pertained till then to the monastery of Vercelli, was given by Eugenius IV.

[2] Removed to its present position by Nevile in 1600 ; see p. 132.

[3] p. 102 n.

The Colleges

Christ's and S. John's, and even in that second gateway of King's Hall which is the present entrance gate of Trinity.[1] The only gateway in Cambridge which varies completely from these models is Alcock's at Jesus, which is much lighter in character. The xvi century gateways of Caius are "the first specimens of the revival of stone work."[2] The ornamental gateway is a distinctive feature of Cambridge college architecture. The room over the gate was used as a muniment room ; in S. John's the chamber in the tower serves this purpose.

Caius College In 1557 Doctor John Keys (whose name A.D. 1557. was Latinised as Caius) built and incorporated with Gonville Hall a college for scientific research and medical studies—the illustrious society which has since been known as Gonville and Caius College.

Keys or Caius was one of the great physicians of the xvi century ; physician to Edward VI., Mary, and Elizabeth, and President of the College of Physicians. He was a Yorkshireman by race but a native of Norwich, and had been Principal of Physwick hostel which was at that time attached to Gonville Hall. Italian universities had turned his mind from the study of divinity to that of medicine and he became a doctor in that faculty at Padua in 1541, two years after leaving Cambridge. At Padua he lived with one of the earliest anatomists —Vesalius ; and he himself lectured for twenty years

[1] See p. 133.   [2] Willis and Clark.

141

THE HALL OF TRINITY COLLEGE FROM NEVILE'S COURT

This is sometimes called the Cloister Court, and was built at the expense of Dr. Nevile about 1612. The principal building in this picture is the Dining Hall with its beautiful oriel window. Passing up the steps and through the passage we enter the Great Court, where we get another fine view of this Hall. Lord Byron occupied rooms in Nevile's Court.

on anatomy to the surgeons in London, at the request of Henry VIII.[1] He was Master of the college of which he was co-founder, but regularly spent the emoluments on fresh buildings at Caius. He was not only a great naturalist, the first English anatomist, a great physician, and an eminent classic,[2] but also a distinguished antiquary, and to him we owe one of the most valuable histories of the university. He had withal "a perverse stomach to the professors of the gospel," and clung like Metcalfe of S. John's and Baker of King's to the old religion and the old ways of worship.[3] He is buried in the college chapel, and the simple words *Fui Caius* are inscribed over him. The foundation-stone of Caius he had himself inscribed: *Johannes Caius posuit sapientiae* ; " John Caius dedicated it to knowledge."

He built his college in two parallel ranges, east and west ; a chapel and the Master's lodge occupying the north side. On the south was a low wall with a gateway. "We decree," he writes in the statutes of Caius, " that no building be constructed which shall shut in the entire south side of the college of our foundation, lest for lack of free ventilation the air should become foul." This appreciation of the all-importance of air and sun to living organisms was more than three hundred years in advance of his time. If his instructions be not carried out, he says, the health of the college will be impaired, and disease and death will ensue. Closed quadrangles had been built in Cambridge ever

[1] iii. p. 179. [2] iii. p. 174. [3] iii. p. 180.

The Colleges

since the erection of Pembroke College, but no more were built there after the time of Caius.[1] Andrew Perne of Peterhouse was a contemporary stickler for hygienic conditions in the colleges ; he saw to it that only pure water should be available " for the avoiding of the annoyance, infection, and contagion ordinarily arising through the uncleanness " of King's Ditch " to the great endammaging " of health and welfare.

The college founded by Gonville is still known as Gonville Court in the joint college ; but the other buildings are entirely new and make a modern show at the corner of King's Parade not necessarily justified by the modernness of the science pursued within their walls.

In the xv century Gonville was peopled with monastic students : it is said that when Humphrey de la Pole and Gresham were studying there the other scholars were nearly all religious. If the monks of Ely, Crowland, Ramsey, and Walden lived at Monks' hostel, the monks of Norwich priory had been allowed by a special papal exemption to continue to frequent Gonville and Trinity Halls, as they had done since Bateman's time.[2] The Suffolk monks of Butley, black Benedictines from Bury, Cistercians from Lewes, and Austin canons

---

[1] Closed courts, however, continued to be built at Oxford ; a late instance being the second court of S. John's built by Laud so that his college should not be outshone by its Cambridge namesake.

[2] Bull of Sixtus IV. 1481. The bull recites that in the time of William Bishop of Norwich the Norwich Benedictines had been accustomed to lodge at Gonville and Trinity Hall where Bateman had made convenient arrangements for them. When the pope proceeds to say that Benedict XI. had required all Benedictines who wished to study in Cambridge to live *in certo alio collegio dictae universitatis*, "deputed ad hoc," he is mistaking the

NEVILE'S GATE, TRINITY COLLEGE

To the left are the College kitchens and on the right
is Bishop's Hostel.   The buildings on the left are
among the most ancient in this college.   Through
the picturesque old gateway we see up the lane into
Trinity Street.

Cambridge

from Westacre in Norfolk were also to be found there.[1] Gonville Hall was always regarded as the papal favourite at Cambridge ; yet by 1530 Nix Bishop of Norwich in a letter to the primate Warham asserts that not one of the clerks at Gonville but "savoured of the frying pan."

Caius has always been a doctors' college ; Harvey, Glisson the anatomist, and a long roll of eminent surgeons and physicians here received their education. Jeremy Taylor and Sir Thomas Gresham the only one of the Merchant Adventurers known to have been at a university, and founder of the Royal Exchange, were also sons of this house ; as was Samuel Clarke (*b.* Norwich 1675) the metaphysician, " the lad of Caius."

There are 22 fellows and some 36 scholars and exhibitioners, the value varying from £100 down to £20. There are also two chapel-clerkships (£38 for one year), and the Tancred medical studentships each worth £100 a year.

Emmanuel 1584. We now come to the last two colleges to be founded in the xvi century. Emmanuel was founded by Sir Walter Mildmay, Chancellor of

authorisation of Monks' hostel 50 years before for the papal Constitution of 150 years before, as he mistakes Benedict XI. for Benedict XII. The suggestion that he refers to University Hall (the *hospicium universitatis*) is certainly erroneous : the words above quoted simply mean "in the said university" and not "the college called university college" : there was no such house for monks in Cambridge between 1347 and 1428, when "the college deputed in the said university ad hoc"—Monks' College—was founded. Benedict's Constitution does not specify whether the religious are to dwell in common, or not. [1] Cf. Magdalene, p. 127.

The Colleges

the Exchequer to Elizabeth, in 1584, his object being to plant the seed of Puritanism in the university. The site he chose was the suppressed house of the Dominicans, and Ralph Symons, the architect who worked with so much skill and judgment at S. John's and under Nevile at Trinity, converted the friary buildings into the Puritan college. The friars' church is now the college hall and the library which at one time served as a chapel was it is said the convent refectory. The college chapel was built, from Wren's designs, by Sancroft Archbishop of Canterbury (1668-78); and the college itself was rebuilt in the xviii and xix centuries. Emmanuel has preserved an evangelical character, the relic of its original Calvinism in doctrine and Puritanism in discipline; and the clerical students of Ridley Hall are recruited chiefly from here. " In Emmanuel College they do follow a private course of public prayer, after their own fashion "; the chapel used was unconsecrated, the communion was received sitting. The contrast must have been all the greater at this time—the beginning of the xvii century—when incense was burning and Latin was sung in other Cambridge chapels.

The name of Emmanuel College recalls the movement with which it was connected later in that century: when Whichcote, Cudworth, Smith, and Culverwell of Emmanuel, and More of Christ's led the van of philosophic thought.[1] Besides Cudworth, Emmanuel

[1] v. p. 286. Cudworth was afterwards Master of Clare, then of Christ's; Whichcote became Provost of King's.

TRINITY COLLEGE BRIDGE AND AVENUE,
    WITH GATE LEADING INTO THE NEW
    COURT

The Bridge was built in 1763 by Wilkins. The trees
in the Avenue in foreground were planted in 1671-72.

Cambridge

has nurtured at least four eminent representatives of learning and science, Flamsteed, Wallis, Foster, Horrox; and one great statesman, Sir William Temple; and as a representative churchman, Sancroft who was also Master of the college. Samuel Parr was here; and William Law, the author of the " Serious Call," was a nonjuring fellow. Harvard went from Emmanuel to America where he founded the university which bears his name.

There are 16 fellowships, 30 scholarships, and 4 sizarships.

Sidney Sussex, the last of the xvi century colleges, was also built in Elizabeth's reign, on the site of the Greyfriars' as Emmanuel rose on the site of the Blackfriars' house. Frances Sidney, daughter of Sir William Sidney and wife to the third Earl of Sussex, bequeathed the money for the foundation, and her executors purchased the property from Trinity College. The ubiquitous Ralph Symons was the architect ; but the college was modernised in the early xix century. There are two courts : the hall and lodge in one, the chapel and library in the other. In this last is a x century pontifical from a northern diocese, probably Durham. The character of the college has always remained Protestant, this and Emmanuel being the first Protestant foundations in the university. Oliver Cromwell was enrolled a member the day of Shakespeare's death, and Fuller the ecclesiastical historian was here for many years. Sterne the founder of the

146

The Colleges

Irish College of Surgeons, Archbishop Bramhall, Henry Martyn,[1] May the poet, and Seth Ward are among its worthies. Edward Montague, Earl of Manchester, of whom the historian writes that he "loved his country with too unskilful a tenderness" was a member of this college, and carried out Cromwell's destructive programme at his university. No one mentions the founder of Sidney Sussex without saying that she was aunt to Sir Philip, and it is a title of honour even for the founder of a college : did not Fulke Greville have himself described in his epitaph as "Frend to Sir Philip Sidney" ?

There are 10 fellows and 36 scholars on the foundation, besides sizarships of the value of £27 a year.

Downing 1803. One college has been built at Cambridge in modern times. The founder, who bequeathed his property for the purpose, was Sir George Downing of Gamlingay Park, Cambridgeshire, whose father was a graduate of Clare. Wilkins (the architect of the modern portions of King's and Corpus and of the New Court of Trinity) began the structure in 1807, but he only completed the west and east sides. The town has since grown up to the college, which has large pleasure grounds. A "Downing" professorship of law and another of medicine were also endowed by the founder. Six of the 8 college fellowships must be held by students of law or medicine ; and there are 10 scholars on the foundation.

[1] p. 126.

147

CAIUS COLLEGE AND THE SENATE
HOUSE FROM ST. MARY'S PASSAGE

On the left is the Senate House built 1722-30.
The building facing the spectator is the South Front
of Gonville and Caius College by Waterhouse (1870).
Through the railings on the right is the Tower of
Great St. Mary's. The street is King's Parade.

Cambridge

Taking the place of the older hostels, but inversely as regards their relative proportion to the colleges, there are now 6 hostels, colleges in all but university status, with resident students reading for the usual university examinations. There are also two post-graduate hostels. The oldest of these are *Newnham* (1871) and *Girton* (1873) which are described in another chapter. *Cavendish College* on the Hills Road was opened in 1876 by the County College Association and admitted students from sixteen years old. It was recognised as a public hostel (November 9, 1882) but was closed nine years later.

Ridley Hall was erected in 1880 for theological students who have taken their degree. Its object is the maintenance of Reformation principles.

Selwyn College was founded in 1882, by subscription, in memory of Bishop Selwyn, and for the maintenance of Church of England principles, to whose members it is restricted. This institution occupies a somewhat anomalous position in the university, for it is the only hostel on avowedly "denominational" lines publicly recognised by and therefore forming part of the academic society. Cambridge has set its face against the recognition of colleges intended to meet the interests of one religious section of the community to the exclusion of others, on the ground that members of all religious communities may now receive instruction in any of the colleges, and suffer no interference with their religion, and also in pursuance of the main principle that a university education is of greater use

148

The Colleges

and value when young men are not classed and separated according to their religious divisions. Thus when the Catholic hostel of *S. Edmund* applied for recognition in 1898, the " grace " was refused, in spite of the fact that many members of the university unconnected with any religious denomination, voted in its favour. *S. Edmund's House* was founded by the Duke of Norfolk in 1897, and is for clerical students working for a tripos or other advanced work recognised in the university. It ranks as a licensed lodging house. A Benedictine hostel, *Benet House*, was founded in the same year, and supported by the father of the present abbot of Downside. A few professed monks, who are entered as members of Christ's or some other college, pursue there the usual university course.

Westminster College is a post-graduate college for the Presbyterian Church of England, founded in Cambridge in 1899 (removed from London).

Cheshunt theological *College*, founded by the Countess of Huntingdon in 1768, has just been removed to Cambridge, and is there lodged in temporary premises. Undergraduate and post-graduate students are received, the former being non-collegiate members of the university. Students and staff must be of the Evangelical Reformed faith, but are free to enter the ministry of the established or any Free Church responding to that description.

These four last are the result of the abolition of the test act (1871) which kept our universities closed both to catholics and nonconformists : but Benet and

149

THE GATE OF VIRTUE, GONVILLE AND
CAIUS COLLEGE

This picture represents the Court built by Caius,
who refounded the College. The Gate of Humility
faces the spectator. This is the west side, and over
the gate are the words Io CAIVS POSVIT
SAPIENTIAE 1567. These words are taken from
the inscription on the foundation stone.

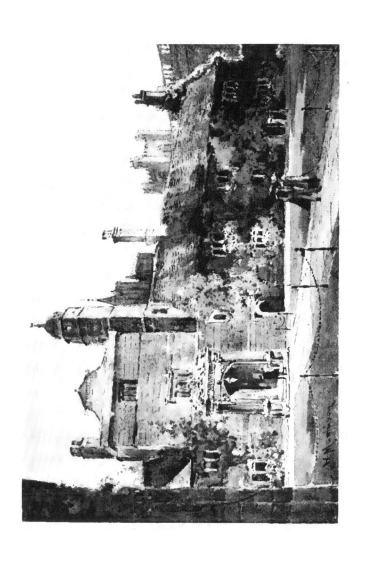

Cambridge

S. Edmund's houses were projected when the prohibition to catholics, maintained by Cardinal Manning, was withdrawn.

A note on the nationality of Cambridge founders.

Hugh de Balsham, founder of Peterhouse, 1284, Cambridge. Ob. 1286, bur. before the high altar, Ely.

Hervey de Stanton, founder of Michaelhouse, 1324. Ob. York 1327, bur. in S. Michael's church near his college.

Richard de Badew, founder of University Hall, 1326, Chelmsford, Essex.

King's Hall, Edward II. and Edward III., 1337.

Elizabeth de Clare, founder of Clare Hall, 1338 b. at Acre of Norman settlers in England Wales and Ireland ; married to two Irishmen. Ob. 1360, bur. Ware, Herts.

Marie de Chatillon, founder of Pembroke Hall, 1347. French, married a Welsh earl. Ob. 1377, bur. in the choir of Denney Abbey.[1]

Edmund Gonville, founder of Gonville Hall, 1348. East Anglian. Ob. 1351.

William Bateman, founder of Trinity Hall, 1350, East Anglian (b. Norwich). Ob. 1354, bur. Avignon.

Two Cambridge guilds, founders of Corpus Christi College, 1352.

William Byngham co-founder with Henry VI. of God's House, 1439, 1448 (Rector of S. John Zachary,

London ; Proctor of the university in 1447) (Fuller pp. 150, 161).

King's College, Henry VI., 1441.

Margaret of Anjou, founder of Queens' College, 1448, French. Ob. 1482, bur. at the cathedral of Angers.[2]

Elizabeth Woodville, co-founder of Queens'. Northants. Ob. 1492, bur. at Windsor, near Edward IV.

Robert Woodlark, founder of S. Catherine's, 1473, b. Wakerly near Stamford, Northants. Ob. 1479.

John Alcock, founder of Jesus College, 1495, b. Beverley, Yorks. Ob. 1500, bur. at Ely.

Margaret Beaufort, founder of Christ's and S. John's Colleges, 1505, 1509, b. Bletsoe, Beds.[3] Ob. 1509, bur. Westminster Abbey, in the south aisle of Hen.VII.'s chapel.

John Fisher (her coadjutor) b. Beverley, Yorks. Beheaded 1534, bur. in the Tower.

Magdalene College [first founded by the Fen abbeys and Walden 1428] Henry and Edward Stafford 2nd and 3rd Dukes of Buckingham, then Thomas first Baron Audley of Walden 1544. The two former (whose family came from Staffordshire) were beheaded 1483 and

---

[1] The spot is marked by the black tombstone in the present farmyard, half way between Cambridge and Ely.

[2] At her own request made to Louis XI. The tomb was destroyed during the Revolution.

[3] The seat of the Bedfordshire Beauchamps, her mother's family.

The Colleges

1521, and bur. at Salisbury, and Austinfriars, London.[1] Lord Audley b. Essex, ob. 1544, bur. Saffron Walden.

Trinity College, Henry VIII., 1546.

John Caius, founder of Caius College 1557. Yorks, but b. Norwich, ob. 1573, bur. in the college chapel.

Sir Walter Mildmay, founder of Emmanuel College, 1584, Chelmsford, Essex. Ob. 1589, bur. at S. Bartholomew the Great, London.

Frances Sidney, founder of Sidney Sussex College, 1595, Kent (the family came from Anjou with Henry II.). [Her father and husband were both Lords deputy for Ireland, and her father also President of Wales.] Ob. 9th March 1589, bur. Westminster Abbey.

Sir George Downing, founder of Downing College, 1803, Cambridgeshire. Ob. 1749, bur. Croydon, Cambridgeshire.

It will be seen that the university owes most to Cambridge itself and East Anglia ; and next to two counties which have always been in strict relation to it, Yorkshire and Essex. Two of the founders of colleges were French. Both Welsh and Irish names have been from the first represented, but Cambridge owes nothing to Scotland.[2] Even as late as 1535 when Henry issued the royal injunctions to the university during the chancellorship of Cromwell, there were students from every diocese and district of England, and from Wales and Ireland, at Cambridge, but Scotland is not mentioned.[3] Of the 4 countesses who founded colleges, one was twice married to Irishmen, and two married Welshmen.

[1] A headless skeleton found, before the middle of last century, near the spot where tradition says that Henry Duke of Buckingham suffered, is presumed to be that of the duke, of whose burial there is no other record. Hatcher's *History of Salisbury*, 1843.

[2] Elizabeth Clare was heir to her brother who fell at Bannockburn : Marie Chatillon was widow of Valence Earl of Pembroke who fell in the wars against Bruce. The only Scotch benefactor was Malcolm the Maiden who endowed the nunnery of S. Rhadegund ; but this was before colleges were built.

[3] "*Ex omni dioecesi et qualibet parte hujus regni nostri Angliae, tam ex Wallia quam ex Hibernia.*" There were, however, Scotchmen at Cambridge in the xiv c., i. p. 37.

151

THE GATE OF HONOUR, CAIUS COLLEGE

In the background on the right appear the buildings
of the University Library, one of the Turrets of King's
Chapel in the distance, and the Senate House is seen
on the left.

Cambridge

Of the 14 (non-royal) men founders (including the third Duke of Buckingham and Fisher) 5 were East Anglian (3 Cambridgeshire), 3 were East-Saxons, 3 Yorkshiremen, one a Northamptonshire man, and one came from Staffordshire. To Beverley the university owes Fisher and Alcock, to Chelmsford Badew and Mildmay, to Norwich Bateman and Caius.

Of the 6 women founders, two were French (Chatillon and Queen Margaret) one was of French extraction (Sidney), the Clares were Normans, Elizabeth Clare and Chatillon were Plantagenets through Henry III. and Edward, Margaret Beaufort and Buckingham by descent from Edward III.; Elizabeth Woodville was half French through her mother Jaquetta of Luxembourg, daughter of Peter Comte de Saint-Paul. Thus, curiously enough, two of the women founders hailed from Anjou (Margaret and Frances Sidney) and two from Saint-Paul (Chatillon and Elizabeth Woodville).

Scope of their foundations. The colleges they founded favoured different provinces.

Marie Valence, wished French fellows to be preferred to others of equal merits, and, failing these, scholars from the college rectories.[1]	Margaret of Anjou's college was, by Andrew Doket, allied with the Cambridge Greyfriars.
Gonville wished to benefit East Anglian clergy.	Margaret Beaufort and Fisher favoured the northern districts of Richmond, Derby, Northumberland, Cumberland, Westmoreland, York, Lancashire, and Nottingham, from which half at least of the scholars were to come.
Bateman wished chiefly to benefit clergy of the diocese of Norwich.	
Henry VI. decided that failing scholars from the parishes of Eton or King's, Buckinghamshire and Cambridgeshire should have the preference.	Sidney Sussex College was, by its "bye-founder" Sir Francis Clerk, endowed for students from Bedfordshire.

[1] To this day Pembroke fellowships are open to men "of any nation

The Colleges

The special character given to Peterhouse by Balsham was the studious pursuit of letters, arts, Aristotle, canon law or theology. There were to be 2 scholars for civil and canon law, and one for medicine ; and poor bible-clerks were to be instructed in grammar.

Hervey de Stanton founded Michael-house for clergy, and for the study of theology.

Marie Valence founded Pembroke for the study of arts as well as theology.

Elizabeth de Burgh founded Clare for general learning. Three poor boys were to be instructed in grammar, logic, and singing.

Edmund Gonville made the 7 Arts the foundation for a theological training. (Bateman abolished its theological character.)

William Bateman founded Trinity Hall for the study of law only.

The two Guilds of Corpus Christi and the Blessed Virgin founded their college for scholars in sacred orders, and for the study of theology and canon law.

William Byngham established God's House for the study of grammar among the clergy of the north-eastern counties.

Henry VI. required all the scholars of King's to be candidates for sacred orders, and made theology and arts the principal but not the exclusive faculties.

Margaret of Anjou made theology the principal study at Queens', and in her college law was only tolerated. The master of arts

must either teach the *trivium* and *quadrivium* for 3 years, or devote the same time to the liberal sciences or Aristotle.

Robert Woodlark made his fellows restrict their studies by vow to "philosophy and sacred theology" —his college of S. Catherine was founded to promote Church interests exclusively.

John Alcock required that the scholars of Jesus College when they had graduated in arts, should devote themselves to the study of theology. Canon law was prohibited, but one out of the 12 fellows might be a student of civil law.

Margaret Beaufort founded Christ's for the study of grammar, arts, and theology, but law and medicine were excluded.

Edward III. and Henry VIII. founded King's Hall and Trinity College for general learning.

John Caius founded his college for the pursuit of science.

Sir Walter Mildmay founded Emmanuel for clergy who should maintain the principles of the Reformation.

Sir George Downing founded his college for the study of law and medicine.

and any county," whereas at other colleges (as e.g. Corpus) the restriction is to "any subjects of the king, wherever born." Cf. Jebb's "*Bentley,*" p. 92.

THE FIRST COURT OF EMMANUEL
COLLEGE

Cambridge

Hence Michaelhouse, Gonville, Corpus, God's House, King's, Catherine's, Jesus, and Emmanuel were destined for a clerical curriculum only.

Bateman contemplated the union of the diplomatic career with the clerical ; and although there were many jurists' hostels his is the only college founded and en-dowed for the exclusive study of law. Caius is the only college founded and endowed for the natural sciences and medicine ; but in the xiii century Balsham, in the xvith Caius, and in the xixth Downing, all provided for medical studies. Similarly in the xiii, xiv, and xvi centuries Balsham, Edward III., Elizabeth de Burgh and Henry VIII. each founded a college for the pursuit of general knowledge.[1]

Wealth of the university. Sources of revenue. Throughout the xiiith, xivth, and xvth centuries the university was certainly a very poor corporation. It took a hundred years to build three sides of the Schools quadrangle, and the money for the important schools of Philosophy and Civil Law collected by Chancellor Booth in the xv century was only got together by taxing the university.

The university as distinguished from the colleges has never been a wealthy society, and its sources of revenue are now much the same as they have always been. There are the capitation fees of members of the university. Fees for matriculation, for the public examinations, and for graduation, and proctors' fines.

[1] See divinity, canon and civil law, medicine, arts, and grammar in the next chapter, pp. 164-7.

The Colleges

The income of Burwell rectory and of a farm at Barton. The trading profits of the University Press ; and one new source of income—the annual contribution from each of the colleges, in proportion to its revenues, provided for by statute in 1882. The vice-chancellor delivers an annual statement of expenditure, which includes the upkeep of the Senate House and Schools, of the University church, the Registrary's office, the observatory, museums and lecture rooms, and a yearly contribution to the library : the salaries of professors and public examiners, and the stipends and salaries of university officers and servants.[1]

College wealth and property. The original property of colleges was in land, benefices, and plate. The portable property was laid by in a *chest* kept in the muniment room : here title deeds, charters, rare books, college plate, and legacies *in specie* were treasured ; the last being drawn upon for the purpose for which they were bequeathed until exhausted. Benefactors to a college presented it with a "chest," and hence the "University Chest" is still the name for its revenue. Queen Eleanor presented a "chest" of a hundred marks to the university in 1293 ("The Queen's Chest") ; and Elizabeth, Duchess of Norfolk, enriched the public treasury with a thousand marks in the reign of Henry VII. when the "chests" had been "embezzled to private men's profit" ; a gift "which put the uni-

[1] To these must be added : insurance, rates, and taxes, repairs, legal expenses, printing, and stationery, gifts made by the university, and the *honorarium* paid to the university preacher.

THE OLD COURT IN EMMANUEL
COLLEGE

The large stained-glass window of the Hall is seen on
the right, and beyond that the window of the Combination Room.   The Dormer window of Harvard's
room is seen on the extreme left.

versity in stock again." [1]   The "Ely Chest" was given in 1320 by John sometime Prior of Ely and Bishop of Norwich, and the other principal givers were country parsons, university chancellors, a "citizen of London" in 1344, and Thomas Beaufort, Duke of Exeter ("Exeter's Chest") in 1401.

The wealth of the colleges differs greatly. Trinity college has a gross income of over £74,000 and the next richest college is S. John's. The poorer colleges have gross incomes varying from 4 to £9000.[2] The proportion contributed at Cambridge and Oxford for the royal loan of 1522 is interesting. At Oxford, New College and Magdalen contributed most, more than eight times as much as Exeter and Queens' (£40) which gave least.[3] At Cambridge, King's College and King's Hall were the richest corporations and contributed the same sums as New College and Magdalen Oxford.

[1] Fuller.

[2] Magdalene, S. Catherine's, Downing, Queens', Peterhouse, Corpus, and Trinity Hall are the small and least wealthy colleges, and in this order. All the others have a gross income of over £10,000 a year. The income of all the colleges is published annually in Whitaker.

[3] University College contributed £50.

CHAPTER III

THE UNIVERSITY AS A DEGREE-GIVING BODY

[pp. 157-164] Meaning of a degree—the kinds of degrees—the bachelor—the ancient exercises of the schools called acts, opponencies, and responsions—the sophister—questionist—determiner—master—regent master—the degree of *M.A.*—introduction of written examinations—the tripos.

[pp. 164-189] The subjects of study and examination : the *trivium* and *quadrivium*—grammar—Aristotle's logic—rhetoric—the three learned faculties—the doctorate—development in university studies—the development of the mathematical tripos—the senior wrangler—the classical tripos—Greek at Cambridge—the moral sciences tripos—philosophy at Cambridge—the natural sciences tripos—science at Cambridge—the language triposes—list of the triposes—changing value of the examination tests—the double tripos—present conditions for the *B.A.* degree—modern changes in the examinations—standard of the ordinary and honour degree, examples.

[pp. 189-201] Method of tuition at Cambridge—the lecture—the class—the weekly paper—the professorial chairs—readerships—lectureships—Lambeth degrees—degrees by royal mandate—honorary degrees—the "modern subjects"—and the idea of a university.

A UNIVERSITY differs from other scholastic institutions in conferring "degrees." Having taught a man his

157

THE LAKE AND NEW BUILDINGS,
EMMANUEL COLLEGE

The building is known as the Hostel, and was erected
between 1885 and 1894.

subject it offers him a certificate that he in his turn is able to teach it : the "degree" originally signified nothing more nor less than the graduate's competence to profess the faculty in which it was obtained. This certificate of proficiency referred to the "three faculties" of theology, law, and medicine, to which was added later "the liberal arts." The titles of "master," "doctor," and "professor" were at first synonymous. A master was a doctor in his subject, capable of professing it. The title of "master," however, clung to the faculty of arts, that of "doctor" to the three liberal or learned professions.

The following degrees are now conferred : in arts, the bachelor and master (*B.A.*, *M.A.*) ; in divinity, the bachelor and doctor (*B.D.*, *D.D.*—formerly *S.T.P.*, *sacrae theologiae professor*) ; in laws, bachelor master and doctor (*LL.B.*, *LL.M.*, *LL.D.*[1]) ; in medicine, bachelor and doctor (*M.B.*, *M.D.*) ; in music, bachelor, master, and doctor (*Mus.B.*, *Mus.M.*, *Mus.D.*) ; in surgery, bachelor and master (*B.C.*, *M.C.*). Besides which a doctorate in science (*Sc.D.*), and a doctorate in letters (*Litt.D.*), are conferred on graduates in laws or in either of the last four faculties who have made some original contribution to the advancement of science or learning.[2]

[1] See p. 167.

[2] A man's university and the faculty in which he has graduated are shown by the hood : the Cambridge master's hood is black silk lined with white silk ; the bachelor's black stuff hood is trimmed with white rabbit fur. The doctors in the three faculties wear scarlet silk hoods lined with pink and violet shot silk (*D.D.*), cherry silk (*LL.D.*) and magenta silk (*M.D.*).

B.D.'s wear a hood of black silk inside and out ; *LL.M.'s* wear

Degrees

The title of bachelor originally marked the conclusion of a period of study ; it was not a degree, and bestowed no faculty to teach.   Here, as elsewhere, a bachelor was an apprentice or aspirant to another status or position ; and he remained *in statu pupillari* as he still is in theory to-day.[1]

It is only in modern times that the conferring of a degree follows upon a set written examination.   For six hundred years the aspiring bachelor and master obtained their status by public disputations in the schools.   Public exercises, called " acts, opponencies and responsions," were regularly held during the period of probation, and the student advanced to the degree of master by steps which recall the rites of initiation in the catechumenate. After his first year the " freshman " became a " junior sophister "[2] in one of the faculties, and began to attend the school disputations, without however taking part in them.   In his fourth year, as senior sophister, he qualified to be " questionist," and presented himself as such at the beginning of Lent with ceremonies which turned him into a bachelor ; ceremonies in which

an *M.A.'s* hood ; *LL.B.'s,* a *B.A.'s* hood ; *M.B.'s* a black hood lined with scarlet.

The *Mus.Doc.* wears a brocaded hood lined with cherry satin ; *Mus.Bac.* black silk lined with cherry silk and trimmed with rabbit fur ; *Litt.D.* scarlet silk inside and out ; *D.Sc.* scarlet, lined with shot pink and light blue silk.

[1] Thus the *knight bachelor* is one enjoying the titular degree and rank of knighthood, without membership of any knightly order, to the companionship of which he is supposed to be an aspirant.

[2] The study of sophistry or dialectic, which preceded Aristotle's analytical logic.

159

THE CLOISTER COURT, SIDNEY
SUSSEX COLLEGE

The new buildings on the left of the picture were
designed by Mr. J. L. Pearson and erected in 1890.
In the distance we see the large mullioned window of
the Hall, which is part of the old college building
begun 1596.

Cambridge

the Cambridge bedell figures as a veritable deacon. The procession was formed on Ash Wednesday and introduced into the arts schools by the bedell, who exclaimed : " *Nostra Mater, bona nova, bona nova!* " and " the father " (the presiding college senior) having proceeded to his place, the bedell suggested to him the stages of the ceremony : *Reverende pater, licebit tibi incipere*, etc. After this day the new bachelor was no longer a questionist but a "determiner" who determined in place of responding to the propositions raised in the schools. This status continued through Lent, and hence the incepting bachelor was described as *stans in quadragesima*.[1]

The master of arts. In due course the bachelor "commenced master of arts," the inception taking place in Great S. Mary's church on the day of the "Great Commencement" the second of July. This is the traditional time of year for the granting of degrees, and the ceremony is still called "Commencements" in Cambridge and in universities which, like Dublin, are derivative institutions. The status now attained was that of *regent master, i.e.* a junior graduate whose

[1] Junior and senior sophister and bachelor : Fuller writing of Northampton says : "But this university never lived to commence Bachelor of Art, Senior Sophister was all the standing it attained unto. For, four years after," etc.

On tutors' bills a century ago the style of *dominus* was always given to bachelors, that of "Mr." to masters ; the undergraduate had to be content with "freshman" or "sophister." The bachelors are still designated *dominus* in the degree lists ; a style which reminds us of the clerical "dan" of Chaucer's time, and the Scotch "dominie" for a schoolmaster. For the degree ceremonies and processions see *Peacock, Appendix A.*

Degrees

business it was to teach the subjects he had himself been taught, for a period of five years ; after which he became a non-regent, or full master.[1] The obligation to teach was part of the university theory of studies ; so that when a Cambridge professor of our own time astonished his hearers by declaring " I know nothing of political economy, I have not even taught it " he was speaking in the spirit of the university maxim *disce docendo*. It was the scholar who had taught who was called *magister* and *doctor* in old times, not the men who, as is the case nowadays, " go down " with no other qualification than that of the bachelor and are nevertheless allowed in due time to write *M.A.* after their names. For the *degree* of *M.A.* has virtually ceased to exist : no one now " commences master," and the master of arts is simply the bachelor who has spent three years away from the university, in which he has had time to forget what he once knew. Indeed as between the master and the bachelor the case is often inverted, and if the former is an ordinary degree man and the latter an honours man, it is the latter who is the master in his subject while the former is little else than a tyro. That the degree of master carries with it not one iota more of scholarship or experience is certainly not understood by the public, but the fact that it is understood elsewhere supplies the reason

---

[1] Regent : *regere* like *legere*, to teach ; cf. the *doctores legentes* and *non-legentes* of Bologna : *regere scholas*, and *officium regendi* occur in Bury school records, xii c. (Brit. Mus. Add. MSS. 14,848, fol. 136). A congregation of the Cambridge masters, regents and non-regents, met in S. Mary's church as early as 1275.

DOWNING COLLEGE FROM THE EN-
TRANCE IN REGENT STREET

These buildings are in the classical style and are all
nineteenth-century work.

why such a small proportion of men now proceed to take it. [1]

Written examinations. It was not till the xviii century that written examinations were introduced, and from the day of their introduction the practice grew and flourished. Originally teaching and tests had both been oral, it was only as books became cheaper that the book in a measure supplanted the teacher, the written examination came to supplant the public acts and disputations, and *the writing down of knowledge* became the characteristic feature of Cambridge training. "Then know, sir, that at this place, all things—prizes, scholarships, and fellowships—are bestowed not on the greatest readers, but on those who, without any assistance, can produce most knowledge upon paper." "Read six or eight hours a day, and *write down what you know*," is a tutor's advice ninety years ago.

The tripos. The *tripos*, although it did not take shape till the middle of the same century derives its name from a custom of the xvith. On the day when the bachelor obtained his public recognition he had as his opponent in discussion one of the older bachelors who posed as the champion of the university. He sat upon a three-legged stool "before Mr. Proctor's seat" and

---

[1] It must be realised that the degree in arts always differed from degrees in theology law and medicine inasmuch as these latter implied competence to exercise the corresponding professions. There was no such corresponding profession in the case of arts, except that of the schoolmaster. The clergyman, lawyer, or doctor at least exercised himself in these subjects, but the "artist" unless he was a regent-master, or a *magister scholarum* elsewhere, left his studies when he left his university.

Degrees

disputed with the senior questionist. This stool or *tripod* was eventually to provide a name for the great written examination of succeeding centuries—the *tripos*. The champion bachelor was addressed as " Mr. Tripos," and his humorous orations were called "tripos speeches." *Tripos verses* were next written, and on the back of these the moderators, in the middle of the xviii century, began printing the honours list:[1] from this *tripos list of names* the transition was easy to *tripos* as the name of the examination itself—the tripos examination. These disputations degenerated in Restoration times to buffoonery, but the principle of examination made steady progress,[2] and there were probably no tripos speeches after the Senate House was built.   In the xvi and xvii centuries, however, great personages had acts and disputations performed for their entertainment ; and the tastes of Elizabeth and her Scotch successor were consulted when "a physic act" was kept before the former, while "a philosophy act" was reserved for James.

There were declamations, which did not escape Byron's ridicule, in the xix century, but the last general public "act" was kept in 1839.   The *viva voce* examination in the "Little go" which was only discontinued 14 years ago, and the *viva voce* and the "act" for the

---

[1] "The Tripos is a paper containing the names of the principal graduates for the year. It also contains 2 copies of verses written by two of the undergraduates, who are appointed to that employment by the proctors."—Dyer. An extract from one of these sets of tripos verses is given in Dyer, *Hist. Camb.* ii. 89.

[2] It was at this time that the moderators were substituted for the proctors, see p. 183.

medical degree [1] are the only survivals to our day of that oral examination by which the scholar in the public acts constantly responded to the living voice of the *magister*. For the first time in their long history silence settled down upon the schools, and the eye replaced the ear as the channel of knowledge. [2]

Subjects of study. The subjects in which university students *Trivium* and were from the first exercised, were those *Quadrivium*. of the Roman *trivium* and *quadrivium*, and the three faculties of theology law and medicine. A special importance must be assigned to the school of grammar—the first member of the *trivium*—at Cambridge. There is every reason to believe that it flourished there not only in the xiii century, under the patronage of the bishops of Ely, but also in the xiith. It was called the school of glomery (glomery, glamery, grammery) [3] and continued to be of importance till the xvi century, the last degree in grammar being granted in 1542. [4] Degrees in grammar were, nevertheless,

[1] pp. 168, 169.   [2] Cf. p. 189, the lecture.
[3] The derivation is Prof. Skeat's.
[4] The school of glomery was flourishing in 1452 (Ely Register *anno* 1452); but a few years previously, when the statutes of King's College were written, it was understood that grammar would be studied at Eton not at Cambridge. A century later (1549) the parliamentary commissioners introduced mathematics into the *trivium* where it replaced grammar. A school of grammar existed at the university side by side with the school of glomery [see the provision for the teaching of grammar at God's House (below) and Peterhouse and Clare p. 153 of the last chapter]. As late as 1500 there was a *magistrum grammaticae* and a *magistrum glomeriae*, who, *in ejus defectu*, is represented by proctors (*Stat. Cant.*). "The Master of Grammar shall be browght by the Bedyll to the Place where the Master of Glomerye dwellyth, at iij of the Clocke, and the Master of Glomerye shall

Degrees

considered inferior to those in arts. To begin with, grammar was only studied for three years, arts for seven ; grammar made the clerk, arts the professor. The introduction of the " new art," Aristotle's ana-

go before, and his eldest son nexte him." A.D. 1591 (*Stokys in G. Peacock*). By Fuller's time the master of glomery had ceased to exist. His work seems to have resembled the preparatory work of the Previous Examinations at the university to-day.

In the Curteys Register of Bury-St.-Edmund's (in the time of Abbot Sampson xii c.) we have the students of dialectic distinguished from the students of grammar and the latter from other scholars—"*dialecticos glomerellos seu discipulos*," and "*glomerellos seu discipulos indistincte*" ; surely a clear reference to two branches of the *trivium*. The use of the word *glomerel* in O.E. law to signify an officer who adjusts disputes between scholars and townsmen, is obviously the result of a misinterpretation of Balsham's rescript of 1276 "*Inprimis volumus et ordinamus quod magister glomeriae Cant. qui pro tempore fuerit, audiat et dicedat universas glomerellorum ex parte rea existentium . . . Ita quod sive sint scholares sive laici qui glomerellos velint convenire . . . per viam judicialis indaginis, hoc faciat coram magistro glomeriae. . . .*" The form of the latter's oath to the Archdeacon of Ely and the functions which fell to the master of glomery when the school became decadent, may also have led to the mistake (which was made by Spelman as regards the Cambridge glomerels). Cf. i. p. 14, iv. p. 207 *n.*, and Fuller, Prickett-Wright Ed. pp. 52-4. The second of these editors, indeed, was the first to call attention (in 1840) to the irrefutable evidence in the Cole and Baker MSS. as to the meaning of master and school of glomery, and to light on the confirmation from the university of Orléans in the verses of the troubadour Rutebeuf. For glomery, see also *Peacock, Appendix A, xxxii-xxxvi.*

The foundation of God's House in 1439 was due to Parson Byngham's zealous desire to remedy "the default and lack of scolemaisters of gramer," following on the Black Death. In a touching letter to the king (Henry VI.) Byngham points out "how greatly the clergy of your realm is like to be empeired and febled" by the default, and relates that "over the est parte of the wey ledyng from Hampton" to Coventry alone, "and no ferther north yan Rypon," *70 schools* were empty for lack of teachers. "For all liberall sciences used in your seid universitees certein lyflode is ordeyned, savyng only for gramer."

165

lytical logic, increased the importance of the second member of the *trivium* : the name of Aristotle was a name to conjure with, but no new texts came to light to add lustre to the acquirements of the classical grammarian. As to the third member of the *trivium*, public rhetoric lectures were delivered in Cambridge by George Herbert (1620) ; but a century later Steele

A.D. 1712. complains that both universities are "dumb in the study of eloquence." There were still however rhetoric lectures in the xviii century, but they were not about rhetoric, and the public declamations in the senate house must be regarded as the last homage to this most ancient of arts, whose modern successor is the Union debating society.

The three liberal or learned faculties.

If the original Cambridge schools were grammar schools after the pattern of Orléans and Bury-St.-Edmund's, then the introduction of the arts faculty—the trivium and quadrivium—was the first step towards the formation of a *universitas* ; and its appearance in the xii century would account for the university status of Cambridge in the opening years of the xiii century.[1] The first of the three learned faculties to take its place in the university was divinity, and with the rise of the earliest colleges provision was made for the study of the two faculties of theology and law. The faculty of medicine was the last to gain a footing. Cambridge never became famous as a school of any of the faculties in the sense in which Paris represented divinity, Bologna law,

[1] See chapter i. p. 33.

Degrees

Montpellier medicine. The study of the civil and canon law was, however, prominent in the xv and early xvi centuries, but was shorn of its ecclesiastical moiety during the chancellorship of Thomas Cromwell when Peter Lombard and Gratian were banished the Cambridge schools.[1] Of the two universities Cambridge alone retains a recognition of canon law in the title of its bachelors masters and doctors of laws, *LL.B.*, *LL.M.*, and *LL.D.*, a title commuted at Oxford into 'bachelor and doctor of civil law,' *B.C.L.* and *D.C.L.* The medical progress of the early xvi century which had been marked by the foundation in 1518 of the Royal College of Physicians reached Cambridge by means of two great men, Linacre from Oxford and its own distinguished son John Caius. Peterhouse had been the first college to admit medical studies, but our naturalists and physicians of later times, not content with the fare provided for them in England, took their degrees at the continental schools. Medicine, the last to obtain recognition, is now the most prominent representative of the learned faculties at Cambridge. Until 1874 when a theological tripos was formed, admitting to a degree in that subject only, theology was studied as part of the mathematical tripos. Law was taken as an additional subject, and degrees in divinity and law were proceeded to separately, as now.

[1] *Royal Injunctions* to the university of 1535, requiring the denial of papal supremacy. "King Henry stung with the dilatory pleas of the canonists at Rome in point of his marriage, did in revenge destroy their whole hive throughout his own universities," *Fuller*. The last Cambridge doctor in canon law "commenced" in this reign.

Cambridge

Satisfying the examiners in the theological, law, or natural sciences tripos does not admit the student to any but the arts degree. Medical students need not, however, graduate in arts, but may proceed at once, after taking the Previous Examination, to read for the M.B. degree.[1] In addition they must keep an "act," which consists in reading a thesis previously approved by the Regius Professor of Physic. Having read the thesis (of which public notice is given) in the schools, the candidate is orally examined by the presiding Regius Professor of Physic. After this he becomes an *M.B.*[2]

A candidate who has obtained honours in Parts I. and II. of the law tripos or honours in Part I. in addition to an arts degree, is eligible for the degree in laws and may proceed to take the *LL.B.*, the *B.A.*, or both. Any candidate may "incept in law" (*LL.M.*), without further examination, who has taken a first class in both parts of the law tripos. If he has not

---

[1] The usual course is to take the special medical examinations with the First Part of the natural sciences tripos. Sometimes however these are taken in addition to the ordinary *B.A.* degree. The last of the three *M.B.* examinations is divided into two parts, of which Part I. is taken at the end of the fourth year of medical study, and Part II. after six years, three of which must have been spent in medical and surgical practice and hospital work. The keeping of the "act" is not intended to be a mere form, and students are advised to prepare for it during the years of their hospital practice.

[2] The degrees of bachelor of surgery (a registrable qualification) and master of surgery require no separate examination ; the candidate must have done all that is required of a bachelor of medicine ; but bachelors of surgery who are not also masters of arts cannot incept until three years have passed since they took the *B.C.*, and masters of arts must have become legally qualified surgeons.

Degrees

this qualification he must have attained an honours standard in one part of the tripos, or be a qualified barrister or solicitor, or their equivalent in Scotland. In this case he must submit a dissertation on law, its history, or philosophy. The doctorate of laws is obtained after making an application in writing and sending in an original written contribution to the science of law. The *LL.M.* cannot incept till six years have elapsed from the end of his first term of residence, and five years must elapse between the master's and the doctor's degree.

The doctorate. A master of arts or of laws becomes a bachelor of divinity after subscribing certain declarations required by statute and preaching a sermon in the University church. Four years later he must "keep an act" *or* print a dissertation, in Latin or English, upon some matter of biblical exegesis or history, of dogmatic theology, ecclesiastical history or antiquities, or on the evidences of Christianity. The "act" is kept in the same way as that for the medical degree, and includes a *viva voce* examination. To proceed to the *D.D.* the same preliminary formalities as for the *B.D.* must be observed,[1] and a dissertation be printed on one of the same subjects. Five years must elapse between the two degrees, except in the case of a *B.D.* who is also an *M.A.* of at least twelve years' standing. In fact the lapse of time is all that remains of incepting and proceeding to the higher degrees.

---

[1] Whitgift's thesis for the *D.D.* degree (1570) was "*Papa est ille anti-Christus*"—'the pope is himself anti-Christ.'

Cambridge

Development of university studies. Until hard upon the close of the xv century there was no development in university studies. Erasmus in 1516 describes them as having consisted until thirty years previously in nothing but Alexander (the grammar text-book at Cambridge) the " Little Logicals," the old exercises from Aristotle, the *quaestiones* from Duns Scotus. The study of mathematics, the new Aristotle, a knowledge of Greek, had all come within the last few years.[1]

The development of the mathematical tripos. Gradually the study of these " arts " yielded to the mathematical tripos. The subjects which had been intended to embrace a general education dropped out,[2] those which dealt with mathematics or mathematical physics encroached more and more, till in 1747 the historic tripos with which the name of Cambridge is identified was fully established. The conviction of the paramountcy of mathematical reasoning had been emphasised at the university by the discoveries of Newton, and when its mathematical studies were consolidated in the xvii century under the influence of Newton's tutor, Isaac Barrow, " philosophy " was understood to mean the mathematical sciences, and continued to mean this and this only in English mouths till the threshold of our own times.[3] " By the

---

[1] *Erasm. Epist.* (London 1642), *Liber secundus, Epist.* 10. Letter to Bullock dated from the Palace at Rochester, August 31, 1516.

[2] Or were relegated to the previous examinations.

[3] Till then it had meant Aristotle : the statutes of Queens' and Christ's, framed within 50 years of one another, provide for its teaching—"the natural, moral, and *metaphysical* philosophy of Aristotle" ; and even in

Degrees

study of the great relations of form," writes an old Trinity student from the other side of the Atlantic, the Cambridge man acquired that "breadth of reasoning," that power of generalisation, and perception of analogy "in forms and formulae apparently dissimilar," which characterise the scientific mind. A study which bestows accuracy of scholarship, the perception of order and beauty, and "inventive power of the highest kind," was that "in which for two hundred years all, and now more than half of the Cambridge candidates for honours exercise themselves." [1]

Wranglers. Euclid and Newton filled the Cambridge horizon, and summed, as we have seen, all philosophy and all "arts." Theology itself ceased to rival the mathematical disputations which became the business of the schools *par excellence*, and which were of such importance that the name of *wranglers* was exclusively applied to those most proficient in them, and "the senior wrangler" held the first position in the university. To attain this place it was necessary to have "fagged steadily every day" for six or eight hours. The quality of a man's work would tell for nothing in the final result if he had neglected, with this end set before him, to practise that mere

Fuller's time these metaphysics were the study of the bachelor of arts : "Let a *sophister* begin with his *axioms*, a *batchelor of art* proceed to his *metaphysicks*, a *master* to his *mathematicks*, and a *divine* conclude with his *controversies* and *comments* on scripture . . ."

Philosophy, meaning Aristotle, had come in to disturb the peace and the sufficiency of the old 'seven arts.'

[1] William Everett, *M.A.*, 1865.

171

TRUMPINGTON STREET FROM
PETERHOUSE

Part of the new buildings of Pembroke College are
seen on the right, and the Tower of the Pitt Press,
commonly called by undergraduates "The Freshers'
Church," is seen in the distance. The entrance to
Peterhouse is behind the tree on the left of the picture.

W. Matthison

Cambridge

mechanical "pace" which would serve him in the great week.[1]

The classical tripos. In 1822 the classical tripos was added. The history of classical studies at Cambridge is of special interest. The introduction of Greek into this country was a movement due directly to our universities : students of Oxford first learnt the language in Italy, but Cambridge as a university first gave it an academic welcome. The last echoes among Englishmen of the most wonderful idiom the world has heard resounded in the school of York, when John of Beverley, Wilfrid, and Bede could be described as Grecians, and where Alcuin taught Greek. More than seven centuries later the efforts of Fisher chancellor of the university of Cambridge with the co-operation first of Erasmus and then of Croke, re-established Greek in an English seat of learning.[2]

[1] It has been said that senior wranglers are hidden in country rectories and are never heard of again. In a hundred and sixty years (1747-1906) there have been eight senior wranglers who could be placed in the first rank as mathematicians and physicists :

Herschell 1813	Adams 1843
Airy 1823	Todhunter 1848
Stokes 1841	Routh 1854
Cayley 1842	Rayleigh 1865

Paley, in 1763, was the first distinguished senior wrangler. On the other hand Colenso Whewell and Lord Kelvin were second wranglers, so was the geometrician Sylvester ; de Morgan and Pritchard were fourth wranglers ; the learned Porteous was tenth wrangler, Lord Manners (Lord Chancellor of Ireland) was 5th, Lord Ellenborough (Lord Chief Justice) 3rd, Lord Lyndhurst (Lord Chancellor) second.

[2] Another distinguished Oxonian, and East Anglian, Grosseteste, attempted in the xiii c. the re-introduction of Greek into England ; but the foreign linguists whom he invited to St. Albans left no successors.

Degrees

Greek at the universities. Erasmus had given up his dream of studying Greek in an Italian university and had
settled down three years before the close of the century
at Oxford on hearing that Grocyn was teaching there.[1]
He had known some Greek before he went to Oxford,
and he knew but little when he left, for its acquisition
was still his great pre-occupation when he accepted
Fisher's invitation and went to Cambridge. The work
of Grocyn and Linacre left no trace in their own university. When Colet introduced the study of Greek
into his new school, Oxford showed itself hostile ;
when the Greek of Erasmus and Croke had taken permanent hold in Cambridge, the Oxford students rose
up in arms against the Cambridge "Grecians," and
dubbing themselves "Trojans" sought street brawls
with the "Greeks." Finally, Sir Thomas More himself wrote a protest to his old university, which, he
wrote, was engaged in casting ridicule on those who
"are promoting all the interests of literature at your
university, and especially that of Greek." "At
Cambridge, which you were always accustomed to out-
shine, even those who do not learn Greek are so much
persuaded to its study in their university that they
praiseworthily contribute to maintain a salaried professor who may teach it to others."[2]

Colet took Greek into our public schools, in face

---

[1] The west countryman Grocyn (b. 1442) who learnt his Greek in Italy
and returned to teach it in Oxford was, chronologically, the first English
classical scholar since the revival of learning.

[2] "All students equally contributed to his" (Croke's) "lectures,
whether they heard or heard them not." *Fuller.*

Cambridge

of the hostility of his university; it was the Cambridge Grecians settled by Wolsey at Cardinal College who established it at both universities, and it was men like Ascham, Sir Thomas Smith, and Cheke who introduced it as Cambridge learning to the world outside. It has been well said that classics "kept a firm hold on the Cambridge mind." The mantle of Erasmus Croke and Cheke fell upon Bentley and Porson who had no rivals among English classics and critics, and the services rendered by Cambridge as a university in this direction have been maintained by the present generation of scholars.[1]

[1] REVIVERS OF GREEK IN CAMBRIDGE.

First period: Early 1. John Fisher, b. Beverley, Yorks, 1459. Chancellor of
patrons of Greek the university, Master of Michaelhouse, President of
learning, and the Queens', a co-founder of S. John's. Though not himself
group round a Greek classic, one of the chief instruments of its intro-
Erasmus. duction into Cambridge. See also ii. pp. 120-21.

2. John Tonnys, *D.D.* prior at Cambridge and provincial of the Augustinians. Ob. 1510. One of the first men in the university to desire to learn Greek.

3. John Caius, ii. pp. 141-2 (lectured in Greek at Padua after leaving Cambridge).

4. Erasmus, *D.D.* Queens', Lady Margaret Professor of Divinity at Cambridge, and lecturer in Greek. Befriended by Fisher, Warham, Tunstall, and Fox, but opposed by the Oxonian Lee, Abp. of York. Left Cambridge 1513.

5. Richard Fox (Bishop of Winchester) Master of Pembroke College. Introduces Greek learning into his college of Corpus Christi, Oxford, and founds the first Greek lectureship at the sister university.

6. Cuthbert Tunstall (Balliol Oxford, King's Hall Cambridge, and university of Padua) b. 1474. Ob. 1559. Bishop of Durham.

7. Henry Bullock, fellow of Queens' and vice-chancellor.

8. John Bryan, fellow of King's, ob. 1545. Lectured on Greek before the appointment of Croke.

9. Robert Aldrich, fellow of King's, senior proctor 1523-4, Bp. of Carlisle.

Degrees

Colloquial Latin and Greek. By order of Thomas Cromwell " two daily public acts one of Greek the other of Latin "

10. Richard Croke or Crooke, scholar of King's 1506 ; later a pupil of Grocyn's ; studied Greek in Italy at the charges of Abp. Warham. Greek tutor to Henry VIII. Appointed first Reader in Greek at Cambridge 1519 ; and was first Public Orator. Afterwards professor of Greek at Oxford.

11. Tyndale, b. circa 1486, ob. 1536 (resided at Cambridge between 1514-1521, and owed his Greek to that university). Left Oxford for Cambridge, as Erasmus had done, probably on account of the sworn hostility at Oxford to classical learning. See his " Answer " to Sir Thomas More, written in 1530 (Mullinger, *The University of Cambridge* p. 590).

Greek Classics, Second period. Roger Ascham, b. 1515, fellow of S. John's. Reader in Greek and Public Orator in the university. Tutor to Mary, Elizabeth, and Lady Jane Grey.

Sir Thomas Smith, b. 1514, *LL.D.* Queens'. Regius Professor of Law and Reader in Greek at Cambridge, and Public Orator.

Sir John Cheke, b. 1514 at Cambridge, fellow of S. John's. First Regius Professor of Greek. [" Thy age, like ours, O soul of Sir John Cheek | Hated not learning worse than toad or asp, | When thou taught'st Cambridge, and King Edward, Greek " (Milton).]

Nicholas Carr, fellow of Pembroke, who replaced Cheke. Ob. Cambs. 1568-9. (As with other Cambridge men he joined science and classics, and afterwards became a doctor of physic.)

Richard Cox, scholar of King's (v. pp. 272-4). One of the introducers of Greek and the new learning into Oxford.

Francis Dillingham, fellow of Christ's. One of the translators of the English bible.

Dr. Thomas Watts, of Caius, who endowed 7 " Greek scholars " at Pembroke College in the xvi century.

A few later names. Augustine Bryan, ob. 1726, Trinity College. Jeremiah Markland, b. 1693, fellow and tutor of Peterhouse.

Richard Bentley, 1662-1742, of S. John's, Master of Trinity.

Richard Porson, 1759-1808, scholar and fellow of Trinity, Regius Professor of Greek.

Thirlwall, b. 1797, fellow of Trinity, Bishop of S. David's.

were to be held in all the colleges.[1] The Commonwealth Committee tried to revive the colloquial use of
Latin and Greek in 1649, but the use of Latin in halls
and walks ceased in this century, though it lingered in
the college lectures, the declamations, and the " acts
and opponencies."   It lingered also in the college
chapels, but the only relic now remaining is the Latin
grace in hall. The study of the classics themselves
declined at Cambridge during the reign of Charles II.
and Gray laments, while Bentley was still living, that
these studies should have "fallen into great con-
tempt."[2]

W. H. Thompson, ob. 1886, Trinity.   Regius Professor of Greek,
Master of Trinity.

Sir R. C. Jebb, ob. 1906, Trinity, Regius Professor of Greek.

REVIVERS OF GREEK IN OXFORD.

1. William Selling.   Got his love of Greek from Italy.   Taught at
Canterbury.   Afterwards of All Souls' Oxford.

2. Linacre, b. *circa* 1460 and studied at Canterbury with Selling, and at
Oxford under Vitelli, but learnt his Greek in Italy.   Lectured in
Oxford on physic.   Tutor to Prince Arthur.   Ob. 1524.

Inspired by Linacre to start for Italy to learn Greek.

3. Grocyn b. Bristol 1442.   New and Exeter Colleges,
Oxford.   The first to lecture on Greek.

4. William Latymer, educated at Padua, but afterwards
a fellow at Oxford.

5. William Lily, b. Hants. 1468, learnt Greek at Rhodes
and Rome.

6. Colet, b. 1466.   At Oxford and Paris ; learnt Greek in Italy.

7. Thomas More, b. 1480.   Learnt Greek with Linacre and Grocyn.

8. Richard Pace.

[1] Namely "in King's Hall, King's, S. John's and Christ's Colleges,
Michaelhouse, Peterhouse, Gonville, Trinity Hall, Pembroke Hall, Queens',
Jesus, and Buckingham Colleges, Clare Hall and Benet College."   Royal
Injunctions of 1535.

[2] The ancient pronunciation of Latin (so far as it can be recovered)

Degrees

The moral sciences tripos. It was the introduction of the classical tripos which gave a foothold for mental and moral philosophy. Occupation with Greek metaphysics, contact with the Greek mind, brought into relief the one-sidedness of the mathematical mind. It also placed the two methods in sharp contrast. For hitherto a fundamental antagonism between mathematical and metaphysical method had been unsuspected. It was not till the dispute between Whewell and Hamilton that the idea was pressed home that there were two philosophical methods, not one ; that not only the reasoning which begs but the reasoning which questions the premiss has a right to be heard ; that there was a philosophy of formal proof and one of philosophic doubt ; that axiomatical reasoning lay on the one side, and the enquiry into the validity of the reasoning process itself on the other.

Psychology. It was indeed by way of psychology that this other philosophy gained a foothold in the university. It was the contact with the scientific temper of Cambridge of psychology and psycho-physics—the modern science

has been taught, as an alternative, at Cambridge for the last 25 years, and has of late been widely adopted there, as elsewhere. Perhaps at the bottom of the preference for English Latin there lies the notion that without it Latin would no longer be the English scholar's second tongue. The simple retort is that with it Latin is no longer (has not been for centuries) a common medium, the second tongue, of European scholars. Anglicised Greek is due to Sir John Cheke and Sir Thomas Smith, though it was promptly abolished at the time by Stephen Gardiner then chancellor of the university, and opposed also by Caius. "Nor mattereth it if foreigners should dissent, seeing hereby we Englishmen shall understand one another," so Fuller explains the position.

Cambridge

par excellence, the point of contact between the experimental method and mental philosophy, the fine flower of science since Darwin, its complement, its interpreter—which ensured the introduction of a moral sciences tripos. This it was which won recognition for an organon other than the mathematical. Metaphysics captured Cambridge based upon psychology, and here the two have never been divorced.

The problem of education at Cambridge before 1851 had been entirely concerned with the mutual relations of mathematics, physics, and classics. The two historic triposes had between them ousted even Locke and Paley, the relegation of which to the ordinary degree work nullified, for all serious philosophic purposes, the "grace" of 1779 which had devoted a fourth day to examination in "natural religion, moral philosophy, and Locke." [1] Whewell who had lectured in 1839 as professor of casuistry on moral philosophy, was chiefly instrumental eleven years later in forming the new tripos. The college which took the leading part was S. John's, where the Rev. J. B. Mayor was fellow and afterwards examiner ; and the first man admitted to a fellowship for his attainments in this direction was a Johnian who came out senior moralist in 1863. When the tripos was framed, within twenty-five years of the final disappearance of all mental

[1] Paley continued to keep his traditional hold on Cambridge through the divinity paper in the "Little Go" which is based upon the "Evidences for Christianity." On the other hand logic has recaptured the place which Aristotle held in the general curriculum by being admitted, since 1884, as the alternative subject for Paley's "Evidences."

Degrees

philosophy from the higher schools at Cambridge, it included papers on logic and psychology, on metaphysics, ethics, political philosophy and political economy. The political subjects now form a tripos to themselves, the Economics tripos created in 1903. Hort was a candidate in the first examination (1851) and L. B. Seeley in the third : until 1861, when Whewell and Leslie Stephen were among the examiners, the tripos was taken in addition to one of the others, and did not confer a degree.[1]

That vampire of the Cambridge schools, mathematics, had absorbed not only philosophy and the arts but also the natural sciences. It had been however through one of the great metaphysicians, Robert Clarke, that Newton's physics had taken their place in the Cambridge curriculum, and Locke and Newton were there side by side, and had entered there together. It seemed, then, a simple revival and continuance of these traditions when the natural sciences tripos was formed in the same year as the moral sciences.

Empirical science at Cambridge. Empirical science at Cambridge dates from Linacre and Caius. The Puritan masters of the university discountenanced science, discouraged the university's higher mathematics, but were led by their liking for the open bible greatly to favour the study of Greek. It is a remarkable fact that the natural ally of the reform movement was "Greek" not natural

---

[1] Lord Maynard of Wicklow (S. John's College) endowed a professor of logic at Cambridge in the reign of James I., with £40-50 a year.

For university activity in philosophy in the xvii c. see chapter v. pp. 284-90.

PEASHILL

The Chancel of St. Edward's Church is seen behind
the stalls in the roadway, and the Tower of Great
St. Mary's in the distance. On the right is the Old
Bell Inn and the old town pump is in the foreground.

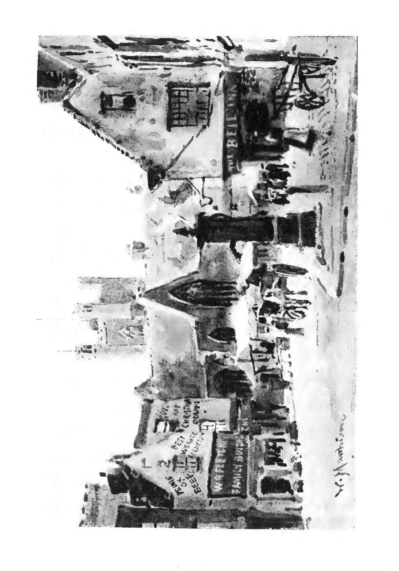

science.[1] Greek and "heresy" were equivalents ; Caius, the ardent champion of medicine and empirical science in Cambridge, was one of the last to cling to the old "popishe trumpery."[2] Just two hundred years before the publication of the "Origin of Species," someone writes to Sir Thomas Browne the author of *Religio Medici*, from Darwin's college at Cambridge, saying that there were then (1648) "so few helps" at the university for the student of medicine and science. With the Restoration scientific interests were revived, London setting the fashion to the seats of learning. But even at the close of the xviii century—that dark age of the universities—there was a professor of anatomy and there were lectures on "human anatomy and physiology" at Cambridge.[3] A few years later there was no physiology and the only physical study was astronomy.[4] Such

[1] One must not forget, however, that both the remarkable men who planted the study of the experimental sciences in Cambridge were distinguished 'classics' as well as scientists.

[2] Letter of Vice-Chancellor Byng to Burleigh then chancellor of the university, 14 Dec. 1572, in which he advises him of a "greate oversighte of Dr. Caius" who had long kept "superstitious monuments in his college." "I could hardly have been perswadid," he continues, "that suche things by him had been reservid."

"Some since have sought to blast his memory by reporting him a papist ; no great crime to such who consider the time when he was born, and foreign places wherein he was bred : however this I dare say in his just defence, he never mentioneth protestants, but with due respect, and sometimes, occasionally, doth condemn the superstitious credulity of popish miracles. . . . We leave the heat of his faith to God's sole judgment, and the light of his good works to men's imitation," writes old Fuller.

[3] Chairs of anatomy, botany, geology, and astronomy had been created in the first quarter of that century. See also Peterhouse p. 153.

[4] For the natural sciences professorships, see pp. 190-92, and *n.* p. 192.

Degrees

was the state of affairs two or three decades before the creation, in 1851, of a tripos which included physiology, comparative anatomy, chemistry, geology, botany, and mineralogy. The examination now comprises papers in 8 subjects, and is divided into two parts : chemistry, physics, mineralogy, geology, botany, zoology and comparative anatomy, human anatomy, and physiology. In the second part the last paper is upon human anatomy and vertebrate comparative anatomy. Cambridge owes its present prominent position as a teacher in the scientific world to the remarkable development of its scientific laboratories and equipment. For the purposes of the natural sciences tripos it possesses some of the finest laboratories and museums in the kingdom. The great Cavendish laboratory was built in 1874, the chemical in 1887, the engineering in 1894-9, the new medical school in 1904 with the museum of geology, while the same year saw the erection of the most complete botanical laboratory in England. Cambridge therefore which is "the most ancient scientific school in the country" is also among the best equipped.

The study of modern languages. Within a century of the decay of Norman French in England, a knowledge of modern languages began to assume value. Throughout the Tudor epoch it was those ecclesiastics and lawyers who were also linguists to whom the diplomatic posts and the secretaryships of state were entrusted. Latin did not cease to be the common official medium, but the growth of national dialects gave to a knowledge of these

181

the importance which they must always possess for the diplomat and the trader. "Esperanto" will not take its place until nothing is spoken anywhere but Esperanto.

Some progress was made in these studies in both the universities in the xvi century :—"Petrarch and Boccace in every man's mouth—the French and Italian highly regarded : the Latin and Greek but lightly," writes Gabriel Harvey to Spenser : but the xixth opened at Cambridge barren of anything linguistic, ancient or modern, eastern or western, except the uncouth Latin of the schools.[1] The first languages tripos was formed in 1878 for the Semitic languages ; the Indian languages tripos (1879) now forms part, with the Semitic tripos, of the Oriental languages tripos created in 1895. In 1886 the "medieval and modern languages" tripos came into being.

List of the triposes. The complete list of Cambridge triposes with the date of their introduction is as follows :—(1) Mathematical 1747.[2] (2) Classical 1822. (3) Moral Sciences 1851. (4) Natural Sciences 1851. (5) Law 1858.[3] (6) Theological 1874. (7) Historical

---

[1] "In barb'rous Latin doom'd to wrangle" writes Byron of the Cambridge of his time.

[2] The year is counted from the beginning of the academic year, *i.e.* Oct. 1747—the first degrees were taken in 1748.

[3] A classified list of civil law graduates exists from the year 1815. There used to be a university *title* S.C.L. (Student of Civil Law) in relation to the civil law classes. The Act of 20-21 Vict., disestablishing civil law in the courts, led to a revolution of law studies at Cambridge. From then dates the abolition of the old quaint ceremonies and disputations connected with this faculty.

Degrees

1875.[1] (8) Medieval and Modern Languages 1886. (9) Mechanical Sciences 1894. (10) Oriental Languages 1895. (11) Economics 1903.

Changing value of examination tests. The value of the tests to which degrees have been attached in the past has varied considerably, and the same is true of the present. The *M.A.* degree in the xvi and following century was obtained with little or no examination ; the disputations, as we have seen, were often idle forms, but the improvement in methods dates from 1680 when the proctors were replaced by *moderators* as overseers in the sophisters' school. Fifty years later the building of the Senate House opened the new era, and the next twenty years (1730-50) saw rapid progress ; so that the Cambridge degree was still something better than the Oxford when at the end of that century aspirants for degrees at both universities were adequately described as " term-trotters." [2] The conspicuous university learning of the xvii century was untested and unstimulated by any adequate examination test ; but earlier still the sheer number of years passed at a university must have had a value which is now lost. Seven years was the rule at Cambridge in the xv, xvi and xvii centuries, and the early history of the oldest of Cambridge colleges shows

[1] From 1870, before the creation of the history tripos, examinations were conducted in a mixed law and history tripos.

[2] Among educational reformers in the second half of the xviii c. Dr. John Jebb must not be omitted. To him is due the annual test examinations of tripos students called 'the Mays,' and perhaps also the " Little-Go." He was a distinguished scientist, and member of Peterhouse.

OLD HOUSES NEAR ST. EDWARD'S
CHURCH AND ST. EDWARD'S PASSAGE

This Passage leads from the Market into King's
Parade. Part of the South side of St. Edward's
Church is seen on the right. The Reformers Bilney,
Barnes, and Latimer preached here. The Three Tuns
Inn, praised by Pepys for its good liquor, formerly
stood in this passage.

us the Peterhouse students residing *all the year round*. Nowadays the standards of the honour and "poll" degree[2] are so wide apart that the terms bachelors and masters of arts applied equally to all degree work, are misleading. "He only wanted to take his degree, he did not work much" someone said to me a short time ago, and one felt one knew that degree. The honours class standard is also variable, and "a good year" raises the first class standard unduly.

The double tripos. The condition which characterised Cambridge studies before 1850 was that the mathematical tripos was obligatory on all candidates for honours. Between 1823 therefore and 1850 every classic was obliged to pass in one of the three classes of the mathematical tripos—he had, that is, to satisfy the examiners in two triposes. The results were often curious. Men like Macaulay, who became fellows of their college, were "ploughed" in the tripos, and professors of classics wrote *M.A.* after their names in virtue of a "poll" degree. The native repugnance to mathematical method in some men's minds was constantly shown and at all stages of the university curriculum ; Stratford Canning was "sorely puzzled" and indeed "in an agony of despair" over the study for which he was a "volunteer" at King's, and Gray refused to graduate rather than pursue it. On the other hand the Cambridge "double first" meant a degree unrivalled in any part of the world.[3]

---

[1] Cf. chap. ii. p. 61 and chap. iv. p. 241.   [2] "Poll," οἱ πολλοί.
[3] In 1835 Goulburn (afterwards Bishop of Trinidad) was second

Degrees

The present conditions for obtaining the *B.A.* degree are (*a*) residence for nine terms within the precincts of the university [1] (*b*) satisfying the examiners in one of the examinations, or groups of examinations to which a degree is attached. One may satisfy them in one of four ways : (1) by reading for and obtaining 'honours' [2] (2) by taking the Previous, General, and Special examinations of the ordinary degree [3] (3) by

wrangler and senior classic ; in 1828 Selwyn, another bishop, was senior classic and sixth wrangler. For the 2 triposes cf. iii. p. 170.

[1] "Within 2½ miles in a direct line" from Great S. Mary's. For the academic year see iv. p. 241, and *n.* p. 182.

[2] Part I. of most of the divided triposes entitles to the degree. Advanced and research students are entitled to the *B.A.* and higher degrees after receiving a "certificate of research" and residing for 6 terms at the university.

[3] The Previous Examination or "Little-Go," as it is popularly called, consists of two parts, the first containing 5 papers on (*a*) one of the four Gospels in Greek (set book) (*b*) a Latin classic (set book) (*c*) a Greek classic (set book) (*d*) simple unprepared passages in Latin (*e*) simple Latin and Greek syntax. Since 1884 a Greek or Latin classic may be substituted for the Greek Gospel. Part II., since June 1903, consists of 5 papers on (1) Paley's Evidences, for which since 1884, elementary logic may be substituted (2) geometry (3) arithmetic (4) elementary algebra (5) subjects for an English essay from some standard English work or works. Until 1903 the geometry paper was exclusively on Euclid's lines, and required knowledge of the first three books and of parts of the vth and vith books. To qualify for admission to an 'Honours' examination a student must pass in certain subjects 'additional' to the ordinary Previous Examination. He is now allowed to choose between (1) additional Mathematics (Mechanics and Trigonometry) (2) French (3) German.

A student must satisfy the examiners both as to grammar and orthography in answering the questions—a last relic of the grammar studies of the university !

The General Examination, taken by those who read for the ordinary degree, includes (in Pt. I.) (1) a Greek classic (2) Latin classic (3) mechanics (4) simple trigonometry [(5) English passages for translation into Latin prose]. (Pt. II.) (1) The Acts of the Apostles in Greek (2) English history, selected

being 'allowed the ordinary degree,' which may happen when a man fails to be placed in any class of a tripos, but when his work is allowed to count as tantamount to period (3) subjects for an English essay, from the selected period (4) elementary hydrostatics and heat [(5) a paper on a Shakespeare play or on Milton's works]. The 5th paper in each part is not obligatory.

The Cambridge General Examination for the ordinary degree leaves much to be desired.

The Special Examination for the ordinary degree may be in one of the following subjects : (a) *Theology* (b) *Political Economy* (c) *Law* (d) *History* (e) *Chemistry* (f) *Physics* (g) *Modern Languages* (h) *Mathematics* (i) *Classics* (k) *Logic* (l) *Geology* (m) *Botany* (n) *Zoology* (o) *Physiology* (p) *Mechanism and Applied Science* (q) *Agricultural Science* (r) *Music*. The standard for the subjects *k, l, m, n, o*, is that of the papers on those subjects in the first part of the moral and natural sciences triposes. The standard in the Theological Special examination may be judged from the following : Pt. I. (1) Outlines of O. T. history (2) a gospel in Greek [(3) history of the Jews from the close of O. T. history to the fall of Jerusalem]. Pt. II. (1) Selected portions of historical and prophetical books (2) one or more of the epistles in Greek (3) outlines of English Church history to 1830 [(4) selected portion of historical books of O. T. in Hebrew. (5) outlines of Early Church history to the death of Leo the Great. (6) paper on a selected period of English Church history]. (7) Essay subjects on the subject matter of papers (1) (2) and (3). But paper (3) in Pt. I. and 4, 5, and 6 in Pt. II. are not obligatory. Law Special examination :—Pt. I. (a) some branch of English constitutional law (b) English criminal law [(c) select cases in illustration (voluntary)]. Pt. II. (1) elementary English law relating to real property (2) English law of contract or tort, or similar. [(3) select cases in illustration (voluntary).] (4) Essay on the subject matter of (1) and (2). The first part of the Historical Special examination consists of 3 papers on English history before 1485, the third on a special period being optional. Pt. II. contains 5 papers (1) outline of general English history from 1485-1832. (2) outlines of English constitutional history for the same period (3) a period or a subject in foreign history (4) a special period of English history. [(5) an essay, optional.] The Mathematical Special is all elementary. The Classical Special is on the lines of the Previous Examination—set papers on portions of two Greek and Latin prose and two Greek and Latin poetic authors ; to which is added an unprepared Greek and an unprepared Latin translation and a Latin prose

Degrees

the examinations of the ordinary degree. (4) by being
"excused the General," which happens when a man
has failed in the tripos examination, but his work is

composition. The papers on Greek and Roman history belonging to Pt. I.
(Greek) or Pt. II. (Latin) are optional. Candidates for all these examinations may present themselves again in case of failure.

The standard of the tripos examination may be gauged by the following
examination schedules for (A) Classics (B) Moral Sciences. (A) Pt. I. 15
papers—4 composition papers ; 5 translation ; (10) History of words and
forms, and syntax, in both classical languages. (11) Short Greek and
Latin passages relating to history and antiquities of Greece and Rome for
translation and comment. (12) A paper on history and antiquities. (13)
Same as 11, with reference to Greek and Roman philosophy, literature,
sculpture and architecture. (14) Same as 12 (the questions on Greek
philosophy being on portion of a set book). (15) Essay.
Pt. II. Examination in 1 or 2 of the 5 following sections : (1) Literature
and criticism (2) ancient philosophy. (3) history. (4) archæology. (5)
language. The following are examples of Sections (1) and (5) : I. (a)
Questions on the history of Greek literature and passages illustrating Greek
literary history or criticism for translation and comment. (b) The same,
Latin. (c) Passages from Greek and Latin authors for interpretation,
grammatical comment, or emendation ; on the paleography and history of
Greek and Latin MSS., and the principles of textual criticism ; questions
on textual criticism of a Greek or Latin author (set book). (d) A special
author (set book) or a special department of Greek or Latin literature.
(e) paper of essays. V. (a) Greek etymology and history of Greek dialects.
Greek syntax. (b) Latin, collated with cognate Italic dialects, and syntax.
(c) Easy passages from Sanskrit authors (set books) for translation and comment, and simple Sanskrit grammar. (d) and last, general questions on the
comparative grammar and syntax of the Indo-European languages. Early
Indo-European civilisation. Indo-European accent. Greek and Italic
alphabets. The Italic dialects. The whole of these two examinations,
with the exception of one portion of paper 14 in Pt. I. and one portion
of papers c and d in Pt. II. Section I., deal with unseen Greek and Latin
authors.

(B) Moral Sciences :—Pt. I. *Psychology* (2 papers). Standpoint, data, and
methods of psychology. Its fundamental conceptions and hypotheses.
Relations of psychology to physics, physiology, and metaphysics. (a)

187

Cambridge

counted as putting him half way towards the ordinary degree. The *aegrotat* is a fifth way. If a man who has read for honours or for the ordinary degree falls sick, he is allowed to answer one or two of the examination papers only, and if he shows adequate knowledge

analysis of consciousness. (*b*) sensation and physiology of the senses—perception. (*c*) Images and ideas. (*d*) Thought and formation of concepts. Judgment. (*e*) Emotions, and theories of emotional expression. (*f*) Volition—pleasure and pain—conflict of emotions. [In the 2nd part, advanced knowledge on these subjects is required, plus a knowledge of the physiology of the senses and nervous system, etc., and of mental pathology in its relation to psychology.]

Logic (2 papers). Province of logic, formal and material. Relation of logic to psychology, and to the theory of knowledge. (*a*) names and concepts, definition and division, predicables. (*b*) classification of judgments and propositions. Theory of the import of propositions. (*c*) laws of thought, syllogisms, symbolic logic. (*d*) induction and deduction. (*e*) observation and experiment, hypotheses, classification, theory of probabilities. (*f*) inference and proof. Fallacies. [In the 2nd part, advanced knowledge of these subjects and of the controversies connected with them is required.]

Ethics (1 paper) (*a*) moral judgment, intuition, and reasoning, motives, pleasure and pain, free will and determinism (*b*) ends of moral action—right and wrong—moral sanctions—obligation—duty—pleasures and pains. (*c*) types of moral character. Principles of social and political justice. (*d*) The moral faculty, its origin and development. (*e*) relation of ethics to psychology, sociology, and politics.

Two papers on political economy and an essay paper exhaust Pt. I.

For those who proceed to Pt. II., two papers on metaphysical and moral philosophy (as below) must be answered, one on the general history of modern philosophy, and *one* or *two* of the 3 following papers (A) Psychology II. ; (B) Logic II.; (Special) history of modern philosophy (subject announced each year) ; *or* (C) papers in politics and in advanced political economy :

Metaphysical and moral philosophy :—(*a*) analysis of knowledge, material and formal elements of knowledge, self-consciousness, uniformity and continuity of experience. (*b*) identity and difference, relation, space and time, unity and number, substance, cause. (*c*) certainty, and necessities of thought. (*a*) fundamental assumptions of physical science—causality,

Degrees

of these is granted a degree, but is not placed in any class.[1]

There have been frequent changes and regroupings in all the examinations described, and other reforms are in contemplation. In 1850 the Universities Commission led to radical changes at both universities. It is now proposed to simplify greatly Part I. of the mathematical tripos, placing the candidates in divisions in alphabetical order, and thus abolishing the senior wrangler.[2] This classification is the rule in the second parts of all the large triposes, all of which have been divided since their formation. The abolition of compulsory Greek in the Previous Examination is bruited and re-bruited, but for the moment the question has been set at rest (May 1906) by a decided negative vote of the senate.

The lecture and class. The method of tuition at Cambridge consists of the lecture, the class, the weekly paper, and the examinations. " Reading " has, naturally, taken the place of oral teaching to a large extent, but the lecture still holds its place in the university. In the view of many of the seniors that place is still too

continuity etc. (e) sources and limits of knowledge, relativity of knowledge, phenomena, and things in themselves. (f) fundamental assumptions of ethics, absolute and relative ethics, intuitionism, utilitarianism, evolutionism, transcendentalism. (g) mechanical and dynamical theories of matter, relations of mind and matter, problem of the external world, idealism, dualism, freedom of intelligence, and of will, good and evil in the universe, teleology.

[1] Even if the candidate answer most of the tripos papers the conditions of the *aegrotat* degree preclude his being placed in any one of the classes. Edmund Spenser the poet and Lancelot Andrewes the scholar-bishop were both on the *aegrotat* list of Pembroke College—in 1571—before, however, this necessarily implied absence from any of the university " acts."

[2] Since going to press, this change has been effected.

189

Cambridge

large a one : the lecture at which copious (often verbatim) notes are taken is, no doubt, in many instances thrown away, especially in those subjects in which the lecturer simply goes over ground covered by the existing text-books. The class permits of lecturer and student discussing difficulties, and here the college tutor's rôle is also of first importance ;[1] the weekly paper (usually a " time paper," to be answered in three hours) tests progress in the subject, and teaches a man how to " write down what he knows," and to do so in a certain given time.

Professorships. There was no salaried professorship in the university until Lady Margaret founded her chair of divinity in 1502. Before this, tuition in each faculty had been assigned to its doctors, the tuition in arts was left in the hands of the masters of arts. The next three professorships to be founded were also in the 3 faculties : the Regius of Divinity by the king in 1540, the Regius of Civil Law in the same year, and the Regius of Physic.[2] Henry also founded Regius professorships of Hebrew and Greek. In 1632 Sir T. Adams founded the Arabic, and in 1663, Henry Lucas, M.P. for the university, the Lucasian of Mathematics ; the Knightbridge of Moral Philosophy was founded by a fellow of Peterhouse in 1683. Between that date and 1899 (when the professorship of Agriculture was founded) 35 professorships have

---

[1] See chap. iv. p. 225.

[2] This professorship was an expansion of the natural science lectureships founded by the great Linacre.

Degrees

been endowed, 16 of which are in natural sciences and medicine, 5 for languages, 4 for history and archæology, 2 more for law, 1 for mental philosophy and logic, and 3 more for divinity, one of which, the Norrisian, is tenable, and is now held by, a layman. Fisher and Erasmus were the first holders of the Lady Margaret professorship, and Selwyn, Lightfoot, and Hort held it between the years 1855 and 1892. Bentley and Westcott held the Regius professorship (1717, 1870). Sir T. Smith was the first to hold the Regius of Civil Law, which was also held by Walter Haddon, and by Sir Henry Maine when he was twenty-five years old, Glisson of Caius was one of the distinguished holders of the Regius of Physic (1636) Metcalfe of S. John's and Cudworth both held the Hebrew professorship, Sir J. Cheke was the first to sit in the chair of Greek following on three such great predecessors and professors of Greek at Cambridge as Erasmus, Croke, and Sir Thomas Smith. Isaac Barrow (1660) Porson (1792) and Sir R. C. Jebb (1889-1906), all Trinity men, have also held it. The Lucasian of Mathematics was held by Barrow, then by Isaac Newton, then by his deputy Whiston of Clare, then by Sanderson of Christ's, and the chair was filled in the xix century by Airy and Sir George Stokes. Roger Cotes was the first to hold the Plumian of Astronomy (1707) founded three years previously by the Archdeacon of Rochester, who endowed it with an estate at Balsham. Professor Adams, the discoverer of Neptune, held the Lowndean of Astronomy and Geometry (1858-1892).

MARKET STREET AND HOLY TRINITY CHURCH

In this picture Holy Trinity Church (of which Charles Simeon was incumbent) with its spire may be seen on the left. The cool grey building in the middle of the picture is the Henry Martyn Hall, a modern structure. In the distance is seen the Tower and North side of Great St. Mary's.

Cambridge

The Regius of Modern History (George I. 1724)[1] was held by the poet Gray, by Sir J. Stephen, Charles Kingsley, Sir J. Seeley, and Lord Acton : the Cavendish professorship of Experimental Physics (founded by Grace of the Senate 1871) was first filled by Clerk Maxwell and Lord Rayleigh ; F. W. Maitland (ob. Dec. 1906) held the Downing of Law ; and the new Quick professorship of biology has just been offered to an American graduate.[2]

Next in dignity to professors are the Readers in the different subjects, who act as a sort of suffragans and assistants to professors ; and next to these come the lecturers in branches of knowledge which range from comparative philology to electrical engineering, from medical jurisprudence to ethnology.[3]

Lambeth degrees and degrees by royal mandate. The Pope was the fountain of graduate honour in the middle ages and conferred degrees in all the faculties, and he does so still. Doctors and masters from Rome would receive

[1] A chair of history was endowed by Fulke Greville, Lord Brooke, with £100 a year, in the reign of Charles I. It no longer exists.

[2] A list of the professorships, with date of creation and emoluments, and of the readers and lecturers, appears in the University Calendar every year.

There were no less than 7 chairs of medicine and natural science before 1851 when the tripos was created. The chairs existed, but with no scientific school to support them.

[3] In 1524 the executors of Sir Robert Rede, Lord Chief Justice, endowed *tres liberae lecturae* in humane letters, logic, and philosophy ; and many distinguished men have been invited to deliver this annual lecture. The Hulsean lecture was founded in the xviii c.

The first *exhibitions* were founded in the xiii c. by Kilkenny, 9th Bishop of Ely, Balsham's predecessor, for "2 priests studying divinity in Cambridge."

Degrees

incorporation at Cambridge, and Englishmen without a degree would be given, on occasion, a degree by the Pope.[1] The general statute of Henry VIII. conveying A.D. 1534. to the primate all licences and dispensations which had heretofore "been accustomed to be had and obtained from Rome," transferred the faculty of conferring degrees in England from the Pope to the Archbishop of Canterbury. This faculty had, until the date of the statute, formed part and parcel of the legatine powers, and had been exercised as such by Wolsey. It was among the more important powers transferred under the statute, relating to licences of the taxable sum of £4 and over, and required confirmation by Letters Patent under the great seal, or enrolment in Chancery. The right was exercised by successive archbishops, and every faculty so granted rehearsed the authority of parliament by which authority the said power was now vested in the see of Canterbury. In the reign of George I. the power was for the first time disputed. The then Bishop of Chester refused to induct a Lambeth *B.D.* and a law suit followed, as a result of A.D. 1722. which a prescriptive and statutable right was made out for the practice. The matter was then carried by appeal to the King's Bench and decided in favour of the archbishop, three years later, in 1725.

From the accession of Charles II. till the end of the A.D. 1660-1700.

---

[1] Towards the end of the xv c. we have several instances of papal degrees conferred on members of religious orders which were followed by incorporation and full membership of Cambridge university. Thus *frater Steele* "of Rome" was incorporated in 1492, and *frater Raddyng* as a doctor five years later.

Cambridge

century the usual recipients were members of one or other of the universities, and when this was not the case incorporation in Cambridge university was granted with the proviso that no precedent was thereby created. Between 1539, when Cranmer created a *D.D.*, and the accession of Charles II., only seven instances of archiepiscopal degrees are recorded.[1] Over 450 were conferred between 1660 and 1848, and some 334 have been conferred since.[2] A Cantabrigian primate confers the Cambridge hood, an Oxonian the Oxford. There have been many instances of the incorporation of men who were recipients of the 'Lambeth degree' in one or other of the colleges. The Lambeth *M.A.* does not include membership of the Senate or of Convocation.[3]

During Stuart times there were several examples of the conferring of degrees by royal mandate; a custom commuted to the now traditional compliment, when a sovereign or prince receives a degree, of conferring degrees on any persons he may wish associated with him in the honour. Lord Stratford de Redcliffe, whose

[1] 1539 Eligius Ferrers, *D.D.*; 1544 a Venetian *B.A. ad eundem*; 1559, *circa*, a *B.D.*; 1615 an *M.A.* created *B.D.*; 1617 the same; 1619 an *M.A.*; 1635 the archdeacon of Essex *M.A.*, is created *B.D.*

[2] Archbishop Sumner (1848-62) 120 degrees; Langley (1862-68) 46; Tait (1868-82) 101; Benson (1882-96) 55; Temple (1896-1903) 12.

[3] Degrees in the 3 faculties are conferred without examination. Since Aug. 1858 degrees in medicine have carried with them no qualification to practise.

All candidates for the *M.A.* must pass an examination in preliminary arithmetic, Greek gospels, and English language and literature: the two classical languages, modern languages, mathematics, mental and moral sciences, and the natural sciences, forming 6 subjects from which the candidate must choose two, and the standard enforced being "that of candidates for honours at the universities." The Stamp Duty and other expenses reach at least £55.

Degrees

studies at Cambridge were interrupted by diplomatic missions, was created *M.A.* by royal mandate.

Ad eundem. *Ad eundem* degrees, admitting a graduate to the same degree which he already enjoys elsewhere, are granted by all universities ; but such degrees are no longer granted at Cambridge as a simple right.[1]

Honorary degrees, and the idea of a university. The university confers other " complete " or " titular " degrees on certain persons who have not qualified for them by residence and examination at Cambridge. A list of those on whom this honour has been bestowed since 1859 is printed in the Cambridge Calendar. The complete degrees are conferrable upon members of the royal family, privy councillors, bishops and bishops designate, peers,[2] the judges of the High Court, the deans of Westminster, of the chapel royal Windsor, and of Cathedral churches.; and also upon heads of colleges in the university, and other distinguished persons who already have a Cambridge degree and are either conspicuous for merit or holders of university office. Titular degrees may be conferred on Englishmen or foreigners of conspicuous merit.

A propos of a recent list of ' birthday honours ' a weekly literary newspaper reminded us " that commerce, politics, and retired generals are not the only vitalizing forces in this country " ; it blamed a public which it described as " increasingly illiterate and sheepish," and adjured the universities to make no " concessions

[1] An *ad eundem* was given in 1501 to a Roman graduate by grace of the Senate.   [2] See iv. p. 218.

GREAT ST. MARY'S, FROM TRINITY
STREET

Here we only get a glimpse of the Tower of the
Church with King's Parade in the distance. In the
foreground on the right is Caius College.

to popular prejudice" but "to confine the honours they are able to give to those who deserve them." It is in fact ludicrous and absurd that the universities should be expected to come in with their blessing in cases of non-academic success, and that degrees should be mere acclamations of popular verdicts. The public should have every reason to regard these as the blue riband of academic attainment in contrast with the attainments of successful ignorance or successful vulgarity, or indeed with all those kinds of success which are sufficiently rewarded by the *vox populi*, and in other ways. It is expected that a university should set a limit to the assumption that every good and perfect thing is at the beck and call of the mere plutocrat, and should confer its honours and seat in its rectorial chairs only those persons who present academic qualifications. When one sees with what punctilious assiduity every mark and brand of tradesman and tradesmen's interests receives recognition nowadays, one turns with anxiety to the Cambridge list of honorary degree men. The university's awards have not yet however been assigned to people who have grown rich on "Trusts," business 'slimness,' or industries like the canned meat industry; whose title to recognition is that they have been successful speculators. How very nice it would be if instead of installing gasometers in the leper colonies or sending the latest pattern of trichord overstrung grand piano to the deaf and dumb schools of Europe and America, some rich man, with a less pretty taste for publicity, should endow the university with a million pounds

Degrees

sterling ! Should he be the recipient of an honorary degree ? Would it not be churlish to refuse it ? If anything could increase one's respect for the benefactor it would be *his* refusal of this kind of recognition of his services. However there is no harm in very occasional exceptions, because these shout the exceptional circumstances and confuse no one. It is different altogether when to create an honorary degree list Mr. Anybody and Mr. Nobody are called upon to step up. It seems a simple programme that periods marked by dearth in merit should also be marked by dearth of awards, but when did a simple programme ever prove attractive from the days of Naaman downwards ?

When we say that neither the elementary nor the advanced studies of a university exist simply with a view to providing the members of the community with a profession or the means of making their living, we say what is a little less obvious, and trench on ground which is hotly debated. Thousands upon thousands, it may be urged, have always gone to a university to learn a profession, and thousands who have not had this end in view have yet gone up there with no intention of acquiring learning. The university has always prepared for the professions, why not for the industries ; why should it not comprise technical colleges ? Hitherto, however, the universities have prepared men for the learned professions, and there is a difference between learning philosophy, theology, biblical exegesis, jurisprudence and political philosophy, or physiology and comparative anatomy for the purposes

Cambridge

of a life profession, and learning agriculture, forestry, military tactics, or mining engineering. The growth of great branches of industry has however been as great as the growth of knowledge and the sciences; the conditions of modern life are entirely and altogether changed, competition extends far beyond the industrial world, to the universities themselves, and to the struggle for existence of knowledge for its own sake. Without supposing that this last condition will be permanent, one may still think that the universities could not refuse to teach what are called " the modern subjects," which means industries like scientific agriculture or electrical engineering that have more money in them than the professions. In a way, too, it is only a turning of the tables ; when the learned professions were studied it was because they promised the profitable careers.

It need not by any means be competition which urges the university to undertake the 'modern subjects' ; it may be, and it is, the persuasion that its rôle does not end with creating a career, that a university possesses advantages extrinsic to the degree taken, or even the work done at it. The truth perhaps is that the present conditions of life afford an object to universities as far-reaching as has ever been allotted to them since their foundation. In these days of haste, and unchewed cuds of learning, they can suggest the value of leisure—and when a man is now sent to Cambridge or Oxford this fact alone is some security that he and his are content not to put haste and quick

Degrees

results above and before everything else. The lazy man we have always with us, the man in a hurry is a modern product, and suffers from a modern disease with which a university is better able, by latent influence and tradition, to deal than any other institution. And when it has taught the value of intellectual digestion, the number of those things which can only be well learnt by being gradually learnt, and in due season, has the university nothing more to teach ? Our modern malady of haste, of quick methods, and quick results has a commercial basis, a certain standard of values and returns which is best so described. The academic spirit is the antagonist of this spirit, of the love of publicity, the self-advertisement, the liking for cheap and unearned rewards. Even as a business maxim it is being preached again that work done for its own sake is the only lasting work. The university may be a bulwark against false values in life, against the restlessness which is confounded with action, the constant change which is not the same thing as adaptation, against the prejudice that certain good things are not always and everywhere ends in themselves. And there is another conspicuous service which a university can perform. The commercial standard is the root of our social vulgarity, and the academic life has been in all ages that ' simple life ' of which we hear so much. It is not necessary for generations of Englishmen to grow up to regard ' poverty as a crime,' or to subscribe to the worship of mere prosperity and success. A university may always be a protest against these and other mental vulgarities, against even that debasing of the good coin of the King's English in which Milton saw the incipient undoing of a nation. What better place for combating the last ridiculous refuge of English *mauvaise honte*—the shamefacedness which prefers to speak one's own language incorrectly? Something every man at least who reads for a tripos must learn about the uses of work, about its respect, something about breadth of view and accuracy of detail—and also about the legitimate support which such work is in life. It will be said that a man's personal character and his home life inculcate all these things and give him the means to meet the shafts of outrageous fortune. But what the university can give him which his own personal character and probably his home surroundings cannot, is the way to set about making of learning a possession for ever. Some nice person said "mathematics is such a consolation in affliction," and there is much to be said for the point of view.

A university can teach these things because, unlike technical colleges or seminaries for the professions, it exists first and foremost for the advancement of learning. Traditionally inseparable from this is its other object—education; and together they provide the tests it applies to all such questions as 'how far it shall adapt itself to a commercial standard.' For a university is not only a place of higher studies, it is the nursery of study; and to instil the love of learning for its own sake will always be required of it. In the

Degrees

words of Elizabeth of Clare : " When skill in learning
has been found, it sends out disciples who have tasted
its sweetness." In the last resort universities must
stand for these things ; the day when they cease to do
so the idea of a university will have oozed out of them.
Like all good things the university will bring forth
from its treasure things new and old. We shall not
look for degrees in cricket, but there may be degrees
in agriculture, degrees in engineering, degrees in
forestry. Why not, if a degree signifies a diploma of
competence ? But there should be degrees and degrees.
There should be licentiates in the technical arts by the
side of bachelors and masters in the liberal arts : the
university must claim to mete with its own measure,
and to teach its own lesson to all sorts of men. *Hinc
lucem et pocula sacra.*

CHAPTER IV

COLLEGIATE AND SOCIAL LIFE AT THE UNIVERSITY

University and college officers :—chancellor and vice-chancellor—
the senate—graces—proctors—bedells—the master of a college
—the vice-master or president—the fellows—unmarried and
married fellows—the combination room—dons' clubs—
'Hobson's choice'—the dons of last century—classes of
students :—scholar—pensioner—fellow-commoner—sizar—
age of scholars—privileges of peers—position of the sizar—
college quarters and expenses—'non-colls'—early discipline
—jurisdiction of the university in the town—present discipline :
—the proctors—fines—'halls'—'chapels'—town lodgings—
expulsion—rustication—'gates'—the tutor—academical dress
—cap and gown—the undergraduates' day—the gyp—the
college kitchen—'hall'—'wines'—teas—the May term—
idleness—rioting—modern studies and tripos entries—athletics
—the Union Society—Sunday at Cambridge—scarlet days—
academic terms and the long vacation—multiplication of
scholarships—class from which the academic population has
been drawn and careers of university men :—the Church—
the rise of an opulent middle class—the aristocratic era
—English conception of the benefits of a university—
examples of the classes from which the men have come—
recruiting grounds of the university—popularity of colleges
—numbers in the colleges—religion at Cambridge—Cambridge
politics—university settlement at Camberwell—married dons
and future changes.

WE have seen that it is of the essence of a university

Collegiate and Social Life

that it should be both a learned and a learning body, and that from the first the academic group consisted of "masters" or licensed teachers, and of scholars maintained on the college foundations. Contemporaneously with the growth of the college we find at the head of the university a chancellor, and at the head of the college its principal or "Master." [1]

The chancellor. A chancellor was originally a cathedral officer whose business it was to grant licences to teach.[2] His connexion with schools of learning seems to be due entirely to the authority which diocesans exercised in the granting of these licences, especially in the faculties of theology and canon law. It is then as a bishop's officer that he makes his appearance at our universities ; at Cambridge as the local officer of the Bishop of Ely, at Oxford as the local officer of the Bishop of Lincoln. "The chancellor and masters" of the university of Cambridge are first heard of together in Balsham's rescript, in the year 1276 ;[3] but Henry III.'s A.D. 1275-6. letter to the university written six years earlier is A.D. 1270. addressed to "the masters and scholars of Cambridge

---

[1] Cf. ii. pp. 52-3.

[2] The *cancellarius scholasticus* of a cathedral chapter.

[3] The earliest chancellor of whom we have a mention belongs to the year 1246 (*Baker MSS.*). A list of chancellors exists from the year 1283, and is reprinted in Carter, *History of the University*. Among xiv c. chancellors belonging to great families, we have—

Stephen Segrave 1303-6
Richard le Scrope 1378
Guy de Zouche 1379
John de Cavendish 1380
John de Burgh 1385.

See v. p. 307 *n*. The name recorded in 1246 is Hugo de Hottun (Hatton ?).

university." It may then be assumed that before this date the chancellor was still an episcopal emissary rather than an academic chief, but that from about this time he began to be chosen by themselves from among the regent-masters of the university, although with the approval of the Bishop of Ely. This approval was not dispensed with until in 1396 a member of the noble family of Zouche became chancellor; and the chancellor's independence of the Bishop of Ely for confirmation of his title was made absolute by

A.D. 1402. Boniface IX. six years later.

Vice-chancellor. The office was annual. The same man, however, was often appointed again and again, and Guy de Zouche himself had been chancellor in 1379 and again in 1382. Bishop Fisher who retained the chancellorship until his death in 1534 was the first chancellor appointed for life.[1] As soon as it became customary to elect as chancellor of the university some personage who would be able to represent its interests in the world outside, a vice-chancellor performed all those functions which before fell to the chancellor, and the position and functions of the present vice-chancellor are exactly equal to those of the old academic chancellor.[2] The first political chancellor succeeded the greatest of what, for distinction, I have called the

[1] By acts of the university 1504 and 1514.

[2] Fuller places the first vice-chancellor in the year 1417, after Stephen le Scrope and Repingale Bishop of Chichester had held the chancellorship —1414 and 1415. Men "of great employment" began then to fill the position, and hence, he says, the necessity. 1454 is however the date of the earliest vice-chancellor usually given, and there were only intermittent

Collegiate and Social Life

academic chancellors of the university. Thomas Cromwell took the post left vacant by Fisher's martyrdom and held it till his own downfall in 1540. The chancellorship is now held by the owner of a traditional Cambridge name, Spencer Cavendish 8th duke of Devonshire.

The chancellor is appointed "for two years" or such further time "as the tacit consent of the university permits." Under this proviso the appointment is practically for life. The vice-chancellor is appointed from among the heads of houses, and the office is annual. In each case the appointment is in the hands of the senate, or legislative body of the university which consists of all resident masters of arts and of those non-resident *M.A.'s* who have kept their names upon the university register.

Senate and graces. The meetings of the senate take place in the Senate House and are called congregations. In these, degrees are conferred and "graces" are considered ; a "grace" being the name for all acts of the senate, or motions proposed for its acceptance.

Resident members of the senate form the "electoral roll," and elect the council.[1] Lastly the executive body

appointments between then and 1500. In that year Richard Fox was chancellor, and Henry Babington vice-chancellor, and was succeeded in 1501 by John Fisher *who filled both offices.* In 1413 a friar was chosen as "president" of the university in the absence of Chancellor Billingford sent by Henry V. with the Bishop of Ely and the chancellor of the sister university to Rome.

[1] In this body, which was created by act of 19th-20th Vict., are concentrated the powers of the houses of regents and non-regents, the ancient governing body of the university. Its 10 members are chosen from the roll.

Cambridge

consists of the chancellor, the high steward,[1] the vice-chancellor, a commissary appointed by the chancellor, and the *sex viri* who adjudicate on all matters affecting the senior members of the university, are elected " by grace of the senate," and hold their office for two years.

A.D. 1603. The university has sent two members to parliament since the first year of James I. The exercise of the parliamentary suffrage belongs to the whole senate and is the one exception to the rule which obliges every member to record his vote personally in the Senate House.[2] The total number of members of the senate is 7192 ; the total number of members of the university is 13,819, this latter including all bachelors of arts and undergraduates in residence, and all *B.A.'s* whose names are on the books pending their proceeding to the degree of *M.A.*

Proctors. After the vice-chancellor no officers are so much in evidence as the proctors. Their duties are twofold : they conduct the congregations of the senate, and they maintain discipline among the undergraduates. There are 2 proctors elected annually, to whom are joined 2 pro-proctors, and 2 additional pro-proctors. The pro-proctors have not the standing of the proctors as university officials, but they exercise the same

[1] The high steward is elected in the same way as the chancellor. He appoints a deputy who must be approved by the senate. The Cambridge high stewardship has been frequently held by favourites of the sovereign ; Elizabeth gave it to Leicester, and Henry VII. to Empson. The present holder, Lord Walsingham, bears a name intimately connected with the history of the university.

[2] At the last parliamentary election, January 1906, the university electorate numbered 6972.

Collegiate and Social Life

authority over the men.[1] Other executive officers are the public orator, who is "the voice of the senate"[2]; the university librarian, the registrary, the university marshal (appointed by the vice-chancellor) and the bedells.

Bedell. If the proctor is the procurator of the academic society, the bedell is the executor of its mandates. The bedells attend the (chancellor or) vice-chancellor on all public occasions, bearing silver maces, and, like the beadles of all guilds and corporations, they summon members of the senate to the chancellor's court.[3] For bedel or bedell is an obsolete form of beadle retained in the ancient corporations of Oxford and Cambridge. As a town or parish officer the beadle brought messages and executed the mandates of the town or parish authority. The apparitor of a trades guild was also

[1] The proctors are appointed according to a statutory cycle—they are nominated by the colleges in turn, two colleges nominating each year. The proctors at Oxford originally represented the north countrymen and the south countrymen. Entries of Cambridge proctors exist from 1350. The office, of course, is kin to that of the procurator of monastic orders; and the Cambridge proctors supervised Stourbridge fair, the markets, weights and measures, and all those matters which affected the supply of provisions for the university or its finances : to which were added their scholastic functions.

[2] The first public orator was Richard Croke ; Sir T. Smith, Sir J. Cheke, Roger Ascham, and George Herbert the poet, all held the office. Caius supposes that the master of glomery was university orator, whose duty it was to entertain princes and peers and to indite the epistles of the university on great occasions. He supposes also that as "senior regent" he collected and counted the suffrages in all congregations : the *Statutes* however show us this officer in company with two *junior regents* sorting the votes cast for the proctors. See also iii. p. 164 *n.*

[3] Thus a guild order in 1389 runs : the alderman "ssal sende forthe the bedel to alle the bretheren and the systeren."

Cambridge

called a " bedel," and it is, no doubt, as a guild officer that he appears in our universities and has taken so firm a footing there.

The bedell was the servant of a faculty, and also of a " nation " in the continental universities : hence at Cambridge one was the bedell of theology and canon law, the other of arts. They arranged and announced the day and hour of lectures. For many centuries Cambridge had an esquire and a yeoman bedell ; but the latter was abolished in 1858. Apparently the yeoman bedell was not a member of the university, and he may have been a townsman.[1] The two esquire bedells of the present day are nominated by the council of the senate, and elected by the latter body.[2]

The Master. Distinct from the university authorities are the college authorities. The foremost of these is the Master of each college. This officer used to be *primus inter pares*, the senior among the fellows or teaching

---

[1] We find Archbishop Laud writing of Oxford : " If the university would bring in some bachelors of art to be yeomen-bedels . . they which thrived well and did good service might after be preferred to be esquire-bedels."

[2] The first esquire or armiger bedell on the Cambridge register is Physwick in the xiv c. ; no one else is entered for this office till 1498 when Philip Morgan held it. After him there is another esquire bedell in 1500. The yeoman bedell probably stood in the same relation to the esquire bedell as the trumpeter to the herald. The herald did not blow his own trumpet and the esquire bedell of the university was doubtless not a macebearer. The original two bedells, nevertheless, used to go before the chancellor and masters *virgam deferentes* ; and Balsham in 1275 arranges that *the bedell of the master of glomery* shall not carry his stave on these occasions, but only when on his superior's own business. A bedell is mentioned in the xiii c. hostel statute referred to on p. 51.

Collegiate and Social Life

body of his house. The change to the later "splendid isolation" of the "Head" is expressed architecturally in the relative positions of the Master's lodging, as we can see it to-day in the old court of Corpus—the simple room leading to the dining hall and the college garden with a garret bedroom above it—and the palatial dwellings which in one or two of the colleges no longer form part of the main buildings. It is one which has a curious chronological parallel with the change that took place in the relative positions of a cathedral dean and chapter after the Reformation. The old college Master, like the old university chancellor, and the cathedral dean, was, officially and residentially, part and parcel of the body he represented. After the Reformation all these positions were shifted. The college Master became in appearance, what the cathedral dean had become in fact, "a corporation sole," while the university chancellor was translated to supra-academic spheres, and no longer resided even in the university city. "Sixty years since," writes a present member of the university, "society at Cambridge was divided broadly into two classes—those who were Heads and those who were not." Ludicrous stories are told of the pride which inflated "the Heads," who at times resented being accosted not only by the inferior undergraduate but by the fellows of their own college. The provost of King's of just a hundred years ago was referred to familiarly by his irreverent juniors as 'Tetoighty.'[1]

[1] Letter of Rennell to Stratford Canning, Nov. 16, 1807.

THE LAKE IN BOTANIC GARDENS

Many different kinds of trees surround this winding water, the banks of which are lined with a variety of rushes and reeds, and are inhabited by many sorts of water-fowl.

Cambridge

Heads of colleges have not only the statutory powers conferred on them by their college, but as assessors to the vice-chancellor they join with him in the government of the university. Their powers were largely increased by the statutes of 1570 which Whitgift procured from Elizabeth ; and in 1586-7 it was decided that the vice-chancellor should always be chosen from their number.[1] The modern " Head " emulates the old academic Master, is *primus inter pares* amongst his fellow collegians, and is no longer dreadful to his juniors.

There are only two exceptions to the title of Master held by all heads of colleges. The head of King's College, like the head of Eton, is styled Provost, and the head of Queens' College is styled President.[2]

The vice-master is called the president. His position is like that of a prior under an abbot, or a subprior in a priory : the one representing the college outside and ruling over the community, the other ruling in the house and having the authority in all which concerns its management.

With the Master and vice-Master are associated the fellows, the dean, the tutors, lecturers, chaplains, and the bursar.[3]

[1] Until 1534 only those who had graduated doctor were elected to the office.

[2] Principal (see vi. p. 339 *n.*), warden, keeper, proctor, and rector are all titles which at one time or another were familiar in Cambridge.

[3] In the xviii c. the colleges had already 4 lecturers in rhetoric, logic, ethics, and Greek. Cf. the provisions in the statutes of Christ's College xvi c. The college *bursar*, the purse-bearer of his college, is its treasurer and oeconomus : a senior and junior bursar are appointed.

Collegiate and Social Life

Fellows. " I can never remember the time when it was not diligently impressed upon me that, if I minded my syntax, I might eventually hope to reach a position which would give me three hundred pounds a year, a stable for my horse, six dozen of audit ale every Christmas, a loaf and two pats of butter every morning, and a good dinner for nothing, with as many almonds and raisins as I could eat at dessert," writes Trevelyan in his " Life and Letters " of Macaulay whose appreciation of a Cambridge fellowship fell nothing short of reverence.

The fellows are the foundation graduates, as the scholars are the foundation undergraduates of a college. They are more ; they are, corporately, its masters and owners. Financially, a fellowship is represented by the dividend on the surplus revenue of a college.[1] As this surplus revenue varies while the fellows are a fixed number, the value of fellowships varies, but may not now exceed £250 a year. A fellow enjoys as a rule other emoluments, as tutor, lecturer, librarian, bursar, of his college, so that his pecuniary position is by no means represented by the value of the simple fellow-ship. All fellowships are now bestowed for a term of years ; life fellowships being held by those only who are on the staff of their college, who have served it, that is, in a tutorial or other official capacity.

Married and unmarried fellows. Until the last quarter of the xix century fellows had to be bachelors. The rule against married officials was first relaxed, after the

[1] The decreasing value of the statutable stipends in the xvii c. led to the adoption (in 1630) of the new scale of payments.

Cambridge

Reformation, in favour of heads of houses; Dr. Heynes, President of Queens' in 1529, having been the first married Master.[1] Fifty years later the fellows of King's complained that the wife of their provost had been seen taking the air on the sacred grass of the college court, where, nevertheless, her husband declared she could not have set her foot twice in her life. Early in George III.'s reign a movement was afoot among the fellows of a different character: in 1766 Betham of King's writes to Cole that the university had been in a most violent flame: "young and old have formed a resolution of marrying"; "the scheme is—a wife and a fellowship with her." In the "sixties" certain colleges began to admit married fellows, while in others a fellow might marry if he held university office, as professor or librarian. No fellowship nowadays is confined to unmarried men.

This is one of three radical changes which the university has undergone in the last thirty years. The abolition of the Religious Test Act which severed the strict connexion of our universities with the Church of England, the marriage of fellows, and the appointment of men not in clerical orders to fill the chief university and college offices, have gradually changed the face of university life, secularising it and socialising it, bestowing on it, definitely, a lay and undenominational character which is perhaps not so far from its

[1] He signed the university instrument which was presented to Henry renouncing the pope's supremacy; Ridley, who was proctor at the time, signed after him.

primitive ideal as sticklers for the connexion of the universities with the Church would have us believe. It is no longer an advantage to be in orders at Cambridge : they do not help you to a fellowship for this is given to the best man in open competition ; even heads of colleges need no longer be clergymen, and only one collegiate office, that of the dean, is still preferably bestowed on a parson. The results are curious. Clerical fellows are popular, but theology is a neglected subject in the big colleges and the theological chairs are not centres of influence. At the same time every college enjoys clerical patronage, which can be exercised in favour of its deserving sons ; and every college, besides its dean, appoints chaplains for the maintenance of the chapel services.[1] Clerical fellows, it is true, are now in a minority, but there seems to be no reason why the clerical don should cease to abound, as he has always abounded, in our university cities. A university education has become more not less valuable for a clergyman now that it enables him to meet men whose beliefs differ widely from his own ; now that the right to display an academic hood in church is no longer prized as its chief advantage.[2]

[1] From 1741 two chaplains were appointed in each college, to replace the fellows who before this used to take the chapel services in rotation. The Trinity College rule which provided that a fellow engaged in instruction in his college for ten years kept his fellowship for life or until he married, made the first rift in the obligation to take orders within a certain period after election, or forfeit the fellowship.

[2] An American student, 20 years before the abolition of the Religious Test Act, was scandalised at the manner in which the reception of the

Cambridge

Among the ' dons ' the centre of social life has always been the combination room. It represents that pledge of civilisation the with-drawing-room, the room contiguous to the banqueting-hall, where the pleasures of the spirit steal an advantage over the pleasures of the table. The rudeness which marked the period of the early renascence, from court to convent, in England, clung also to our academic life, and it is not till the last quarter of the xvi century that we find the fellows first provided with table napkins, and learn that the enterprising college which made the innovation exacted a fine of a penny from those who continued to wipe their fingers on the tablecloth. The temptation to this latter practice must indeed have been great ; for the fork which made its appearance at the dawn of the renascence in France was unknown in England two hundred years later. It is only in the course of the next, the xviith, century that the combination room emerges as a more or less luxurious apartment ; the subsequent addition of newspapers, magazines, and easy chairs marking in turn the rise of journalism and the higher standard of comfort. The dons of Charles II.'s time who had to be content with the " London Gazette " supplemented the lack of news by social clubs. " The Ugly Faces " club dined periodically in what was then the ugliest of college halls—Clare. " The

sacrament was used as a mere condition for obtaining the certificate of fitness for orders. Men who had not made 3 communions in their college chapel during their stay, came up afterwards for the purpose, and received thereupon a document certifying that they had entirely satisfied " the vice-chancellor and the 8 senior fellows " of their fitness for their vocation.

Collegiate and Social Life

Old Maids' Club" flourished in the early xix century, with Baker the antiquary, Tonstall, and Conyers Middleton as members. The first " news letter " was however laid on the table of Kirk's coffee-house in Charles's reign. The first flying-coach, following the example of Oxford which had run a coach to London in one day, sped to the Capital in 1671.[1]

When the xix century opened there was no general society in Cambridge. It was more out of the way of polite England than Oxford, and many dons whose homes were at a distance spent the whole year in their colleges, emphasising the faults and therefore detracting from the virtues of small learned societies. The dons in the xvi century, say at S. John's College, had been a brilliant company who bestowed as much on the Elizabethan age as they took from it : but the xviii century closed upon a period of dulness and reaction, in which the rudeness of material civilisation met a social uncouthness little calculated to recall the university of Spenser, of Burleigh, of Bacon. The intimacy between the fellows and their head was a thing of the past ; the familiarity between scholar and don had been replaced by "donnish-

---

[1] In the same century Hobson, who died in 1630 at a great age, was the famous Cambridge carrier and kept the first livery stable in England. His numerous clients would find a large stable full of steeds from which "to choose" (with bridle whip and even boots provided) ; but everyone was expected to take the horse next the door : hence 'Hobson's choice,' which has become an English household phrase, as has another Cantab expression, 'constitutionalize' for walking. Yet another phrase is 'tawdry,' the name given to the flimsy gaily coloured chains which were sold at Barnwell (now Midsummer) fair on the eve of S. Awdrey's day. Hobson was immortalised by verses of Milton's.

PARKER'S PIECE

This large open space in the centre of Cambridge is one of the Town's playgrounds. In the distance is the Roman Catholic Church, and the boundary wall of the Perse Grammar School, just behind the trees on the left.

ness" which kept the undergraduate at arm's length; the blight of the artificial and stilted, the sterile and pompous aristocratism of just a century ago had settled down upon the university. Isolated in this eastern corner of England, just before the enormous impulse to travelling brought by railways, just after the cosmopolitan spirit which took even the English-man abroad—the sense of a debt to Italy, of a continental comradeship—had finally ceased to exist, Cambridge dons at the dawn of the xix century had perhaps fathomed the lowest social depths. But before this century passed a social change more wonderful than the material changes around them metamorphosed university society. The unmannerly don married; and the sex which makes society, the sex which suffers no social deterioration when left to its own devices—the aristocratic sex—was introduced as the don's helpmeet. More still—worse still—she was introduced in the same quarter of a century as what the weak-kneed among us cry out upon—his rival. It is the same donnish bachelor, separated by a gulph from the social amenities, wedded to ingrained habits and some eradicable prejudices, who suffered women to come to Cambridge and take what they could of the intellectual advantages he himself enjoyed. The historian of the great movements of the age we live in will record with interest this proof of the traditional open-mindedness which has never deserted the Cantabrigian, which has never failed to respond to the sacred dual claims of the age and the intellect.

Collegiate and Social Life

Classes of students. The learned body which congregates in the combination rooms is the *ecclesia docens* of the university; the learning body—the *ecclesia discens*—includes all members of the university below the degree of *M.A.*, and is divided into four or five classes. The most important of these from the academic point of view is the scholar, and for at least two centuries after colleges were built the only resident students were these students on the foundation.[1] To them were joined in course

---

[1] Colleges were not at first built for the 'undergraduate.' The scholar of the xiii, xiv, and xv centuries was the *socius* (fellow) of to-day. His clerical position was that of a young man in minor orders, his scholastic that of a bachelor in art. He attended the schools of the doctors and masters, and was assisted by his fellowship and by exhibitions in the learned faculties to study for the degrees (master of art, and doctor in the faculties). The pensioner, who might or might not be an undergraduate in standing and who lived at his own charges, was provided for in the hostel. It was not till the visitation of 1401 that we find *socii* and *scholares* distinguished; and when King's College was founded in the same half century its scholars were young students and nothing else. Nevertheless, although such was the original conception of the endowed college—at Peterhouse, Michaelhouse, Pembroke, Corpus—the later developments were outlined from the first. The bible clerks at Peterhouse were poor students not of the standing of bachelors, and a proviso in the statutes enabled the college to maintain " 2 or 3 indigent scholars well grounded in grammar " when its funds shall permit. At Clare (1359) the sizar was regularly recognised. At Pembroke (1347) there were in addition to the "major scholars" 6 "minor scholars" who might fit themselves to be major scholars. At King's Hall (Statutes Ric. II.) boys from 14 years old were admitted. At Christ's (1505) the standing of the scholar was defined by requiring him to give instruction in sophistry; but the pensioner was contemplated for the first time as a regular inmate of the college. In fact the *perendinant* who ate at the college tables became, before the middle of the xv c., the *commensalis*; the class being fully recognised 50 years later in the *convivae* of Christ's. There were no fewer than 778 *convivae* or pensioners in the colleges in the time of Caius 1574.

As to the age at which youths went up, it was not until the xix c. that the university was finally regarded as the complement to a full 'college'

Cambridge

of time the *pensioners*, youths who paid for their board and lodging, the class which now makes up the great majority of undergraduates. Two other classes were added. The peers and eldest sons of peers with other *fellow-commoners*—a class which has fallen into practical desuetude but is not obsolete—and the *sizars*. The peers enjoyed some privileges which would not be coveted nowadays—they could make themselves conspicuous on all occasions by their clothing, and they could take a degree without working for it. The younger sons of peers and the richer undergraduates also messed at the fellows' table, and were therefore called "fellow-commoners": the advantages of this arrangement did not end with the better treatment in hall, for the companionship of the fellows and seniors of his college must have proved a welcome stimulus to an intelligent young man.[1] Lastly, there were and are the

(public school) course elsewhere. The grammar boys at Clare and Peterhouse, the richer youths at King's Hall, and the glomery students, must always have kept Cambridge peopled with little lads: but when grammar disappeared altogether (in the xvi c.) from the university curriculum, scholars continued to go up very young. In the xvi c. Wyatt went to S. John's at 12, Bacon and his elder brother to Trinity at 12 and 14; Spenser was in his 16th year. In the xvii c. George Herbert was 15, so was Andrew Marvell, Milton had not attained his 15th year; Newton went to Trinity at 17, and Herschell to S. John's at the same age. Pitt was a precocious exception in the xviii c. at 14.

All the scholars of the early colleges were to be indigent; the one exception was King's Hall, but the proviso appears again in the statutes for King's College.

We may note that All Souls' Oxford retains the characteristic of the ancient college foundations, in being a college of fellows only. The title "students" for the fellows of Christchurch recalls the same intention.

[1] When Gresham went to Gonville in Hen. VIII.'s time the fellow-

Collegiate and Social Life

" sizars," the poorer students, not on the foundation or the college, who pay smaller fees and receive their commons gratis.[1] The sizar of fifty years ago used to wait on the fellows at dinner and dine off the broken victuals, reinforced by fresh vegetables and pudding.

When Macaulay summed the advantages of a Cambridge fellowship he omitted perhaps the chief, the college residence which like " the good dinner " is to be had " for nothing." Fellows and scholars receive their college quarters gratis ; but the rest of the under-graduate population pays for its lodging. It is housed in its 17 colleges, the new hostels which are springing up on all sides, and the licensed lodgings in the town. The cost of the college bed and sitting room a term varies from £3 to three times this sum. Service adds £2 or £3 a term. Small lodgings with service can be had in the less good streets for £5–£7 ; good rooms from £8 to £10, while more than £12 is only charged in the best positions, or near the big colleges. The expense of college rooms is augmented by the prepayments for furniture (the average valuation of the permanent furniture is £20, but the sum may be as low as £10 or as high as £40), by the " caution money," about £15, returned at the end of the term of residence, the admission fee (varying with the college from 6/8 to £5) and the matriculation fee £5. During residence there is also an annual payment of £9–15 towards the

commoner had just made his appearance. Cambridge was full of them in the reign of Elizabeth.

[1] Jeremy Taylor was a sizar, Newton and Bentley sub-sizars.

219

upkeep of the college and its servants, and the tuition fee, which covers all lectures in one's own college, and varies from £18 to £24 a year.

It was to obviate the necessity of paying these fees that the system of non-collegiate students, familiarly called "non-colls," was devised in 1869. While the expenses of an undergraduate who is a member of a college average about £165 a year, £60 in excess of this and £60 less representing the higher scale of expenses on the one hand and the minimum on the other, the undergraduate who lives in lodgings and *is not a member of any college* can live for £78 a year (if he does not require "coaching" or private tuition which costs about £9 a term) and it is just possible to take the *B.A.* degree after a three years' residence which has cost you at the rate of £55 a year.

Fifty years ago the minimum cost of living at Cambridge for a pensioner was £150 and double this sum involved no extravagant outlay. A fellow-commoner required £800 a year and could not live on less than £500. These were the aristocratic days of English universities and they were in sharp contrast to the time when scholars were poor, begged their way to and from college, and were included among vagabonds in the statute of 1380 directed against mendicancy. But the entertainment in those days was also widely different. Two fellows shared not only a room but a bed, or a two-bedded room would be shared by a fellow and two poor scholars. It was not till the xvi century that each fellow had a bed to himself and a room to himself if space permitted.[1] The dining hall was a comfortless room where rude fare was served at a tresselled board to guests who sat upon wooden stools. The conditions of the xiii and xiv centuries were not greatly bettered in the xvth and xvith, and Erasmus found it hard to stomach the fare at Queens' College at a time when the Cambridge ale appears to have been no improvement on the "wine no better than vinegar" which came from the surrounding vineyards.

Early discipline. The little lads who thronged the streets of Cambridge in the xiii century were under little or no discipline. They ran up debts with the Jews, who had established themselves there in the opening years of the previous century, fought the townsmen, and had few duties to society beyond making their own beds, a work certainly performed by university scholars in the xiii and xiv centuries and enjoined on the boys of the famous schools founded in the xvth. It was this custom of doing your own work, at least until you became an advanced student when the little boys did it for you, which was the origin of "fagging" in our two most ancient schools connected respectively with our two universities—Eton and Winchester.[2] Even this amount of work, however, was not expected of fellow-commoners in the xvi century, who frequently got out of hand, though few of them have left us so delightful a reminder of their misdeeds as the young Earl of

[1] Statutes of Christ's College.

[2] The scholars of Eton were directed to recite the Matins of our Lady while making their beds.

221

Cambridge

Rutland has done in a letter to his mother who had complained of his behaviour : " I do aseure your Ladyship that the cariage of myselfe both towardes God and my booke, my comeliness in diet and gesture, shall be such as your Ladyship shall hear and like well of."

With the great era of college building in the succeeding century, the founders' statutes make their appearance ; and in days when monks were birched and nuns were slapped the college stocks held in durance vile the fellow who had presumed to bathe in any stream or pool of Cambridgeshire, while the college hall resounded to the strokes of the birch which visited the scholar for the same offence. College discipline was supplemented by university discipline, and the academic authorities shared legal powers with the town authorities until recently. The jurisdiction of the university extended not only to matters affecting its members, but to a *conusance* in actions which affected the townsmen.[1] The last attempt to exercise the right of im-

[1] This right was given up in 1856. The legal powers and privileges of the university date from the xiii c. and the reign of Henry III. . *Ita tamen quod ad suspensionem vel mutilationem clericorum non procedatis, sed eos alio modo per consilium universitatis Cantabr. castigetis* is the clause inserted in 1261 in the matter of a quarrel between students from the north and south parts of the realm. The privileges granted to the university by Edward III. include the power of imprisoning offenders ; and even the king's writ could not be invoked to free them. In the 10th year of Edward's reign the university chancellor maintained this right both over scholar and townsman. The oath taken by the mayor of Cambridge to maintain the "privileges liberties and customs of the university" dates from the same reign (when the mayor bailiffs and aldermen were obliged to swear to respect the chancellor's rights). When the riots of 1381 led to a suspension of the town charter its privileges were transferred to the university, till the restoration of the charter in 1832.

Collegiate and Social Life

prisoning undesirable characters in the "Spinning House" was made by the vice-chancellor in 1893 ; but the incarceration of a young woman on this occasion caused so much indignation in the town that it led to the final disallowance of all the vice-chancellor's powers, in this direction, which were waived by the university in 1894.

Present discipline —proctors, fines, "hall," "chapels." University discipline is in the hands of the vice-chancellor and his court,[1] and the proctors. College discipline in those of the dean[2] and tutors. Two proctors perambulate the town every night, each accompanied by two servants known to the undergraduate as the proctor's "bull-dogs." They take the name of any offending student and bring him up next morning if necessary before the vice-chancellor. They can also send men back to their college or rooms, enter lodgings, and exact fines. When the youth of 19 or 20 leaves the higher forms of a public school and comes to the university, he is treated as a man, and leads a man's life guided by himself. But he becomes also a member of a great society, existing for certain purposes. If he is a man, he is a very young one ; and if he guides his own life he has only just begun to do so. He lives in his own house —for his college room, like the Englishman's dwelling, is his castle—but he must be at home by 10 p.m.

[1] The vice-chancellor's court for persons *in statu pupillari* is composed of the vice-chancellor and six heads of colleges elected by grace.

[2] It will be observed that the academic dean possesses disciplinary functions like his predecessor and prototype the monastic dean. The academic dean is also the presiding official at the chapel services.

TRINITY BRIDGE, KING'S COLLEGE
CHAPEL IN THE DISTANCE

This is one of the many charming views on the Cam
at " the Backs " of the Colleges.

Cambridge

This is the first point of discipline. The gates of colleges and the outer doors of lodgings are shut at 10, and any one who presents himself after that hour, without his tutor's permission, has his name taken by the college porter, or by the lodging proprietor who acts *in loco janitoris*. He must also dine in hall, if not every day at least five times in the week, which must include Sunday. The third restriction on his liberty is (or at least was originally) a care for his soul. The obligation to attend chapel so many times a week resolves itself now into two attendances in the week and generally two on Sunday. No means of enforcing this are however taken nowadays, and the men are generally left free to judge for themselves in this respect, though 'moral suasion' is exercised by the deans except in the case of nonconformists and conscientious objectors. Fifty years ago 8 "chapels" were expected ; but if a pensioner kept 6 and a fellow-commoner 4, he was left untroubled by his dean. In New England at the same epoch no less than 16 attendances at chapel every week were required, seven at unseasonable hours ; a burden which was tolerated with more cheerfulness by the New Englander than were the 8 "chapels" by his Cambridge contemporary.

Town licences. The licensing of all lodgings and places of
Expulsion entertainment [1] to which undergraduates
"rustication"
"gating." may go, is the hold which the university
has over the town. Its sanctions for the undergraduate are fines and expulsion ; breaches of

[1] Undergraduates may not give entertainments in taverns or public halls

college rules being visited by " gating " and expulsion. A man can be expelled for any cause which in the judgment of the university or the college warrants it. If a man thus expelled from the university society refuses " to go down "—to leave Cambridge—he cannot live in any licensed lodging house in the town.[1] A man may also be sent down for a term, which is called " rustication," an epithet which suggests to him that he has forfeited the society of men of polite learning. If a man misbehaves himself he can be " gated," *i.e.* the porter receives instructions not to let him out after a certain hour—and it may be any hour the authorities choose to fix and for any length of time.

The tutor. The college tutor is the official who supervises the undergraduate's academic career. He advises him what subject to read for, what examinations to take, what books to master. The career of a mediocre man is often made and that of a first-rate man heightened by an able tutor, and Cambridge has boasted some very great men in this capacity. The mathematical genius of Newton was quickened by having for his tutor Isaac Barrow ; Whichcote of Emmanuel, Laughton of Clare, and Shilleto of Trinity were eminent as tutors and

without permission of their tutor : even then more than 5 men *in statu pupillari* cannot meet together in a public place without a further permit from the proctor.

It was agreed in 1856 that the licence of any ale house was liable to be revoked if a complaint in writing was made by the vice-chancellor to the Justices of the Peace.

[1] Lodging house keepers sign a hard and fast undertaking with the Lodging-house Syndicate. They cannot let to other than members of the university without permission.

Cambridge

"coaches"; and "coaching" supplements, for a very backward or a very advanced student, the lectures of college and university.[1]

The cap and gown. The academic appearance of a university owes much to the traditional cap and gown worn by all its members. A bonnet and gown are very ancient appanages of the learned professions of divinity law and medicine—they were the dignified apparel of doctors in the three faculties. Short hose had not become fashionable when universities sprang into existence, and the clerk or scholar even if he were not destined for major was very usually in minor orders: the gown is therefore a fitting distinction for those learned societies which have never ceased their corporate existence, and have carried into modern times, as a special dress, items of attire which like clerical vestments, the cassock, the monastic habit, and the friar's tunic were proper to the age which saw their rise.

The distinctive features of academic dress are simply survivals of this ordinary dress of the period: the ceremonial hood is the hood which was worn in everyday life in the xiith the xiiith xivth and xvth centuries.[2]

---

[1] The tutor probably made his first appearance at King's Hall; his office was firmly established by the middle of the xvi c. (later Statutes of Clare College, 1551), and marks the epoch when students other than those on the foundation were also firmly established as college inmates. Before the xviii c., however, the official tutor of to-day was not known; any fellow whom the master designated filled the post. In some colleges the tutor is appointed for life; at Trinity for a term of 10 years.

[2] Like all other items of headgear the derivatives of the hood acquired ceremonial significance. The removable hood of the xiv c., which was slung over the shoulder or attached to the arm, became the *capuce* of the

Collegiate and Social Life

If we had looked in at the priory church of Barnwell on a day when the novices made their profession we should have seen each one enter dressed in the black habit or gown, a cloak of fur, and the "amess[1] over his head": and when he walked out he was already vested with the *capam nigram* of the canon. Here, then, we have all the elements of early academic dress; the homely Gilbertine canons, so familiar in the Cambridge thoroughfares, wore it in white; for it was the dress of the more respectable, the decently clad, clergy and clerks as well as of those most respectable and regular clergy, the canons. The dress of the better looked-after scholars on the college foundations differed but little from this. No doubt the scholars of Peterhouse habitually wore the clerical *vestis talaris*[2]—the gown to the ankle—but the special item of academic attire adopted at Cambridge appears to have been the *capam nigram*.[3] The majority of scholars in the hostels

dignified clergy, of the doctors in the 3 faculties, rectors of colleges, and others in authority. It is preserved today in the *pellegrino* of the Roman Church. The hood itself appears to have gained this ceremonial importance in the xv c.; and it is in the middle of that century that the hood as head-gear disappears, and is replaced by the various caps and bonnets which were formed from it.

[1] The amess was a capuce of fur.

[2] Statutes of Peterhouse 1338-1342. The same is prescribed for the junior students of King's Hall (temp. Richard II.). Precisely the same regulations—for the tonsure and *vestis talaris*—were made for the scholar at the university of Paris.

[3] This accorded with the custom at Bologna and at Salamanca (xiv c.)— *una capa scolastica . . . foderata sufficienter pellibus pecudis.* At Salamanca each scholar received annually one cappa lined with sheepskin, and one unlined, and a lined hood.

Cambridge

and grammar schools observed no general rule as to costume,[1] but the scholars of any standing wore the black cappa of the canon ; and the hood, lined with sheepskin or minever, was becoming—even in the xiv century—the habitual, and therefore distinctive, dress of foundation scholars when they "commenced" bachelor or master.[2] The hood indeed was probably restricted to an academic use before this century closed, for there is a statute of the year 1413 ordering hoods of kid or lambskin to be worn. The incepting Cambridge bachelor,[3] then, wore a *cappa*, a fine hood was gradually restricted to the master of arts.

The soft bonnets or caps—of doctors, bishops, jurists, canons—are derivatives of the hood, as is the stiff cap —the biretta, as is the mitre itself. The xviii century Cambridge student still wore a soft round cap, like that worn to-day by the Italian university student and quite recently adopted in France : but the Paduan doctors had adopted the stiff square cap in the xvi century, and our own students revolted against the round cap in 1769, and thereupon accomplished the

---

[1] The object of most of the rules regarding scholars' dress seems to have been to enforce sumptuary restrictions, and impose something clerical and sober in appearance—*decenter et honeste* are the words used in the statutes of King's Hall. The same is true of similar regulations in Italian universities.

[2] The cappa (with a hood?) probably constituted the *speciem scholasticam* which pseudo-scholars in the town were forbidden to imitate. (*Statuta Antiqua*, statute 42.)

[3] An order of the time of Henry V. (documents Nos. 90, 91 in the Registry) requires the Cambridge bachelors to dress like those at Oxford ; which probably referred to the black *capuce* or hood of the Oxford bachelor ?

Collegiate and Social Life

feat which neither Archimedes "nor our Newton" had attempted :

> For all her scholars square the circle now.[1]

The chancellor of the university wears a black and gold robe. Scarlet is the colour of the doctors' gowns, as it still is of the papal doctors of divinity. The physician of Chaucer's time wore his furred scarlet gown, and scarlet gowns and corner caps were worn by the Cambridge doctors when the Cromwells entertained James I. on his way from the north in 1603.

The master wears a full-sleeved gown of stuff or silk ; the bachelor's gown has two flowing bands hanging loose in front ; the undergraduate's gown is both scantier and shorter than these ; but 'Advanced Students' wear the bachelor's gown, without the loose bands. The academic gown of English universities is now black, but the earlier violet gown of Trinity is recorded in the present blue gown of its undergraduates, a blue gown being also worn by the neighbouring college of Gonville and Caius.[2] The gowns of certain colleges are distinguished by little pleats in the stuff or bars of velvet.

Peers and eldest sons of peers, in the first half of the

---

[1] This feat was celebrated by verses inscribed : *Mutantque Quadrata Rotundis*. A square cap (called both 'scholastic' and 'ecclesiastical') was recognised as the proper head-gear for Cambridge fellows graduates and foundation-scholars in the later xvi. c. Pensioners were to wear a round cap.

[2] For the coloured gown see *infra*.

xix century, wore the black silk gown and tall silk hat of an *M.A.*,[1] and on great occasions a more splendid dress adorned with gold tassels and lace. Fellow-commoners wore a gown with gold or silver lace and a black velvet cap ; the younger sons of peers being known as " Hat-fellow-commoners " because they wore the *M.A.'s* silk hat instead of the velvet cap.

Most of the pensioners at Cambridge in the xviii century (but not the fellow-commoners) used to wear a sleeveless gown called a "curtain." [2] Neither the clerical cassock nor the *capam nigram* in fact account for the undergraduate's dress of later or present times ; the original of which, I think, is to be found in the sleeveless gown or coat, called *soprana*, of the ecclesiastical colleges founded between the xv and xvii centuries. Two of the peculiarities of the *soprana* are still traceable. The bands of the bachelor's gown may be seen attached to the black coat of the *Almum Collegium* founded in 1457 by Cardinal Capranica, to the violet and black dress worn by the Scotchmen,[3] to the red coat of the college founded by Ignatius Loyola, and the blue of the Greek College founded by Gregory XIII. ; while

[1] The *pileum* placed on the head of the new master of arts in the xv ? and xvi centuries, probably symbolised the termination of the *status pupillaris.* Cf. *Haec mera libertas, hoc nobis pilea donant ;* and *servos ad pileum vocare* (Livy). The tall silk hat signified the same thing. It was worn by young *M.A.'s,* and by the 'Hat-fellow-commoners,' and is still worn by *M.A.'s* on a visit to their *alma mater* though not by resident 'dons.'

[2] This was not worn at Trinity, King's, and one or two other colleges.

[3] It is interesting to note that the Scotch universities retain the violet gown. The Scots' College in Rome (founded in 1600) dresses its collegians in a violet cassock, over which is a black *soprana.*

Collegiate and Social Life

one string, adorned with the papal arms, is left on the *soprana* worn by the Vatican seminarists : these are leading strings, denoting the state of pupilage.[1] The Cambridge scholar's and bachelor's gown is black—the descendant of the full black *cappa*—but as we have just seen the coat or gown of the ecclesiastical colleges is of different colours, and the ancient gowns of Trinity and Caius still record this variation.

Every one *in statu pupillari* must wear cap and gown after nightfall, on Sunday,[2] at examinations and lectures (except laboratory demonstrations), when visiting the vice-chancellor or any other official on academic business, in the library, the Senate House, and the university church : professors and others usually wear the gown while lecturing, and all dons wear it in chapel and hall.

The under-graduates' day. A twentieth century undergraduates' day does not differ from those recorded in his diary by Wordsworth's brother when he was a freshman at Trinity in 1793.[3] This is how he was employed during the Reign of Terror and within a few days of the execution of Marie Antoinette :—" Chapel. Lectures. Considered of a subject for my essay on Wed-

---

[1] Bachelors of arts whether they be scholars reading for a fellowship or young graduates preparing for the 'Second Part' of a tripos, are still *in statu pupillari*. Perhaps, then, the more important gown, the bachelor's, retained this vestige of the older dress which has been lost in the modification undergone by the undergraduates'. That the strings indicate a state of dependence is confirmed by their being found on the dress of the pope's lay chamberlains called *camerieri di cappa e spada* ; the papal palfrey men and other domestics being also provided with them.

[2] A custom now dying out.

[3] Christopher Wordsworth became Master of his college.

231

nesday se'nnight. Drank wine with Coleridge. Present the *Society*. Chapel. Read 'Morning Chronicle.' Found in it an ode to Fortune, by Coleridge, which I had seen at Rough's yesterday. Read *ratios* and *variable quantities*, and Burton's Anatomy of Melancholy." It was indeed rather in its outer than in its inner circumstance that the life even of the xiii and xiv century undergraduate differed from that of the xxth. Then as now he listened to doctors in their faculties and his own college seniors expounding the mysteries of art and science ; then, as now, he supplemented these lectures with private reading, then, seated upon a wooden stool in a corner of a crowded room, or in the college library, or best of all in the college meadows ; now, in a comfortable arm chair or stretched upon a sofa in his private sitting room.[1] Then, as now, he caroused or discussed " the universe " with his friends, as his nature suggested. Then, as now, he made early acquaintance with the river Granta and knew each yard of the flat roads round the university town. Even the periodical outbreak between " town and gown " belongs

---

[1] Studies were much later additions in the colleges, and at first a room would be fitted with 8 or 10 'studies,' alcoves or cabinets 5 ft. 6 in. by 6 ft., which would be eagerly hired by students. Sometimes the studies were furnished by the pensioners with the necessary desk and shelves. No attempt at decoration of college rooms appears to have been made till the poet Gray placed scented flowers in his window and bought Japanese vases of the blue and white china afterwards to become so fashionable—which caused much remark. When young peers came up to Cambridge attended by their tutor and an ample *suite* the colleges were much put about to lodge them, and we find Lady Rutland as early as 1590 sending hangings for her son's with-drawing-room at Corpus.

Collegiate and Social Life

as much to the xiii century as to the most recent history in the xxth.[1]

Lectures take place in the morning, " coaching " and private study usually in the late afternoon and evening. Two to four is the chosen time for recreation, and the chief recreations of the Cantab used to be the road and the river. The latter runs familiarly past the windows of his college rooms, and invites him as he steps forth from the threshold of his college court. Boating, swimming, or fishing, the student of a bye-gone day found in the Granta a never-failing and an inexpensive resource. Cambridge fish as we have seen has always been famous, and the Merton scholars poached upon the townsmen's fishing rights long before the xiii century was out.

"Your success in the Senate House" said a well-known tutor "depends much on the care you take of the three-mile stone out of Cambridge. If you go every day and see no one has taken it away, and go quite round it to watch lest any one has damaged its farthest side, you will be best able to read steadily all the time you are at Cambridge. If you neglect it, woe betide your degree. Exercise, constant, and regular, and ample, is absolutely essential to a reading man's

[1] The enmity of 'town and gown,' a consequence, no doubt, of the thronging of our university towns with an alien population, is traditional, and we first hear of it in 1249 before any colleges were built. Fifty years later (in 1305) the townsmen attacked the gownsmen, wounding and beating both masters and scholars "to the manifest delaying of their study" says the King's letter on the subject (33rd of Edw. I.). Bad relations between 'town and gown' prevailed throughout the reign of Elizabeth. Cf. v. p. 261.

success." And the reading men have taken the lesson to heart. No roads until the era of bicycles were better tramped than the flat Cambridge roads which lend themselves so well to this form of recreation ; pair after pair of men, tall and small, a big and a little together, used to keep themselves informed as to their state of repair, or lose the sense of space and time in discussions on the modern substitute for "quiddity" and *essentia*, or the social and biological problems which are newer even than these.

Once back in his college the persons on whom the undergraduate's comfort most depends are the college cook the bedmaker and the "gyp." The last calls him, brushes his clothes, prepares his breakfast, caters for him, serves his luncheon, waits on him and his friends, and carries back and forth the little twisted paper missives which, as an American noticed fifty years ago, Cambridge undergraduates are perpetually exchanging. All these services the gyp may have to perform for a number of other men. The only woman servant is the "bedmaker" whose name sufficiently describes her official business, but who for the great majority of modern students discharges the functions of gyp. The college kitchen is a busy centre. Here is prepared not only the hall dinner but all private breakfasts and luncheons served in college rooms ; and most of the college kitchens supply luncheons and dinners to residents in the town if required. Dinner in hall costs from one shilling and tenpence to two shillings and a penny, according to the college ; bread and butter

Collegiate and Social Life

called "commons" can be had from the buttery for 6d. a day ; a breakfast dish at a cost of from 6d. to 1/ ; and at some college halls a luncheon is served at a small fixed charge.[1]

A hundred years ago the undergraduate dressed for "hall" with white silk stockings and pumps and white silk waistcoat. A few wore powder, the others curled their hair, and he was a bucolic youth indeed who omitted at least the curling. "Curled and powdered" the Cambridge scholar wore his hair even in the xiv century provoking the indignation of primates and founders. A hundred and fifty years ago beer was served for breakfast, and only Gray and Walpole drank tea. Even fifty years ago the food was roughly served and in an overcrowded hall. It was however abundant, and extras like soup, confectionery, and cheese could be "sized for" *i.e.* brought you at an extra charge. The food provided consisted of plain joints and vegetables, with plenty of beer. The fellows' table and the side tables of the bachelors were better served.

"The wine," the famous entertainment which followed the old four o'clock dinner fifty years ago, has yielded place to coffee and tea. In the May term teas assume new proportions ; for during the

[1] The allowance per head per week for food or "commons" was at Michaelhouse 12d. in 1324, and no more was allowed in the xvi c. at Christ's and S. John's. The allowance at Jesus College was 4d. a week in excess of this, and this was the sum which Archbishop Arundel had sanctioned for fellows' commons earlier in the century (1405). Peterhouse statutes made no provision, but the Bishop of Ely as visitor restricted commons to 14d. a week in 1516. Mullinger, *Hist. Univ. Camb.* p. 461.

term which is fateful to the reading man as that preceding the tripos examination, the idle man turns work time into play, invites his friends and relatives up to Cambridge, and entertains his sisters at "the races." It is not indeed to be supposed that the majority of undergraduates are to be found keeping themselves awake with black coffee, a damp towel bound about their brows, while they burn the midnight oil. Even the harmless necessary "sporting of one's oak" is no longer "good form." In days when you advertise for a curate and a schoolmaster who is a good athlete the very thin literary proclivities of the bulk of Englishmen cannot be held to be on the increase. What one might legitimately hope for is that athletics should prove a safety-valve to the natural "rowdyism" of the non-reading man ; so that if school and university sports cannot make a scholar they might at least turn out something not unlike a gentleman. Last October (1905) proved a "record" in the number of men "going up," and November proved "a record" in the number of men who should have been "sent down." What took place is fresh in our memories ; and it will not quickly be forgotten that while the undergraduates of one university were shouting their disgrace, a well-known bishop was signalising (and exaggerating) the disgrace of the other ; and we may choose between the merits of leaguing with the town blackguard to kick policemen at Cambridge or indulging the vice which changed the name of "wines" at Oxford to "drunks." At the rejoicings for Mafeking the iron railings and

Collegiate and Social Life

posts were torn up along the 'backs,' and everything combustible from drays to handcarts was "commandeered" to make a bonfire on Market hill, where many panes of glass in the surrounding houses were smashed. Proctors' "bull-dogs" were rolled over in the mud, and the proctors treated to the dignity of a "chairing."[1] The bonfire on Market hill is a development of a traditional ritual more amusing and less dangerous: you drag out your own and your friends' furniture and make a bonfire in the middle of the college "court."

Would it be impossible, among so many good rules, to make cap and gown obligatory at both universities between the hours of 9 and 12 ? The spectacle of youths hugging golf clubs on the Oxford station at ten o'clock in the morning cannot be extraneous to examination results which show that not 3 men in 4 who matriculate, take the *B.A.* At Cambridge there is good promise in the large increase of scientific students who take advantage of the facilities afforded by its laboratories : more men entered for the "doctors' college" in October 1905 than for any other, except of course Trinity ; and even "the sporting college" has been a principal contributor to the number of medical graduates. Since 1883 there has been a board of Indian Civil Service studies, and the universities between them send up far the larger number of

[1] Undergraduates have perhaps shown a tendency to get out of hand since the day a few years back when some of the dons invited an expression of their opinion, apparently expecting that a serious question affecting the university would receive illustration from a little hooliganism.

THE TOWER OF ST. JOHN'S COLLEGE
CHAPEL FROM THE RIVER

Trinity College Library lies on the right, through the trees.

Cambridge

candidates for this service. A board of agricultural studies was instituted in 1899, a diploma in agriculture is now awarded, also one in sanitation, and geographical studies are encouraged by prizes. Since 1899 when the tripos was divided, the Historical has become one of the larger triposes and in 1905 had the highest number of entries after the Natural Sciences.[1]

University athletics. The traditional rivalry in sports has of course been that between the two universities. The inter-university boat race was begun in 1836, and the first 4 races were won by Cambridge, as was also the first race rowed in outriggers in '46. Of the 63 races run, Oxford has won 6 more than Cambridge ; Cambridge has won 4 out of the last 5, and has also won by the greater number of lengths (in '49 by "many," and in 1900 by 20).[2] The great inferiority of the 'Cam' to the 'Isis' is partly compensated by the excellent style of rowing which Eton

---

[1] In June 1905 there were 647 tripos candidates, 146 for the Natural Sciences, 127 for History, 111 Classics, 95 Law, 63 Mathematics, 28 Mechanical Science, 25 Theology, 13 Modern Languages, 5 Moral Sciences, 5 Economics, 1 Oriental Languages. The year before Natural Sciences was also at the top of the poll with 131 graduates ; the Classical came next with 112, the Mathematical 67, History 63. Some 30% therefore take Natural or Mechanical Sciences, and some of the mathematical students stay on for scientific work. The far larger number of men now take the First Part of the Mathematical, Classical, or Natural Sciences tripos in their third year, which gives them the B.A., and do not proceed to the Second Part. For the proportion of First and Second classes obtained cf. vi. p. 356 n.

It was, however, only very gradually that the classical and other triposes worked their way to an equality in popularity with the mathematical. It was not till 1884, after the division of the tripos, that the classical men were slightly in excess of the mathematical (see chap. iii.).

[2] On the other hand Oxford has had 9 wins in succession.

Collegiate and Social Life

traditions carry on into Cambridge. The happy connexion between Cambridge and Eton established by Henry VI. has never ceased to link the most aristocratic English school with the more democratic of the English universities, and many boys come to the "light blue" university already wearing her favours. In football the two universities have shown equal prowess ; Cambridge cricket is superior (the inter-university match was started in 1839 and Cambridge won the first 6 matches), but Cambridge golf is inferior. In athletics (1868-1906) Cambridge has from the first shewn herself superior.

The Union Society forms another distraction well calculated to turn out the English ideal of a university man—a man, *id est*, ready for public affairs. It was founded in 1815 by the *union* of three already existing debating societies, the present building was erected in 1866 and fitted up as a club. Stratford Canning (Lord Stratford de Redcliffe) and Blomfield, afterwards Bishop of London, belonged to one of these earlier "spouting clubs" in 1806, where Palmerston and Ellenborough both "laid the foundation" of their parliamentary fame. The college ball and the college concert are also crowded into the student's seven weeks of residence in the May term, taking the place of the plays which formed the staple entertainment in the xvi and xvii centuries. The modern "A.D.C." has been rendered famous by the "Greek Plays" which were inaugurated twenty-five years ago with a performance of "Ajax."

Cambridge

Sunday at Cambridge. But the round of work and play comes to an end with Sunday, and the university has preserved the festival aspect of this day, the day when continental beadles and *gens d'armes* don their fine plumes and when what is bright and gay rather than what is dull and grave is mated to the idea of a day of rest. The college courts—the outdoor centre and rallying point of college life—are thronged with men gay in surplice or gown [1] as they were thronged on that Sunday 370 years ago when Stephen Gardiner Bishop of Winchester found two hundred dons assembled "as is their wont" and buttonholed the men who were likely to pleasure his grace in the matter of the divorce. That fine day in the xvi century was no doubt a repetition of many fine days in the centuries preceding it, for it is always fine in Cambridge on Sunday. And Sunday after Sunday the undergraduate has received a lesson in dignities, as he circled becapped and begowned on the cobbled paths round the greater luminaries becapped and begowned tranquilly stepping on the college grass. The modern undergraduate does not remember a time when a pathway ran across the turf from corner to corner of the college courts, as it did in Clare Hall, in the old court of Corpus, and in William of Wykeham's foundation at Oxford. On "scarlet days" the courts are

[1] The wearing of the surplice in chapel on Sundays and holidays by all undergraduates, scholars, and bachelors, is a very interesting historical survival at Cambridge, which has successfully resisted the attacks of Puritanism. It is worn by all members of a college on 'white nights' (vigils and feasts), and is the ancient dress of the canon and of clerks of all grades at divine service.

still more gay, for the doctors then appear in their scarlet.[1]

The gowns in the court clothe the learned and the unlearned, and make a present of as brave an academic appearance to the rowdiest of non-readers as to the future senior wrangler. The academic year is divided into 3 terms of 8 or 9 weeks each : half the year only is therefore passed at Cambridge. For serious study the intervals are too long and the 'long vacation term' has become the reading man's term *par excellence* ; all the colleges are then half full, the numbers being swelled by the medical students. The multiplication of extra-collegiate scholarships has not told all one way. Parents who used to make sacrifices to send a son to the university now count upon a scholarship, with the result that on the principle of 'light come light go' less use is made of opportunities. The university authorities look to the "advanced students" (of whom there are now 60 or 70 in residence) who are staying up for research work or come from other universities, for solid academic achievement.

Class from which the academic population has been drawn. There is no more interesting enquiry connected with our subject than that concerning the classes from which the academic population has been recruited at different epochs, and the careers for which the university has fitted its members.

[1] " Scarlet days " are Easter, Christmas, Ascension, Whitsunday, Trinity Sunday, All Saints, the first Sunday in November (when benefactors are commemorated) and Commencement Tuesday (the next before June 24). The vice-chancellor may appoint other days.

Cambridge

The Church has always remained the most constant client of academic advantages : it was the churchmen who on the decline of the monasteries and when the universities were established as learned corporations, exchanged the cloister for the college education. The dissolution of the monasteries and the breach with Rome left the universities as the only representatives of the faculty of theology ; and during the last century, especially, if a man were destined for the Church he went—*ipso facto*—to Cambridge or Oxford even though he were the only member of his family to do so. In the xv as in the xvi centuries it was chiefly men destined for the faculties of theology and law who frequented the universities, and then, as always in their history, the poorest scholar lived side by side with the youth of family and influence.

The lawyers, perhaps, have gone in equal proportions to a university or to one of the Inns of Court ; many have gone to both. The great change to be observed is as regards students of the third faculty, medicine. In the xix century the doctor and the tradesman's son did not go to a university ; but this century, as we have seen, has already been marked by the enormous accession of medical students at Cambridge. The gradual growth of a powerful middle class resulted in the later xvi century in filling the universities with the sons not only of the older yeomanry of our shires but of the new Merchant Adventurers, often themselves men of gentle blood and coat armour. It is perhaps from this century that the idea began to prevail that an academic education was the proper education of a gentleman. Of this century it was true as it had been true of no other that "the civil life of all English gentlemen" is begun at Oxford or Cambridge. Statesmen and ministers, the political and the diplomatic careers, were recruited at the universities, and university-trained canonists and lawyers like Cranmer and More, and churchmen like Wolsey and Gardiner were chosen to be the ambassadors and secretaries of state. Ascham complains to Cranmer that sons of rich men "who sought only superficial knowledge" and "to qualify themselves for some place in the State" overran the university, and both universities soon became, in Macaulay's words, the training ground not only of all the eminent clergy, lawyers, physicians, poets, and orators, but of a large proportion of the "nobility and opulent gentry" of the country.

In England men belonging to what have, hitherto, been the governing classes have always sought advantages which would doubtless be less apparent in countries where nobility and gentry are synonyms and where government is not carried on by means of two such institutions as the House of Commons and the House of Lords. A *noblesse* which gives no scions to the professions or to a representative chamber has seldom sought academic distinction. The man destined for parliament for the diplomatic service and the government office—occupations which an acute American observer has said are chosen by Englishmen as the business of their lives "without studying any other

UNIVERSITY BOAT-HOUSES ON THE
CAM—SUNSET

This view is taken near Stourbridge Common and
the bend of the river known as Barnwell Pool, looking towards the town.

Cambridge

profession "[1]—prepared himself in no other way than by three or four years spent at the university, with or without graduating there. It was not however till the nineteenth century opened that the distinctively aristocratic trend of a university was defined. Throughout that century the university was *par excellence* the seminary of the English gentleman, and the parson. A few bankers' sons might be put into their fathers' counting houses, a few government officials might place their sons at an early age in a government office, but the exception only proved the rule.

Examples. Let us look at some examples of the class from which Cambridge was recruited through the xvi and xvii centuries. Hugh Latimer (*b.* 1491) was the

xvi c. son of a yeoman farmer ; Sir Thomas Wyatt (*b.* 1503) was the son of a knight. The father of Matthew Parker (*b.* 1504) was a Norwich merchant ; Bacon (*b.* 1561) and his brother, fellow-commoners of Trinity, were sons of the Lord Keeper and nephews of Burleigh. Fletcher (*b.* 1579) the dramatist, was the son of the Bishop of London, and his cousins the poets were sons of Elizabeth's Master of the Requests and ambassador

xvii c. to Russia.[2] In the xvii century Herrick the poet (*b.* 1591) was the son of a goldsmith established in London ; Waller (*b.* 1605) a nephew of Hampden's, a man of large private fortune ; Cowley (*b.* 1618) was

[1] Everett, *On the Cam.* Everett's father was United States ambassador at the Court of S. James', and he himself was a graduate of Trinity College.

[2] Wolsey, son of a well-to-do Suffolk butcher, was sent to Oxford, but Thomas Cromwell, who was the son of a blacksmith, probably was not educated at a university.

Collegiate and Social Life

son to a city grocer ; Marvell (*b.* 1620) son to a York-shire clergyman ; while Temple was the son of an Irish Master of the Rolls. In the latter half of the xvii century we still hear of " the farmer's son newly come from the university "[1]—Bentley was one of them —and at the same time we hear that Tuckney, Whichcote's tutor, " had many persons of rank and quality " under him at Emmanuel College. In the xviii century, Pepys' (*b.* 1703) father was a tailor, the Wordsworths were sons of a north country attorney, Sir William Browne (*b.* 1692) was the son of a physician.

Recruiting schools. Men of low origin were sent up, and have always been sent up, to the universities through the beneficence of patrons, and the poor tailor Stow was enabled to write his history owing to the patronage of Archbishop Parker who sent him to Oxford. Through the xv and early xvi centuries the monastic and other convent schools supplied university students. Bale (*b.* 1495) had been educated by the Norwich Car-melites, Coverdale (*b.* 1487) had been an Austinfriar at Cambridge. At the present day the big grammar schools, and in especial the Norwich grammar school which educated Nelson, send every year a contingent of students, as they have done since the reign of Edward VI. If we take the sporting representatives sent from the two universities the year before last, 23 from Oxford and 21 from Cambridge, we shall find that one third of the Cambridge men hailed from the greater public schools,

[1] *The New Sect of Latitude-men,* 1662.

245

Cambridge

Eton, Charterhouse, and Rugby.[1] Our colonies are also a recruiting ground, and with them Cambridge is favourite university.[2]

The number of undergraduates entered this academic year (1906-7) was the largest on record, totalling 1021. The reputation and the popularity of colleges of course wax and wane : for the past two years the largest number of entries (excluding Trinity) has been for Caius and Pembroke, Emmanuel coming next, and then S. John's.[3] The number of non-collegiate students is steadily increasing.

Religion at Cambridge. There are no 'high Church' centres among the colleges, and there is no 'broad Church' movement among the undergraduates. The 'broad Church' movement is among the younger dons

[1] Eton—Cambridge and Oxford—3 each ; Oxford had 3 from Winchester, all the rest coming from the lesser public schools, Haileybury (3), and church schools such as Radley.

[2] A very interesting symptom is the recent election of an American fellow at Trinity and Christ's Colleges.

[3] In the time of Caius the number of students was 1783 (see p. 217 n.). Trinity held 359 of these, John's 271, Christ's 157, King's 140, Clare 129, Queens' 122. Magdalene and S. Catherine's were the smallest with 49 and 32 respectively. The remaining 6 colleges held between 62 and 96 students each, except Jesus which had a population of 118. A hundred years after Caius the numbers were 2522. 3000 is about the maximum at either university since the xiii c. At Cambridge the undergraduate population at the present date (October 1906) exceeds 3200, with over 350 resident bachelors, and about 650 *M.A.'s* and doctors, 400 of whom are fellows.

Cf. with the figures given on p. 206. A man may keep his name on the boards of his college by a payment varying from £2 to £4 a year. The number of men "on the boards" of the university includes all those on the boards of their colleges and has grown in 150 years from 1500 (in 1748) to 13,819 in 1906-7.

A.D. 1573.

A.D. 1672.

Collegiate and Social Life

and in connexion with the University Settlement. There are nonconformists in every college, but the reunion with Christendom which begins at home finds no advocates among other university men. As usual there is at Cambridge no particular 'school' of religious thought. There is however just now a decided religious movement among the undergraduates, almost exclusively connected with the 'high Church' parish of S. Giles. The majority of the men make little religious profession, but there is no violent reaction such as agitated Oxford in the 'forties' and 'fifties,' and the yearly increasing number of scientific students inclines to a pantheistic rather than a materialistic standpoint.

Cambridge politics. The undergraduate population is decidedly conservative, as the university has always been. At the present moment both sides of the fiscal controversy are represented, the distinguished Cambridge economist Dr. Cunningham advocating tariff reform, while the Professor of Political Economy is a free-trader.

The university settlement in Camberwell. The "slumming" movement made an early appeal to the younger members of the university. Their present work in south London was begun over twenty years ago, and "Cambridge House" has existed for ten years in a district which has been called "the largest area of unbroken poverty in any European city." The workers are all laymen, 11 out of the 17 colleges being represented by resident Cambridge men, while an under-

247

DITTON CORNER, ON THE CAM

From this spot the boat races are viewed. Behind the elms is the village of Ditton, and the building we see is Ditton Church.

graduate secretary in every college assists in furthering the movement.

Married dons. We saw at the beginning of this chapter that the aspect of the university had changed with the marriage of fellows, tutors, and officials ; and in time this factor must greatly modify the conditions of life at our universities. Both of these are now overrun with children's schools, and there can be little doubt that all the boys (and many of the girls) will go to college. The natural profession for many of these, owing to the father's influence with his college and the son's inherited inclinations, will be academic. It would certainly not be to the advantage of our seats of learning if they became in this sense close corporations. It is obvious that this would mean less movement of ideas and less opportunity for the outside world to affect the university ; and if a large number not only of the teachers but of the scholars belonged to such a caste as this, if the profession of teaching were handed down from father to son, the situation would not be unlike that which threatened Europe when Gregory VII. interposed and made the Christian world his executor in enforcing clerical celibacy. A new tuitional field would be open to the young graduate in the numerous schools of Cambridge and Oxford, but this would only accentuate the vicious circle of an education which might come to suggest the ecclesiastical seminary rather than the English university. Perhaps, too, a young man loses more than half the social and worldly advantages of a college life if when he "goes up to the university" he does not change his habitat.

The married fellow cannot begin life again elsewhere after the 5 or 10 years' teaching at his college which used to precede his departure for a benefice : the old bachelor, if he stayed on, no longer taught, and new men took his place in the lecture room. But now a fellow cannot renounce the lecture room, for he and his family cannot live on the fellowship. Lecturers are therefore often men past the prime of life, and moreover men who no longer live in daily contact with the undergraduate. New blood comes in seldom, and percolates slowly. On the other hand valuable men stay who would under the old system have left. The influx of the "monstruous regiment" will not however, one hopes, diminish an advantage at present possessed by the seniors at our centres of learning— a general equality of fortune which frees university society from the laborious vulgarity that travails the soul elsewhere, from the general "ponderousness," as someone has called it, of English life. At least Gray's advice to Wharton not to bring his wife to Cambridge would now be quite out of place ; the "few" women are no longer "squeezy and formal, little skilled in amusing themselves or other people," and the men are no longer "not over agreeable neither."

CHAPTER V

UNIVERSITY MEN AND NATIONAL MOVEMENTS

Men who owe nothing to a university—40 great Englishmen—
Cambridge men : the scientists, the poets, the dramatists, other
literary men, the philosophers, the churchmen, lawyers and
physicians, the statesmen. (pp. 250-260.)

National movements : King John and the barons—the
peasants' revolt—York and Lancaster—the new world—
Charles and the Parliament—James II. and the University—
the Declaration of Indulgence—the Nonjurors—William and
Mary and Cambridge whiggery—Jacobitism and Toryism at
Cambridge in the reign of Anne—George I. and Cambridge—
modern political movements. (pp. 260-269.)

Religious movements : Lollards, the early reformers, the
question of the divorce, Lutheranism at Cambridge, later
reformers and the Reformation, the English bible, and service
books, the Cambridge martyrs, the Puritans, the Presbyterians,
the Independents, the Latitudinarians, the Deists, the
evangelical movement, the Tractarian movement, anti-calvinism.
(pp. 269-281.)

Intellectual movements : the New Learning and the age
of Elizabeth—the Royal Society—the Cambridge Platonists
—modern science. (pp. 281-291.)

Connexion of Cambridge founders and eminent men with
the university : early Cambridge names—a group of great
names in the xiii and xiv centuries—Cambridge men in the
historical plays of Shakespeare—genealogical tables of founders
—Cantabrigians from the xv century to the present day—Cambridge men who have taken no degree. (pp. 291-309.)

250

Cambridge Men

WHAT part is played by a university in the life of a people? This can only be gauged by its output of men, its influence on great movements, the trend and character of the learning it fosters and the opinions it encourages.

During the centuries in which the English universities have existed, the first degree of excellence has been reached in every department of human knowledge and activity by men whom no university can claim. Shakespeare, Bunyan, Hawkins, Raleigh, Drake, the Hoods, Howard of Effingham, Clive, Warren Hastings, Marlborough, Nelson, Wellington, Scott, Dickens, Keats, Browning, were at no university; the same is true of Smollett, Richardson, and Sheridan. It is noticeable, nevertheless, that the literary names cited include none but poets and novelists. Among scientific men and philosophers, Bishop Butler, Faraday, J. S. Mill, Huxley, Lubbock (Lord Avebury), Spencer, G. H. Lewes, Buckle, and Grote were not trained at universities—even among the great educationalists, the founders of colleges in our universities and of great public schools, few received an academic education. Some careers, again, are entirely outside the sphere of university influence—admirals and great captains, sailors and soldiers, do not go to universities, and among inventors hardly one hails from a seat of learning. Art, also, is not fostered by an academic atmosphere; painters, architects, and musicians owe nothing to it; and although universities adorn themselves with professorships of the fine arts, and of music, it is not to

Cambridge

them that we go for definitions of art, or for an output of artists. In Orlando Gibbons, indeed, Cambridge possessed a native musician whose compositions and unrivalled technique as an organist place him in the first rank of musical Englishmen ; but while nearly every English artist owes something to a *wanderjahr* in Italy, scarcely one ever resided at a university.

Nevertheless if we were to take a short list of representative Englishmen, of the men who have influenced and shaped the national life, its religion, its politics, its thoughts, who have helped to realise the English genius and to make England what it is, we should find that a large proportion of those who could have been educated at Cambridge or Oxford were in fact university men. In the following list those who have had a preponderant influence on English education from the vii century onwards, are included :—

```
vii-viii c. Bede. †
    vii c. Hild. * † ¹
   viii c. Alcuin. * †
     ix c. Alfred. †
    xii c. Stephen Langton    .    .    (Paris).
        „   Grosseteste *  .      .    .    Oxford (and Paris).
   xiii c. Roger Bacon  .    (Paris) and Oxford.
        „   Edward I. †
    xiv c. Wyclif  .    .    .    .    Oxford.
        „   Chaucer    .    .    .    Cambridge.
        „   William of Wykeham * ² .    none.
 xiv-xv c. Lady Margaret. * †
```

¹ Those marked with an asterisk are included principally for their influence on education.
² *Or* Walter de Merton.

Cambridge Men

xv-xvi c.	Colet *	Oxford.
„	Bishop Fisher * . .	Cambridge.
„	Wolsey	Oxford.
xvi c.	Sir Thomas More . .	Oxford.
„	Cranmer . . .	Cambridge.
„	Ascham * . . .	Cambridge.
„	Elizabeth. †	
„	Drake	none.
„	Raleigh [1] . . .	none.
„	Sir Philip Sidney . .	Oxford.
„	Lord Bacon . . .	Cambridge.
xvi-xvii c.	Shakespeare . . .	none.
„	Harvey	Cambridge.
„	Cromwell . . .	Cambridge.
„	Milton . . .	Cambridge.
„	Jeremy Taylor .. .	Cambridge.
„	Bunyan	none.
„	Locke	Oxford.
„	Newton	Cambridge.
xvii-xviii c.	Marlborough . . .	none.
xviii c.	Wesley . . .	Oxford.
„	Clive	none.
xviii-xix c.	Nelson † . . .	none.
„	Pitt . . .	Cambridge.
xix c.	John Stuart Mill . .	none.
„	Darwin	Cambridge.
„	Gladstone [2] . . .	Oxford.
„	Florence Nightingale. † [3]	

[1] Raleigh was entered as a boy for Oriel College but never resided there.

[2] Gladstone was by race a pure Scotsman, but was English by birth and breeding.

[3] Miss Nightingale is taken as a representative of the work of Howard, Clarkson, Shaftesbury, Hannah More, Mrs. Fry, and others of the same noble army among whom she is perhaps typical for the English adventuresome and pioneer spirit.

It would not be possible to choose 40 great Englishmen whom every one

Cambridge

Of these, 9 could not have been at a university and are marked †, but of the remaining 31, 23 were at a university; 12 at Cambridge, 10 at Oxford. Two were at both Paris and Oxford, and one was at Paris.

In this chapter, however, our concern is with the great men produced by the one university. There are two fields in which Cambridge is and always has been

should agree to be among the 40 greatest, or the best types in the lines indicated. Some great English names—as e.g. Simon de Montfort—do not appear for the same reason which excludes William the Conqueror, viz. that they were not Englishmen.

The following is a short analysis :—

(1) *Men representing English Learning and education :*	(2) *English Churchmen :*	(3) *English Religion :*	(4) *English politics :*
Hild.	Stephen Langton.	Wyclif, Ox.	Alfred.
Bede.	Robert Grosseteste,	Lady Margaret.	Stephen Langton.
Alcuin.	Ox.	More, Ox.	Grosseteste, Ox.
Alfred.	William of Wyke-	Jeremy Taylor, C.	Edward I.
Grosseteste.	ham.	Bunyan.	Elizabeth.
William of Wyke-	Fisher, C.	Wesley, Ox.	Cromwell, C.
ham.	Wolsey, Ox.		Milton, C.
Lady Margaret.	Cranmer, C.		John Locke, Ox.
Dean Colet, Ox.	Jeremy Taylor, C.		Pitt, C.
Bishop Fisher, C.			Gladstone, Ox.
Thomas More, Ox.			
Roger Ascham, C.			

(5) *Literature and makers of English language :*	(6) *Philosophers :*	(7) *English Science :*	(8) *English Adventure :*
Bede.	Locke.	Roger Bacon, Ox.	Drake.
Chaucer, C.	Mill.	Francis Bacon, C.	Raleigh.
Ascham, C.		Harvey, C.	Clive.
Philip Sidney, Ox.		Newton, C.	Nelson.
Shakespeare.		Darwin, C.	Nightingale.
Francis Bacon, C.			
Milton, C.			
Bunyan.			
Locke, Ox.			

254

Cambridge Men

facile princeps. She has nurtured all the great scientists, and all the great poets. The discoveries of world-wide importance have been the work of Cambridge men— such were the three which revolutionised the science of the world, the laws of the circulation of the blood, of gravitation, of evolution. From Bacon the founder of experimental philosophy to Darwin and Kelvin, every great name is a Cambridge name, if we except indeed the few who like Wallace, Humphry Davy, Faraday, and the elder Herschell owe nothing to a university.

Literature. If the scientific pre-eminence of Cambridge is unquestioned, her poetical pre-eminence is no less absolute. Chaucer, Spenser, Marlowe, Milton, Dryden, Gray, Wordsworth, Byron, Tennyson called her mother. In the long list of English poets every poet of first rank (excluding Shakespeare and Keats who were at no university) was at Cambridge, except Shelley who was expelled from Oxford.

The dramatist movement from Marlowe to Shirley is one of the most important in our literature. Here for the first time in English history a group of Englishmen set themselves, on leaving the university, to earn an independence by literature—and the opportunity offered them was writing for the players. The dramatists were, with but few exceptions of which the greatest is Shakespeare himself, university men ; and of these all who were epoch-marking hail from Cambridge. The list is headed by the first English tragic poet, Christopher Marlowe, Shakespeare's great predecessor ; and Ben

THE FITZWILLIAM MUSEUM—EVENING

In the distance are seen the square tower of the Pitt
Press and Pembroke College. Behind the trees are
Peterhouse and the Congregational Church.

Cambridge

Jonson the greatest of his younger contemporaries was also a Cambridge man. Lyly who created the art tradition of English comedy, went to Cambridge from Oxford and there graduated *M.A.* Lodge after leaving Oxford went to Avignon, took his *M.D.* degree there, and on returning to England went to Cambridge. Shirley, the last of the dramatists, went from Oxford to Cambridge.[1]

The sonneteers had preceded the dramatists, and the first writer of an English sonnet was another Cambridge man, Sir Thomas Wyatt.[2] Surrey whose university, if he went to one, was certainly Cambridge, wrote the first blank verse. The first English essayist was Bacon, and he takes his place in literature by another title, because he was the first to adapt our language as the vehicle for a scientific literature. Of the five men who in the great days of the flowering of English poesy wrote about the art of verse Spenser, Webbe, Harvey, Sidney, and Puttenham, the first three, whose contribution is also the most important, were Cambridge men.

All literary initiative, indeed, between the xiv and xviii centuries appears to have come from the one university; the epoch-making representatives of our literature, that is, were Cambridge men: Chaucer, Spenser, Marlowe and Ben Jonson (in defect of Shake-

[1] See the list of dramatists below.

[2] Sonneteers : Wyatt, Cambridge. Surrey, Cambridge ? Thomas Watson, Oxford ? Philip Sidney, Oxford. Samuel Daniel, Oxford. Lodge, Oxford to Cambridge. Drayton, none.

Cambridge Men

The Dramatists.

Greene	(Cambridge).
Lyly	(Oxford to Cambridge).
Peele	(Oxford).
Lodge *(disciple of Greene)*	(Oxford to Cambridge).
Christopher Marlowe	(Cambridge).
Kyd	(none).
Shakespeare	(none).
Ben Jonson	(Cambridge).
Nash	(Cambridge).
Chapman	(?)
Marston	(Oxford).
Dekker	(nothing known).
Thomas Heywood	(Cambridge).
Middleton	(nothing known).
Munday	("The pope's scholar in the seminary at Rome ").
Fletcher *(12 years at Benet College)*	(Cambridge).
Beaumont	(Oxford).
Webster	(nothing known).
Massinger	(Oxford).
Rowley	(nothing known).
Ford	(Oxford ?).
James Shirley	(Oxford to Cambridge).

The Novelists.

Richardson	(none).
Fielding	(University of Leyden).
Defoe	(none).
Steele	(Oxford).
Smollett	(none).
Sterne	(Cambridge).
Goldsmith	(none).

And the 7 great names of our century :

Jane Austen.	
Scott	(none).[1]
The two Brontës.	
Thackeray	(Cambridge).
Dickens	(none).
George Eliot.	
Meredith	(none).

---

[1] Scott attended the law classes at Edinburgh university.

Cambridge

speare), Bacon, Milton, Dryden.[1] The first history of
English literature also comes from the hand of a
Cantabrigian, John Bale. There are two other classes
of English literature to which reference must be made.
The novelists as we have already seen have not been
alumni of our universities, partly because this is a field
in which women have attained the highest rank, partly
because there seems to be that something more of the
artistic afflatus in the novelist's craft and that something less of the academic, as compared with the other
forms of literature, which we should à priori have
certainly predicated of poetry also. A list of the
novelists, from Mrs. Afra Behn to George Meredith
would however show how different is the case of the
novelists to that of the poets.

The last branch of literature, the importance of
which is much greater than its literary merit, is
journalism. Here, too, Cambridge led the way, though
here, as elsewhere, it has not maintained its position.
It was Roger Le Strange who as sole licenser and
authorised printer and publisher of news, printed the
first number of the " London Gazette " ;[2] and Andrew

---

[1] "The first of the great English writers in whom letters asserted an
almost public importance." In the new 'republic of letters' Dryden
was "chosen chief"; "He had done more than any man to create a
literary class"; "he was the first to impress the idea of literature on the
English mind." Master "alike of poetry and prose, covering the fields
both of imagination and criticism . . . Dryden realized in his own personality the existence of a new power which was thenceforth to tell steadily on
the world . . . our literature obeyed the impulse he had given it from the
beginning of the eighteenth century till near its close."—J. R. Green.

[2] The first number appeared in November 1665 and was called "The

Cambridge Men

Marvell's newsletters to his constituents at Hull were among the earliest attempts at parliamentary reporting.

The learned   When we turn to philosophy, we find that
professions.   Cambridge has been singularly poor in
metaphysicians, logicians, and political philosophers.
Edinburgh, Aberdeen, Glasgow, and Oxford all precede
her. Among eminent representatives of 'the learned
faculties Cambridge had, with the exception of Segrave,
Bateman, and Beaufort, no great churchmen in the
xiv century. In the xvth it can boast that it nurtured
Thomas Langton,* Fox,* Rotherham,* Alcock,* Tunstall, and Fisher.* In the next century Cambridge has
it all its own way, the succession of primates is hers,
and nearly every one of the prelates who took the
leading parts in that busy century were Cambridge
alumni : Fox,* Gardiner,* Latimer,* Ridley,* Cranmer,*
Parker,* Grindal,* Whitgift,* Bancroft.[1] In the xvii
century Andrewes,* Cosin,* Williams * the opponent
of Laud, Taylor, Stillingfleet, and the primates Bancroft, Sancroft, Tillotson, Tenison, represented the
university.

Cambridge has also contributed her large share of
the lawyers, lords chancellors and chief justices of

Oxford Gazette," the court being at that time at Oxford on account of the
plague which was then raging in town.

[1] The succession of archbishops of Canterbury from 1486 is : Cardinal
Morton, Oxford ; Warham (1500), neither university ; Cranmer, Cambridge ; Pole, Oxford ; Parker, Cambridge ; Grindal, Cambridge ; Whitgift, Cambridge ; Bancroft (1604), Cambridge.

Among the names given above, those with an asterisk were further
connected with their university as founders, Masters and fellows of colleges,
or as chancellors.

Cambridge

England, from Thorpe, Cavendish and Beaufort in the reigns of Edward III. and his successors to Booth, Rotherham, Alcock, Fox, Ruthall, Goodrich, Wriothesley, Gardiner, Heath, Coke, the two Bacons, Williams, Guilford and Lyndhurst in later times. The great physicians, Caius, "Butler of Cambridge," Gilbert, Hårvey, Wharton, Sydenham,[1] Paris, Grew, Sir William Browne and Sir Samuel Garth, were all Cambridge men, and illustrate the early history of medicine from the xvi century to the xixth.

Statesmen and diplomatists. The roll of Cambridge statesmen is not less distinguished : the two Cecils, Walsingham, Boyle 'the great earl' of Cork, of whom Cromwell said that had there been one like him in every province it would have been impossible for the Irish to raise a rebellion ; Cromwell himself, Sir W. Temple, Halifax, Walpole, Chesterfield, Pitt, Castlereagh, Wilberforce, Stratford de Redcliffe, Palmerston.

National movements. The first great national movement in which the groups of scholars and teachers settled at Cambridge and Oxford could have taken part was the conflict with King John under the leadership of Stephen Langton, and the Barons' war led by Simon de Montfort. Cambridge clerks were implicated in the former, for as soon as Henry III. came to the throne he ordered the expulsion of all those excommunicate scholars who had joined Louis the Dauphin, the Barons' candidate for the throne of England ; and it is surmised that Hugh de Balsham

[1] Sydenham took a medical degree at Cambridge.

Cambridge Men

later in the century favoured the side on which Simon de Montfort fought. It was at Cambridge too that the Dauphin held his council after the demise of John. Much had happened at the university between this struggle in the xiii century and the latter part of the A.D. 1378-1381. xivth when the peasants' revolt again raised the standard of rebellion. The university was no longer a mere aggregate of poor scholars and unendowed teachers, it had long grown into a privileged corporation possessing fine buildings and a full treasury. As such, peasant and burgess bore to it no good will, and Wat Tyler's riots were seized as the opportunity to burn the university charters, ransack the colleges, and mishandle the masters and scholars. At the neighbouring manor-house of Mildenhall (which had formed part of the historic dowry of Queen Emma the mother of the Confessor) Prior John of Cambridge who was acting at the time as abbot of Bury-St.-Edmund's, was murdered by the mob. In 1381 Buckingham, after dispersing the revolted peasantry in Essex, held 'oyer and terminer' at Cambridge, and the town was among the few which was exempted from the general pardon.

Wars of the Roses. Through the next great national crisis Cambridge was Lancastrian. The men of letters of this party, its poets and historians, were Cambridge men, members of Cambridge colleges—Warkworth, Skelton, the Pastons. The Lancastrian sympathies of the university dated indeed from the time of "the good duke" and of John of Gaunt, both of whom befriended it and became patrons of one of its important colleges; and the intimate connexion with the House of Beaufort, which began when Cardinal Beaufort studied at Peterhouse,[1] culminated when Lady Margaret Beaufort, the mother of Henry VII., crowned by her singular benefactions the sympathies of the university for the House of Lancaster. Edward IV. had not loved Cambridge, had indeed robbed Henry VI.'s college of its revenues; but it was there that the royal houses laid down the sword to join in a work of scholarly peace, and few episodes in the annals of a university are more interesting than the building of Queens' College by Margaret of Anjou and Elizabeth Woodville, and the labours of Lady Margaret in whose son were at length reconciled the rival claims of York and Lancaster.

The colonisation of the new world. We have seen that a Washington lies buried in the ancient chapel of the first Cambridge college, and we are to see further on that the impulse which set the "Mayflower" on her course proceeded from a Cantabrigian. The oldest of the 'pilgrim fathers' was a Peterhouse man, persecuted in England for his 'Brownist' opinions. There were many university men among the first settlers, but they were chiefly from the one university; and 'Cambridge' was the name which rose to their lips when they christened the town in the great state of Massachusetts where they first set foot. Thomas Hooker, one of the founders of Connecticut, was a Cambridge graduate and exercised great influence

---

[1] Cf. the Duke of Exeter, ii. pp. 58 *n.*, 156.

Cambridge Men

among the New England settlers. John Eliot, "the Indian apostle," had graduated at Cambridge in 1622 ; and Harvard, the 'Cambridge' of the new world, was founded by another of her sons.

_{The Parliament and the Stuarts.} No sooner had America been colonised by these exiles for their faith than the English revolution brought about the changes which would have kept them in this country. Both universities declared for the king. The loyalty of Oxford is a household word, and it certainly was not diminished by the fact that Charles had his headquarters in the university town : but Cambridge loyalty was not less ; the university plate was sent to Charles at York in _{A.D. 1642-4.} 1642, and among the chests which reached Oxford there were some which arrived safely at the colleges and never arrived anywhere else.[1] The royalist poet was a Cambridge man with a Devonshire cure, Robert Herrick. Cambridge also supplied 'the first cavalier poet' John Cleveland, who lost his fellowship for the king, Abraham Cowley, ejected in the same way _{A.D. 1643.} by the Puritans, and yet another poet and yet another fellow in Richard Crashaw, a royalist born in the year that Shakespeare died, who on refusing to sign the Covenant retired to Paris where he was employed on royalist business by the exiled queen. Isaac Barrow, too, whose father lost everything for the royal cause, and had been with Charles at Oxford when Isaac went up to Trinity, refused the Covenant ; and lived to find himself in an increasing solitude amidst

[1] The plate of Queens' College is preserved at Oxford to this day.

263

Cambridge

the growing Puritanism of the university. A royalist
A.D. 1645. sermon preached by Brownrigg (Bishop of Exeter)
deprived him of the Mastership of S. Catherine's, and
Queens' College was entirely depopulated by the
Parliament men.

But contemporary with Herrick and Crashaw there
were Cambridge men still more famous, and they
espoused the parliamentary cause. Chief of these was
the Cambridge poet on the parliament side, John
Milton. Both universities suffered severely from the
Roundheads, yet together they contributed the chief
actors against the king. From Cambridge came
Cromwell, Milton, and Hutchinson, from Oxford
Ireton, Hampden, and Pym. Anti-monarchical and
Puritan opinions were, however, only grafted on the
university as a result of the violent measures and the
wholesale ejectments carried out by Cromwell and his
agents.[1]

A.D. 1657. By the middle of the xvii century Cambridge had
become Puritan, though here she was outstripped by
Oxford which had been Puritan fifty years earlier,
before Elizabeth died. Among the "regicides" many
were university men ; Andrew Marvell and the young
Dryden at Cambridge were friends to Oliver : but the

[1] Chief of whom was the Earl of Manchester, like Cromwell himself
a Cambridge man. Cromwell and Lord Grey of Wark had "dealt very
earnestly" with the Heads of colleges to extract a loan of £6000 for the
public use. The earnest dealing included shutting most of them up till
midnight. Cromwell on their refusal declared he would have taken
£1000 ; not that that sum would have been of any service, but because it
would have shown that they had one of the universities on their side. All
that Cambridge had, however, was sent to Charles.

Cambridge Men

Presbyterian Wallis, a member of Emmanuel College and later one of the founders of the Royal Society, protested against the king's death warrant which met with the approval of such men as Milton, Hampden, and Hutchinson.

The university and James II. The Restoration was welcomed at both universities. The scheme to secure a Protestant succession and the attempt to exclude James now agitated men's minds. The 'bill of exclusion' was condemned both at Oxford and Cambridge; and the earlier Rye House plot was met at the latter by the deposition of Monmouth at that time chancellor of the university. To the loyal addresses sent by both Cambridge and Oxford on the coronation of James II., Cambridge added a condemnation of the attempt to alter the succession. The attitude of the bench of bishops was not less emphatic—only two prelates could be found to sign the invitation to William of Orange.[1] It was with these facts before him that James set to work to affront a loyal clergy and the two loyal seats of learning; and thus gave to each a rare occasion of proving their quality. The king first attempted to force the hand of the universities, and began by ordering Cambridge to confer the *M.A.* degree on a Catholic. A.D. 1687. This was refused. The vice-chancellor, and with him eight fellows (one of whom was Isaac Newton) was cited to appear at Westminster before the High Commission. Oxford was much more harshly treated, and there is nothing in the history of either university to

---

[1] Compton and Trelawney.

surpass the splendid resistance of Magdalen College to tyranny, during which it was twice depleted of its fellows. The Declaration of Indulgence, however admirable in itself, struck a blow at constitutional principles, and introduced the dangerous corollary that he who could loose *motu proprio* could also bind. The loyal archbishop of Canterbury, a graduate of Emmanuel, with six other prelates refused to publish the Indulgence, and were sent to the Tower. Lloyd of S. Asaph, Lake of Chichester, Turner of Ely, and White of Peterborough were Cantabrigians; Ken of Bath and Wells and Trelawney of Bristol, Oxonians.[1] Perhaps never since the primacy of Stephen Langton had the Church in England been so popular, or shown itself so ready to slough the servilism which attends on state Churches.

The nonjurors. In the following year five of the seven staunch prelates who had withstood James, refused to take the oath of fealty to William and Mary. The primate, with Turner, Lake, White, and Ken, to whom were joined Lloyd of Norwich[2] and Frampton of

A.D. 1688.
A.D. 1689.

---

[1] There had been a previous meeting at Lambeth Palace in which Turner, White, Tenison (then rector of S. Martin's) and Compton, the suspended Bishop of London, took part. All were Cambridge men except Compton. At a consultation of London clergy Tillotson, then Dean of Canterbury, Sherlock, Master of the Temple, Stillingfleet, Archdeacon of London and Dean of S. Paul's, and Patrick, Dean of Peterborough, supported Edward Fowler (an Oxonian) in a declaration that they were unable to publish the Indulgence. Every one of these men was from Cambridge.

[2] He had not received his call in time to sign the protest of the seven bishops. Lloyd was at Cambridge, Frampton at Oxford.

Gloucester, headed some 400 of the clergy as 'Non-jurors.' Under Sancroft the non-juring clergy established a schism in the English Church which lasted till the xix century. The Cambridge Sherlock had at first the greatest influence among them, but neither he nor Ken followed them in the subsequent schism. If another Cambridge man, Jeremy Collier, was the ablest of the nonjurors, Dodwell, a Dublin man, and professor of Ancient History at Oxford, was the most erudite.

The House of Hanover. Although, as we have seen, the two bishops who signed the invitation to William were Oxford men, Oxford had no love for the ' Roman-nosed Dutchman,' and William had no love for Oxford. Halifax, William's henchman, and Nottingham, the leaders of the party which placed William and Mary on the throne, hailed respectively from Cambridge and Oxford : but it was the favour with which Cambridge greeted the accession of the new sovereigns that became the seed of its whiggery. During the reign of Anne, nevertheless, an anti-Hanoverian spirit spread among the younger men. Not only were there Jacobites A.D. 1702-14. among the undergraduates and the junior dons, but a political party was forming which represented the permanent elements in Toryism when separated from Jacobitism. Amongst this party high churchmanship also found refuge. The non-juring clergy still left at the university lived there in close retirement, and helped to swell the ranks neither of the nascent Jacobitism nor the new high churchism. A new vice- A.D. 1714.

Cambridge

chancellor, favourable to the House of Hanover, followed a Jacobite predecessor just in time to present a loyal address to George I. on his accession. This was rewarded by the splendid gift of Bishop Moore's library ; while at Oxford, where the Jacobites were more noisy and had just made the anniversary of the Pretender's birthday the occasion for a disturbance, two Jacobite officers were placed under arrest, and a troop of horse was quartered in the city. These events gave rise to the following couplets :

A.D. 1715.

> (Oxford) The King observing with judicious eyes,
> The state of both his Universities,
> To one he sends a regiment ; for why ?
> That *learned* body wanted *loyalty*.
> To th' other books he gave, as well discerning
> How much that *loyal* body wanted *learning*.

> (Sir Wm. Browne The King to Oxford sent his troop of horse :
> for Cambridge) For Tories own no *argument* but *force*.
> With equal care to Cambridge books he sent :
> For Whigs allow no *force* but *argument*.

Modern politics. When we come to modern politics, the parts are played on the political stage at Westminster.

In the radical matter of parliamentary reform, the first step was made by one of Cambridge's great sons, the younger Pitt, fifty years before a Whig ministry led by Earl Grey, another Cantabrigian, laid the Reform Bill on the table of the House. The claims of America to self government and freedom from taxation were upheld by both the Pitts, by Fox and by Burke, and

268

opposed by Samuel Johnson. The Whigs, as we know, were, as a whole, of Johnson's mind in the matter.

Cambridge opposed the Manchester school ot Liberalism—and Catholic emancipation, Free-trade, Reform bills, and Home Rule for Ireland were all measures which received no support from the Whig-Conservative university.

⁊ Philanthropy seems to be as far removed from the academic purview as art or practical politics : none of the great humanitarian movements which dignified the xix century took their rise in Cambridge ; but Clarkson and Wilberforce were Cambridge men, and Grey A.D. 1807-34. abolished slavery itself in 1834.

Religious movements. The Lollards. In the century succeeding that which saw the historical birth of our two national universities, the first breath of the early renascence was wafted to our shores: but that dual aspect of the later movement which haunted and shaped its whole course in England had been presaged in a remarkable way, and in Wyclif Oxford gave a fore-runner of the religious renascence a hundred years before the advent of the humanistic. Even when Henry IV. ascended the throne, Ralph Spalding, a Carmelite friar, was the only person of note at Cambridge suspected of Lollardry ; and when Archbishop Arundel A.D. 1401. set himself to crush Wyclif's movement at the two universities, the Cambridge harvest was of the poorest.

The Reformation. But with the blaze of the renascence the reform movement passed from Oxford to Cambridge. Great national movements, as we have

UNIVERSITY CHURCH OF GREAT
ST. MARY

The original church dates back at least to the thir-
teenth century and was partially rebuilt in 1351. The
present edifice is Perpendicular Gothic, and was begun
in 1478 and not completely finished until 1608. It
is the largest Parish Church in Cambridge, and the
University sermons are preached in it.

seen, are seldom the consequence of an opinion of the Schools. The struggles of the barons, the parliamentary wars, the restoration, the revolution which placed William and Mary on the throne, were not prepared in any university. But there is one exception—and the prime part in that reawakening of the human mind which issued in the English Reformation, must be assigned to the university of Cambridge. Here was laid the intellectual and historical basis of the reformed religion, and Cambridge produced the men and the minds which created the ecclesiastical order, the liturgy, and the service books deemed suitable to the reformed faith. The stones of Cambridge are indeed a monument to the academic and intellectual form of Protestantism, as the cathedral at Orvieto is a monument to the crudest form of eucharistic doctrine.

The end of the xv century found Cambridge very happily situated. It met the dawn of the religious awakening with a galaxy of men representing the noblest spirit of the time : Fisher, Fox, Thomas Langton, Alcock, Rotherham, even Lady Margaret herself and Erasmus, belonged to Cambridge in a sense which did not apply to Colet and More at Oxford. They constitute a group of Cambridge 'reformers before the Reformation' who were eager patrons of the New Learning ; and the epoch was marked there by the rise of important college foundations. As a result, the university benefited to an extraordinary degree by gifts of religious lands made not by the hand of the despoiler but by the friends of the old faith. Peterhouse had itself been one of the earliest known instances of the conversion of religious property to secular purposes ;[1] but in the xv and early xvi century the instances crowd upon us. Henry VI. bestowed on King's College and on God's House land from the alienated priories ; Alcock obtained from the Pope the dissolution of the Benedictine nunnery which he converted into Jesus College ; Lady Margaret endowed Christ's College with abbey lands ; her stepson the Bishop of Ely dissolved the Canons' House of S. John's bestowing its property upon the new S. John's College ; and Mary gave monastic property to Trinity.

But the hopes raised in England by the spirit of catholic reform were defeated : and it is again to Cambridge that we must look for the next group of men in the march of events—Tyndale, Cranmer, and Latimer all drew their inspiration from Cambridge.

The divorce of Catherine. Closely allied to the movement for reform was the question of the divorce, and Cranmer, less scrupulous than Wolsey, was the first to suggest a legal solution in the king's favour. The Church and the universities were invited to emit a (favourable) judgment on the point ; and as a result of the tactics to this end the junior leaders at Oxford pronounced in its favour, while the opinion elicited from Cambridge really left the matter where it was before. The university declared that Henry's marriage with his brother's wife was illegal if the previous union had been consummated, but no answer was given to

[1] See ii. p. 57, the dissolution of the friars of the Sack.

271

the second question—whether the pope possessed the dispensing power. This was no answer at all, and undermined neither the king's position nor the pope's.

Lutheranism. Meanwhile, at the Austinfriars, a Lutheran movement had sprung up. Here, as elsewhere, the community to which Luther himself belonged led the way in the Protestant revolt. Barnes, the Augustinian prior, was the centre of a group of reformers who met at the White Horse inn ; and Miles Coverdale, one of his friars, learnt his reforming principles at the Cambridge friary. The meetings at the White Horse were to have consequences which affected the other university. Clerke Cox and Taverner were to form part of the little group of Cambridge scholars who took possession, at Wolsey's bidding, of Cardinal College, and to provoke the cry of the warden of Wykeham's house : "We were clear without blot or suspicion till they came !" The famous "Oxford Brethren" were the Cambridge nucleus of the Reform in the sister city.

The English bible and service books. The travail of the times, indeed, passed through a series of men who came from the one university—the laboratory of the Reformation was at Cambridge. The English Bible comes from

A.D. 1524-68. its hands : Tyndale was the earliest worker, and Coverdale produced the first complete English bible in 1535-6. "Cranmer's bible" appeared in 1540 ; "Matthew's" bible (1537) was the work of the Cambridge martyr John Rogers who had also assisted Tyndale. Amongst the latter's assistants had been

Cambridge Men

Roy, a Cambridge Franciscan, and Scory, a Cambridge Dominican.[1] The "Bishop's bible" was published under the auspices of the Cambridge primate, Parker; and other scholars associated in the work of translation were Clerke and Dillingham of Christ's, Layfield, Harison, and Dakins of Trinity, Sir Thomas Smith, and Bishops Andrewes and Heath.[2] Erasmus' New Testament had appeared under the auspices of Warham, and of three Cambridge men, Fisher, Fox, and Tunstall.[3]

The service books owe as much to the one university: it is the 'Cambridge mind' which sets its seal on these formularies. The Cambridge scholars were the best prepared men: Cranmer knew more about liturgies than any one among the reformers; no one but Andrewes was the equal of the catholic divines in patristic knowledge. The prayer book as it stands is in the main Cranmer's work; Cox and Grindal were on the Windsor Commission which compiled the Communion service in the first Prayer-book of 1549. Nine years later Elizabeth entrusted the revision of Edward VI.'s 1552 Prayer-book to Parker, and Cox and Sir Thomas Smith were among the revisers. In the final revision

[1] Scory, Bishop of Hereford, had been given preferment by Cranmer on the dissolution of the Dominicans; he was put into the see of the deprived Catholic bishop Day of Chichester, a King's man, and was one of Parker's consecrators. In 1554 he renounced his wife and did penance before Bonner. The other Day of King's, Bishop of Winchester and brother of the Catholic prelate, was an ardent reformer.

[2] Heath of Clare College was successively Bishop of Rochester and Worcester, and Primate of York.

[3] Cuthbert Tunstall, who had come to King's Hall from Oxford, and afterwards studied at Padua, was himself one of the translators of the 1540 bible.

Cambridge

of 1660 Cosin rendered great services; and even when the still-born attempt was made to revise the liturgy in the reign of William and Mary, the task was once more assigned to Cambridge men, Tenison, and Patrick who was set to mutilate the collects.

The Articles of Religion in their original form and number were the work of Cranmer, their reduction to Thirty-nine was the work of another Cambridge primate, Parker.[1] Whitgift drew up for Elizabeth the famous "Lambeth Articles"; and when the vexed subject of the Athanasian creed agitated the ecclesiastical commission of 1689 as it is agitating the national Church now—then, as now, when Cambridge heads of houses, professors of divinity, and deans and tutors of colleges have signed a declaration in favour of its excision from the public services, two Cambridge men protested—the one against its retention, the other against its unqualified damnatory clauses.[2] Dryden had already made a similar protest.

Long however before the reformers had a free hand, Burleigh in his retirement in Lincolnshire had jotted down the names of the eight learned men most fit to carry out the Reform and to settle its formularies when a Protestant queen should succeed. Seven of these men hailed from Cambridge.[3]

---

[1] See ii. p. 84. Corpus Christi College.

[2] Tillotson and Stillingfleet, the most prominent churchmen in the reign of James II.

[3] They were Matthew Parker of Corpus, Cox of King's, Grindal of Pembroke, Bill and Pilkington of S. John's, May and Sir Thomas Smith of Queens', and David Whitehead.

Cambridge Men

It was not only in what concerned scholarship that the travail of the Reformation belonged to Cambridge. It gave, in the person of Fisher, the only member of the episcopal bench who died for denying the royal supremacy. Early in the reign of Henry VIII. the first group of Cambridge Lutherans gave other martyrs : Bilney, like Barnes, had carried his faggot and recanted Lutheran opinions before Wolsey, but afterwards took new courage and went to the stake for them. The cause left smouldering by the death of Barnes, Bilney, and George Stafford (a fellow of Pembroke) was rekindled by Latimer. Henry himself had examined another Cambridge reformer, John Nicholson ("Lambert") who denied the corporal presence in the eucharist, and that royal and rigid sacramentarian had condemned him. "Pleasant Taylor" "making himself merry with the stake" was another Cantabrigian.[1] The first man to die for his faith when Mary's reign opened was Rogers of Pembroke[2] ; and "the hardiest" of the Marian Martyrs was another Cambridge man, Bradford. As she had nurtured the only martyr-bishop on the Catholic side, so Cambridge nurtured the Protestant group of prelates who died at the stake : Cranmer, Ridley, and Latimer are three Cambridge martyrs whose only title to be known as "the Oxford martyrs" is that Oxford burnt them. It

[1] Rowland Taylor of Christ's College, a Suffolk rector, suffered in 1535. Latimer who had argued on the Catholic side at the university, was persuaded to Protestantism by Bilney. With Bilney Thomas M'Arthur, a fellow of S. John's and then Principal of S. Mary's Hostel, recanted.

[2] Rogers b. 1509 at Birmingham. Burned at Smithfield Feb. 1555.

must not be forgotten, also, that one of the fifteen heroic London Carthusians, martyred at Tyburn in 1535, was William Exmew of Christ's.

The death of Fisher, chancellor of the university, was followed by a wholesale ejection of the professors of the ancient learning, and the man who died for his denial of that 'anglican solecism' the royal supremacy was immediately succeeded by the man who first suggested it to Henry—Thomas Cromwell.[1]

The Puritan. The next religious movement in the country was the Puritan, against which we know that Elizabeth fought as lustily as Henry had combated Lutheranism. Despite the fact that there were Puritan nuclei, as there had earlier been Lutheran nuclei, at Cambridge, Puritanism was eventually imposed on the university only by the same violent means as had banished the old religion—wholesale ejections. The Anglican heads of colleges were turned out, under Oliver, to be replaced by Puritan Masters, in precisely the same way as Thomas Cromwell had replaced the Catholics by men who accepted the royal supremacy.

Early Presby- One of these early nuclei of Puritanism terianism. was fomented by Thomas Cartwright, and Thomas Aldrich, Master of Corpus, became the leader of the Cambridge Puritans. Cartwright was one of the first Presbyterians, and canvassed the English counties in the interest of that form of Church govern-

[1] It was Cromwell who, as chancellor, began to wean the university from the pope ; and he removed its papal script—bulls, briefs, and dispensations—which was not returned till such time as he judged the substitution of the king for the pope to be complete.

ment. The movement was checked by Elizabeth, and Cartwright was driven from his professorship. Later on the Puritan Tuckney was Regius professor of Divinity as Cartwright had been Margaret Professor. Presbyterianism was not congenial to the university : Hall Bishop of Norwich, the satirist who was a contemporary of Shakespeare, and Archbishop Williams the life-long opponent of Laud, both went to the Tower for protesting against the acts of the Long Parliament, and Hall though he was a noted ' low-churchman ' remonstrated against the proposed abolition of episcopacy. Among still more eminent Cantabrigians, Jeremy Taylor was as much opposed to its abolition as Milton favoured it : but when, in 1643-4, the Westminster Assembly met, Wallis the Cambridge scientist acted as its secretary, the Oxonian Selden being another of the thirty laymen present at its deliberations.

The Brownists or Independents. Milton had no liking for the Westminster Assembly ; with Cromwell he sympathised with the rising Independent Congregations who took their principles from the Brownists of Elizabeth's time. Of the five movements which were still to sweep over the face of religious England, two originated in Cambridge. How inept the university is to the creation of such schools of thought, how alien to its genius such creations are, may be gauged by the comparatively puny character of these two movements. The Brownists and the Cambridge Platonists do not suggest a world set ablaze ; but though ineffective as

277

Cambridge

schools both of them represented far-reaching principles, and have left a lasting impression on Anglo-Saxon religion. It is easy to show this in the case of the Brownists : for Browne was the spiritual father of the Pilgrim Fathers, of the men who colonised a continent to obtain space to form those free Church communities which many Englishmen regarded as the logical completion of the principles of the Reformation. The English refugees at Amsterdam were disciples and adherents of Robert Browne, and it was a little company A.D. 1620. of Brownists which eventually set out in two ships for the new world, one of which—the " Mayflower "— reached what is now the State of Massachusetts. The Brownists were the first party of separatists from the newly established Church in England, and the old and new worlds recognise in them the true spiritual forbears of all Independent and Congregational Churches; whose ecclesiastical polity requires that each congregation should suffice to itself, be complete in itself.

The Latitudinarians. In the next century arose the liberal church movement of Hales, Chillingworth, and Jeremy Taylor. Falkland, the great layman who inspired it, had been educated at Dublin university, but was entered for S. John's College as early as 1621, and claimed in after life, in a letter to the then Master, to have been a member of that society. Taylor was a Cambridge man who had removed to Oxford ; Hales and Chillingworth were both distinguished Oxford scholars. The distinction made by Taylor and Chillingworth between essential and non-essential articles of

278

Cambridge Men

belief was very far ahead of the theoretical and practical narrowness of the German Protestantism around them. The problem at issue was stated by Stillingfleet,[1] " fresh from the generous intellectual life of Cambridge," on the eve of the Restoration : Does there exist, in regard to Church government, any such *jus divinum* as would prevent men, under the stress of circumstances, learning from each other, and arriving at unity ? The doctrine of *accommodation* stated in his *Eirenicum*, though it was not in advance of the earlier speculation of Ussher, Chillingworth, Taylor, and Hales, anticipated later developments of theological speculation with which we are all familiar.

Deism. The xvii and xviii centuries saw the rise and progress of Deism. Lord Herbert of Cherbury[2] " the father of deism " was educated at Oxford ; the great opponent of his doctrines was the Cambridge philosopher Samuel Clarke. Nevertheless deism was not a university movement. Bolingbroke, Morgan, and Blount (1654-93) were at no university ; Shaftesbury (b. 1621) and Tindal had been at Oxford ; Woolston and Anthony Collins (b. 1676) had been at Cambridge ; and Toland after a residence at three other universities, retired to Oxford. Conyers Middleton, librarian of Trinity, was another opponent of the deists. Like unitarianism, deism undoubtedly responds to a certain temper of English religious speculation and senti-

[1]. Falkland, *b.* 1610. Chillingworth born and educated in Oxford. Taylor born and educated in Cambridge. Stillingfleet, *b.* 1635, fellow of S. John's, bishop of Worcester. [2] *ob.* 1648.

ment, but apparently to no very wide-spread temper ; and the success of English deism was consummated not here but on the continent.

The Evangelical movement. The evangelical movement is entirely associated with the names of John and Charles Wesley and Whitfield—with a group of Oxford men. There was no principle of ecclesiastical polity and none of philosophy underlying it : it was a fervent religious revival begun within the Church of England and ending outside it, and as such the great influence it has exerted would appear to have presented few attractions for the Cambridge mind.

The Tractarian movement, and the earlier Cambridge movement. The 'Tractarian movement' which also arose as a renewal of religious life in the Church of England, was, like Wesleyanism, due exclusively to Oxford men. A still earlier 'High Church' movement—a ritualistic movement before 'Tractarianism'—had however found its home in Cambridge under the auspices of Andrewes, Wren, and Cosin. These three men, later bishops of Winchester, Ely, and Durham respectively, established a type of Reformed churchmanship not only more tolerant and scholarly than Laud's but one which was more genuinely a university movement ; for it was indigenous—its patrons were all heads of Cambridge houses—and it did not meet, as did Laud's efforts at Oxford, with dislike and rejection at the university. Two hundred years passed before the Tractarian movement at Oxford reproduced its likeness and tendered it to Englishmen as the *vera effigies* of the Church of

Cambridge Men

England.[1] The influence on religion of Charles Simeon
and other Cambridge men in ante-Tractarian days
should also be remembered; neither should it be
forgotten that the liberal anti-Calvinistic churchmanship
of Peter Baro and Overall was first taught by Cambridge
men.

The age of
Elizabeth and the
New Learning. The pre-eminence of Cambridge during
the age of Elizabeth would be in itself
sufficient proof of its relation to the New
Learning—to the revival of letters and of Greek, the
rise of experimental science, and the theological speculations of the century.   Round Elizabeth there gathered
from the first to the last days of her reign a brilliant
group of men—scholars, poets, tutors, prelates, lawyers,
statesmen, philosophers, travellers, explorers.   Every
name we chance upon, every man who influenced the
court, the letters, the science of the day, hails from
Cambridge.   The tutors of Henry VII., Henry VIII.,
Edward VI., Mary, and Elizabeth had all been
Cambridge men, and Cambridge men were appointed
as their physicians and chaplains.   Names like those of
Skelton, Fisher, Erasmus, Croke, Tyndale, Ascham,
Sir Thomas Smith, and Cheke ; of Spenser, Gabriel
Harvey, Marlowe, and Ben Jonson ; of Bacon, Gilbert,
Harvey and Caius, conjure up a picture of the scholar-
ship of the age, of the new stir in thought, letters,
and learning.   Let us look at two other well-
defined groups of Elizabethans—the statesmen and the

[1] Cf. Peterhouse pp. 58-9, and Emmanuel p. 145. For religion in
Cambridge at the present day, see iv. pp. 246-7.

Cambridge

churchmen. The two Cecils, Walsingham, Haddon and Fletcher (Masters of the Requests), Bacon, Knollys, Sussex, Smith, and Mildmay were all Cambridge men ; and so were all Elizabeth's great prelates : Lancelot Andrewes, her chaplain, and dean of Westminster, and the primates Parker, Grindal, and Whitgift : and they represented every party in the country. Fulke Greville the most fortunate of the Queen's favourites, Sir John Harrington her godson, and Essex, were also Cambridge men. Among the gallant little company of the first adventurers one only is known to have studied at a university, and he was at Cambridge : Sir Thomas Gresham conducted the expedition fitted out by Raleigh which resulted in the discovery of Virginia—named after the virgin queen—and in the introduction of the tobacco leaf. Cavendish, a Corpus man, brought to England the tobacco called after him. Clifford, third earl of Cumberland, a Trinity man, was one of the early privateers and navigators ; and young Roger Manners, of Queens' and Corpus, went the "Islands Voyage" with Robert Devereux who had studied at Trinity. Even Drake, who was at no university, is known as a Cambridge benefactor, and was as we have seen a large subscriber to the chapel of Corpus Christi College.

In the last place the New Learning of the Tudor age was carried from Cambridge to the sister university. It was so well understood that Cambridge represented this new learning that Wolsey went there for the men who, by colonising Cardinal College, were to introduce it at Oxford ; and Fox of Pembroke founded a belated *Corpus Christi College* with the express purpose of erecting a monument in Oxford to the Renaissance.

The schoolmasters. The last half of the xv century brought with it the great schoolmasters. Mulcaster of Eton and King's was master of Merchant-Taylors' on its foundation ; Colet's school, S. Paul's, sent to Cambridge for its second head, and five of its first eight head masters were Cambridge and King's men. King's College has supplied a large proportion of the Provosts and head masters of Eton, many of the famous masters of Harrow, and a King's man counts as the creator of Rugby " as it now is." Ascham's " Schoolmaster " was epoch-making, and his connexion with his university was much closer than William Lily's with Oxford.

The Royal Society A.D. 1660-62. The brilliant epoch of Elizabeth spent, intellectual life smouldered during the reigns of the first two Stuarts and the Protectorate, to be renewed and rekindled not by fresh literary activity but by the inquisitive temper which invaded the nation as it emerged, with the Restoration, from civil conflict and the slough of doctrinal wrangling. This inquisitiveness took shape in the institution of the Royal Society. The *foyer* of the Royal Society was London, although some of its most distinguished members migrated later with Wilkins to Oxford. Of the eminent men who formed the first Royal Society Wallis, Wilkins, Foster, Jonathan Goddard, Sir William Ball, Lawrence Rooke,

Cambridge

Sir William Petty, Ward the mathematician, Ray, Woodward the mineralogist, Flamsteed, Sloane, Boyle, Halley, Chief-Justice Hale, Lord Keeper Guilford, with Sprat the Bishop of Rochester (its historian), Cowley and Dryden (its poets), and Sir Robert Moray —Wallis, Foster, Rooke, Ray, Woodward, Flamsteed, Guilford, Cowley, and Dryden, were Cantabrigians. Four of the most prominent, Ward, Boyle, Sloane and Ball, were at no university; Goddard went from Oxford to Cambridge where he graduated; Petty though he became Professor of Anatomy at Oxford was educated at foreign universities; Moray was at S. Andrews and Paris; Wilkins, Halley, Hale, and Sprat were at Oxford. Among the first fellows there came from Oxford Christopher Wren, John Evelyn, Hook of the microscope, Sydenham : More the Platonist, Sir William Temple, Willughby the ornithologist, and Grew, came from Cambridge. Two more of Charles's courtiers joined Moray, Kenelm Digby from Oxford, and Villiers Duke of Buckingham from Cambridge.

The Cambridge Platonists. The next movement in English thought was both religious and philosophical. When Latitudinarianism ceased to be ecclesiastical it passed from Oxford and became identified with the sister university.[1] Here it was handled by a group of

---

[1] Burnet, the historian of the movement, writes : "They loved the constitution of the church, and the liturgy, and could well live under them ; but they did not think it unlawful to live under another form. . . They continued to keep a good correspondence with those who differed from them in opinion, and allowed a great freedom both in

284

men, from the two colleges Emmanuel and Christ's, so as to embrace a moral and political philosophy, to which the term *Platonist* is only aptly ascribed if it be meant to stand for the "mass of transcendental thought"; that traditional Platonism of the speculative schools which had succeeded one another down the centuries, always at war with nominalism and constantly asserting the transcendent character of moral ideas and the reality of free will. Hobbism came to assail this position; for Hobbes applied Bacon's method to the moral and social order, and found the basis for them in certain obvious facts of human nature. The spirit of enquiry set afoot by the Cambridge Platonists was none the less real because it was opposed to such tenets. They set themselves, in fact, to enquire whether authority and tradition should guide men in matters of faith. They asserted that reason was supreme, and they sought to place Christianity again—to place Protestantism for the first time—under the protection of that noble spiritual idealism which the great thinkers of the early Church had chosen for the new faith; to penetrate Christianity with philosophy.[1]

The early Latitudinarianism was merely an essay in liberal ecclesiastical polity. The new movement was something more, something finer. Cambridge now

philosophy and in divinity; from whence they were called men of latitude. And upon this, men of narrower thoughts and fiercer tempers fastened upon them the name of Latitudinarians."

[1] "Within the bosom of Protestantism they kindled for the first time the love of this nobler speculation." (*Tulloch, vol. 1. p. 24.*)

Cambridge

gathered up the floating philosophical speculation which existed in the xvii century side by side with the intense absorption in dogmatic wranglings, the rapid growth of sects—of Anabaptists, Antinomians, anti-Trinitarians, Arians. "A kind of moral divinity," as Whichcote's tutor, the Puritan Tuckney, cried out in alarm, was to be substituted for theological polemic. The movement indeed was due to the combination of a higher spirituality than the Puritan with the new spirit of bold enquiry in moral and speculative fields[1]—it constituted a Cambridge reaction against the trammels of Puritanism. It was the first of all English religious movements (not excepting Wycliffism) to ally a growth of the religious sentiment with the demand for a wide and liberal theoretical basis to theology. At the head of this theological movement stands Benjamin Whichcote (b. 1609) tutor of Emmanuel, who numbered among his pupils Wallis, Smith, and Culverwell, and who was afterwards Provost of King's. Ralph Cudworth (b. in Somersetshire 1617) is perhaps the central figure : he is great as a moral philosopher, great in his impartial statement of an opponent's case, great even in his freedom from the party and political heat which con-

[1] Cf. Tulloch, *Rational Theology in England in the xvii century* (1872) vol. 2. p. 13, to whose able and interesting account of the movement I am very much indebted. "They sought," writes Tulloch, "to confirm the union of philosophy and religion on the indestructible basis of reason and the essential elements of our higher humanity" : and again : "It is the glory of the Cambridge divines that they welcomed this new spirit of speculation " and "gave it frank entertainment in their halls of learning." "Their liberalism takes a higher flight" than that of Hales and Chillingworth.

sumed his contemporaries.[1] In John Smith (*b.* 1616) of Emmanuel[2] the movement becomes more speculative, his was the finest and most richly stored mind, and his "Select Discourses" perhaps mark the culminating point of the Cambridge school. There remains Henry More (*b.* 1614) the better known name, of Christ's College, the exponent of Descartes, the ardent follower of Plato, from whom he learnt "that something better and higher than the knowledge of human things constitutes the supreme happiness of man." His *Enchiridion ethicum* and *Enchiridion metaphysicum* were the text books of the school.

This academic group forms, as Tulloch points out, not only "one of the most characteristic groups in the history of religious and philosophical thought in England," but one of the most homogeneous. Whichcote's aphorism "There is nothing more unnatural to religion than contentions about it" sums an epoch in religious thought. Questions of Church order and Church policy were left aside, to philosophise ; the clash of ecclesiastical parties ceased to trouble, and an academic enquiry into the relation of philosophy to religion takes its place. Neither Puritan nor Presbyterian had brought any such liberating attitude towards theology, for which indeed the early Protestantism cared not one jot, but which has never entirely died out of England since the speculations of the Cambridge

---

[1] His *True Intellectual System of the Universe* was published in 1678.

[2] Afterwards fellow of Queens', Hebrew lecturer and Greek praelector.

Cambridge

Platonists.[1]   The Englishman—fed with the crude dogmatism of Luther, the arid ecclesiasticism of Laud, the dull fancy of the Puritan, and the intolerance of all three—now for the first time was called dispassionately to consider the claims of the philosophical reason, the eternal distinction between essential and non-essential —a distinction anathema to the ordinary Protestant— fundamental and non-fundamental, between the reality and the figure ; to the claims, in fine, of those onto- logical verities on which belief in the revealed verities ultimately depends.   A "rational Christian eclecticism" was for the first time presented to Protestants, and in so far anticipated the principle upon which the problems of the present day attend for solution.   The values to be assigned to the notions of " orthodoxy," of dogma— who around them had ever thought of such things before !   At Oxford it has always been a question of form, of Church order ; but at Cambridge a question of substance, an enquiry into the criteria of truth, the credentials of theories.

Nevertheless, the Cambridge Platonists were in- effective.   Their philosophy lacked a touchstone, concentration ; and they allied its fate to a ridiculous bibliology.   For More, who taught at the university which gave us our school of biblical critics—Erasmus, Colenso, Westcott, Lightfoot, Hort—the wisdom of the Hebrew had been transmitted to Pythagoras, and

---

[1] Whichcote's moral and philosophical style of preaching now replaced " that doctrinal style which Puritans have curiously always considered to be more identical with the simplicity of Scriptural truth."   Tulloch.

from Pythagoras to Plato, who thus becomes the heir of divine (the Hebrew) philosophy. Such a doctrine was a serious embarrassment to a cause in the age of Hobbes ; it meant that the rational and critical *criteria* of the day went unutilised, and no doctrine can withstand such a charge. There was, too, a certain lack of the spirit of adventure, that gallant spirit which is not out of place even in philosophy, and of the courage which belongs to enthusiasm. The appeal to reason made by Hooker had debouched as Latitudinarianism ; Laud and George Herbert had both opposed it ; but Puritan England was stronger than both and would have none of either. The Platonists stood between them—called upon the Laudian to modify his conception of authority, upon the Puritan to admit the claims of reason, enriched Latitudinism with a philosophy. They were not listened to. None the less the *via media* they offered has penetrated English thought. The Englishman favours reason but is no Hobbist, he must have his God behind the machine ; he likes the supremacy of reason with a nebulous Plato behind it—not the real Plato, but a Plato to hurl as a weapon in the face of the materialist, without understanding too much about it. The 'Cambridge mind' hit on a middle term, a resting place for speculation and for faith, which suits the Englishman in the long run better than either Laud or Hobbes. In Cudworth we have that mind typified—that union of toleration with half lights which triumphs in England. Very bold speculation is not the English-

ADDENBROKE'S HOSPITAL IN
TRUMPINGTON STREET

This building, as we now see it, was remodelled by Sir
M. Digby Wyatt 1864-65.

man's *forte*. His intellect in such *gesta* is not clear-cut, and his practical sense is always compatible with un-turned-out-corners of mysticism, prejudices, reverences false and true—all the haziness made by those useful half lights loved by a people who do not like to be mystified, but do not wish to be too much enlightened.

And if we ask why Cambridge should be Platonist, the answer is because it always resisted the Aristotelianism of the Schools. Reaction against scholasticism had brought Plato to Florence in the xv century, it made Plato at home in Cambridge in the xviith. We have called Cambridge the laboratory of the Reformation ; there too, we see, was made the first attempt to reconcile Protestantism with philosophy : in undoing the servitude of the latter to religion, which had been the mark of the middle ages, the Cambridge Platonists did away with medievalism, joined hands, behind its back, with that Neo-Platonism of the Alexandrine schools which had influenced the early Church, defied, of course, scholasticism, and prepared the place for our modern moral sciences tripos.

Modern science. We have already seen that Cambridge is the representative in England of the scientific movement which has changed the face of the modern world. It may perhaps be pretended that the stages of its development in Europe have been marked by the great men emanating from this one university. The names of Bacon, Gilbert, Harvey, Flamsteed, Newton, Darwin, are signposts of the direction which science was to take and landmarks of its achievements.

Cambridge Men

William Gilbert the discoverer of terrestrial magnetism and of the affinity of magnetic and electric action, was praised by Galileo, while Erasmus called him "great to a degree which is enviable." Flamsteed began that series of observations which initiated modern astronomy, Horrox came still earlier, and they have been followed by such Cantabrigians as Newton, Nevil Maskelyne, Herschell, Airy and Adams. Newton and Darwin are two of the greatest names in the history of the physical and physiological sciences—they stand out as creators of epochs in the march of human knowledge : on Newton's statue in Trinity chapel are inscribed the words *qui genus humanum ingenio superavit*—of whom else could they be spoken ?— Darwin has revolutionised our thoughts in spheres far removed from those directly affected by his great hypothesis.

When we turn to consider the relation of these distinguished sons to the university which bred them, it is interesting to find how close this has always been. From the first makers of Cambridge to the last, from its earliest distinguished sons to its latest, the individual's relation to the university has been a close one and the same names come down the centuries and create a homogeneity in Cambridge history which has certainly not received its due meed of recognition. A group of persons — of families — is already assembled in this remote eastern corner of England in the xiii and xiv centuries which contains the elements of our university history : Stantons, de Burghs, Walsinghams,

Cambridge

Beauforts, Clares, Greys, Pembrokes are there — and Gaunt and Mortimer the roots of Lancaster and York. If we had looked in upon the town earlier still, in the xi and xii centuries, we should have found Picot—the ancestor of the Pigotts whose name is recorded in Abingdon Pigotts hard by—who succeeded to the honours of Hereward the Wake[1] and who founded the church dedicated to the Norman saint Giles; Peverel who brought the Austin canons to Cambridge, Clare, de Burgh, Fitz-Eustace (or Dunning) and, by the side of these companions of the Conqueror, the sons of the soil — the Frosts and Lightfoots. In the xiii century there were the Dunnings assisting the Merton scholars to establish themselves, Mortimer endowing the Carmelites, the Veres[2] establishing the Dominicans, de Burghs, Walsinghams, Walpoles, and Bassetts,[3] the Greys, and Manfields,[4] and "Cecil at the Castle"—all of whom appear in Edward I.'s Hundred Rolls.

The name of Clare figures on every page of the history of the Plantagenets. The first Gilbert de Clare had been employed to terrorise the East Anglians who held out against William; another Gilbert is at the head of the barons, his son is the guardian of Magna

---

[1] The Conqueror gave him the barony of Bourne in the fen.

[2] The de Vere of Matilda's time had been her faithful adherent; Cambridgeshire was one of the ten English counties in which the Veres held lands, and they were the benefactors of the Cambridge Dominicans.

[3] See also i. pp. 19, 44, ii. p. 110 *n.* and p. 296.

[4] Manfield was nephew to Castle-Bernard another Cambridge landowner.

Cambridge Men

Charta, and *his* granddaughter founded Clare College. She also built the Greyfriars house at Walsingham in 1346, was, with her kinsmen the Monthermers a great benefactor to the first Augustinian priory founded a hundred years earlier at Stoke Clare [1] and found time A.D. 1248. to send timber from her estates towards the building of the king's Hall, as Queen Elizabeth sent a similar gift just two hundred years afterwards to the king's college of Trinity. The Clares had received 95 lordships in Suffolk, which formed "the honour of Clare," and they gave their name to the county in Ireland. Through Ralph de Monthermer the founders of Clare and Pembroke were allied, for he was Elizabeth de Clare's stepfather, and afterwards brother-in-law to Aymer de Valence (see Tables I, II).

We first hear of the de Burghs in 1198 when A.D. 1198. Thomas, brother to Hubert the king's chamberlain, became guardian to a Bury ward. In 1225 a de Burgh A.D. 1225. was bishop of Ely, and a hundred years later John de Burgh the 4th earl of Connaught and 2nd earl of Ulster married with Elizabeth de Clare. Towards the end of the xiv century another de Burgh, author A.D. 1385 of the "*Pupilla oculi*," was chancellor of the university, and it is he who purchased the land of S. Margaret's hostel in 1368.

The connexion of the Mortimers with Cambridge also dates from the xiii century : Guy de Mortimer A.D. 1291.

---

[1] Dugdale, *Monasticon* p. 1600. Stoke in the deanery of Clare was within the liberty of S. Edmund. The Augustinian hermits, as we have seen, came to Cambridge about the same time.

Cambridge

figures in the Cambridge Hundred Rolls as the bene-factor of the Carmelite friars, and sixty years later Thomas, son of Sir Constantine de Mortimer, ceded land for King's Hall.

The name of Walsingham occurs as that of a prior of Ely in 1353. The Walsinghams held two manors

A.D. 1344. in Suffolk, besides land in Cambridge part of which was sold to the king for the site of King's Hall.

A.D. 1290-1299. There was a Ralph Walpole bishop of Ely, and subse-quently of Norwich in the time of Edward I., who gave a messuage to Peterhouse as early as 1290. The Wal-poles continued to figure on the roll of this college till in the xvi century the Walpole of that day fled with the Jesuit Parsons to Spain after the trial of Campian ; he became vice-rector at Valladolid but was eventually martyred at York five years before the close of the century. Robert and Horace Walpole continued the Cambridge traditions of their family.

With the xiv century other names appear : the Scropes, Gonvilles, Stantons,[1] the families of Cambridge and of Croyland, Haddon,[2] Zouche,[3] and Cavendish, and last but not least Valence, and the house of Gaunt and Beaufort.

The connexion of the Scropes with Cambridge

---

[1] Stanton is a Cambridge place-name ; other names derived from places in the district (besides of course 'Cambridge' and 'Croyland') being Walsingham, Walpole, Gaunt, Balsham, Bourne, Chatteris, Haddon, Milton, Newton, Caxton, Drayton, Brandon, Connington, Shelford ; and Chancellor Haselfield (1300, 1307) probably took his name from Haslyngfield. Long Stanton was the seat of the Hattons.

[2] The name appears early in the fen country as that of an abbot of Thorney—xiv c.   [3] Cf. iv. p. 204.

Cambridge Men

probably dates from the earlier half of the xiv century. Scropes, as we have seen, figure among the chancellors of the university in that century, and were allied not only to the Mortimers but to the Gonvilles : when therefore we find the representative of the house of Valence who is also a grandson of Roger Mortimer, and whose son married a descendant of the founder of Clare, engaged in a political intrigue with Gaunt, Scrope, and the Master of Pembroke in 1371, and A.D. 1371. the Scropes[1] Greys and Mortimers conspiring with Richard Earl of Cambridge[1] early in the next century, A.D. 1414. we gain a very definite impression of a Cambridge *coterie*.

> "——Cambridge, Scroop, and Grey, in their dear care,
> And tender preservation of our person"——

are the words which Shakespeare puts into the mouth of Henry V. before his discovery of their treachery.

Shakespeare and Cambridge men. Indeed the historical plays of Shakespeare, from the dawn of our university history in the reign of John to its zenith in that of Henry VIII., place prominently before us our Cambridge protagonists. In "King John" the names of Louis the Dauphin, Chatillon, and de Burgh recall the Cambridge

---

[1] 2nd son of Edmund Langley. His wife was Anne Mortimer greatgranddaughter of Elizabeth de Burgh, Duchess of Clarence ; the son of Hastings, who figures in the earlier conspiracy, married her granddaughter.

Richard's son was earl of Ulster and lord of Clare in right of his mother. The sons of Edw. III.—Clarence, Gaunt, Edmund Langley, and Thomas of Woodstock—were all allied to founders of Cambridge colleges (see Tables I, II, III). Scrope's brother Stephen was chancellor of the university ; see p. 94, 94 *n.*

history of two centuries. Chatillon is here the ambassador of Philip of France who calls upon John to surrender his "borrowed majesty" into Prince Arthur's hands ; and in the next century Marie de Chatillon and Elizabeth de Burgh are building colleges. Sir Stephen Scrope figures in "Richard II." In "Henry IV." Scroop Archbishop of York and Edward Mortimer, and in "Henry V." the Earl of Cambridge, Scroop, and Grey, appear. In "Henry VI.," with Beaufort, Mortimer, Suffolk, Somerset, Buckingham and Stafford, Stanley, Woodville, and Margaret of Anjou —all of whom were to play a part in Cambridge history— we have Bassett of the Lancastrian faction, and Vernon representing the Yorkists. The *dramatis personae* of this play thus include the *dramatis personae* of King's and Queens' Colleges, of Haddon Hall, of Magdalene, and Christ's. In "Richard III." Rotherham of York appears, with many others who belong to Cambridge in the xv century ; while in "Henry VIII." even Dr. Butts of Gonville, Henry's physician, is not omitted.

xv c.　　In the xv century we have some new names. Zouche is there still, and Scrope, and Bassett, and Beaufort, but there are also Langton, Stafford, Pole, xvi c.　Brandon, Stanley, and Babington. In the xvi century Stanley, Brandon, Stafford, Sidney, Audley, Bacon and Cecil, are all prominent names.

These various groups are not independent. The annexed pedigrees will show us that the Clares, Mortimers, de Burghs, Audleys, and Staffords had intermarried : that Valence and Chatillon, Mortimer,

Cambridge Men

Grey, and Hastings, formed one family ; that the Beauforts, through John of Gaunt, joined the house of Edward III. to the house of Tudor, and were allied to the Staffords, Nevilles, and Stanleys ; that the Scropes were allied to the Mortimers, the Staffords again to the family of Chatillon and to the Woodvilles : the Sidneys to the Brandons, the Brandons to the Greys, the Greys to the Woodvilles ;[1] and that the xvi century Audleys intermarried with the Greys as the xiv century Clares had wedded with the Audleys ; that through Mortimer, Stafford, Hastings, and Grey, the founders—Clare, de Burgh, Chatillon, Valence, Beaufort, Stafford, Woodville, Audley, and Sidney —form one clan. Before we proceed with the list of well-known Cambridge names from the xvi century onwards, let us notice in passing that certain titles have always clung to Cambridge, no matter who bore them : such are Pembroke, Huntingdon, Buckingham, Suffolk, Leicester.[2]

---

[1] "In all which time, you, and your husband Grey, were factious for the house of Lancaster." *Richard III.* Act i. scene 3.

[2] Pembroke held by the Clares, Mareschalls, Valence, Hastings. Huntingdon by David of Scotland and Malcolm the Maiden, by Hastings, and Grey. Buckingham by Stafford and Villiers. Suffolk by Pole, Brandon, Grey, and Howard. Leicester passed from the Beaumonts to the de Montforts, from the earls of Lancaster to John of Gaunt, the Dudleys and the Sidneys (p. 42 *n.*).

<pre>
        Henry of Lancaster Earl of Lancaster and Leicester,
                        ob. 1345.

  William de Burgh, last = Matilda = 2ndly Ralph Stafford.
  Earl of Ulster.

                Elizabeth de Burgh = Lionel Duke of Clarence.
</pre>

TABLE I.

PEDIGREE OF CLARE

Gilbert de Clare, ob. 1229 =	Isabella, daughter of William Mareschall,
Earl of Hertford and Gloucester,	Earl of Pembroke in right of his wife
descended from Richard, founder	Isabella de Clare, and granddaughter of
of the House of Clare (whose	Richard de Clare, 2nd Earl of Pembroke,
4th son was abbot of Ely) and	surnamed " Strongbow " (who married
great-grandson of Richard the	a dau. of the Irish prince Dermot).
Fearless, Duke of Normandy.	
The family settled in Wales	
in the xii c. Gilbert (ob. 1148)	
being created Earl of Pembroke	
by Stephen in 1138. Attests,	
with Hubert de Burgh, John's	
charters to the town of Cambridge.	

Richard, ob. 1262 = Matilda de Lacy, dau. of the
Earl of Gloucester and Lord of Earl of Lincoln.
the Honour of Clare. He
and his father were
the acknowledged heads of the
baronage and guardians of
Magna Charta.

Gilbert, 1243-1295 = in 1290 Joan,
Earl of Gloucester, Clare and dau. of Edw. I.
Hertford, called 'the red.' The = 2ndly Ralph de
greatest of the barons in the Monthermer.
reign of Edw. I. Supported de
Montfort till after the battle of
Lewes. Endowed Merton scholars.

Gilbert killed at	Eleanor = Hugh le	Margaret = 1st Piers	Elizabeth Lady of the
Bannockburn June 24	Despenser.	Gaveston.	Honour of Clare, b. at
1314, one of the		= 2nd Hugh	Acre during the crusade
" ordainers."		Audley.	c. 1291-2.
			FOUNDER OF CLARE
			COLLEGE.
			married = 1st John de Burgh
			3rd Earl of Ulster
			and 4th Earl of
			Connaught.
			= 2nd Lord Verdon.
			= 3rd Roger d'Amory.

Margaret = Ralph Earl of Stafford,	William = Matilda, dau. of Henry
ob. 1372.	last Earl of Earl of Lancaster. She
	Ulster. = 2ndly Ralph Stafford.

Elizabeth de Burgh = in 1352 Lionel Duke
Lady of the of Clarence second
Honour of Clare.[1] son and heir of Edw.
III. The title de
Clarentia is taken
from his wife, Lady of the Honour
Philippa de Clarentia = Edmund Mortimer of Clare, and is also recorded in
Earl of March. that of Clareneeux, or Clarence,
king-of-Arms, an heraldic title
Philippa = John Hastings derived from the duke's.
Earl of Pembroke.

The descendant of the Duke and Duchess of Clarence became Edward IV., and the 'honour of Clare' was thenceforth merged in the crown, and now forms part of the duchy of Lancaster.

---

[1] From her, her grandson Mortimer Earl of March derived the title of Earl of Ulster.

TABLE II.

PEDIGREE OF VALENCE

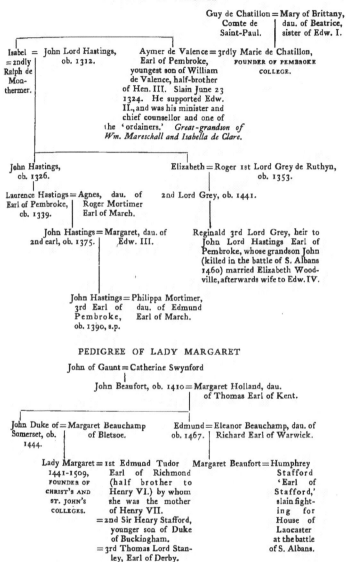

Guy de Chatillon = Mary of Brittany,
Comte de   dau. of Beatrice,
Saint-Paul.   sister of Edw. I.

Isabel = John Lord Hastings,   Aymer de Valence = 3rdly Marie de Chatillon,
= 2ndly   ob. 1312.   Earl of Pembroke,   FOUNDER OF PEMBROKE
Ralph de   youngest son of William   COLLEGE.
Mon-   de Valence, half-brother
thermer.   of Hen. III. Slain June 23
1324. He supported Edw.
II., and was his minister and
chief counsellor and one of
the 'ordainers.' *Great-grandson of*
Wm. Mareschall and Isabella de Clare.

John Hastings,   Elizabeth = Roger 1st Lord Grey de Ruthyn,
ob. 1326.   ob. 1353.

Laurence Hastings = Agnes,   dau. of   2nd Lord Grey, ob. 1441.
Earl of Pembroke,   Roger Mortimer
ob. 1339.   Earl of March.

John Hastings = Margaret, dau. of   Reginald 3rd Lord Grey, heir to
2nd earl, ob. 1375.   Edw. III.   John Lord Hastings Earl of
Pembroke, whose grandson John
(killed in the battle of S. Albans
1460) married Elizabeth Woodville, afterwards wife to Edw. IV.

John Hastings = Philippa Mortimer,
3rd Earl of   dau. of Edmund
Pembroke,   Earl of March.
ob. 1390, s.p.

PEDIGREE OF LADY MARGARET

John of Gaunt = Catherine Swynford

John Beaufort, ob. 1410 = Margaret Holland, dau.
of Thomas Earl of Kent.

John Duke of = Margaret Beauchamp   Edmund = Eleanor Beauchamp, dau. of
Somerset, ob.   of Bletsoe.   ob. 1467.   Richard Earl of Warwick.
1444.

Lady Margaret = 1st Edmund Tudor   Margaret Beanfort = Humphrey
1441-1509,   Earl of Richmond   Stafford
FOUNDER OF   (half brother to   'Earl of
CHRIST'S AND   Henry VI.) by whom   Stafford,'
ST. JOHN'S   she was the mother   slain fight-
COLLEGES.   of Henry VII.   ing for
= 2nd Sir Henry Stafford,   House of
younger son of Duke   Lancaster
of Buckingham.   at the battle
= 3rd Thomas Lord Stan-   of S. Albans.
ley, Earl of Derby.

Lady Margaret was the representative of John of Gaunt and the House of
Lancaster, as Elizabeth de Clare was the ancestor of the House of York.

TABLE III.

PEDIGREE OF THE DUKES OF BUCKINGHAM

Edward III.

Thomas of Woodstock=Eleanor de Bohun.
(youngest son) Duke of
Gloucester and Earl of
Buckingham, ob. 1397.

Edmund Earl of Stafford=Anne Plantagenet, sister and heiress of Hum-
ob. 1404.   phrey Plantagenet Earl of Gloucester and
                    Buckingham (he died unm. 1399).
                    She had previously married Thomas 'Earl
                    of Stafford,' and her son by her 3rd husband,
                    William Bourchier, married Anne, dau.
                    of Richard Woodville Earl Rivers.

Humphrey Stafford=Anna Neville, dau. of Ralph
created Duke of Buck-   Earl of Westmoreland.
ingham, ob. 1460.

Humphrey styled=Margaret Beaufort, great-
'Earl of Stafford,'   granddaughter of John
slain fighting for   of Gaunt.
the House of   (See Table II.)
Lancaster 1455.

Henry 2nd Duke=Katharine Wood-
of Buckingham,   ville, sister of
beheaded 1483. Elizabeth, wife to
                     Edw. IV.

Edward
3rd Duke of Buckingham,
FOUNDER OF BUCKINGHAM COLLEGE
beheaded 1521. Great-grandson
through his mother of Peter Comte
de Saint-Paul. [See Table II.]

PEDIGREE OF AUDLEY OF WALDEN

Thomas 1st Lord Audley of Walden=2ndly Elizabeth Grey, dau.
          (1488-1544)   of Marquess of Dorset.
FOUNDER OF MAGDALENE COLLEGE.

Eleanor=1stly Despenser.   Margaret=1stly Dudley Duke of
      =2ndly Lord Zouch   Northumberland (beheaded).
        of Mortimer.   =2ndly Thomas Howard
                                             Duke of Norfolk (beheaded).

Thomas was very possibly descended from the ancient family of that name which
intermarried with the Clares, Staffords, and Greys.

TABLE IV.

PEDIGREE OF STAFFORD AND AUDLEY

Edward Stafford = Eleanor Percy, dau. of
3rd Duke of | 10th Earl of Northumberland.
Buckingham,
beheaded 1521.
FOUNDER OF BUCKINGHAM
(now Magdalene) COLLEGE.

Thomas Howard = Elizabeth Stafford
2nd Duke of | (2nd wife).
Norfolk, ob. 1554. |

Henry Howard Earl = Frances de Vere,
of Surrey (the poet) | dau. of John Earl
beheaded 1547. | of Oxford.'

Thomas Howard = 2ndly Margaret, dau. of
3rd Duke of Norfolk, Thomas Lord Audley of
beheaded 1572. Walden, widow of Robert
Dudley. *Daughter of the
founder of Magdalene
College.*

Henry Howard
Earl of Northampton,
ob. 1624 (King's
Coll. Cambs).
Chancellor of the
University.

Their son Thomas Howard (ob. 1626) was created Earl
of Suffolk, and was Chancellor of the University.

PEDIGREE OF SIDNEY

Nicholas Sidney = Anne, sister of William Brandon,
| father of Charles Duke of Suffolk.

Sir William,
ob. 1553.

Thomas Ratcliffe Earl = 2ndly Frances,
of Sussex, ob. 9 March 1589,
Lord Deputy for FOUNDER OF SIDNEY
Ireland, 1557. SUSSEX COLLEGE.

Sir Henry = Mary, dau. of
ob. 1586, | John Dudley
President | Duke of
of Wales | Northumber-
and Lord | land.
Deputy for |
Ireland. |

Sir Philip Sidney = a dau. of
ob. 1586. Sir Francis
Walsingham.
She married
2ndly Robert
Devereux Earl of
Essex (beheaded 1600),
and 3rdly Richard de Burgh
the 'great Earl' of Clanricarde.

Robert Sidney
created Earl
of Leicester,
ob. 1616.

Henry Herbert = 3rdly Mary.
Earl of Pem-
broke (2nd earl
of this line).

301

Cambridge

The names of great Cantabrigians hardly ever appear singly in the annals of the university, and as there are family groups among founders so there are also among its other benefactors and distinguished representatives. Babington, Bacon, Beaumont, Bryan, Cavendish, Cecil, Coleridge, Darwin, Devereux, Fletcher, Greville, Harvey, Langton, Lightfoot, Lytton, Manners, Montague, Neville, Newton, Palmer, Shepard, Taylor, Thackeray, Temple, Wordsworth—all form such groups, and have provided the university not only with great names, but with a family history.

No name has clung more steadily to Cambridge than Babington—it was known there at least as early as the xv century, and was that of the 25th abbot of Bury in the time of Henry VI. Henry Babington was vice-chancellor in 1500; Dr. Humphrey Babington built the two sets of rooms on the south side of Nevile's court known as 'the Babington rooms,' in 1681, and his family have given prominent members to the university ever since. One of the Bacons was the last Master of Gonville, and Nicholas Bacon and his two sons were at Corpus and Trinity. Beaumont is a Peterhouse name; but in the reign of Elizabeth Dr. Robert Beaumont was Master of Trinity and vice-chancellor, and a Beaumont was Master of Peterhouse in the xviii century. Towards the end of the xiv century William Cavendish was fellow and master of the same college, and John Cavendish had been chancellor in 1380. In Gray's time Lord John Cavendish was at Cambridge, in the next century Henry

Temp. Ric. ii. 1380-1397.

Cambridge Men

Cavendish the scientist ; and the connexion of this family with the university has never been severed.

The Cecils appear at Cambridge with the rise of Burleigh's family in Elizabeth's reign, and they were connected with the Bacons a family which also came into prominence at the same time ; the great Bacon was Burleigh's nephew, and the Cecils were kinsmen of other celebrated Cambridge men—Cheke, Hatton, Howard, and the founder of the Brownists. Moreover one of the early Cecils had been made water Temp. Hen. viii. bailiff of Whittlesey ('bailiff of Whittlesey mere') and keeper of the swans in the fen district. William, first Lord Burleigh, was born in his mother's house at Bourn—the place which gave its name to the barony held successively by Hereward, Picot, and Peverel. The third and fifth lords married with the Manners, the sixth with a Cavendish. Both the Cecils of Elizabeth's time were chancellors of the university ; Burleigh's eldest son Thomas Earl of Exeter and Lady Dorothy Nevill his wife gave no less than £108 a year to Clare Hall, and 'Mr. Cecil' was moderator when James visited the university in 1615. Darwin had been preceded at Cambridge by old Erasmus Darwin, botanist and poet, the 'Sweet Harmonist of Flora's court' as Cowper calls the ancestor of the man who gave us the great harmonizing hypothesis of the century.[1] Fletcher is another Cambridge name. Fletcher Bishop of London was at Corpus, so was his

---

[1] Cowper was not himself at Cambridge, but he lived near by and frequently visited his brother a fellow of Benet College.

son the dramatist; Giles the brother of the bishop, one of Elizabeth's ambassadors, was at King's, his two poet sons were Cambridge men, and there was a scientific Fletcher at Caius in the xvi century. Greville or Grenville is another Cambridge name: Fulke Greville, first Lord Brooke (whose mother was a Neville) was at Jesus College, so was his cousin the second lord, whose father had been sent to Trinity in 1595 by Robert Devereux Earl of Essex with a letter of advice on Cambridge studies written by another old Cantabrigian, Bacon. The first Lord Lansdowne in the time of Charles II. and Sir Bevil Greville (ob. 1706) were both at Trinity.

The Suffolk name of Hervey is another which has always figured in Cambridge — there was Hervey Dunning in the xiiith and Hervey de Stanton in the xiv century; a Harvey succeeded Gardiner and Haddon in the Mastership of Trinity Hall, of which he was a considerable benefactor, and was vice-chancellor in 1560, Gabriel Harvey, a kinsman of Sir Thomas Smith's, was a fellow of this college and of Pembroke, William Harvey was at Caius. Langton[1] is an ancient and honoured name; it was that of the 6th Master of Pembroke, of John Langton chancellor of the university in the time of Henry VI., of Thomas Bishop of Winchester, and other Cambridge men. Lightfoot is a name which was known in the fen before the Conquest, and was that of the eminent Cambridge

[1] Langley and Langham were both names known at Cambridge in early days.

Cambridge Men

Hebraist two hundred years before the Bishop of Durham studied there. The Lyttons have been known at the university since the xvii century, Sir Rowland Lytton the antiquary was a member of Sidney Sussex College[1] and Bulwer Lytton was at Trinity Hall. The Montagues and Montacutes have been important since the day when Simon Montacute Bishop of Ely befriended Peterhouse. Through the xvii century, the first Master of Sidney Sussex, Richard Bishop of Norwich (the antiquary), the 2nd Earl of Manchester, and Charles Montague (afterwards Lord Halifax) who, with Prior, replied to Dryden's " Hind and Panther," were all Cambridge men ; and Sir Sidney Montague of Barnwell was one of Charles I.'s Masters of the A.D. 1627. Requests. We have seen how the Nevilles intermarried with the families of Cambridge founders ; Henry Neville was proctor, and vice-chancellor in 1560 ; Thomas Nevile was 8th Master of Trinity[2] and vice-chancellor, and 6th Master of Magdalene, where the name was again recorded in the last Master of the college (Lord Braybrooke). There was a Newton at Cambridge, 6th Master of Peterhouse, con- A.D. 1381. temporary with Beaufort, Thorpe, Scrope, and de Burgh. In the middle of the xvi century another Newton was vice-chancellor ; fifty years later Fogg Newton was Provost of King's and vice-chancellor in the 8th of James I., and an Isaac Newton unknown to fame

[1] He married Anne daughter of the first Lord St. John of Bletsoe, a descendant of Margaret Beauchamp the mother of Lady Margaret.
[2] See Trinity College pp. 135, 7, 9.

Cambridge

entered for Peterhouse about the same time as the discoverer of the law of gravitation entered Trinity. Palmer is another well-known name : a John Palmer was proctor in the reign of Elizabeth, Edward Palmer was fellow of Trinity in the reign of Charles I., and Edward Palmer Professor of Arabic, the sheikh Abdullah, was a Cambridge man. Skeltons have been found at A.D. 1391. the university since a proctor of that name who flourished in the days of Richard II. ; Shepards since the days of Elizabeth when there was a proctor of that name ; Jeremy Taylor was kin to Rowland Taylor the Cambridge martyr ; and Palmerston continued the tradition of the Temples. The Sternes had played a part in Cambridge before the days of Laurence Sterne ;[1] Thackeray followed other members of his family to the university, and there have been Wordsworths at Cambridge ever since the poet went to S. John's and his brother Christopher was Master of Trinity.

Other Cambridge names claim attention. There had been Latimers and Ridleys at Cambridge before the Protestant martyrs. Aldrich belongs to the xvi and xvii centuries. Byngham was not first heard of when the parson of S. John Zachary built God's House, but is the name of no less a personage than the first Master of Pembroke (Thomas Byngham), and another William Byngham was proctor A.D. 1570. in the year when Whitgift was vice-chancellor. One of the Bassetts was proctor as late as 1488, and Roger

---

[1] His ancestor Dr. Richard Sterne was one of the Masters ejected for refusing the Covenant.

Cambridge Men

Ascham's father in the xvi century was steward to the great Yorkshire house of Scrope ; Mildmay, the founder of Emmanuel, was brother-in-law to Sir Francis Walsingham, and was allied to the Ratcliffes.[1] There were Days before the Days of King's ; the Harringtons—allied to the Montagues, Stanleys and Sidneys—were Cambridge men ; a Hatton was proctor in 1499 and later Provost of King's, and the Hattons of the time of Elizabeth and her successors—who intermarried with the Montagues—were all benefactors of Jesus College.[2] The northern Percies have often taken part in Cambridge affairs, and Percy Bishop of Carlisle was chancellor of the university in the time of A.D. 1451. Henry VI. Roger Rotherham was Master of King's Hall before the days of the great chancellor. There were Somersets at Cambridge from the days of Henry VI., and a Stafford was proctor the year Henry VIII. beheaded

> ———bounteous Buckingham
> The mirror of all courtesey.

---

[1] In the Mildmay-Ratcliffe alliance, the two Protestant foundations of the xvi c. meet. The Ratcliffes, in addition to the alliance with Sidney, intermarried with the Staffords and Stanleys.

Beside the xv c. Bynghams and Bassetts and Percies, and the xiv c. names so often recorded, it should not be forgotten that few early figures in the university are more interesting than that of Chancellor Stephen Segrave mentioned on pp. 203 and 259. Segrave was Bishop of Armagh and titular bishop of Ostia. He had been a clerk in the royal household, and was the champion of the university against the friars. It will be remembered that Nicholas Segrave—a baron of de Montfort's parliament in 1265—had been one of those defenders of Kenilworth who held out in the isle of Ely till July 1267.

[2] Cf. pp. 203 n., 294 n.

Cambridge

Stokys and Stokes was a well-known name before Sir George Stokes went to Pembroke ; Sedgwick was on the papist side in the controversy held before Edward VI.'s commissioners ; Tyndale, like Aldrich, belongs to the xvi and xvii centuries. Fitzhugh is a name which flourished at the university in the xv and early xvi centuries. Parker, Paston,[1] Morgan, Cosin and Cousins, and the various forms of Clark are constant Cambridge names. In modern times Macaulay, Trevelyan, Paget, Maitland, and Lyttelton should be added.

The subject of university men must not be dismissed without noticing how many of the most distinguished Cantabrigians never earned a degree. We have already seen (in chapter iii.) that in some periods of greatest intellectual achievement the examination tests at the university were wholly inadequate : what follows is a list of great and prominent men who took no degree at all :—Bacon, Byron, Macaulay (fellow of Trinity), Gray (professor of history),[2] Morland the hydrostatician,[3] Woodward the founder of mineralogy,[4] Donne, Fulke Greville, Parr the classic, Sir William Temple, Cromwell, Pepys and Mildmay both of whom were conspicuous benefactors of the university, Dryden who received his degree by dispensation of

---

[1] One of the Pastons married Anna Beaufort a great-granddaughter of John of Gaunt.

[2] Gray took the *LL.B.* on returning to the university.

[3] Morland improved the fire engine and invented the speaking trumpet —one of his trumpets is preserved in the library at Trinity. He was 10 years at Cambridge, and was assistant to Cromwell's secretary, Thurloe.

[4] Woodward went to Cambridge when he was 30 years old.

the Primate, Stratford de Redcliffe who was created
M.A. by royal mandamus, Palmerston who graduated
"by right of birth." There was no one so important
as Macaulay in 1822 when his name was absent from
the tripos list, no one so great as Darwin in the tripos
lists of 1831 when he took an ordinary degree.

The Oxford roll of non-graduates is not less dis-
●tinguished : Sir Thomas More, Sir Matthew Hale,
Sir Christopher Hatton, Sir Philip Sidney, Wolsey,
Massinger and Beaumont the dramatists, Shaftesbury,
Gibbon, Shelley—while Halley the astronomer took his
M.A. by royal mandamus, and Locke's degree was
irregular. Dublin university has not a dissimilar tale to
tell ; Burke failed to distinguish himself there, and
Swift was given a degree *speciali gratia.*

CHAPTER VI

GIRTON AND NEWNHAM

Etheldreda of Ely and Hild of Whitby connect the school of York
with the monastery of Ely—English women and education—
the four "noble and devoute countesses" and two queens at
Cambridge—the rise of the movement for university education
—two separate movements—Girton—Newnham—rise of the
university lecture movement—Anne Clough—the Newnham
Halls and Newnham College—the first triposes—the "Graces"
of 1881—social life at the women's colleges—character and
choice of work among women—the degree—status of women's
colleges at Cambridge and Oxford—and status elsewhere.

THE foundation of the women's colleges is of sufficient
importance to call for a chapter in any history of the
university, even if they did not in themselves awaken
so much general interest. Cambridge cannot be otherwise than proud of its position as pioneer university
in the higher education of the women of the country;
the women's colleges count as one of its glories and
stand to it in the relation which Spenser gave to the
river Ouse :

> My mother Cambridge, whom as with a crowne
> He doth adorne, and is adorn'd of it.

310

Girton and Newnham

They belong to its atmosphere of vitality and growth, their presence adds something to that air of newness and renewal which has never been absent from the university town.

Etheldreda of Ely and Hild of Whitby were of the same blood, kin to Edwin and Oswy. They founded two of those famous double monasteries for women and men, one of which became the greatest school in England, the other the nursing mother of the university of Cambridge.[1] The histories of the School of York and of the School which was to rise on the banks of the Granta had therefore been linked together since the vii century by Hild and Etheldreda. Was any prevision vouchsafed to Hild, that mother of scholars, of the day just twelve hundred years later when two women's colleges were to rise by the side of the great school in the diocese of Ely ? The centre of learning which had Etheldreda of Ely for one of its patrons was certainly propitious to women ; but Cambridge had another patroness—whose name was among the earliest to be invoked in the town after the coming of the Normans —that Rhadegund who ruled the first nuns and the first double monastery in France, who was ordained a deacon by S. Médard, in whose convent study came

---

[1] The original double monastery of Ely did not become Benedictine till 970. See i. p. 12. Etheldreda ('S. Audrey') was the daughter of Anna king of the East Angles, and of Hereswitha sister of Hild, and wife to Oswy king of Northumbria. She thus united in her person the destinies of the northern provinces and East Anglia (where she was born) a union which has been perpetuated in the university of Cambridge. She was born *circa* 630, and died in 679. As "the Lady of Ely" her will, living or dead, was held to decide the fortunes of the city.

THE GREAT BRIDGE—BRIDGE ST.

This view is painted from the old Quay side. The
water-gate of Magdalene College is seen on the right,
and in the distance is the Tower in the New Court
of St. John's College rising above the tree-tops.

next to prayer, who lectured each day to her spiritual children, and whose learning is recorded with admiration by one of her monks, the poet-bishop Venantius Fortunatus.[1]

Perhaps there is no country with a long history where women have played a smaller part on the national stage than England. But a conspicuous exception must be made—in education they have played a great part, and this part was nowhere greater than in Cambridge. We have the little group of college builders who lived in contiguous centuries—Elizabeth de Clare, Marie de Saint-Paul, Margaret of Anjou, and Margaret of Richmond—to prove it : but the activity of the xiv and xv centuries was equally apparent between the viith and xth. It was Saxon nuns who carried learning to Germany, and the rôle of the great abbesses in those centuries, while it must be reckoned among the exceptions to the inconspicuous part played by women in English history, also served prominently the cause of education.[2]

The " two noble and devoute countesses " who built Clare and Pembroke, and whom Margaret of Anjou desired to imitate, realised perhaps more than anyone else in the xiv century the extraordinary joy of launching those first foundations with their promise for the

[1] i. p. 16. Her name was given to the only monastic house in Cambridge. Rhadegund was abbess of Ste. Croix A.D. 519-587.

[2] It is sufficiently remarkable that a conspicuous rôle pertained almost exclusively to Englishwomen who were of the blood royal. This is true in the case of the great abbesses, and from the time of Hild and Etheldreda to that of Lady Margaret.

future:[1] but it was something of this joy which was reserved for their descendants who saw the rise of Newnham and Girton. It was, indeed, not to two but to four noble and devoute countesses[2] that Cambridge owed its most efficient co-operation in the great periods which mark its history—the dawn of the renascence in the xiv, the threshold of our modern life in the xv, and the consolidation of the religious movement in the xvi century:[3] and if Queens' College was built by Margaret of Anjou "to laud and honneure of sexe femenine" Cambridge has repaid her by extending the significance of her ambition.

The women's colleges which we now see did not, then, begin the connexion of women and the university, they completed it. It is a curious thing when one looks down a list of Cambridge benefactors to find that from a college to a common room fire, from a professorship to a Cambridge "chest," from the chapel to a new college to the buttress of a falling college, from a university preacher to a belfry,[4] the names of women never fail to appear as benefactors, but appear in no other way. Not once until the xix century did any

[1] For the circumstances in which Clare and Pembroke were founded, see chap. ii. pp. 67-8 and 69, 71-2.

[2] The countesses of Clare, Pembroke, Richmond, and Sussex.

[3] Erasmus' "three colleges" which represented for him the university and its new learning were Queens', Christ's, and S. John's, all founded by women.

[4] Lady Mildred Cecil gave money to the Master of S. John's "to procure to have fyres in the hall of that colledg uppon all sondays and hollydays betwixt the fest of all Sayntes and Candlemas, whan there war no ordinary fyres of the charge of the colledg." And pp. 72, 86, 120, 155.

Cambridge

woman benefit from the learning which her sex had done so much to inaugurate, to sustain and consolidate.

In the year 1867 the idea of founding a woman's college and of associating the higher education of women with the university of Cambridge began to take shape.[1] No movement of the century, it may confidently be affirmed, has done so much to increase the happiness of women, and none has opened to them so many new horizons. If men look back on the years spent at the university as among the happiest in their lives, so that everything in later life which recalls their *alma mater*— not excluding the London terminus from which they always "went up"—borrows some of its glamour, the university life meant all this, and more, for women. To begin with it repaired a traditional injustice, the absence of any standard of individual life especially for the unmarried ; the neglect of every personal interest, talent, or ambition, which a woman might have apart from looking after her own or other people's children. The Reformation, in itself, had done singularly little for women. Puritan views were of the kind patronised

---

[1] A pioneer committee had been formed in October 1862 to obtain the admission of women to university examinations ; Miss Emily Davies was Hon. Secretary. The first step taken was to secure the examination of girls in the university Local Examinations which had been started in 1858, and a private examination for girls simultaneously with that for boys was held on the 14 Dec. 1863. These examinations were formally opened to girls in February 1865 (*infra* p. 358). Meanwhile the Schools Enquiry commission of the previous year had brought into relief the absence of any education for girls after the school age. The commissioners were memorialised, and the immediate outcome was the scheme for a college, and the formation of a committee to carry it into effect. Cf. pp. 317-18 *n.*

Girton and Newnham

by a Sir Willoughby Patterne, and no step had been made towards recognising women's claims as individuals since the days when convents had in some measure certainly admitted these, a fact which probably sufficed to make the convent turn the scale on the side of happiness.

Girton and Newnham are the outcome of two contemporaneous but separate movements. In 1867, as we have seen, the moral foundations were laid of a college in connexion with Cambridge university where women should follow the same curriculum and present themselves for the same examinations as men. In 1869 the late Professor Henry Sidgwick, fellow of Trinity, and afterwards Knightbridge Professor of Moral Philosophy, suggested that lectures for women should be given at Cambridge in connexion with the new Higher Local Examination which the university had that year established for women all over England. To-day, more than thirty years after the building of the two colleges, Newnham and Girton are as alike in character as two institutions can be, but this likeness is the consequence of changes on both sides. The view taken by the promoters of Girton was that if women were to be trained at the university by university men they should undergo precisely the same tests, and take precisely the same examinations as men. Professor Sidgwick contented himself with a scheme for relating the higher education of women to university teaching, and not only accepted but encouraged a separate course of study and a separate examination test. Girton represents the principle that a woman's university

VIEW OF CAMBRIDGE FROM THE
CASTLE HILL

The central object in the picture is the tower of St.
John's College Chapel, with the tower of Great St.
Mary's a little to the right and King's College Chapel
to the extreme right. In the middle distance on the left
is Jesus College and the Round Church, and nearer to
us we look down upon the roofs of Magdalene College.
The building on the right in foreground is St. Giles'
Church, the original foundation of which takes us
back nearly to the Conquest. In the extreme distance
is the rising ground known as the Gog-Magog Hills.

education should closely resemble that which the centuries had evolved as the best for men. Newnham was started to further a scheme of education as unlike the men's as preparation for the higher work made possible. The one grew out of a claim to have the same examination as men ; the other was the outcome of an examination established expressly for women. Events have not justified the second scheme. If women's education was to be connected with the university, the only permanently satisfactory way was, clearly, to follow the curriculum already traced out. If this was not actually the best which could be devised, the foundation of women's colleges was not the moment to attempt to alter it. A "best" created for women would always have been thought to be a second best. There were in fact not one but two objects set before all who interested themselves in these things—to get higher education for women, and to win recognition for their capacity to do the same work as men. Among the founders of women's colleges many had present to their minds something further than the advantages of education—they looked forward to a time when women should participate in the world's work, and have a fair share in the common human life ; not a fair share of its labour, for this had never been lacking, but of the means, the opportunities, and the recognition enjoyed by men.

Women and the ordinary degree. Girton at once prepared its students for the university Previous Examination, and claimed that they should be examined for both the ordinary and the honour degree. Newnham at first prepared its students for the Higher Local examinations and the triposes, discountenanced the Previous Examination and would not allow its students to prepare for the Ordinary degree. In the event, Newnham has had to abandon the examination which was the original *raison d'être* of its existence, and Girton has had virtually to abandon its claim to examination for the ordinary degree. This means that every woman who takes a degree takes it in honours : the same is true of no college of men in Cambridge except King's. The founders of Newnham considered it a waste of time for women to come to the university to qualify themselves for that Ordinary degree which graces the majority of our men, and which represented such a mysterious weight of learning to sisters at home in the old days. This decision has a double *ricochet*—it is good for the colleges, for only the better women come up ; it is bad for many women who, like many men, are unfit to do tripos work and who might yet enjoy from residence at Cambridge the same advantages—direct and extraneous—which the ' poll ' degree man now obtains.

Girton.   The first committee for the future Girton College met on December 5th 1867 ; [1] but the founda-

[1] There were present Mrs. Manning, * Miss Emily Davies, * Sedley Taylor, and * H. R. Tomkinson. * Madame Bodichon, who was ill, was not present, but George Eliot wrote to her four days before the meeting, à propos of an appointment to see one of the members of the committee : "I am much occupied just now, but the better education of women is one of the objects about which I have *no doubt*, and I shall rejoice if this idea of a college can be carried out."

On the General Committee of Hitchin College the bishops of Peter-

tion of Girton dates from October 16. 1869 when a hired house at Hitchin, midway between Cambridge and London, was opened to six students at a time when it was not thought advisable to plant a women's college in Cambridge. The college at Hitchin[1] was carried on under serious tuitional and other disadvantages—lecturers from the university, for example, were paid for the time occupied in the journey—and in 1873 the college was removed to Girton, a village two miles out of Cambridge.

The manor and village of Girton. The manor of Girton on the Huntingdon road—the old via Devana—belonged in the xi century to Picot the Norman sheriff of Cambridge who expropriated part of its tithes for the endowment of the canons' house and church of S. Giles which is passed by Girtonians on their way from the college to the town. In the xvi century the manor provided a rent charge for Corpus Christi College. Earlier still it was the site of a Roman and Anglo-Saxon burial ground (discovered in a college field in 1882-6). The college itself is built on old river gravel.

borough and S. David's, the Dean of Ely, Lady Hobart, Lord Lyttelton, Prof. F. D. Maurice, Sir James Paget, Rt. Hon. Russell Gurney, M.P., Miss Anna Swanwick, and Miss Twining, sat with several others. On the Executive Committee were Mme. Bodichon, *Lady Goldsmid wife of Sir Francis Goldsmid elected liberal member for Reading in 1866, *Mrs. Russell Gurney, Prof. Seeley, Dean Stanley, and the members of the 1867 committee : while a Cambridge Committee included Professors Adams, Humphry, Lightfoot, Liveing, Drs. J. Venn, T. G. Bonney, the Revv. J. Porter, R. Burn, T. Markby, W. G. Clark ; Henry Sidgwick, and Sedley Taylor. The asterisked names denote those who also constituted with 11 others the first members of Girton College (p. 321).

[1] Incorporated from 1872 as Girton College.

Girton and Newnham

The founders. The final decision to build near but not in the university town was taken at the last moment when Lady Augusta Stanley, wife of Dean Stanley, refused both money and moral support if it were decided otherwise.[1] Lady Augusta Stanley who thus determined a step which has not proved advantageous to Girton was not, however, one of the founders of the college. This honour is due in the first place to Madame Bodichon (Barbara Leigh Smith before her marriage) and to Miss Emily Davies, daughter of Dr. Davies, rector of Gateshead, who elaborated the scheme together. The first thousand pounds which made possible the realisation of the scheme was given by the former, whose activity in all causes for the advancement of women's interests was crowned by her gifts to the first women's college : part of her capital was made over in her life-time to Girton which became her trustee for the payment of the interest until her death in 1891, and of certain terminable annuities afterwards.[2] The third founder was Henrietta wife of the 2nd Lord Stanley of Alderley and daughter of the 13th Viscount Dillon,[3] a munificent donor to the college, who joined

[1] Two or three of the Cambridge colleges were built at a distance from the schools and the centre of the town : thus Alcock described Jesus College as "the college of the Blessed Virgin . Mary, S. John Evangelist, and S. Rhadegund, *near Cambridge*." Hitchin in Hertfordshire, the first site of Girton, was one of the homes of the English Gilbertines, a double order for men and women which was also established in Cambridge. i. p. 19 and *n*.

[2] This was followed by a bequest of £10,000.

[3] It is interesting to find the names of Dillon and Davies continuing in the case of the first college for women at Cambridge the Irish and Welsh traditions of college founders. It is perhaps still more interesting to find

319

GIRTON COLLEGE—EVENING

These buildings were designed by Mr. Waterhouse.
They are of red brick, and were first occupied in 1873.

Cambridge

the movement in 1871, before the removal from Hitchin, and who died in 1895.

The college. The picturesque and collegiate-looking building which arose in 1873 for the accommodation of 21 students, was thus the first residential college for women ever built in connexion with a university. It was, like Pembroke, the result of a woman's intention to found and finish a *domus seu aula scholarium*, the scholars being, for the first time, of the sex of the founder. Subsequent building in 1877, 1879, 1884, 1887 (when Jane C. Gamble's legacy enabled the college to house 106 students) and finally between 1899 and 1902, has greatly increased its capacity, and the college now holds 150 students in addition to the Mistress and the resident staff. It contains a large hall, libraries, reading room, lecture rooms, a chemical laboratory, chapel, hospital, and swimming bath ; and its position outside the town gives it the advantage of large grounds, some thirty acres being divided into hockey fields, ten tennis courts, an orchard, and kitchen garden ; while a seventeen acre field, purchased with the Gamble bequest in 1886, is utilised as golf links and woodland. Over the high table in the hall are the portraits of the three founders ; Madame Bodichon is represented painting, reminding each generation of students that one of their founders was a distinguished and delightful artist.

that on her mother's side Lady Stanley was descended from the companion-in-arms of de Burgh the "red earl" of Ulster, and that a Dillon inter-married with the heiress of the 2nd earl of Clare, names honoured as those of the woman founder of one of the first Cambridge colleges.

Girton and Newnham

Government. The college is governed by its members,[1] from whom is drawn the Executive Committee, three members of which are indirectly chosen by the old students. The Executive Committee appoints the Mistress and college officers, but the Mistress nominates the resident staff with the exception of the bursar, junior bursar, librarian, and registrar. The fees for residence and tuition are thirty-five guineas for each of the three yearly terms, and they include "coaching." Students may be in residence who are not reading for a tripos, the goal of the great majority. A great part of the preparation for triposes is done at the college by its own resident staff. The first Cambridge degree examination taken by women was in 1870 when five of the six Hitchin students were examined for the Previous Examination;[2] and the first tripos examination taken by women was two years later when three of these students passed in the classical and mathematical triposes.[3] In scholastic successes, Girton trained the first wrangler (Miss Scott, equal to 8th wrangler 1880), the first senior moralist (Miss E. E. Constance Jones, the present Mistress of Girton), and the only senior

[1] See the original committee *supra* pp. 317-18 *n*. The existing members elect the majority of new members. The first official recognition of the existence of the college was made in 1880 when the Council of the Senate elected three members of the college from among its number, and so exercised a power conferred on it in the original articles of association.

[2] The college still prepares for this examination; at Newnham it must be prepared for at the student's own expense. It is however now usually taken by all students before coming up.

[3] Classics: R. S. Cook (Mrs. C. P. Scott) and L. I. Lumsden. Mathematics: S. Woodhead (Mrs. Corbett) senior optime.

Cambridge

classic (Miss Agnata Ramsay, now wife to the Master of Trinity) ; and was the first to obtain first classes in the classical tripos.[1]

Among scholarships and exhibitions are six foundation scholarships the gift of private persons ; the scholarships of the Clothworkers', Drapers', Goldsmiths', and Skinners' Companies and of the Honourable the Irish Society ; in addition to which there are other valuable scholarships and studentships due to private benefactors, and the Gamble, Gibson, Montefiore, Metcalfe, and Agnata Butler prizes.[2]

Former Girton students.　Former Girton students not only fill posts all over Great Britain and Ireland as head or assistant mistresses in high schools, grammar schools,

---

[1] This was in 1882. First class honours in this tripos did not become usual until women came up better prepared from schools. A Cambridge man, however, writing in 1873 declares that a man may be a wrangler when his mathematical knowledge was contemporary with his admission to the university, but that "no one was ever placed in *any* class of the (classical) tripos who came up to the university knowing only the elements of Greek grammar. . . . The classical man, if plucked," (*i.e.* in mathematics) "loses 10 years' labour"—the time spent in classics from early school days. Women, nevertheless, belied this dictum from the first ; many have not known even "the elements of Greek grammar" when they came up, and few indeed have 10 years' Greek studies on their shoulders when they take the tripos.

[2] The Claude Montefiore prize was founded in memory of the donor's wife, who was at Girton. The Agnata Butler prize is awarded to classical students by the Master of Trinity and his wife. One of the early scholarships, offered by Mr. Justice Wright, was described as "a year's proceeds of an Oxford fellowship." Dr. W. Cunningham, fellow of Trinity College, assigned, in 1898, the entire profits of his book *Growth of English Industry and Commerce* towards a fund for publishing dissertations of conspicuous merit written by certificated Girton students. The above-named city companies have always been generous donors to the women's colleges.

Girton and Newnham

and women's colleges, but they are to be found holding the professorship of mathematics and a classical fellowship at Bryn Mawr College Pennsylvania, in the high schools of Pretoria, Bloemfontein, and Moscow, in women's colleges at Toronto and Durban, as mathematical or other tutors in Queen's College London, Queen's College Belfast, and Alexandra College Dublin. A Girtonian is vice-president of the British Astronomical Association, computer at Cambridge Observatory, assistant inspector to the Scotch Education Department, lecturer in modern economic history in the university of London, a fellow of the university of London, on the staff of the Victoria History of the Counties of England, assistant on the staff of the English Dialect Dictionary (just published) ; while one is secretary and librarian of the Royal Historical Society, and another (a *D.Sc.* of London) is a fellow of the same society. Old students are also to be found as educational missionaries in Bombay and Calcutta, as members of the Missionary Settlement for University Women in Bombay, and of the Women's Mission Association (S.P.G.) at Rurki ; as medical missionary at Poona, as missionaries at Lake Nyasa, and in Japan, and the principal of the North India Medical School for Christian Women is also a Girtonian. In special work, a Girtonian is H.M.'s principal lady inspector of factories, one of H.M.'s inspectors of schools, a Poor Law guardian, a deputy superintendent of the women clerks' department of the Bank of England, and on the secretarial staff of the Tariff Commission. An old

THE BOATHOUSE ON ROBINSON
CRUSOE'S ISLAND

On the upper river at the back of King's Mill, not far from Queens' College. Across the bridge in the distance and behind the trees on the left is Coe Fen, and on the right is Sheep's Green.

Cambridge

Girtonian is the only woman member of the Institution of Electrical Engineers, and the only woman to hold the Hughes Gold Medal of the Royal Society.

All other colleges which have been founded or will be founded for women owe a debt to Girton for upholding the principle of equal conditions and equal examination tests in the university education of women and men. Its promoters always kept steadily before them the two ends of women's education, and never moved from the position that "what is best for the human being will be found to be also the best for both sexes." To them it is mainly due that when Plato's ideal of equal education of the sexes came at length to be realised, after women had waited for it more than two thousand years, it was not upon a basis of separate examinations for women, and separate tests so designed as to elude comparison.[1]

Newnham. The village of Newnham which is approached from the "Backs" of the colleges, and

---

[1] The committee of 1862 had had (as we see) for its avowed object the "obtaining the admission of women to university examinations": the subsequent committee (of December 1867) was formed "for the establishment of a college holding to girls' schools and home teaching a position analogous to that occupied by the universities towards the public schools for boys." The following was the reply given by the first named committee when approached in March 1868 with a view to a joint memorial asking for "advanced examinations for women" :—"That this committee, believing that the distinctive advantage of the Cambridge University Local Examinations consists in their offering a common standard to boys and girls, and that the institution of independent schemes of examination for women exclusively tends to keep down the level of female education, cannot take part in the proposed memorial to the university of Cambridge for advanced examinations for women above the age of eighteen."

Girton and Newnham

which, until 1880, was also accessible by a ferry over Coe fen, played an important part in the early history of the university. It was the site given to the White-friars, who had been the first arrivals in Cambridge, and who from the time of their appearance there as romites till they became the sons of S. Theresa were the most conspicuous community in the town. The first general of the Carmelites—an Englishman—had been a contemporary of the founder of the first college, and it was at Newnham that he visited his friars in the middle of the xiii century, at the convent there which is described in the Hundred Rolls and the Barnwell Chartulary.[1] In the same century William de Manfield left his lands in Newnham to the scholars of Merton. In the next (the xiv) century the manor of Newnham was given to Gonville Hall by Lady Anne Scrope, and both Sir John Cambridge and Henry Tangmer, who were aldermen of the guilds of the Blessed Virgin and Corpus Christi, gave or bequeathed lands and houses they held in Newnham to the new college which the guilds had built.[2] The Carmelites moved later to the A.D. 1291.

---

[1] "The brethren of Mount Carmel had a site at Newnham where they dwelt and where they founded their church, which site they had of Michael Malherbe" (Hundred Rolls ii. 360). "Here they made many cells, a church, a cloister, and dormitory, and the necessary offices, sufficiently well constructed, and here they dwelt for 40 years" (Barnwell Chartulary). See i. p. 20.

[2] Scroope Terrace occupies part of the ground of Newnham Manor. Like the other great benefactors of colleges, Lady Elizabeth Clare and Lady Margaret Beaufort, Lady Anne was three times married. Her mother was a Gonville. Corpus Christi College benefited by tithes and houses in the manors both of Girton and Newnham (p. 318).

QUEENS' LANE—THE SITE OF THE OLD
MILL STREET

The Towers of Queens' College Gateway are seen on
the left, through the trees on the right is St.
Catherine's College, and in the distance a portion of
King's College.

present site of Queens' and the adjoining ground, and the edge of their property is skirted by every Newnham student on her way to lectures either through Silver Street or King's College. This new residence was the gift of Sir Guy de Mortimer and was in the busy university centre—Mill Street in the parish of S. John Baptist—so that the friars still heard the sound of the horn which was blown at the King's Mill to tell the miller at Newnham that he might begin to grind. Beyond the mill was Newnham Lane, which stretched to Grantchester.[1]

Like Peterhouse which was adapted and built for the " Ely Scholars," the Hall at Newnham was the outcome of a students' association :—the North of England Council for the Higher Education of Women, of which Miss Clough was president, and the association formed to promote the interests of the Higher Local students were its real progenitors.

As soon as the removal from Hitchin had been decided, it was hoped that the students already settled in Cambridge and the Girton community might form one body ; but the decision to build away from the town put a stop to any such scheme. The standpoint of the promoters of Newnham had always diverged in some particulars from that of the promoters of Girton. The former wished to reduce the expenses of

[1] Those who held that Grantchester and Cambridge were but one and the same town, told us that the principal part lay on the north, towards Girton, while Newnham Lane, beyond the mill, extended as far as Grantchester " the old Cambridge " : *Ad Neunhamiae vicum, ultra molendinam, que se longius promovebat versus Grantacestriam.* . . . (Caius).

a university education to the minimum, and they wished, too, that it should be completely undenominational, while a clause in the constitution of Girton provided for Church of England instruction and services. Finally, the question as to which preliminary and degree examinations should be preferred by women was still pending.[1]   But when the moment came to hire and build a house of residence, the advantage was all on the side of Newnham.   Work began in a hired house in the centre of the town with five students, in the October term of 1871.[2]   These quarters were too noisy, and Miss Clough, who loved a garden, found an old house set in a large garden and orchard, with the historic name of Merton Hall, and moved there in 1872.   A supplementary house in Trumpington Street was taken next year, and there were then in residence 14 students in Merton Hall, 7 in Trumpington Street, and 8 in town lodgings.   In 1875 Newnham Hall was built on one side of Coe fen and Newnham Mill, as

[1] It may be recorded here that Madame Bodichon's scheme was for a college (a) *in* Cambridge (b) with the same intellectual conditions and tests as applied to men and (c) free of denominationalism.   A chapel was not erected at Girton till after 1895.   Of Mme. Bodichon as a pioneer it has been said that she had the singular faculty for realising in her imagination exactly what she wanted, down to the last detail—the creative power.   Her failing health for the last fourteen years of her life made impossible the active share in the work which had been so ungrudgingly undertaken by her between 1867 and 1877 ; but her interest extended to every student who went up to Girton, and she was at pains to know them and to find out from their conversation how the college might be improved.

[2] This house, 74 Regent Street, had been hired by (Professor) Henry Sidgwick in the spring of the year at his own financial risk, and here Miss Clough came in September.

MERTON HALL

An old house in the Merton Estate district.

Cambridge

Peterhouse had been built on the other. So that Newnham students frequented the streets of Cambridge from the first, and had their house of residence in the town two years before the sister community settled at Girton. The founders of Girton had been the first to ideate a women's college in connexion with university teaching, but Newnham was the first college for women to take its place by the side of the historic colleges in Cambridge.

Let us now retrace our steps for a moment. In March 1868 the North of England Council memorialised the university to obtain advanced examinations, and in the following year Cambridge instituted the examinations for girls over eighteen since known as the Higher Local Examination. In the autumn of the same year (1869), as we have seen—the year which saw the establishment of the future Girton community at Hitchin—the organisation of the Cambridge lectures for women was mooted under the auspices of Mr. Henry Sidgwick. The first meeting was convened at the house of Mrs. Fawcett, whose husband was then Professor of Political Economy at the university, and whose little daughter, the future senior wrangler, was peacefully cradled at the time in a room above. The result of this meeting was the formation of a committee of management consisting of members of the university, and of an executive committee, and the programme of a course of lectures was printed for the following Lent term 1870.[1] The original scheme in-

[1] The names of the 16 men (one being a Frenchman) who first lectured to women at the university are treasured at Newnham. Six were S. John's

cluded a students' house where women from a distance could be lodged. Two students applied in the autumn term of 1870 for permission to reside in Cambridge, and were received into private houses in the town. Meanwhile in response to an appeal, originating with Mrs. Fawcett, exhibitions of £40 for two years for students attending the lectures had been given by John Stuart Mill and Helen Taylor, and before the year closed it was found necessary to open a house of residence. In March 1871 the post of head of a house of residence was offered to Miss Anne J. Clough.

men, 4 Trinity, and the other colleges represented were Christ's, Queens', and Caius. They were :

†F. D. Maurice.	†W. K. Clifford.
†W. W. Skeat.	J. Venn.
†J. E. B. Mayor.	†A. Marshall.
J. Peile.	Prof. C. C. Babington.
W. C. Green.	T. G. Bonney.
M. Boquel.	P. T. Main.
†Prof. Cayley.	G. M. Garrett, Mus.D.
J. F. Moulton.	S. Taylor.

Dr. (afterwards Sir) Michael Foster, Adam Sedgwick, Frank Balfour (all of the Physiological laboratory) H. Sidgwick, Mr. Archer-Hind, Dr. E. S. Shuckburgh, and Mr. Keynes were also among the earliest lecturers.

The general committee then formed included the first 3 of these names, and Nos. 7, 8, and 10 ; with Prof. Adams, Mr. Henry Jackson, and Mr. (afterwards Sir) R. C. Jebb. The Executive were : Prof. Maurice, Mr. T. G. Bonney, Mr. Ferrers (afterwards Master of Gonville and Caius) Mr. Peile (now Master of Christ's) Mrs. Adams (the wife of the Lowndean professor) Mrs. Fawcett (the wife of the professor of Political Economy) Miss M. G. Kennedy, and Mrs. Venn (the wife of Dr. Venn of Caius) H. Sidgwick and T. Markby, Hon. secretaries, and Mrs. Bateson (the wife of the Master of S. John's) Hon. treasurer.

Certain courses of lectures in the public and inter-collegiate lecture rooms were open to women from 1873—22 out of the 34. A few years later 29 were open, and now all are open.

Cambridge

Anne Clough. We know more about Miss Clough than about any founder or first principal of a college on which he or she left a personal mark. Of the life and thoughts of others, with the exception perhaps of Bateman in the xiv century and Fisher in the xvith, we know singularly little. Anne J. Clough was born on January 20, 1820, at Liverpool. Through her Newnham received, what Girton missed, the impress of a strong individuality, now placed by "great death" at a distance which enables us to focus and appraise it. Her father's family was of Welsh origin and traced itself to that Sir Richard who was agent to the great merchant-adventurer, Sir Thomas Gresham. To her Yorkshire mother, Anne Perfect, she and her brother, the poet Arthur Hugh Clough, owed their literary interests. In appearance she was of middle height and spare—an old woman of that Victorian epoch in which she was born, out of whose eyes looked the soul of the twentieth century, and after. She seemed indeed to have two personalities—the white hair and an uncertain gait typified the one, but the eyes, very dark and very bright, would lift unexpectedly in the midst of a conversation, and then the visitor would receive a revelation ; he would see no more the old woman but the woman who must always be young, the stamp of an inexhaustible energy, that shrewdness with an unconquerable idealism close behind, an atmosphere about her of uncouth poetry.

For she was no artist. She had not that which separates the artist from the man of ideas, or the

330

dreamer, or the seer—expression. No poetical imagination was ever more tongue-tied. She spoke by actions,
and used words only as indications of thoughts. Her
speech was compared by a former student to the works
of early painters, before command over the material had
been obtained, but where " sheer force of character and
feeling had risen over the difficulties." She was an
idealist, but she could never understand the value of
an abstract principle. Her interest was always in the
individual, in the career, and she came to no matter,
to no person, with a store of general principles ready
for the case. She wanted to give women not merely
learning, but a life of their own, to call out interests,
to satisfy their individuality. She liked to find in them
many and marked vocations, for she understood the
dignity of all work and had no disdain of common
things. She wanted every one to have a place and an
office in life, and must perforce fit the squarest bits
into a round hole, so intolerably pathetic was it to her
that they should have no hole. You could not " hand
her the salt or open the door for her " without
receiving " some recognition of your individuality "
a student said of her. This recognition of the individuality of women and of the human and practical
sides of higher intellectual training was her contribution to the movement in which she took so great a
part. And the contribution was all important.

She had besides a strong belief in the value of
academic advantages. It was in order that some
crumbs of things academic might fall to the teachers

in elementary schools, that she arranged the summer meetings of University Extension Lecture students. Miss Clough's belief in happiness—in people's right to happiness—was the source of most delightful qualities. She had waited, she said, for her own till she was fifty years old, and it had come to her with Newnham. She insisted on the little pleasures "which bring joy by the way." Nothing was too small to engage her own attention, and her educational qualities lay in awaking similar interest in others, as her moral disposition led her to share and so to increase the common stock of interests and supports in life. And so on the rare occasions when she left the college boundaries she would recount to the students at her table or in her room all that had interested her during her absence. She busied herself over the minutest details of their health or well-being, and finding that two students made a simple supper upstairs on Sunday, she arrived at the door carrying a good-sized table, because she had noticed there was none convenient for the purpose. Newnham was for her a big house, and the students were grown-up daughters in a delightful family not yet realised elsewhere, each of whom had her own place in the world, her own personal life, its rights and liberties. Yet the "head" who habitually intervened in small college matters (with a total lack of power of organisation, which in the administration of Newnham she left to others) and who was frequently agitated and over anxious about them, balanced these things by a life-long habit of interest in large public affairs, and, what was more strange, by a very real serenity. She did not think the individual should be sacrificed to the college, or " to a cause, however good." She never lived in a small milieu—even Newnham.

She constantly exercised a simple diplomacy, not divorced from sympathy—with independent-minded students, with university dons who viewed Newnham with disfavour, and in generally vain attempts to conciliate high theory with prudent practice. It was here that her characteristics sometimes jarred on the early students, among whom were many ardent spirits, people whose presence there at all was the consequence of a struggle *à outrance* with convention and prejudice ; and who resented Miss Clough's temporising ways, as though the first maker of Newnham were a backslider in the matter of first principles. They thought her indirect and timid. She was neither. She had real courage, not only as her biographer has said " audacity in thought "[1] but audacity in execution. She was staunch and tenacious, and might be found taking an individual's part against the whole college ; and whether the help she gave was moral or financial, no one ever knew of it but herself. Neither did she always prefer the most brilliant or useful student, but would take under her wing the apparently most insignificant. She had no fear of the unusual, though the younger students thought so, and it was " her indifference to abstract principle " which made them

[1] *Memoir* of her aunt, by Blanche Athena Clough, Arnold, 1897—to which I am indebted for many of these details.

sometimes judge that she despised ideals. She had also a singular frankness—a singular directness—when speaking with others face to face ; her important things were said at odd moments, odd moments were her opportunities. Neither did she compromise ; she went all the way round and came out at the same place. This expedient made it quite unnecessary to override obstacles, and her aphorism " my dear, you must go round " was received with hostile scorn by a student seated on the high horse of abstract considerations. Indeed Miss Clough was not a fighter in the sense that she could neglect the quantity of others' feelings : and her desire that people should not be offended was part of a sympathy, not of a timidity, which could not be conquered. The working of her mind is shewn in the saying : " If we watch, we may still find a way to escape " — because to her there was no inevitable where her sympathies were engaged. Her diplomacy led her to keep her notions to herself, so that they should not be nipped in the bud by the frost of hostile criticism.

" My dear, I did wrong " was the disarming reply to a very young student who asked her " as one woman to another " whether she considered she had been justified in a certain course of action. Her singleness of purpose—the absence of all vanity—a complete disinterestedness, shone on all occasions. Her never failing search after the right course she once tried to express by saying to a student : " You must remember that I try to be just but I don't always succeed " ; and she criticised the performance with complete detachment from the personal equation.[1]

Among the ideas which seethed in her brain was the training of students as doctors to work among Hindu women ; and one of the last things she interested herself about was a school for girls at Siam. She wanted teachers trained to teach.[2] She urged students to know at least one country and one language besides their own. Her liking for new people, her interest in foreigners, especially in Italians, and in travel, was part of a spirit of adventure with which she was largely endowed. She liked old students to go to the colonies, and her interest in such doings never flagged. Her hold on the xx century was foreshadowed in the interest she took during the last years in the Norwegians, and in Japan. She felt very special sympathy with elementary teachers who receive small encouragement for highly important and difficult work. Even the monotonous life of the country clergy claimed her attention, as did a Sunday class for working men inaugurated by one of the students—which she visited, taking the keenest interest in the handwriting of the men, in the books they read. Her relations with her servants were always delightful, and she found time in the midst

---

[1] In her diary written the year she came of age she writes that honour and praise were not what she cared for. "If I were a man I would not work for riches or to leave a wealthy family behind me ; I would work for my country, and make its people my heirs."

[2] This she lived to see accomplished. A training college for women was proposed by Miss Buss in 1885 and Miss E. P. Hughes was its first principal and guiding spirit at Cambridge. Out of this grew the latter's Association of Assistant Mistresses.

of a busy life to teach the Newnham house boy to write.

She sometimes spoke at the college debates, and usually, as a student remarked, " spoke on both sides." On college anniversaries she would make short addresses, and point the connexion of study with life—" examinations demand concentration, presence of mind, energy, courage," qualities which " come into use every day " : or she would tell students " to bear defeat, and to try again and again " ; or she would quote the American who said we should not complain about things which can be remedied, or which cannot be remedied ; and add : " there is great strength in these words."

Her religion was unconventional like her mind ; full of aspiration, but lacking in definiteness. She spoke of it as " a longing towards what is divine," as " arising from the contemplation of the divine." She spoke of " bringing our hearts into a constant spirit of earnest longing after what is right " and added in language which discovers the burning thought and the halting utterance that made strange partnership in her : " There is no occasion, then, of kneeling down and repeating forms to make prayers."

One of the last acts was to preside on February 3, 1892 at a meeting which recommended the Council to build a college gateway ; the gateway which was to symbolise the concentration of the work—for the public pathway had just been closed—and the *tollite portas* to ever fresh generations of students. Its bronze gates are the old students' memorial of her.

Girton and Newnham

And on the morning of October 27, 1892, she died, in her room on the garden at Newnham, looking out at the gathering light of the new day.

She was buried with the honours of the head of a college, the Provost and fellows of King's offering their chapel for the purpose. She lies in the village church-yard of Grantchester, the *civitatula* which Bede describes where the sons of Ely monastery came to fetch the sarcophagus for S. Etheldreda. So in her death she is not divided from the great memories which link the history of the university to that of the movement to which she gave her life.

The first 28 students came into residence in Newnham Hall on October 18th 1875, and found the moment no less thrilling because they approached the door of their *alma mater* across planks and unfinished masonry. More room was at once needed, and "Norwich House" in the town was hired. In 1879 the Newnham Hall Company and the Association for promoting the Higher Education of Women [1] amalga-mated, and as "the Newnham College Association for advancing education and learning among women in Cambridge" built the second, or North Hall. Thus Newnham Hall became Newnham College. A public pathway led between the two halls, and this was not closed till 1891 ; but in 1886 a still larger building, containing the college hall, was erected, and called

---

[1] The Association formed to promote the interests of students working for the university Higher Local examinations ; see p. 326. The Newnham Hall Company was constituted in 1874 to build the first Hall.

NEWNHAM COLLEGE, GATEWAY

This shows the east front, and is called the Pfeiffer Building. The whole of the buildings are in the Queen Anne style, and were designed by Basil Champneys. The Bronze Gates were placed here as a memorial to Miss Clough.

Cambridge

Clough Hall, the original Newnham ("South") Hall becoming the "Old Hall," and the North Hall becoming "Sidgwick Hall." Lastly the two original halls were joined by the "Pfeiffer building"[1] and the college gateway in 1893, and in 1897 Mr. and Mrs. Yates Thompson presented a fine library, the pretty old library of Newnham Hall which had been built in 1882, being converted into a reading room. The land for the three Halls was purchased from S. John's College, the hockey field is on Clare land, and the total acreage is about ten and a half acres. The college holds 160 students, a few 'out students' being affiliated to one or other of the halls—and consists of a large hall, capable of seating 400 persons, a smaller hall and reading room in each building, the library, nine lecture and class rooms, gymnasium, small hospital, chemical laboratory, and the Balfour laboratory in the town which is a freehold of the college. The grounds contain two fives courts, lawn tennis courts, and a hockey ground. In the hall are the portraits of Miss Clough, Professor and Mrs. Sidgwick, and Miss M. G. Kennedy, as the four people who had given most of their life work to Newnham.[2]

The fees vary from £30 to £35 a year according to

[1] The cost of which was mainly defrayed by a bequest for the benefit of women left by Mrs. Pfeiffer and her husband.

[2] Mrs. Sidgwick is the daughter of the late James Balfour and of Lady Blanche Cecil, who was the sister of one Prime Minister as Mrs. Sidgwick is of another. Miss M. G. Kennedy is the daughter of the late Benjamin Hall Kennedy, one of the revisers of the New Testament with Lightfoot, Westcott, and Hort; fellow of S. John's, Canon of Ely, and Regius Professor of Greek, in whose honour the Latin professorship was founded.

the rooms occupied. The college is governed by a Council, and presided over by a Principal, Old Hall Sidgwick Hall and Clough Hall having each a resident vice-principal.[1] Miss Clough hoped to effect a real and lasting union between the old students and Newnham—that the college might be the support of the students, and the students of the college. It was a principle she had always present to her mind, and she herself did much to realise it. School and college have long bestowed this advantage on men, which is reinforced by the support men are accustomed to give to each other ; but all this is lacking for the woman who goes forth into the world to fend for herself. University life might however do much to supply the want, and it is to be hoped that women will form a tradition on the point, as men have done. The constitution of the college at least preserves some part of its first Principal's idea, old students have from the first had a share in the government and a place on the Council.

Candidates for entrance must pass the College Entrance examination (of the same standard as the university Previous Examination), unless they have already taken equivalent examinations. The greater number read for a tripos, but students may follow special lines of study. As to its university successes— the first tripos to be taken was the Moral Sciences

[1] The style of Principal was, as we have already seen, used for the chief of a hostel in the university ; it was also the title of the head of the *domus universitatis*, University Hall (1326).

Cambridge

(1874), and here Newnham students at once obtained the highest honours.[1] In 1876 Sir George Humphry,[2] as one of the examiners for the Natural Sciences tripos, when he met his fellow examiners said " I don't know, gentlemen, who your first is, but my first is a man called Ogle." The man called Ogle was a Newnham student.[3] In 1883 first classes were obtained in the Second Part of the Classical tripos, but Newnham waited till 1885 for its two first wranglers. In 1890 the University Calendar inserts in its Mathematical tripos list : " P. G. Fawcett, above the Senior Wrangler." Miss Fawcett obtained (it was reported) several hundred marks above the university senior wrangler Bennett of John's. It is customary to ring the bell of Great S. Mary's in honour of this *enfant gaté* of Cambridge university ; but Mr. Bennett stopped the ringing, and a bonfire at Newnham celebrated the occasion. In the History tripos two Firsts were obtained in 1879, and this tripos has frequently been duplicated with another —the Moral Sciences, Modern Languages, Mathematical, Classical, or Law. The first woman to take the two historic triposes, mathematical and classical, together, was Miss E. M. Creak in 1875. The first examinations in the Medieval and Modern Languages tripos were passed in 1886, 1887, and 1888, when

[1] See page 355. 1874 was the year in which Prof. James Ward was alone among the men in the first class when two of the examiners thought Mary Paley (Mrs. Marshall) should be there also, and two placed her in the second : no one doubts that Miss Paley attained the first class standard of any other year.

[2] Professor of Anatomy.   [3] Afterwards Mrs. Koppel.

Girton and Newnham

Firsts were obtained, and 30% of first classes have been taken in this tripos. Newnham has indeed been remarkable from the beginning for the number of its first class honours in the university lists.

Former Newnham students. There have been 880 honour students, and the total number of past and present students is 1600.[1] Like the Girtonians, old Newnhamites are to be found engaged in all kinds of work and in every corner of the world, and like Girton they have their large share of the teachers in the County and High schools of the country ; the towns which are perhaps most conspicuous for the number of Cambridge 'graduates' being Norwich, Exeter, Cambridge, and Birmingham. Among the mathematicians one is lecturer on Physics in the London School of Medicine for Women, another is mathematical lecturer at the Cambridge Training College, a third is warden of the House for Women Students at Liverpool, a fourth (who took the Natural Sciences as a second tripos) is senior physician in a Bombay hospital. Others are lecturers in the Civil Service Department of King's College London, and others again are teaching in Toronto, Cape Town, the Training College of Cape Colony, in Nova Scotia, the diocesan school at Lahore,

---

[1] October 1906. There are at Newnham 6 scholarships worth £50 a year, 1 of £70, 1 of £40, and 2 of £35. There is also a studentship of £75 and another of £80 a year, tenable for one year or more. Of these, two are for natural science students, one for a classic.

Through the munificence of private donors Newnham has been enabled to appoint 4 fellows of the college, and a fund is being formed which it is hoped will place these fellowships on a permanent basis.

THE GRANARY ON THE CAM

Coe Fen is on the left, and Prof. George Darwin's
House on the right of the Granary. This view is
taken close to Queens' College.

Cambridge

and at an Indian mission school; one is assistant investigator in the Labour Department of the Board of Trade, another who was secretary for secondary education in the Transvaal is now Chief Assistant on the Education Committee (Executive Office) of the L.C.C. The classics are engaged as classical tutors in Columbia University, in Trinity College Melbourne, at Mysore, and Cape Colony, at the Girls' High school at Poona, and as lecturers on history in University College Cardiff, on Method in the Chancery Lane Training school of the L.C.C., as assistant to the Professor of Humanity at Aberdeen, and as members of the educational committees of the Staffordshire County Council and Newcastle Town Council. The moralists have posts as lecturers at Newnham, as Mistress of Method at University College Bristol, and in the training department of the government school for girls at Cairo, as member of the Chiswick education committee, and as sub-warden of the Women's University Settlement at Southwark; and a senior moralist was first Principal of the Training College Cambridge. The natural scientists lecture on physiology in the London School of Medicine, on chemistry in Holloway College, are to be found in the geological research department of Birmingham University, as Quain student of botany in University College London, and as assistant demonstrator in geology to the Woodwardian professor at Cambridge. One is in Bloemfontein, one is sanitary inspector at Hampstead, another assistant curator of the museum at Cape Town, and another in the missionary

Girton and Newnham

school at Tokio ; and a daughter of a late master of
S. John's is a market gardener.   The historical students
are to be found teaching in New Zealand, Johannesburg,
Bloemfontein, and Winnipeg, lecturing in English
literature in Birmingham University, assisting the
Professor of Education and assistant secretary in the
faculty of commerce and administration in Manchester
University, Principal of S. Margaret's Hall Dublin,
of the Cambridge Training College, of the Diocesan
school at Lahore, of the missionary school at Kobé,
Japan, superintendent of the women students in
University College Bangor, and on the Education
committee of the Somerset County Council.   The
Medieval and Modern Languages students are to be
found as tutor and lecturer in French at University
College Bristol, as readers in German at Bryn Mawr
College Philadelphia, lecturers in English and French
at Holloway College, mistress of the Ladies' College
Durban, and of the convent school Cavendish Square.
Teaching in Queen's College Barbadoes, in Londonderry,
Brecon, and Guernsey (Newnham and Girton students
are to be found in both the Channel Islands), Vice-
principal of the Samuel Morley Memorial College
London, and, not least interesting, lecturer at the
University Extension College Exeter.   One is assistant
librarian of the Acton library Cambridge, another almoner
of King's College hospital, and a third is on the Education
committee of the Gateshead County borough Council.

Among the 658 who have not taken triposes,[1] among

[1] These include many who read for a tripos, and a large number who

343

the usual number of principalships and head and assistant mistress-ships of schools and colleges, we find old students lecturing in History at the Women's College Baltimore, demonstrating in Physics at Bryn Mawr College Philadelphia, lecturer at Smith College Northampton U.S.A., Professor at Wellesley College Massachusetts, tutor at Owens College Manchester, head of the Presbyterian school Calcutta, head mistress of the Church Missionaries' High school Agra, warden of the Women's University Settlement Southwark (and ex-vice-principal of Newnham College), and Principal of Alexandra College, Dublin (*LL.D.* of Dublin *honoris causa*). One is clinical assistant at the Royal Free hospital, another is in the superintendent's office at Guy's, a third is a physician at Newcastle-on-Tyne and member of the County borough Education committee. There is a lecturer in botany at Holloway, the director of a lyceum at Berlin, a teacher and superintendent of a class for blind women (Association for the Welfare of the Blind), a clerk to London university, a member of the council of Queen's College London, and the secretary of the Association of University Women Teachers. These old students are also to be found in Toronto, the West Indies, Vancouver, New South Wales, New Zealand, Pietermaritzburg, Natal, Johannesburg, North China, New York, and Christiania ; and on the Education committees of the Dorset, Herefordshire, and West Sussex County Councils, on the

in early days passed in the various Higher Local "Groups," besides all who have taken special courses of study.

Girton and Newnham

Croydon Education committee, and lecturing on English literature and on classical archaeology.

A large number of students take the tripos with a view to tuition, with which the above lists are, as we see, mainly concerned ; but an account of the literary output of Newnham students is in course of preparation.

Newnham has formed a collegiate character which is partly due to elements in its original constitution, partly to its first principal, and partly to its physical vicinity to the university. To take the last first. The college has always benefited by what one of the professors once described to the present writer as " the life of the university passing through it." It was not only this proximity, but the fact that Newnham was the product of the interest taken by university men in the advanced education of women—(Girton of a just and fully justified claim to university education made by women for women)—which made the acquirement of this character easier : and Newnham has in a marked degree the character of the university which harbours it—its cult of solid learning, its width and range, the absence of all pretentiousness, of that which every man and woman educated at Cambridge abhors as " priggishness." The delightful informality of Newnham and the liking for simple appearances is already outlined in the first Principal's views about the scheme and the new building ; " nothing elaborate or costly " is wanted : " The simple Cambridge machinery will be found all the better and all the more lasting because it suggested

GRANTCHESTER MILL

This picturesque old mill is on the upper river about
two miles from Cambridge, and is a favourite rendez-
vous of boating parties. The walk from Cambridge
to this mill is by 'Varsity men called the Grantchester
Grind. The famous Byron's Pool is just below the
mill.

itself so very naturally, and almost, so to speak, created itself. It is all the better for a college, as for other institutions, when it is not made, but grows." [1] And Newnham was not made but has grown, grown " very naturally " out of the " simple machinery " first designed for it ; has "created itself" because these simple elements suggested the way and the means of growth. There is no chapel at Newnham, all sorts and conditions of men have always been found there, and have worshipped God their own way—" not on this mountain, nor in Jerusalem." Old students sit at its council board, and come up to read in the Long Vacation. Miss Clough governed without rules, in conditions which were not then normal—which were thought indeed to be so abnormal that no company of women could venture to accept them.

If the enthusiasm expended over the two colleges by those who did most for them—the anxiety when things seemed to go wrong, the rejoicing when they went right—be remembered best by those who experienced it, it has had its enduring result in the

[1] Professor Seeley's rendering of her views for use at the public meeting at Birmingham. In a leaflet appealing for funds, Miss Clough said that the Cambridge lectures had been "a free-will offering" made to women by members of the university ; here at Cambridge women of " different occupations, different stations in life, and different religious persuasion " were brought together to receive in common "at least some share of academic education." " If we are right," she says, "in thinking our object one of national importance " the expense should not be thrown on Cambridge residents, "much less should members of the university, who are already giving their time ungrudgingly, be called upon to give money also." The journey to Birmingham was made with Miss M. G. Kennedy, and Mrs. Fawcett addressed the meeting.

movement itself. For nothing great is born without enthusiasm, and this was one of the greatest movements of the century. The lecturers—those "trained and practised teachers" who as an original prospectus declared "were willing to extend the sphere of their instruction " — took no fees, or returned them for several years as a donation to Newnham. Miss Clough not only took no stipend as Principal but helped the college with money ; Dr. and Mrs. Sidgwick, in addition to financial help of every kind, gave up their home in Chesterton and lived in three rooms at the "North Hall" of which Mrs. Sidgwick became vice-principal ; and here Miss Helen Gladstone, Gladstone's unmarried daughter, acted as her secretary. Miss M. G. Kennedy has been honorary secretary of the college since 1875, Mrs. Bonham-Carter its honorary treasurer and Mr. Hudson its honorary auditor. It may fairly be said of Newnham also, that it is partly the outcome of the enthusiastic loyalty of its first students, who have since taken so large a share in its welfare.[1]

The "Graces" of 1881. In the Lent term of 1881 there happened the greatest event in the history of the women's university movement. Three " Graces " were proposed to the Senate (a) should women be entitled to examination in the triposes (b) to a certificate of the place won

---

[1] It is interesting to note that there have been several students at both colleges bearing old Cambridge names, some known there in the xii, xiii, xiv and xv centuries : Bassett, Mortimer, Frost, Gaunt, Bingham, Booth, Parker, Alcock, Skelton, Crook, Bullock, Bentley, Parr, Creighton, Cartwright, Ridley, Day, May, Wallis, Sanderson, Morland, Herschell, Jebb, Sedgwick, Paley, and several others.

347

Cambridge

(c) to the insertion of their names, after that of the men, in all tripos lists, with a specification of the corresponding place attained by them in the men's list? On the eve of the day fixed for the vote—February 24th —the vicar of Little S. Mary's church and a Mr. Potts announced that they would *non-placet* the ' graces,' and as the day dawned some believed that their recruits would swamp the vote. On the same evening Mr. John Hollond, late M.P. for Brighton, was differently engaged in the House of Commons getting members to promise to share in a special train which was to take them to the university by two o'clock to record their votes, and get them back to their places by four when there was to be an important division in the House.[1] The students of Girton and Newnham crowded the roof of the latter college to watch for the pre-arranged signal—a handkerchief tied to the whip of a student who rode along the " Backs " from the Senate House carrying the news. The vote in favour of the Graces had been 398 to 32, and when it was declared the venerable Dr. Kennedy, the distinguished headmaster of Shrewsbury school and at that time Regius Professor of Greek,[2] waved his cap under the eyes of the vice-chancellor like any schoolboy. The loyal friends now came hurrying up to Newnham, one by one, Henry Sidgwick, Miss Emily Davies, Professor Cayley (first president of the College Council) Mr. Archer-Hind, Mr. (now Dr.) J. N. Keynes, and received an ovation from those whose

[1] Some forty members of Parliament voted in favour of the " Graces " on this occasion. [2] See p. 338 *n*.

348

Girton and Newnham

battles they had fought to such a successful issue : and if one of the seniors of the university became a boy in his delight, another Johnian[1] did not fail to cover himself with glory by his verses in imitation of Macaulay's Lay of Horatius, in which "Father Varius" and his friends hold the bridge against progress :

> Then out spake Father Varius
> No craven heart was his :
> ' To pollmen and to wranglers
> ' Death comes but once, I wis.
> ' And how can man live better,
> ' Or die with more renown,
> ' Than fighting against Progress
> ' For the rights of cap and gown ?'

The anniversary has since been kept at Newnham

[1] Another clergyman also—the Rev. E. W. Bowling, afterwards rector of Houghton Conquest, and a light blue champion in the boat race.

Battle of the Pons Trium Trojanorum, Thursday Feb. 24. 1881.

> Aemilia Girtonensis
> By the Nine Muses swore
> That the great house of Girton
> Should suffer wrong no more.
> By the Muses Nine she swore it
> And named a voting day
>
> .　　.　　.　　.
>
> But by the yellow Camus
> Was tumult and affright
>
> .　　.　　.　　.
>
> ' O Varius, Father Varius,
> ' To whom the Trojans pray,
> ' The ladies are upon us !
> ' We look to thee this day ! '
>
> .　　.　　.　　.
>
> The Three stood calm and silent
> And frowned upon their foes,
> As a great shout of laughter
> From the four hundred rose.

349

Cambridge

as " Commemoration " day : and if one touch were needed to complete it it would be found in Miss Clough's reminder to the students that they commemorate not only what women gained that day, but what the university gave that day. There was an amusing sequel to the vote : the official charged with the preparation of the university certificates consulted a confidential clerk as to the colour of the knot of ribbon which is attached to the university seal—" Don't you think blue—the university colour ? " he hazarded ; but was met by the prompt and horrified rejoinder " blue stockings, sir, blue stockings ! " So the colour is green.

Social life. Except under special circumstances the age for admission at Newnham and Girton is 18. Students' quarters at Newnham consist, in most cases, of a bedsitting room ; at Girton each student has a sitting room with a small bedroom leading from it. The necessary furniture is supplied, and can be supplemented according to taste by the student. All students must be within college boundaries by 7 o'clock (but with permission they can be out till 11) and are " marked in " two or three times a day, the chief occasion being the 7 o'clock " hall." Girton and Newnham students, if no other lady is to be present, can only visit men's rooms accompanied by some senior of the college. Visits of men to students' rooms are not permitted, except in the case of fathers and brothers ; but a student cannot ask her brother to her room to meet her college friends, for as Miss Clough observed " the brother of one is not the brother of all." Careful supervision with large liberty and an atmosphere which encourages the students to make themselves the trustees of the rules, characterise both colleges; and women students, as Miss Davies has pointed out, carry on their university life without being subject to the proctorial control which is found necessary in the case of men.

In the early days it required some independence of character to encounter the gibes and the wonder which women's life at the university aroused outside it. People who did not know what a " divided skirt " was, undertook to affirm that all Girtonians wore them : at Newnham some unconventionality in dress was amply concealed by the general dowdiness of the early Newnhamite. The dreaded eccentricities in conduct or clothes would not indeed have killed the movement ; and the authorities did not allow this dread to paralyse the quality of mercy, so that there was in fact small justification for the witty suggestion of a Newnham student that " Mrs. Grundy rampant and two Newnham students couchant" would make appropriate armorial bearings for the college. Nevertheless, as a concession to human weakness, smoking was not, and still is not, tolerated.

Both colleges hold debates in the great hall and also inter-collegiate and inter-university debates. Here are some of the subjects discussed : " Is half a loaf better than no bread ? " " That we spend too much " (lost). " That the best education offered to our grandmothers was more adequate than that offered by the High

MADINGLEY WINDMILL

This old ruin is on a hill near Madingley, about four miles from Cambridge. A great sweep of Fen Country is seen in the far distance. The long range of red buildings in the middle distance is Girton College. On a clear day Ely Cathedral can be seen from the left of the windmill.

Cambridge

Schools of to-day " (lost). The most important society at Newnham, however, is the Political Debating Society, and the lively and absorbing interest in politics shown nowadays by the college is in striking contrast to the general indifference to politics at Girton. This year (1906) in an inter-university debate (Oxford and Newnham) the motion " That this house approves Chamberlain's conception of empire " resulted in a 'draw.' Most of the students of both colleges are members of the Women's University Southwark Settlement, to which they subscribe. There is a Sunday Society and two musical societies in addition to the original Choral Society at Newnham, and societies in connexion with each of the triposes take the place of the select " Jabberwock " and " Sunday Reading Society " of earlier days. The great indoor institution at both colleges is the students' party at 10 p.m. known at Newnham as the " Cocoa." Two to four is the chief recreation hour, and there are college, inter-collegiate, and inter-university hockey, fives, cricket, tennis, and croquet matches. One of the first conveniences provided at Newnham was its gymnasium, where in the early days of the college a senior moralist might be seen leaping over the back of a student who had just been " ploughed " in the divinity of the " Little-Go," and a series of reverend seigniors would engage in a hopping match round the room led by the youngest " first year " who was an acknowledged expert in the art.

The public of a generation ago imagined that

Girton and Newnham

learned women would not marry and that men would specially 'fight shy' of taking to wife women who had done the same work as themselves. It may therefore be recorded that the first Newnham student to take a tripos, who was also the first lecturer appointed at Newnham Hall, married the professor of Political Economy, and that they wrote a book on that subject together. That the first classical lecturer at Newnham married a well-known classic and classical tutor of his college (Trinity) ; that the next Moral Sciences lecturer married the distinguished psychologist who is now professor of Mental Philosophy ; that the first historical lecturer, Ellen Wordsworth Crofts, married Darwin's biologist son Mr. Francis Darwin ; and that the first woman to come out senior classic (a Girtonian) married the Master of Trinity College, himself senior classic of his year.

Writing about the proposed Bedford College for women, in 1848, Frederick Denison Maurice had declared that "The least bit of knowledge that is knowledge must be good, and I cannot conceive that a young lady can feel her mind in a more dangerous state than it was because she has gained one truer glimpse into the conditions under which the world in which it has pleased God to place her actually exists." So "ambitious" a name as "college" for a girls' academy had a novel sound "to English ears." To-day the words which excuse and explain its use sound strange and antiquated in ours. Many of the things about which men have fought and borne the heat of

45

Cambridge

long days will seem incredible to posterity, and the refusal of a 'college' or of university education to women will no doubt be among them. No one else, nevertheless, had given to women the opportunity they wanted when Cambridge gave it. Cambridge returned affirmative answers to each request as it was preferred —in 1863, in 1865, in 1870, and in 1880 when in reply to a memorial signed by 8600 persons praying that the Senate would "grant to properly qualified women the right of admission to the examinations for university degrees, and to the degrees conferred according to the result of such examinations," the Syndicate appointed to consider it returned the memorable answer : "The Syndicate share the desire of the memorialists that the advantage of academic training may be secured to women and that the results of such training may be authoritatively tested and certified." [1] The irony of history required that this memorial, which led to the granting of the Graces, should be rolled and unrolled over the drawing room carpet of a vice-chancellor known to be hostile to the movement. Forty years after F. D. Maurice had penned the words already quoted women had come out at the head of the list in each of the principal triposes. The most striking

[1] The first man to maintain that girls had a right to as good an education as boys, was a *Cantab* (Eton and King's College) a master at the new Merchant-Taylors' school, and afterwards headmaster of Colet's school. Lancelot Andrewes was one of his pupils. This famous Cantab and famous schoolmaster—Richard Mulcaster—also advised that teachers should be trained to teach. In the xviii c. Defoe's appreciation of the woman with 'knowledge'—"well-bred and well-taught"—led to his suggestion that there should be a college for her higher education.

instance of the misjudgment which it is possible to
make about things simply because custom has allowed
no one to try them, occurred at the dinner table of
friends of the present writer when the late Professor
Fawcett, in urging the claims of women to university
education, said : " I don't say that a woman would
ever be senior wrangler, but women would take very
good places." His daughter was to be the first senior
wrangler : but at no other period of English history
would the comparison have been possible by which a
parent could test such capacities in his own child.
After this it is not surprising that lesser men were
unable to gauge the unused powers of half the race ;
and when one spirited person declared he had no
objection whatever to women competing with men
but that he considered the air of Cambridge would not
be beneficial to them, the argument was as reasonable
as any other.

Character and As to the character of the work in which
choice of work. women do best. It had been said that
they would not do well in "abstract" subjects. The
tripos in which they have taken the highest distinction
is the Moral Sciences,[1] where they have been at the
top of the list or alone in the First Class five times,
provoking Punch's cartoon in the ' eighties ' of a girl
graduate entering a first class railway carriage marked
" For Ladies only." Their best work has been done
in pure mathematics, and, agreeing in this with the
men, it is these subjects which they choose for the

[1] For the subjects of this tripos, see iii. pp. 187-189.

355

Cambridge

Second Part of the tripos. In choice of subject the order is as follows (*a*) Mathematics (*b*) Classics (*c*) History (*d*) Natural Sciences (*e*) Languages (*f*) Moral Sciences. The scale of success has been highest in Moral Sciences, then in (*b*) Languages (*c*) Natural Sciences (*d*) Classics (*e*) History (*f*) Mathematics.[1] The classical and mathematical triposes lead to those general tuitional posts for which so many women seek a university education ; the languages tripos is easier for those women who go up without the usual school preparation ; while the lower places in the history tripos do duty for that " ordinary degree " which is not open to women. It is therefore in the moral and natural

[1] *For the 20 years from 1886 to 1906 :—*
Mathematics 345 candidates, 31 wranglers

			First and 2nd classes 56 per cent.
Classics 296 candidates, 54 first classes .	,,	,,	61 ,,
Moral Sciences 83 candidates, 21 first classes (this excludes the triumphs of the first 12 years)	,,	,,	76 ,,
Natural Sciences 246 candidates, 64 first classes	,,	,,	70 ,,
History 290 candidates, 49 first classes .	,,	,,	64 ,,
Medieval and Modern Languages (tripos created in 1886) 246 candidates, 73 first classes . . .	,,	,,	74 ,,

Hence in these 6 triposes the highest percentage of Firsts has been obtained in the Moral Sciences, Languages, and Natural Sciences, Classics coming fourth ; while in the percentage of First and Second classes the order is again : Moral Sciences, Languages, Natural Sciences, followed by History, Classics, and Mathematics.

In the first 10 years 250 students took a tripos, of whom one in five (51) was placed in the first class.

Among the men the percentage of *First Classes* for *the years 1900-1905* is : mathematics 39 per cent, classics 28 per cent. For the subjects chosen by men cf. iv. p. 238 *n.*

356

sciences that there is distinct evidence of choice of
subject : the proportion of women who take the former
is overwhelmingly greater than the proportion of men,[1]
and the taste of women for the natural sciences is as
marked, a fact which might have been foreseen by
those who watched the signs of the times many years
ago.

The degree. The refusal of the degree, of the magic
letters *B.A.* and *M.A.*, to women, need not be discussed here. That women have the same use for the
degree as men is obvious ; that it strains their alleged
liking for self-sacrifice too far to suggest that they
prefer to forgo the legitimate rewards of their work,
not less so ; and it should not be regarded either as
satisfactory or logical that when they do the same work
the men only should have the recompense. Dublin
university has just offered an *ad eundem* degree to all
women who had qualified themselves for the degree at
Cambridge or Oxford—187 have taken the *B.A.*, 121
the *M.A.*, and three have become doctors of letters
or science. The credit of this act belongs to the gallant
Irishman, and the coffers of Dublin university have
thus been enriched, very warrantably, at the expense
of the impoverished coffers of Cambridge which sent
the far larger number of graduates.[2]

---

[1] There are, roughly, 3000 men and 300 women at the university.
Since 1882, 94 women and 168 men have taken this tripos—the proportion
should have been 940 men.

[2] The founders of Girton have been steadfast in demanding the degree.
In 1887, 842 members of the senate signed a petition in favour of it.
Miss Clough had signed a similar petition earlier. The objections to

Cambridge

We have moved step by step from the cautious recommendation of the university that the names of the young girls examined for the Local Examination should not appear, and that no class lists should be published (1865) and the informal examination for the triposes, when for nine years (until 1881) the examiners in the classical tripos "objected to state" what class had been attained, to the present state of things when all the "publicity and intrusion" dreaded forty years back in the case of little girls being examined somewhere privately in the same town as little boys, is annually given to hundreds of women in the highest examination in the country in the midst of the university. There had been prophets who opined that under these circumstances Cambridge would be deserted by the other sex. Visions of the halls of Trinity and John's empty and forsaken, while Girton and Newnham poured forth a ceaseless flow of undergraduates disturbed the sleep of these prophets and seemed worth putting on record in their waking moments. No sooner were the Local Examinations opened to girls in 1865 than the number of boys entered rose from 629 to 1217;[1] and the largest entry of under-graduates on record was that of this present year 1906-7. What has happened? Has a robuster generation of undergraduates arisen, or were the

opening the degrees to women have been adequately met in the pamphlet "Women in the Universities of England and Scotland," Cambridge, Macmillan and Bowes, 1896.

[1] The entries for 1863, when girls were first informally examined, were 639, the next year they rose to 844.

Girton and Newnham

undergraduates of the " seventies " and " eighties "
simply maligned ?

As between the two ancient universities
Cambridge remains the pioneer in the
education of women. The examinations
are open to women at Oxford, but the same restrictions
as to preliminaries and residence are not imposed.[1]
It is, however, by the restrictions imposed that
Cambridge has established the position of its women
students. It has thus bound itself to compare the work
of all tripos students irrespective of sex. While at
Oxford there is no university recognition of the status of
the candidate or of her hall, and no university certificate
of the place obtained, Girton and Newnham are
recognised colleges at Cambridge ; the name of the
successful candidate followed by that of the college is
read aloud in the Senate House and published on the
Senate House door ; and only students presented
by these colleges are admitted to the university
examinations, as is the case with men. Girton and
Newnham each owe something to the other. Newnham
to Girton in the collegiate status now enjoyed by both,

---

[1] Statutes regulating the examination of women, and opening to them
the Mathematical, Natural Sciences, and Modern History schools, were
voted in 1886 by a majority of 464 votes to 321. Responsions and the
other schools were opened to women in 1888, 1890, and 1893 (the
Theological school, Oriental studies, and the *D.Mus.*) and in 1894 the
remaining examinations were opened. Pass and honour examinations are
both open to women at Oxford, and the names of successful candidates
appear in the official lists. The certificate, however, is given by the
Oxford Association for the Education of Women, who restrict it to those
students who have qualified like the men on all points.

Cambridge

Girton to Newnham because the considerable advantages accruing to women students through proximity to Cambridge have been reflected on the sister college. Each displayed a boldness distinctively its own which has been the main source of the success of the movement : Newnham planted her house of students in the university town, Girton asked to follow the same curriculum as men ; and these two things have had a mutually favourable reaction ever since.

The position of women in other universities. In 1856 the first application was made—by Jessie White to London university—for admission as a candidate for the medical degree. A similar request was made seven years later. A supplementary charter establishing special examinations for women was procured by this university in 1869. In 1878 it made "every degree, honour, and prize awarded by the university accessible to students of both sexes on perfectly equal terms." Since 1889 all disqualification for women in Scotch universities has ceased. The Victoria university, by its original charter 20 April 1880, admitted both sexes equally to its degrees and distinctions ; and in 1895 Durham became a "mixed" university. All the more recent universities treat men and women equally.

Index

OF

Names of Persons and of Cambridge Families referred to in the Text

chr. = chancellor, *v.-c.* = vice-chancellor, *proc.* = proctor (of the university), *M.* = master (of a college), *abp.* = archbishop, *bp.* = bishop.

Acre, Joan d', 64 *n.*, 298
Acton, 1st lord, professor, 192, (quoted) 99
Adams, Prof. John Couch 126, 172 *n.*, 191, 291, 318 *n.*, 329 *n.*, Mrs. 329 *n.*, Sir T., founder of chair of Arabic 190
Addenbrooke, Dr. John, 115
Agnes, daughter of Philip the tailor [*Rot. Hund. Cant.*], 42, 43
Aidan, S., 2
Airy, G. B., prof., 139, 172 *n.*, 191, 291
Albert Pr. Consort, chr., 113
Alcock, 347 *n.*
    John, bp. of Ely 76, 150, 152, 259, 260, his arms on the watergate of Coe fen 57 *n.*, probably a Peterhouse man *ibid.*, a pluralist 63, chancellor of England 76 *n.*, obtains dissolution of nunnery from Alex. VI. 115, 271, founds Jesus 115, restores the church of S. Rhadegund 116, his gateway at Jesus 141, scope of his foundation 153, its dedication 319 *n.*, friend of the new learning 270

Alcuin, 1, 2, 172, 252, 254 *n.*
Aldrich, 306, 308
    Robert, bp. 105, 174 *n.*, Thos., Puritan M. of Corpus 276
Alexander VI., 78, 115, 271
Alfred, 8, 252, 254 *n.*
Alfred of Beverley, 3
Alley, Wm., bp. of Exeter, 106
Andrewes, Lancelot, bp. of Ely & Winchester, M. of Pembroke, 74, 189 *n.*, 259, 273, 280, 282, 354 *n.*
Anjou, see *Margaret of*
Anna, king of the East Angles, 311 *n.*
Anne, queen, visits Cambs. 113, Jacobites there in her reign 267
Anselm, S., 101 *n.*
Antony of Padua, S., 23 *n.*
Arthur, Prince (duke of Brittany), 295
Arthur, Prince (Tudor), 176 *n.*
Arundel, abp. 29, 58, 235 *n.*, 269, Wm. FitzAlan, earl of 75
Ascham, Roger, 3, 126, 173, 174, 175 *n.*, 207, 243, 253, 254 *n.*, 281, 283, 360
Athelstan, 32, 87 *n.*
Audley, 296, 297, 298
    Thos., Ld., founder of Magdalene Coll.

361

46

76, 129, 150, (quoted) 129, pedigree 300, 301
Audrey, S., see *Etheldreda*
Augustine, S., of Canterbury, 2
Austen, Jane, 257

Babington, 296, 302
  abbot of Bury 302, Prof. C. C. 329 *n.*, Henry, v.-c. 205 *n.*, 302, Humphrey, Dr. 302
Bacon, 244, 296, 302
  Francis, lord 3, 85, 137, 139, 215, 218 *n.*, 244, 253, 254 *n.*, 255, 256, 258, 281, 282, 285, 290, 302, 303, 308, Sir Nicholas 83, 85, 106 *n.*, 107, 244, 302, Thos., M. of Gonville 302
Badew, Ric. de, chr., 64, 64 *n.*, 150, 152
Baker, Dr. Philip, v.-c. 106 *n.*, 142, Thos., historian of S. John's (1656-1740) 126, 215
Bale, John, bp. of Ossory, 16 *n.*, 20, 20 *n.*, 116, 245, 258
Balfour, Frank, prof., 329 *n.*
Ball, Sir Wm., Royal Soc., 283
Balsham, Hugh de, bp. of Ely 15, 27, 29, 30, 54, 55, 76, 150, 192 *n.* His judgment cited 6 *n.*, 28 *n.*, 203, limits archidiaconal authority in university 14, 28, 37, design to graft secular scholars on the canons' house of S. John 38, 55, 122-123, founds Peterhouse 55-6, 62, his motives for so doing 62, leaves money to build a hall 56, leaves his books to the college 58, 138 *n.*, scope of foundation 153, 154, sides with de Montfort 260, S. Simon Stock his contemporary 325, see *general index*
Bancroft, abp., 99, 116, 118, 259
Bardenay, John de, prior of Benedictine students, 128 *n.*
Barnes, prior, 22, 272, 275
Baro, Peter, 60, 280
Barrow, Isaac, prof., 60 *n.*, 139, 170, 191, 225, 263
Bassett, 44, 110 *n.*, 292, 296, 306, 307 *n.*, 347 *n.*
  Alan (quoted) 68 *n.*, John 306, Philip, chief justice 44, William, proc. 19, 306

Bateman, Wm. bp. of Norwich 76, 150, 152, 153, 259, 330. Changes character of Gonville statutes 67, Gonville's executor 78, 83, Edw. III.'s ambassador 79, founds Trinity Hall 79, motives of the foundation *ibid*, founds the library 80, obtains licences for the 2 college chapels 109 *n.*, Ely hostel conveyed to him 127, Norwich monks come to Cambs. during his episcopate 128 *n.*, 143 *n.*
Bateson, Wm., M. of S. John's 329 *n.*, Mrs. 329 *n.*
Beauchamp, 150 *n.*
  Eleanor dss. of Somerset 299, Margaret dss. of Somerset 299, 305 *n.*
Beaufort, 262, 292, 294, 296-97
  Anna, sister to Ly. Margaret 308 *n.*, Henry, Cardinal, scholar of Peterhouse 58 *n.*, 59, 106, 259, 260, 262, Thos. duke of Exeter 58 *n.*, 156
Beaumont, 202, 297 *n.*
  Charles 62, Francis (the dramatist) 257, 306, Joseph, M. of Peterhouse 62, Dr. Robt. v.-c. 302
Bede, 2, 5, 5 *n.*, 10, 10 *n.*, 172, 252, 254 *n.*
Behn, Mrs. Afra, early novelist, 258
Beket, Thos. à, educated at Merton priory, 44 *n.*
Benedict XI. 143 *n.*, 144 *n.*, XII. 127, 144 *n.*
Benjamin the Jew, his house in Cambridge, 21 *n.*
Benson, abp., confers Lambeth degree, 194 *n.*
Bentley, 347 *n.*
  Ric., 126, 135, 139, 174, 175 *n.*, 176, 191, 219 *n.*, 245
Betham, Edw., fellow of King's, his letter to Cole, 212
Beverley, John of, 2, 172
Bill, Wm., bp., v.-c., 139, 274 *n.*
Billingford, Ric., chr., 205 *n.*
Bilney, Thos., 80, 275, 275 *n.*
Bingham, 347 *n.*, & see *Byngham*
Blomfield, bp., 239
Blount, Chas., the deist, 279
Bodichon, Barbara L. S., 317 *n.*, 318 *n.*, 319, 320, 327 *n.*
Boleyn, 102 *n.*
  Anne 102, 102 *n.*, Henry 102 *n.*, Wm. 102 *n.*

Index of Names

Bolingbroke, Ld., the deist, 279
Bonham-Carter, Mrs., 347
Boniface IX., 204
Bonner, bp., 273 n.
Bonney, T. G., 318 n., 329 n.
Booth, Laurence, abp., chr., 74, 76 n., 154, 260, 347 n.
Boquel, Lucien, 329 n.
Bossuet, has Sherlock for opponent, 60
Bottlesham, John de, bp. of Rochester, M. of Peterhouse (1397-1400), 58
Bowling, E. W., 349, 349 n.
Boyle, earl of Cork, 85, 260, Robt., Royal Soc., 284
Bradford, John, 75, 275
Bramhall, Protestant abp. of Armagh, 147
Brandon, 296, 297, 297 n., 301
   Charles, 1st & 3rd dukes of Suffolk 106, Henry, 2nd duke 106
Brantingham, bp., 27
Braybrooke, see *Neville*
Brodrick, abp., 66
Brontë, Charlotte & Emily, 257
Brooke, see *Greville*
Brown, Ford Madox, 57 n.
Browne, Robert, of Corpus 278, 303, Sir Thos., letter to, from Christ's, Coll. 180, Sir Wm. 61, 245, 260, 268
Browning, Robert, 251
Brownrigg, Ralph, bp., M. of Catherine's, v.-c., 115, 264
Bruce, Robert, 69
Bryan, 302
   Augustine 175 n., John 174 n.
Bucer, Martin, 60
Buckingham, see *Stafford & Villiers*
Buckle, H. T., 251
Bullock, 347 n.
   Henry, v.-c., 111, 170 n., 174 n.
Bunyan, 251, 253, 254 n.
Burgh, de, 291, 292, 293, 296, 297
   Elizabeth de, see *Clare*, Elizabeth jnr., *domina Claræ*, dss. of Clarence 95, 295 n., 297 n., 298, Hubert, earl of Kent 293, 295, 298, John, chr. 203 n., 293, John, bp. of Ely 293, John, 3rd earl of Ulster 64 n., 293, 298, Ric. 2nd earl of Ulster, the 'red earl' 64 n., 320 n., Ric. 'the great earl of Clanricarde' 301,

Thos. 293, William, last earl of Ulster 297 n., 298
Burke, Edmund, 268, 309
Burleigh, see *Cecil*
Burn, Rev. R., 318 n.
Burnet, bp. (quoted), 284 n.
Buss, Miss, 335 n.
Butler, bp., 251
Butler 'of Cambridge,' 260
Butts, Sir Wm., *M.D.*, 296
Byng, Thos. v.-c., 180 n.
Byngham, 306, 307 n.
   Thos. 1st M. of Pembroke 306, Wm., founder of God's House 117 n., 150, 153, 165 n., 306, (quoted) 165 n., Wm. proc. 306
Byron, lord, 139, 163, 255, 308, (quoted) 7, 182 n.

Caedmon, 2
Caesar, 4
Caius or Keys, John 151, 152, 260, 281, founds Caius 78, 141, 142, President of College of Physicians 141, Principal of Physwick hostel 141, studies in Italy 141, lives with Vesalius 141, lectures in London on anatomy 142, the first English anatomist 142, his influence on Cambridge 167, 179, scope of his foundation 153, 154, an eminent classic 142, 174 n., lectures at Padua on Greek 174, opposes the new pronunciation of Greek 177 n., Master of Gonville & Caius 142, antiquary & historian of the university 142, his care for sanitation 142, his inscription on foundation stone & his epitaph in Caius chapel 142, clings to Catholicism 142, 180, 180 n.
Cambridge, earls of 36 n., family of 294, Sir John de 24 n., 132, prior John of 261, Ric. earl of 36 n., 295, 295 n., 296, Ric. earl of, & of Ulster, Lord of Clare 295 n., see *York, duke of*
Cantaber, 4, 20 n.
Canterbury, abp. of, see *Bancroft, Cranmer, Grindal, Langton, Parker, Sancroft, Sumner, Tenison, Tillotson, Whitgift, Whittlesey*
Cantilupe, Nicholas, 20, 20 n.

363

Canute, 10
Capranica, Card., 230
Carlisle, bp. of, see *Aldrich, Close, Goodwin, Law, May, Percy & Scrope*
Carlyle, Thos., 140
Carr, Nicholas, 175 *n.*
Cartwright, Thos., 276, 277, 347 *n.*
Castle-Bernard, a Cambridge name, 292 *n.*
Castlereagh, viscount, 126, 260
Catherine of Alexandria, S., 114
Catherine of Aragon, 114, 121
Cave, Wm., 126
Cavendish, 294, 302, 303
  Henry, the scientist 59, 303, Lord John 302, Sir John de, chr. 203, 260, 302, Wm., M. of Peterhouse 302, Mary, countess of Shrewsbury, benefactor of S. John's 124, 125, Spencer, 8th duke of Devonshire, chr. 205, Thos., the circumnavigator, 282
Caxton, 75, 99, 112
Cayley, Prof., 139, 172 *n.*, 329 *n.*, 348
Cecil, 296, 302, 303
  Wm. lord Burleigh, chr. 126, 215, 260, 282, 303, Thos. earl of Exeter, chr. 303, Robert earl of Salisbury, chr. 126, 260, 282, 303, lady Dorothy (see *Neville*), lady Mildred 313 *n.*, Mr. Cecil, moderator 303, 'Cecil at the castle' [*Rot. Hund. Cant.*] 42 *n.*, 292
Chantrey (quoted), 137
Chapman, Geo. (dramatist), 257
Charlemagne, 2
Charles I. 113, 263, 264 *n.*
Charles II. 113
Charles V., Emperor, Pole's letter to 121, (quoted) 129 *n.*
Chatham, lord, 268, (quoted) 74 *n.*
Chatillon, 69, 296, 297
  Marie de, see *Valence*, Gaucher de, 1st Comte de Saint-Paul 295, 296, Guy de, 299, Walter de 69, pedigree of 299
Chaucer, 3, 88, 89, 252, 254 *n.*, 255, 256
Cheke, Sir John, first Professor of Greek, fellow of S. John's, 105, 126, 174, 175 *n.*, 177 *n.*, 191, 207 *n.*, 281, 303
Chester, Gastrell, bp. of, 193
Chesterfield, Philip 4th earl of, 80, 260
Chillingworth, Wm., 278, 279, 286 *n.*

Clare, 292-293, 296, 297, 297 *n.*, 320, pedigree of 298
  Elizabeth de 64 *n.*, 67, 95, 151 *n.*, 152, 293, 295, 296, 297, 312, 320 *n.*, 325 *n.* Benefactor to Austin priory at Stoke Clare 22 *n.*, 293, founds Clare 64-5, conveyance to her of the *domus universitatis* 65 *n.*, her statutes quoted 67-8, scope of foundation 153, 154, founds Greyfriars of Walsingham 293, sends timber to King's Hall 293, (quoted) 64 *n.*, 86 *n.*, 201, lineage 64 *n.*, 150, 299, pedigree of 298
  Gilbert de (temp. Conquest) 292, Gilbert earl of Hertford & Glouc. (*ob.* 1229) 292, 298, Gilbert 'the red' (father of the founder of Clare) 40, 44, 64 *n.*, 298, Gilbert earl of Glouc. (killed 1314) 65, 151 *n.*, 298
  Richard, earl of Glouc. 22 *n.*, 292-3, 298, Richard de, abbot of Ely 298, Richard, 2nd earl of 320 *n.*
Clarence, Elizabeth dss. of, see *de Burgh*, George duke of 111, Lionel duke of 94, 95, 295 *n.*, 297 *n.*, 298
Clarentia, Philippa de, 298
Clark, 308
  J. W. 8, 31, 32, 44, Rev. W. G. 318
Clarke, Robert 179, Samuel 144, 279
Clarkson, Thos., 126, 253 *n.*, 269
Clerk, Sir Francis, 152
Clerk Maxwell, Jas., first Cavendish Prof., 139, 192
Clerke, Ric., a Cambs. colonist at Cardinal College, 272, 273
Cleveland, John, 263
Clifford, 3rd earl of Cumberland, 282
Clifford, W. K., 329 *n.*
Clive, Robt., 251, 253, 254 *n.*
Close, Nicholas, bp., 105, 327
Clough, Anne J. 326, 327, 327 *n.*, 329, 330-337, 338, 339, 346, 347, 350, 357 *n.*, Arthur Hugh 330, Sir Ric. 330
Coke, Edw., lord, High Steward of the University, 139, 260, (quoted) 100
Cole, Wm. (*ob.* 1782), 66, 105, 212
Colenso, bp., 126, 172 *n.*, 288
Coleridge, S. T., 116, 232, 302
Colet, dean, 173, 176 *n.*, 253, 254 *n.*, 270
Collier, Jeremy, 267

Index of Names

Collins, Anthony, of King's, the deist, 279
Compton, bp., 265 n., 266 n.
Coningsby, Sir Wm., 105
Constantia, wife to Earl Eustace, grants Cambs. fisheries, 116 n.
Cook, R. S. (Mrs. Scott), 321 n.
Cornwallis, 1st marquess, 66
Cosin, Cousins, 308
  John, bp., M. of Peterhouse, 58, 59, 259, 274, 280
Cotes, Roger, 1st Plumian Prof., 139, 191
Cotton, Sir Robert, 139
Courtney, abp. of Canterbury, stays with the Whitefriars, 20
Coverdale, Miles, an Austinfriar at Cambs., 22, 245, 272
Cowley, Abraham, 139, 244, 263, 284
Cowper, Wm., 303, 303 n.
Cox, Richard, bp. of Ely, 105, 175 n., 272, 273, 274 n.
Cranmer, abp., 116, 194, 243, 253, 254 n., 259, 271, 273, 273 n., 274, 275
Crashaw, Ric., 59, 60 n., 263
Crawden, John de, prior of Ely, 127
Creak, E. M., 340
Creighton, 347 n.
Crofts, Ellen, see *Darwin*
Croke (Crooke), first Reader in Greek at Cambs., 105, 172, 173, 174, 175 n., 191, 207, 281
Cromwell, Oliver 22, 146, 147, 253, 254 n., 260, 264, 264 n., 275, 277, 308, Thos. 151, 167, 175, 205, 244 n., 276, 276 n.
Cromwells, the, 229
Crook, 347 n.
Crouchback, Edmund earl of Leicester, 42 n.
Croyland, 294
  Robert de, 132
Cudworth, Ralph, prof., 66, 119, 145, 145 n., 191, 286, 289
Culverwell, Nathanael, 145, 286
Cumberland, Ric., bp., 130
Cunningham, Dr. W., fellow of Trinity, archd. of Ely, 247, 322 n.
Curteys, abbot of Bury, 16 n.
Curthose, Robert, 8

Dakins, Wm., of Trinity, a translator of the bible, 275

Daniel, Samuel, 256 n.
Darwin, 302
  Charles 119, 178, 253, 254 n., 255, 290, 291, 303, 309, Ellen Wordsworth Crofts (Mrs. Francis) 353, Erasmus 126, 303, Francis 353
D'Aubeney, Reiner, 75 n.
David of Scotland, 36 n., 297 n.
David's, S., Thirlwall, bp. of (see also *Thirlwall*) 318 n., see *Langton*
Davies, Miss Emily, 314, 317 n., 319, 348, 351
Davy, Humphry, 255
Day, 307, 347 n.
  George, bp., v.-c., 105, 273 n., W., bp., 105, 273 n.
Defoe, Daniel, 257, 354 n.
Dekker, Thos. (dramatist), 257
De Morgan, Prof., 139, 172 n.
Derby, css. & earl of, see *Ly. Margaret & Stanley*
Descartes, 287
Devereux, 302
  Robert earl of Essex, 139, 282, 301, 304
Devonshire, see *Cavendish*
Dickens, Charles, 251, 257
Digby, Sir Kenelm, 284
Dillingham, Francis, M. of Emmanuel, a translator of the bible, 175 n., 273
Dillon, viscount, 319 n.
Diss, Walter 16 n., 20, Wm. 15 n.
Dodwell, Prof., 267
Doket, Andrew, 109, 111, 152
Donne, John, 139, 308
Downing, Sir George, senr. 66, 147, founder of Downing 147, 150, 153, 154
Downside, abbot of, 149
Drake, Sir Francis, 83, 251, 253, 254 n., 282
Drayton, Michael, 256 n.
Dryden, John, 139, 255, 258, 258 n., 264, 274, 284, 305, 308
Dudley, 297 n.
  Robert earl of Leicester, 297 n., 300, 301
Dunning, 39, 123, 292
  Eustace 42, Hervey 42, 42 n., 304
Durham, William, bp. of, 45 n., & see *Cosin, Lightfoot, Pilkington, Ruthall, Tunstall, Westcott*

Edmund, king & saint, 12 n., 15 n.

Edward I. 64 n., 152, 252, 254 n., 298, 299. Builds Franciscan friary 21, visits Cambs. as Pr. of Wales 36, composes disputes between scholars & townsmen 37, his Scotch wars 69, lodges at the castle 113, visits Walsingham with Eleanor 114, redresses a late dispute 233 n.

Edward II. 150. Obtains from pope European status for university 35, 35 n., maintains scholars there 37, 131, lodges at Barnwell priory 113, gives licence for University Hall 64, intends to found a college 37, 131, 131 n.

Edward III. 88, 94, 150, 152, 153, 154, 260, 295 n., 297, 298, 299, 300. Quarries Cambridge castle for King's Hall 5 n., bestows a hospice on Oriel College, Oxford 18 n., gives licence to Gilbertines 19, creates earls of Cambridge 36 n., fulfils intentions of Edw. II. 37, 131, gives privileges to university 37 n.-38 n., 222 n., issues letters to town of Stamford 46, knights the Master of Pembroke 75, gives licence to Gonville 78, Bateman his ambassador 79, letters about King's Hall 95 n., his arms on Entrance Gate of Trinity 103 n., visits Cambridge 113, builds King's Hall 131, his effigy on Great Gate 131, his gateway at King's Hall 132. See general index

Edward IV. 36 n., 37 n., 86 n., 112, 262, 298,299. His arms in King's chapel 103 n., sequestrates building funds of 104, visits university 112, King's Hall chapel built in his reign 137, robs King's College of revenues 262

Edward VI. 141, 175 n. Continues favour shown by Tudors to Cambs. 37 n., sends foreign Protestants there 60 n., Trinity College built under 135, his tutors Cambridge men 175 n., 281

Edward VII., 113

Edward the Confessor, 261

Edward the Elder, 4

Edwin of Northumbria, 2, 311

Eleanor of Castile, 114, 155

Eliot, George 257, 317 n., John, 'the Indian apostle,' 263

Elizabeth 21 n., 60, 141, 145, 175 n., 219 n., 233 n., 253, 254 n. Apostrophizes Pembroke College 73-4, sends timber for Corpus chapel 83, visits Cambs. 107, 108, 113, 163, completes Trinity Chapel 134, 137, makes Leicester High Steward 206 n., her statutes 28 n., 210, entrusts revision of Edward's Prayerbook to Cambs. men 273, 'Lambeth articles' drawn up 274, her antipuritanism 276, checks Presbyterianism 277, Cambridge men round her 281-2, sends timber to Trinity College 293. See general index

Elizabeth of York, 114

Ellenborough, 1st lord, 59, 172 n., 239

Eltisley, Thos. first M. of Corpus, 82

Ely, bps. of, see Alcock, Andrewes, Balsham, Cox, Felton, Fleetwood, Fordham, Goodrich, Gunning, Holbroke, Kilkenny, Moore, Montacute, Patrick, Stanley, Thirlby, Turner, Walpole, West, Wren. For abbot, prior, & sub-prior of, see Balsham, Clare, Norwich, Walsingham

Harvey Goodwin, dean of, aftw. bp. of Carlisle 317 n.

Emma, queen, 261

Empson, Sir Ric., 206 n.

Erasmus 88, 174, 270, 281, 288, knows Franciscan nuns at Cambs. 25 n., bp. Sampson a pupil of, there 80, Thos. Aldrich a Cambridge friend of 105, lives at Queen's 111, influence of on statutes of Christ's 119, writes lady Margaret's epitaph 120, his description of Cambs. studies at the end of the xv. c. 170, letter to Bullock of Queen's ibid., co-operates with Fisher in introducing Greek 172, studies Greek at Oxford 173, studies Greek at Cambs. 173, teaches Greek there 174 n., his Cambs. supporters ibid., date of leaving Cambs. ibid., motive for leaving Oxford 175 n., holds Margaret professorship 191, cannot stomach Cambridge fare 221, praises Wm. Gilbert 291, his 'three colleges' 313 n., (quoted) 221

Index of Names

Essex, see *Devereux*
Essex, archdeacon of, receives a Lambeth B.D. (1635), 194 *n.*
Ethelbert of Kent, 4
Etheldreda, S., 311, 311 *n.*, 312 *n.*, 337
Ethelred, king of the East Angles, 8 *n.*
Eugenius IV., 140 *n.*
Eustace, earl, 116 *n.*
Evelyn, John, 284
Everett, Wm. (quoted) 171, 213 *n.*-214 *n.*, 243
Exeter, see *Beaufort & Cecil*
Exmew, Blessed Wm., 119, 275

Fagius, Paul, 60
Fairfax, Thos., lord, 126
Falkland, Lucius, viscount, 126, 278
Faraday, Michael, 251, 255
Fawcett, Rt. Hon. H., prof. 328, 329 *n.*, 355, Mrs. 328, 329, 329 *n.*, 346 *n.*, P. G. 328, 340
Fawkes, Francis, the poet, 116
Felix, bp., 4 *n.*
Felton, Nich., bp. of Ely, 75
Fenton, Elijah, the poet, 116
Ferrers, Eligius, receives a Lambeth D.D. (1539) 194 *n.*, Dr., M. of Gonville & Caius 329 *n.*
Fielding, Henry, 257
Fisher, John bp. of Rochester & Cardinal 3, 105, 119, 125, 150, 152, 253, 254 *n.*, 259, 281, 330. Suggests foundation of Christ's to Ly. Margaret 118, co-operates with her 120, her panegyrist 120, 120 *n.*-121 *n.*, perpetual chancellor 120, 204, succeeded by Thos. Cromwell 205, chancellor & vice-chancellor 205 *n.*, Master of Michaelhouse 120, completes foundation of S. John's 120, 124, statutes for 67, 126, President of Queen's 111, establishes study of Greek in Cambs. 172, 174 *n.*, & invites Erasmus 173, upholds Erasmus 174 *n.*, 273, a reformer before the Reformation 120, 270, first Lady Margaret Professor 191, created cardinal priest 121 *n.*, Hen. VIII.'s opinion of 121, Hallam's 121 *n.*, martyred 121, 275, (quoted) 120, 120 *n.*
Fitz-Eustace, a Cambridge name, 292

Fitzhugh, a Cambridge name, 308
Flamsteed, John, 1st astronomer royal, 146, 284, 290, 291
Fleetwood, Wm. bp. of Ely, 105
Fletcher, 302, 303
  Giles, *LL.D.* 282, 304, Giles (poet) 304, John (the dramatist) 257, 304, Phineas (poet) 304, Ric. bp. of London 303, John, of Caius 304
Ford, John, 257
Fordham, bp. of Ely, 61, (quoted) 62 *n.*
Foster, Saml., Royal Soc. 146, 283, 284, Sir Michael, prof., 329 *n.*
Fowler, Edw., aftw. bp. of Gloucester, 266 *n.*
Fox, Edw. bp. of Hereford 105, Ric. bp. of Winchester, M. of Pembroke, chr. (1500) 3, 74, 177 *n.*, 205 *n.*, 259, 260, 270, 273, 283
Frampton, bp., 266, 266 *n.*
Francis, S., of Assisi, 21, 22, 22 *n.*
Frost, 292, 347 *n.*
  Henry, 18, 122 *n.*
Fry, Mrs., 253 *n.*
Fuller, Thos., 5 *n.*, 47, 51, 99, 111, 120, 146, & see *general index*

Galileo, 291
Gamble, Jane C., 320, 322
Gardiner, Stephen, bp. of Winchester, M. of Trinity Hall, chr., 79, 80, 177 *n.*, 240, 243, 259, 304
Garrett, Dr. G. M., 329 *n.*
Garth, Sir Samuel, 260
Gaunt, 294 *n.*, 347 *n.*
Gaunt, House of 294, 297, John of 20, 27, 95, 261, 292, 295 *n.*, 297 *n.*, 308 *n.*
George I., 99, 113, 192, 268
George II., 113
George IV., 138
Gibbon, Edw., 309
Gibbons, Orlando, 252
Gilbert, S., of Sempringham, 19
Gilbert, Wm., 126, 260, 281, 290, 291
Gladstone, W. E. 253, 254 *n.*, Miss H. 347
Glisson, Francis, prof., 80, 144, 191
Gloucester, duke of, see *Clare*
Goddard, Jonathan, Royal Soc., 283
Goldcorn, John, 98 *n.*
Goldsmid, Sir Francis 318 *n.*, lady 318 *n.*

Goldsmith, Oliver, 257
Gonville, 294, 295
    Edmund 77, 78, 150, 152, 153, Sir
        Nicholas 77
Goodrich, Thos., bp. of Ely, 106, 260
Goulburn, bp., 2nd wrangler, 184 n.
Grafton, 3rd duke of, chr., 59
Gray, Thos., prof., 7, 58, 59, 73, 74, 75,
    104 n., 139, 184, 192, 232 n., 235,
    255, 308, 308 n., (quoted) 7, 56,
    74 n., 176, 249
Green, W. C., 329 n.
Greene, Robt., 257
Gregory the Great, 4
Gregory XIII., 230
Gresham, Sir Thos., 78, 143, 144, 218 n.,
    282, 330
Greville, 302, 304
    Fulke, 1st Ld. Brooke 99 n., 116,
        192 n., 282, 304, 308, 2nd Ld.
        304, Sir Bevil 304, (Grenville or
        Granville) 1st Ld. Lansdowne 139,
        304
Grew, Nehemiah, of Pembroke, 260,
    284
Grey, 252, 295, 297, 297 n., 299, 300
    earl 268, 269, lady Jane 113, 175 n.,
        Sir Thos. 295, 296, of Wark, Ld.
        264 n., pedigree of 299
Grindal, Wm., the classic, pupil of
    Ascham 126, Edmund, abp. 74, 99,
    118, 130, 130 n., 259, 263, 274 n.,
    282
Grocyn, Wm., 173, 173 n., 176 n.
Grosseteste, Robert, bp. of Lincoln,
    172 n., 252, 254 n.
Grosvenor, Sir Robert, 94
Grote, Geo., 251
Guest, Edm., bp. of Rochester & Sarum,
    106
Guilford, Francis North, Ld., 260, 284
Gunning, Peter, bp. of Ely, M. of Clare,
    then of S. John's, 126
Gurgentius, 4
Gurney, Rt. Hon. Russell 318 n., Mrs.
    318 n.
Guthlac, S., of Mercia, 12 n.

Hacket, bp. of Lichfield, 138
Haddon, 294
    abbot of Thorney 294 n., Walter,
        v.-c. 80, 105, 191, 282, 304

Hainault, John, count of, earl of Cam-
    bridge, 36 n.
Hale, Chief Justice 284, Sir Matt. 309
Hales, John, 278, 279, 286 n.
Halifax, Geo. Savile, visc. & marq. 260,
    267, see Montague
Hall, Joseph, of Emmanuel, bp. of
    Norwich, 277, Ric., biographer of
    Fisher 119
Hallam, Arthur, 139
Halley, Edm., Royal Soc., 284, 309
Hamilton, Sir Wm., 177
Hampden, John, 244, 264, 265
Harison, Thos., a translator of the bible,
    273
Harrington, 307
    Sir John, 1st Ld., 105, 282
Hartley, David, 116
Harvey, Hervey, 302, 304
    Gabriel 74, 74 n., 256, 281, 304,
        (quoted) 182, Henry, v.-c. 304,
        Wm., 144, 253, 254 n., 260, 281, 304
Hastings, 297, 297 n.
    Henry earl of Huntingdon 111, John
        earl of Pembroke 27, 295, 295 n.,
        Warren 251
Hatfield, Wm. of, 104 n.
Hatton, 203 n., 294 n., 303, 307
    Sir Christopher 309, Ric. Provost ot
        King's 307
Hawkins, John, 251
Heath, Nicholas, abp., a translator of the
    bible, 66, 273, 273 n.
Henrietta Maria, queen, 114
Henry I. (Beauclerk) 18 n., 88. Favours
    the town 8, 36, 36 n., gives it a
    charter 9, charter referred to 5-6,
    6 n., 13, fabled to have studied at
    Cambs. 36
Henry II., 151
Henry III. 6 n., 36, 38, 45, 51 n., 54,
    69, 152. Sends to Cambs. for fish
    11, orders the adherents of the
    dauphin to leave the town 33, 260,
    establishes taxors 33, rescript quoted
    33-34, gives a charter to the univer-
    sity 34, rescripts on behalf of the
    university 35, 47-48, 203, quoted
    30 n., 34 n., 203, withdraws licence
    to found university at North-
    ampton 46, licence quoted 46 n.,
    visits Cambs. 113, privileges of

368

Index of Names

university date from his reign 222 n.
See *general index*

Henry IV., said to have granted stone for a chapel at King's Hall, 5 n.

Henry V. 37 n., 59, 205 n., 228 n. Intended building a college at Oxford 101, betrayed by "Cambridge, Scroop, & Grey" 295

Henry VI. 58 n., 106, 117. Favours Cambs. 37 n., statutes for King's 67, 105 n., 152, 153, imitates Wm. of Wykeham 67, 101 n., portrait of in Pembroke 73, coins money at Cambs. 8 n., invites abbot of Bury to Cambs. 16 n., buys & conveys ground in Cambs. 24 n.-25 n., 101, founds King's College 100, 150, dedicates to S. Nicholas 101, double charter of Eton & King's *ibid*, lays foundation stones 101, 102, 112, his original design for King's 101 n.-102 n., visits Cambs. 4 times 112, lodged in King's Hall 112, 112 n., founds God's House 117 n., 118, 150, bestows church lands on this & King's 271, Byngham's letter to 165 n., half-brother to lady Margaret's first husband 299

Henry VII. 118, 175 n., 281, 299. Favours Cambs. 37 n., chief builder of King's chapel 104, visits Cambs. 5 times 113, accompanied by lady Margaret 114, & by the queen *ibid.*, makes Empson High Steward, 206 n.

Henry VIII. 106, 123, 151, 212 n., 281, 295. Favours Cambs. 37 n., monogram with that of Anne Boleyn in chapel screen at Trinity 102, visits Cambs. 113, Henry & Fisher 121, 121 n., founds Trinity 131, effigy on the Entrance Gate 131, endows college with abbey lands 133, motives for the foundation 133, scope of 133-134, 153, 154, portrait of in Trinity lodge 136 n., invites Caius to lecture on anatomy 142, his divorce from Catherine, how met at the university 240, 271, his injunctions imposing the royal supremacy 167 n., founds the Regius professorships 190

Henry of Huntingdon, chronicle cited, 7 n.
Henry of Orléans, bailiff, 16 n.
Herbert, George 139, 166, 207, 218 n., 289, of Cherbury, lord 279
Hereswitha, 311 n.
Hereward the Wake, 11, 146, 292, 303
Herrick, Robert, of S. John's, 244, 263
Herschell, 347 n.
    Sir John 126, 172 n., 218 n., 291, senr. 255
Heynes, Dr. Simon, Pres. of Queen's, v.-c. 212, 212 n.
Heywood, Thos. (the dramatist), 59, 257
Hild, 2, 252, 254 n., 311, 311 n., 312
Hill, Rowland, 126
Hind, Archer, 329 n., 348
Hobart, lady, 318 n.
Hobbes, Thos., 285, 289
Hobson the Cambridge carrier, 215 n.
Holbroke, John, M. of Peterhouse, chr. (1430), bp. of Ely, 59
Holland, Margaret, 299
Hollond, John, M.P., 348
Honorius I., 28
Honorius III., 111, 127
Hoods, the, 251
Hooke, Robt., Royal Soc., 284
Hooker, Ric. 289, Thos. 262
Hope, Alex. Beresford-, 136
Horrox (Horrocks), Jeremiah, 146, 291
Hort, F. J. A., prof., 139, 179, 191, 288
Hottun, Hugo de, chr. (1246), 203 n.
Howard, 297 n., 300, 301, 303
    of Effingham 251, Henry, earl of Northampton, chr. 301, Henry, earl of Surrey 256, 256 n., 301, John 253 n., Thos. earl of Suffolk, chr. 301, 303 [see *Norfolk*]
Howe, John [*Rot. Hund Cant.*] 42, 43, Walter [*Rot. Hund. Cant.*] 42
Hrostwitha of Gandersheim, 108
Huddlestoo, Sir Robert, 5 n., 113
Hudson, Prof. H. H., *LL.M.*, 347
Hughes, Miss E. P., 335 n.
Hugolina, wife of the Norman sheriff, 17
Hulle, Wm., English Prior of the Order of S. John, 24
Humphry, Prof. Sir Geo., of Downing Coll., 318 n., 340
Huntingdon, css. of 149, earl of, see *David of Scotland & Hastings & 297 n.*

Cambridge

Hutchinson, Col., 59, 264, 265
Huxley, T. H., 251

Ingulph, abbot of Crowland, 13, 13 *n.*
Ingworth, Ric., Franciscan friar, 20
Innocent VI., 72, 75
Ireton, Henry, 264

Jackson, Henry, Prof., 329 *n.*
James I., 113, 116, 163, 229
James II., 265, 266
James, Thos. of King's, Headmaster of Rugby, 283
Jaquetta of Luxembourg, 152
Jebb, 347 *n.*
  Dr. John 183 *n.*, Sir Ric., prof., 139, 176 *n.*, 191, 329 *n.*, (quoted) 153 *n.*
Jessopp, Dr., 10 *n.*, 80
Jocelyn of Bury 16 *n.*, (quoted) 15 *n.*
Jocelyn, John, secretary to abp. Parker, (quoted) 81, 82
Joffred, abbot of Crowland, 12, 122, 127
John, king, 6 *n.*, 11, 32, 36, 113, 260, 295
John XXII., 28, 35, (quoted) 35
John, prior, of Cambridge, 261
Johnson, Samuel, opposes American claims, 269
Jones, Burne 57 *n.*, Miss E. E. C. 321, Inigo 65, 118
Jonson, Ben, 126, 256, 257, 281

Keats, John, 251, 255
Kelvin, Ld., 59, 172 *n.*, 255
Ken, bp., 266, 267
Kennedy, B. H., *D.D.*, prof. 338 *n.*, 348, Miss M. G. 329 *n.*, 338, 338 *n.*, 346 *n.*, 347
Kenton, Nicholas, Carmelite, chr., 20
Keynes, J. N., Dr., 329 *n.*
Kilkenny, bp. of Ely, 38 *n.*, 40, 192 *n.*
King, Edw. 119, Oliver, bp. 105
Kinglake, A. W., 139
Kingsley, Chas., prof., 130, 192
Kirke, Edward, 139
Knollys, Sir Francis, 282
Kyd, Thos. (the dramatist), 257

Lake, of Chichester, one of the 7 Bishops, 266
Lancaster, Henry, the "good duke" of 89, 89 *n.*, 261, earl of 297 *n.*, 298
Lanfranc, abp., 18 *n.*

Langham, 304 *n.*
  Simon, bp. of Ely, afterwards primate, 62
Langley, 304 *n.*
  abp. 194 *n.*, Edmund earl of Cambridge 20, 36 *n.*, 295 *n.*
Langton, 296, 302, 304
  John, chr., M. of Pembroke, bp. of S. David's 101, 304, Stephen, abp. 252, 254 *n.*, 260, Thos., proc. fellow of Pembroke, bp. of S. David's, Winchester, & elect of Canterbury 3, 74, 259, 270, 304
Latimer, 306
  Hugh, bp., 66, 119, 244, 259, 271, 275, 275 *n.*, 306
Latymer, Wm., 176 *n.*
Laud, abp., 143 *n.*, 259, 280, 288, 289, (quoted) 208 *n.*
Law, 59
  Edm., bp. of Carlisle 59, Wm., author of the "Serious Call" 146
Layfield, J., a translator of the bible, 273
Lee, abp. of York, opposes Erasmus, 174 *n.*
Leicester, Henry of Lancs., earl of 297 *n.*, Robt. Dudley, earl of 206 *n.*, de Montfort, earl of 42 *n.*, 260, 261, 298, 307 *n.*, Robt. Sidney, earl of 301, Wm. of [*Rot. Hund. Cant.*] 43 *n.*
Leland, John, 119
Le Strange, Roger, 258
Lewes, G. H., 251
Lichfield, bp. of, see *Hacket, Sampson, Scrope*
Lightfoot, 292, 302, 304
  J. B., bp. of Durham, fellow of Trinity, prof., 3, 139, 191, 288, 305, 318 *n.*, John 115, 119
Lily, Wm., 176 *n.*, 283
Linacre, Thos., 80 *n.*, 125, 167, 173, 176 *n.*, 179, 190 *n.*
Lincoln, bp. of, see *Close, Wickham, Williams*, & general index
Liveing, Prof., 126, 318 *n.*
Lloyd, non-juring bp. of Norwich 266, 266 *n.*, bp. of S. Asaph's, one of the 7 Bishops 266
Locke, John, 178, 253, 254 *n.*, 309
Lodge, Thos., 256, 257
London, Dr., Warden of New Coll. (quoted), 272

370

Index of Names

Louis the Dauphin, 33, 260, 261, 295
Loyola, S. Ignatius, college founded by in Rome, 230
Lubbock, Sir John (Ld. Avebury), 251
Lucas, Henry, founds Lucasian professorship, 190
Lumsden, L. I., 321 n.
Luther, Martin, 272, 288
Lydgate, monk of Bury 4, 88, quoted 7 n., 88 n.
Lyly, John, 256, 257
Lyndhurst, Ld., 139, 172 n., 260
Lyttelton, 308
   4th Ld., 318 n.
Lytton, 302, 305
   Bulwer 80, 305, Sir Rowland 305

MacArthur, Thos., an early Cambs. Protestant, 275 n.
Macaulay, 308
   Thos. Babington, Ld., 137, 138, 139, 184, 211, 308, 309
Maio, P. T., 329 n.
Maine, Sir Henry, prof., 74, 80, 191
Maitland, 308
   F. W., prof., 192, 308
Malcolm 'the Maiden,' 36 n., 116 n., 151 n., 297 n.
Malherbe, Michael, owns land at Newnham, 325 n.
Manchester, earl of, see *Montague*
Mandeville, earl of [*Rot. Hund. Cant.*], 24 n.
Manfield, 292
   Wm. de, 39, 42, 292 n., 325
Manners, 302, 303
   Sir John, 1st Ld. 110 n., lord, Lord Chancellor of Ireland 172 n., lord John (duke of Rutland) 139, Roger son of 1st earl of Rutland, Esquire of the Body to Eliz. 86, Roger 3rd earl of Rutland 111, 222, 232 n., 282
Manning, Card. 150, Mrs. 317 n.
Mareschall, 297 n., 298, 299
Margaret of Anjou 114, 123, 150, 152, 296, 312, founds Queen's 100, 109, her motives for so doing 109, 112 n., 313, dedication 109, 112, scope 153, Eliz. Woodville co-founder with 112, 262
Margaret, lady, 119-120, 125, 133, 150, 252, 254 n., 305, 312, 312 n. Most conspicuous figure in university hist., representative of John of Gaunt 299, joins Ho. of Edw. III. to Ho. of Tudor 297, 299, reconciles Houses of York and Lancs. 262, in her own person, & through alliance with Stafford, stands mid-way between founders of King's Hall Clare & Pembroke & founders of Queens' Magdalene & Sidney 297, 299, 300. Three times married 64 n., 299, 325 n., marries a Stanley 299, reformer before the Reformation 120, 270, friendship with Fisher 120, her sojourns in Cambs. 114, 120, founds Christ's 118, endows it with abbey lands 271, scope of foundation 119, 153, 154, fellows from northern counties 119, 152, bequeaths gold plate 118, statutes 67, 119, founds S. John's 123, alienates gifts to Hen. VII's chapel for this coll. 120 n., institutes first university chairs & preachership 120, 190, bur. Westminster Abbey 120, 150, epitaph written by Erasmus 120, Fisher's panegyric 120 n.-121 n., lineage 118, 152, 297, pedigree 299
Margaret of Montefiascone, S., 109, 112 n.
Markby, T., 318 n., 329 n.
Markland, Jeremiah, 60, 175 n.
Marlborough, duke of, 251, 253
Marlowe, Christopher, 85, 255, 256, 257, 281
Marshall, Alf., prof. 329 n., Roger, benefactor to Peterhouse library, 58 n.
Marston, John (dramatist), 257
Martin V., 28, 28 n.
Martyn, Hen., 126, 147
Marvell, Andrew, 139, 218 n., 245, 264
Mary, queen, 5 n., 60, 113, 134, 136, 141, 175, 175 n., 271, 281
Maskelyne, Nevil, astronomer royal, 291
Massinger, Philip, 257, 309
Matilda, empress, 6 n., 36 n., 114, 292 n.
Maurice, F. D., prof., 139, 318 n., 329 n., 353, 354
Maxwell, James Clerk, prof., 139, 192
May, 347 n.

May, Thos. (dramatist) 147, Wm. bp., M. of Queen's, v.-c. 115, 274 n.
Maynard, Wm. lord, 179 n.
Mayor, J. B. 178, J. E. B. prof. of Latin 329 n.
Médard, S., 311
Meredith, George, 257, 258
Merton, Walter de, bp. of Rochester 38, 76 n., 252 n. His scheme to endow scholars 39, 40, 41, buys land Cambs. 39, 43 n., 45, buys land Oxford, 39, 40, 45, his statutes 40, 41, 68, quoted 39, 40, 41, 45, 68 n., the phrase "at any other university" 45, scheme to found a coll. 43, 54, house of scholars at Cambs. 41, 41 n., 44, 45, buys house called 'school of Pythagoras' 39, 122, founds Merton,Oxford 41, a pluralist 63, his name 44 n., Wm. de 44 n.
Metcalfe, Nicholas, M. of S. John's, 106 n., 126, 126 n., 142, 191
Middleton, Conyers 215, 279, Thos. (the dramatist) 257
Mildenhall, Edmund of 15 n., Robert of, chr., 15 n.
Mildmay, 307 n.
  Sir Walter, founder of Emmanuel College, 76, 119, 119 n., 144, 151, 152, 153, 282, 307, 308
Mill, J. S., 251, 253, 254 n., 329
Millington, Wm., 1st Prov. of King's, 112 n.
Milton, John, 3, 7, 7 n., 118, 119, 139, 215 n., 218 n., 253, 254 n., 255, 258, 264, 265, 277, (quoted) 7, 7 n., 104, 175 n., 200
Monckton-Milnes, Lord Houghton, 139
Monmouth, Jas. duke of, chr., 265
Montague, 302, 305, 307
  Charles, Ld. Halifax (Trinity) 305, Edw. 2nd earl of Manchester 147, 264 n., 305, James, bp. of Bath & Wells, then of Winchester, 1st M. of Sidney 305, Richard, bp. of Norwich 305, Sir Sidney 305, Simon (Montacute), 17th bp. of Ely 28, 28 n., 55 n., 67 n., 123, 305
Montefiore, Claude, 322, 322 n.
Montfort, de, 297 n.
  Simon de, 11, 42 n., 254 n., 260, 261, 298, 307 n.

Moathermer, 293, 298, 299
  Ralph de, 293
Moore, bp. of Ely, 99
Moray, Sir Robert, an original member of Royal Soc.
More, Hannah 253 n., Henry the Platonist 257, 284, 288, (quoted) 119, 145, 287, Sir Thomas 120, 121, 126 n., 173, 175, 175 n., 176 n., 243, 253, 254 n., 270, 309
Morgan, 308
  Philip, second esquire bedell, 208 n., Thos., the deist 279
Morland, 347 n.
  Sir Saml. the hydrostatician, fellow of Magdalene, 308
Morris, Wm., 57 n.
Mortimer, 292, 293, 295, 296, 297, 298, 299
  Anne 295 n., Sir Constantine de 132, 294, earl of March & Ulster 298 n., Edw. 296, Guy de 293, 326, Philippa 295 n., 299, Roger 295, Thos. de 132, 249
Morton, Card., 259 n.
Moulton, J. F., 329 n.
Mowbray, Anne, wife to Ric. of York, 86 n.
Mulcaster, Ric., 283, 354 n.
Munday, Anthony (the dramatist), 257

Nash, Thos. (the dramatist), 257
Necton, Humphrey, Carmelite, 20
Nelson, Horatio lord, 245, 251, 253, 254 n.
Nelson, Edmund (Hobhouse) bp. of, 41, 44 n.
Neville (Nevile), 297, 300, 302, 304, 305
  lady Dorothy, css. of Exeter 303, Henry, proc. 305, Latimer 6th lord Braybrooke, M. of Magdalene 305, Thos. (Nevile) v.-c., M. of Trinity 113, 135, 139, 140 n., 145, 305
Newton, 302, 305
  Fogg, Prov. of King's Coll. (1610-12) v.-c. 305, Francis v.-c. (1562-3) 305, John de, M. of Peterhouse 305, Isaac, fellow of Trinity, prof. 3, 31, 66, 137, 139, 170, 191, 218 n., 219 n., 225, 253, 254 n., 265, 290, 291, Isaac, of Peterhouse 305
Nicholas, S., of Bari, 101, 106

Index of Names

Nicholson, John ("Lambert"), 275
Nightingale, Florence, 253, 254 n.
Nix, bp., 144
Norfolk, Eliz. Talbot, dss. of 86, 155, Margaret Audley dss. of 301, Henry Howard 15th duke of 149 (see also *Howard*)
Northampton, earl of, see *Howard*
Northumberland, see *Percy & Dudley*
Norwich, John, bp. of, prior of Ely, 156, see also *Bateman, Hall, Montague, Nix, Overall, Thirlby, Walpole*
Nottingham, Daniel Finch, earl of, 267

Occam, Wm., 88
Ockley, Simon, professor of Arabic, 111
Odo, monk of Orléans, 14 n.
Ogle, Amy, 340
Oswy, king of Northumbria, 311, 311 n.
Oughtred, Wm., mathematician, 105
Overall, John, bp. of Norwich, M. of S. Catherine's, 28, 115, 126, 126 n.
Oxford, see *de Vere*

Pace, Ric., 176 n.
Paget, 308
Sir James, 318 n.
Paley, 347 n.
Mary (Mrs. Marshall) 340 n., Wm., Preb. of S. Paul's 118, 172 n., & see *general index*
Palmer, 302, 306
Edw., prof. (sheikh Abdullah), 306
Palmerston, Hen. Jno. Temple, visc., 126, 239, 260, 306, 309
Paris, Dr. J. A. 260, Matthew 23 n., 33 n., 55 n., 84
Parker, 308, 347 n.
Matthew, v.-c., abp., 49, 84, 85, 99, 106 n., 244, 245, 259, 273, 273 n., 274, 274 n., 282
Parr, 347 n.
Samuel, 146, 308
Parsons, the Jesuit, 294
Partholin, Spanish king of Ireland, 4
Paston, 261, 308, 308 n.
Sir Wm., 85
Patrick, Simon, bp. of Ely, 266 n., 274
Paul III., 121 n.
Paulinus of York, 2
Peacock, Geo. dean of Ely, Lowndean prof., 139
Pearson, bp., 106, 111, 111 n.

Perse, Stephen, 99 n.
Peele, Geo. (dramatist), 257
Peile, Dr., M. of Christ's, 329 n.
Pembroke, css. of, see *Chatillon*, earls of, 292, 297 n., 298, 299
Pepys, Samuel, 130, 145, 308
Percy, 301, 307, 307 n.
Eleanor 301, Wm., bp., son of 2nd earl of Northumberland, chr. 307
Perfect, Anne, 330
Perne, Andrew, M. of Peterhouse, 58, 60, 99 n., 143
'Peter of Blois,' 13 n., 14, (quoted) 14 n.
Peterborough, Francis Jeune, bp. of, (Oxonian) 317 n., see also *Cumberland, White*
Petrarch, 88
Peverel, 110 n., 292
Pain, 17, 292, 303
Pfeiffer, Mrs., 338
Philip of France, 296
Physwick, Wm., first esquire bedell, 50, 208 n.
Picot, Hugh, baron of Bourne, 17, 292
Pigott, 292
Pilkington, Jas., bp. of Durham, 10th M. of S. John's, 274 n.
Pitt, Wm., 73, 74, 74 n., 100, 218 n., 253, 254 n., 260, 268
Plantagenet, 8 n., 152, 292, 300
Beatrice 69, Joan, see *Joan d'Acre*
Pole, 296, 297 n.
Card., chr. 259 n., (quoted) 121, Humphrey de la 78, 143, Edw. de la, archd. of Richmond 78 (sons of 2nd duke of Suffolk), Wm. de la, earl & 1st duke of Suffolk 117 n.
Porson, Ric., prof., 137, 139, 174, 175 n., 190
Porteous, bp., 172 n.
Porter, Rev. Jas., M. of Peterhouse (1876), 318 n.
Potts, Mr., 348
Prior, Matthew, 126, 305
Pritchard, fourth wrangler, 172 n.
Pugin, Aug. W., 130
Puttenham, Geo., writes of art of poetry, 256
Pym, John, 264

Raddyng, *frater*, of Rome, incorporated as a Cambs. doctor, 193 n.

Raleigh, Sir Walter, 251, 253, 254 *n.*, 282
Ramsay, Agnata (Mrs. Butler), 322, 322 *n.*
Ratcliffe, 307, 307 *n.*
    Thos., 3rd earl of Sussex (crd. *M.A.* 1564), 146, 282, 301
Ray, John, the botanist & zoologist, 115, 139, 284
Rayleigh, 3rd lord, prof., 172 *n.*, 192
Rede, Sir Robt., 130, 192 *n.*
Rennell, Thos., of King's, (quoted) 209 *n.*
Repingale, bp. of Chichester, chr., 204 *n.*
Rhadegund, S., 115, 311, 312 *n.*, 319 *n.*
Richard II., 18, 20, 67, 113
Richard III., 104
Richard of Devon, Franciscan, 21
Richardson, Saml., 251, 257
Richmond, earl of 299, css. of, see *Margaret, lady*
Ridley, 306
    Nicholas, bp., M. of Pembroke, 74, 75, 79, 212 *n.*, 259, 275, 306, 347 *n.*
Rivers, earl, 112
Rochester, Dr. Plume archd. of, 191
Rochester, bp. of, see *Bottlesham, Fisher, Merton*
Rogers, John, 75, 272, 275, 275 *n.*, 307
Rooke, Lawrence, Royal Soc., prof. at Gresham Coll., 283
Rosse, Ld., see *Manners, 3rd earl of Rutland*
Rotherham, Thos., abp. of York, chr., 74, 76 *n.*, 97, 98, 98 *n.*, 105, 115, 259, 260, 270, 307
Roubilliac, sculptor, 137
Routh, E. J. of Peterhouse, senior wrangler, 172 *n.*
Rowley, Wm., dramatist, 257
Roy, Wm., Franciscan translator of the bible, 273
Ruthall, Thos., bp. of Durham, chr., 260
Rutland, see *Manners*

St. John of Bletsoe, Anne, 305 *n.*
Saint-Paul, 152, 296, 300
    Gaucher, 1st comte de 296, Guy comte de, see *Chatillon*, Marie de, see *Valence*
Salisbury, see *Cecil*
Salisbury, bp. of (temp. Hen. VI.), 101

Sampson, abbot of Bury, 15, 15 *n.*, 16 *n.*
Sampson, bp. of Lichfield, 80
Sancroft, abp., 145, 267
Sanderson, 347 *n.*
    (Saunderson), Nicholas, prof., 118, 191
Sandys, Edwin, abp., v.-c., 115
Sanger, Ralph., proc., 98
Savona, Wm. of, printer, 99
Scory, bp. of Hereford, 273, 273 *n.*
Scott, Sir Gilbert, 57 *n.*, 102 *n.*, 124, 125
Scott, Miss E. P. 321, Sir Walter 251, 257, 257 *n.*
Scrope (Scroope), 93, 94, 294, 295, 296, 307
    lady Anne 94 *n.*, 325, 325 *n.*, Henry le, 1st baron Scrope of Masham 94, Henry 3rd baron (beheaded 1415) 295, 295 *n.*, 296, Ric. le, 1st baron Scrope of Bolton, treasurer & Lord Chancellor, 1371, 1378-1381 (ob. 1403) 27, 295, Ric. abp. of York, chr. (1378) 94, 94 *n.*, 203 *n.*, 296, Ric. le, M. of King's Hall, bp. of Carlisle, chr. (1461) 94 *n.*, Stephen le, chr., brother of the conspirator 94 *n.*, 204 *n.*, 295 *n.*, Sir Stephen (brother of Wm. Scrope, earl of Wilts, & aftw. 2nd Ld. S. of Bolton) 296
Scrope & Grosvenor (controversy) 93
Sedgwick, 308, 347 *n.*
    Adam, Woodwardian prof. of Geology, 139, 308, junior 329 *n.*
Seeley, Sir John, prof., 119, 192, 318 *n.*, -Clough (quoted), 346, 346 *n.*, L. B. 179
Segrave, Nicholas, 307 *n.*, Stephen, bp., chr., 203, 259, 307 *n.*
Selden, John, 277
Selling, Wm., 176 *n.*
Selwyn, bp., prof. 98 *n.*, 126, 148, 185 *n.*, 191
Sergius, pope, 27
Sexburga, abbess of Ely, 10
Shaftesbury, Sir Anthony Ashley Cooper, 1st earl of, 253 *n.*, 279, 309
Shakespeare, 146, 251, 253, 254 *n.*, 255, 256, 257, 295, (quoted) 295, 297 *n.*
Shelley, Percy Bysshe, 255, 309
Shepard (Shepherd), 302, 306
    Nicholas, M. of S. John's, proc., 306

Index of Names

Sheridan, Ric. Brinsley, 251
Sherlock, dean, 60, 266 n., 267
Shilleto, tutor of Trinity, 325
Shirley, James (dramatist), 115, 255, 256
Shrewsbury, John, 1st earl of (killed 1453), 86 n., see *Talbot & Cavendish*
Shuckburgh, Dr. E. S., 329 n.
Siberch, printer, 99, 100
Sickling, John, 1st M. of Christ's, 118
Sidgwick, Hen., prof. 315, 318 n., 327 n., 328, 329 n., 338, Mrs. 338, 338 n., 347
Sidney, 296, 297, 297 n., 307 n.
 Frances, css. of Sussex, founder of Sidney Sussex Coll., 145, 151, 152, 312, Sir Philip 147, 253, 254 n., 256, 309, Sir Wm. 146, pedigree of 301
Siegebert, king of the East Angles, 3, 3 n.
Simon Stock, S., 20, 325
Skeat, W. W., 329 n., (quoted) 7 n., 164
Skelton, 306, 347 n.
 John, 261, 281
Sloane, Hans, 284
Smith, John, the Platonist 145, 286, 287, Sir Thos., v.-c. 111, 174, 175 n., 177 n., 191, 207, 273, 274 n., 281, 282, 304
Smollett, Tobias, 251, 257
Somerset, 307
 Dr. John, of Pembroke, proc., 58 n., 76 n., 106, 106 n., 117 n.
Somerset, Sarah Alston dss. of 125, earls & dukes 296, & see *Beaufort* & pedigree 299
Southampton, see *Wriothesley*
Spalding, Ralph, Carmelite, 269
Spelman, Sir Hen. 139, (quoted) 165 n.
Spencer, Herbert, 251
Spenser, Edmund, 3, 7, 7 n., 47, 74, 74 n., 106 n., 124, 139, 182, 189 n., 215, 218 n., 255, 256, 281, (quoted) 310
Sprat, Thos., bp., historian of Royal Soc., 284
Stace, Thos. of Ipswich, 93
Stafford, 296, 297, 297 n., 298, 299, 300, 301, 307 n., & Audley, pedigree 301
 Edw. 3rd duke of Buckingham 128, 129 n., 150, 152, 307, Hen. 2nd duke 129, 150, 151 n., pedigree of

300, John, proc. 307, George, an early Protestant 275
Stanley, 269, 297, 299, 307 n.
 of Alderley, Henrietta, Ly. 319, 319 n., Ly. Augusta 319, dean 318 n., Jas. bp. of Ely 271, Thos. Ld. 299
Stanton, 291, 294
 Hervey de 63 n., 68, 76, 150, 304. Founds Michaelhouse 63, statutes & scope of 67, 68, scope of foundation 153, 154, Robt., original fellow of Pembroke 75, 75 n.
Steele, *frater*, of Rome, incorporated as a Cambs. *D.D.* 193 n., Ric. 257, (quoted) 166
Stephen, Sir J., prof. 192, Sir Leslie 80, 179
Stephen, king, 36 n.
Sterne, 146, 306
 John, 1st pres. of Irish Coll. of Surgeons 146, Laurence 116, 257, 306, Ric., abp., M. of Jesus 116, 306 n.
Stillingfleet, Edw. bp. of Worcester, 126, 266 n., 274 n., 279
Stokes, Stokys, 307
 Sir George, prof., 73, 74, 172 n., 191, 308
Stow, John, 245
Stratford, abp., 88
Stratford de Redcliffe, Ld., 105, 184, 194, 209 n., 239, 260, 308, (quoted) 104 n.
Strype, John, 115, 116
Sudbury, John of, prior of Benedictine students, 128 n.
Suffolk, 296, 297 n., 301
 2nd duke of 78, earls & dukes of 297 n., see *Brandon, Howard, Pole*
Sumner, abp., 106, 194 n.
Surrey, earl of, 256, & see *Howard*
Sussex, 3rd earl, 146, 282, see *Ratcliffe*
Swanwick, Anna, 318 n.
Swift, Jonathan, 309
Sydenham, Thos., 74, 260, 260 n., 284
Symons, Ralph, architect, 145, 146

Tait, abp., confers Lambeth degree, 194 n.
Talbot, Eleanor 86 n., Eliz. see *Norfolk*
Tangmer, Hen., alderman of a Cambridge guild, 325

Taverner, Ric., one of the colonisers of Cardinal Coll., 272

Taylor, 302, 306
  Brook 126, Jeremy 144, 219 *n.*, 254 *n.*, 259, 277, 278, 279, 306, Helen 329, Rowland 275, 275 *n.*, 306, Sedley 317 *n.*, 318 *n.*, 329 *n.*

Temple, 302, 306
  abp., confers Lambeth degree 194 *n.*, Sir Wm. 146, 245, 260, 284, 306, 308

Tenison, abp., 85, 259, 266 *n.*, 274

Tennyson, lord, 139, 255

Thackeray, 302
  Wm. Makepeace, 139, 257

Theodore, abp., 2

Theresa, S., 325

Thirlby, Thos., bp. of Ely, then of Norwich, 80

Thirlwall, bp., 139, 175 *n.* (see *S. David's*)

Thixtil, John, fellow of Pembroke (1519), 74

Thompson, W. H., prof., 176 *n.*
  Yates, Mr. & Mrs., 338

Thorpe, Sir Robt., M. of Pembroke 27, 75, 76 *n.*, 96, 260, 295, Sir Wm. 98 *n.*

Thurloe, secretary to Cromwell, 308 *n.*

Tillotson, abp., 66, 259, 266 *n.*, 274 *n.*

Tindal, Matthew, the deist, 279

Tiptoft, John, earl of Worcester, 112

Todhunter, senior wrangler, 172 *n.*

Tokerham, Ric., proc., 98

Toland, John, the deist, 279

Tomkinson, H. R., 317 *n.*

Tonnys, John, prior of the Cambs. Augustinians, 174 *n.*

Tooke, Horne, 126

Tonstall, Jas., of S. John's, 215

Trelawney, bp. of Bristol, 265 *n.*, 266

Trench, R. C., Protestant abp. of Dublin, 139

Trevelyan, 308
  Macaulay's biographer (quoted), 211

Tuckney, Anthony, Puritan M. of Emmanuel, 245, 277, (quoted) 286

Tudor, see the Tudor sovereigns & *general index*

Tulloch, Principal (quoted), 285 *n.*, 286 *n.*, 287, 288 *n.*

Tunstall, Cuthb. bp. of Durham, 98, 139, 174 *n.*, 259, 273, 273 *n.*

Turner, bp. of Ely, one of the 7 Bishops, 266, 266 *n.*

Twining, Miss, 318 *n.*

Tyler, Wat, 261

Tyndale, 308
  Wm., 175 *n.*, 271, 272, 281

Upton, Jas., headmaster of Taunton school, 105

Urban V., 72

Ussher, abp., 279

Valence, 27, 294, 295, 297, 297 *n.*, pedigree of 299
  Aymer de, earl of Pembroke 69, 150, 151 *n.*, 293, 299, Marie (*or* de Saint-Paul, born Chatillon) css. of Pembroke 74, 77, 150, 296, 312. Founds Pembroke 69, 71, scope of foundation 152, 152 *n.*, 153, statutes of 68, 73, 73 *n.*, founds Denney 25, 25 *n.*, 73, 73 *n.*, lineage 69, 152, 293, 297, pedigree 299

Venantius Fortunatus, bp., monk of Sainte-Croix, 312

Venn, Dr. J. 318 *n.*, 329 *n.*, Mrs. 329 *n.*

Verdon, Theobald Ld., 298

Vere, 36 *n.*, 292, 292 *n.*, 301
  Alice de, css. of Oxford 21 *n.*, Aubrey de, 1st earl of Oxford 36 *n.*, Maud, wife of 8th earl! 111

Vernon, 110, 296
  Dorothy, of Haddon, 110 *n.*

Verulam, visc., see *Bacon, Ld.*

Vesalius, early Italian anatomist, 141

Victoria, queen, visits Cambs., 113, 176 *n.*

Villiers, dukes of Buckingham, 297 *n.*
  Geo. 2nd duke of Buckingham (Trinity College), 99 *n.*, 284.

Wallace, Alf. R., 255

Waller, Edm., 105, 244

Wallis, John, fellow of Queen's, one of founders of Royal Soc., 145, 146, 265, 277, 283, 286, 347 *n.*

Walpole, 292, 294
  Ralph, bp. of Ely & Norwich 294, Robt. 105, 260, 294, Horace 105, 139, 235, 294

Walsingham, 291, 292, 294
  Edm., owns land in Cambridge 132,

Index of Names

Sir Francis 105, 260, 307, Ld. 206 n., prior of Ely 294

Ward, John, bp. of Salisbury, one of the founders of Royal Soc. 284, Prof. James 340 n., Seth 147

Warham, abp., 12 n., 144, 174, 175 n., 259 n., 273

Warkworth, John, M. of Peterhouse, 58, 59, 261

Washington, Godfrey, bur. at Peterhouse, 61, 262

Watson, Thos., early sonneteer, 256 n.

Watts, Wm., of Gonville & Caius, archd., 175 n.

Webbe, Wm., writer on art of poetry, 256

Webster, John (dramatist), 257

Wellington, duke of, 251

Wentworth Ld. Strafford, 126

Wesleys, the 280, John 253

West, Nicholas, bp. of Ely, 105

Westcott, B. F., bp., fellow of Trinity, prof., 139, 191, 288

Wharton, Thos., the anatomist 74, 260, Thos., fellow of Pembroke, Gray's letter to 249

Whewell, Wm., M. of Trinity, prof., 3, 136, 137, 138, 139, 172 n., 177, 179

Whichcote, Benj., the Platonist, 105, 145, 245, 286, (quoted) 287

Whiston, Wm., prof. in succession to Newton, 66, 191

White, bp., one of the 7 Bishops 266, 266 n., Jessie 360 n., Kirke 126

Whitefield, Geo., 280

Whitehead, David, one of the 8 men on Cecil's memorandum 274 n., Wm., poet laureate 66

Whitgift, abp., v.-c. 59, 60 n., 74, 74 n., 139, 259, 274, 282, 306, his thesis for the D.D. 169 n.

Whittlesey, Wm., abp., M. of Peterhouse, 58

Wickham of King's, bp., 105

Wilberforce, John, 126, 260, 269

Wilfrid of York, 2, 172

Wilkins, architect 102 n., 147, John, bp. of Chester, M. of Trinity 139, 283

William the Conqueror, 5, 8, 10, 11, 114, 254 n., 292, 292 n.

William & Mary 266, 267, 276, Wm. of Orange 265, 266, 267

Williams, abp., 124, 125, 259, 277

Willughby, Francis, of Trinity, Royal Soc., 284

Winchester, bp. of, see *Andrewes, Beaufort, Day, Fox, Gardiner, Langton, Montague, Wickham*

Wisbeach, John of, abbot of Crowland, 128 n.

Wolsey, Card., 63, 129 n., 174, 193, 243, 244 n., 253, 254 n., 271, 282, 309

Woodhead, S. (Mrs. Corbett), 321 n.

Woodlark, Robt., chr., founder of S. Catherine's, 105, 114, 150, 153

Woodstock, Thos. of, earl of Buckingham, later duke of Glouc., 261, 295 n., 300

Woodville, 296, 297, 300
Anthony, see *Rivers*, Eliz., co-founder of Queens', 112, 114, 150, 152, 262, 299

Woodward, John, founder of mineralogy, 284, 308

Woolston, Thos., of Sidney Sussex, the deist, 279

Wordsworth, 245, 302
Christopher, M. of Trinity, 136 n., (quoted) 231, Wm. 136 n., 255, (quoted) 7, 74 n., 103, 124, 137

Worsley, Mrs., wife of the M. of Downing, 136 n.

Wren, Christopher 58, 73, 137, 145, 284, Matthew, bp. of Ely 58, 72, 75, 280, his staff & mitre 75

Wright, Mr. Justice, 322 n.

Wriothesley, Sir Thos., of King's Hall? (crd. earl of Southampton 1547), 260

Wulfhere, king of Mercia, 12 n.

Wyatt, Sir Thos., 218 n., 244, 256

Wyclif, John, 27, 252, 269

Wykeham, Wm. of, 27, 63, 67, 101 n., 252, 254 n.

York, abp. of, see *Booth, Heath, Rotherham, Sandys, Scrope, Sterne, Wilfrid, Williams*

York, Cecilia, dss. of 111, Ric. of 86 n., Ric. duke of, 36 n., 295 n. [see *Langley, Edmund*]

Zouche, 294, 296
Guy de, chr., 111, 203, 204, 294, 296

377   48

General Index

(FOR NAMES OF PERSONS SEE P. 361.)

The principal references are in black type.

Abbesses, Saxon, 312, 312 *n.*
Abbey lands and the University, 133, 270-71
Aberdeen University, 259
Abingdon Pigotts, 292
Academic year, the, 182 *n.*, 241
"Accommodation," doctrine of, 279
"Acta," 163, 168, 169, 175, 176, 189
A.D.C., 239
Addenbrooke's Hospital, 115
Additional MSS. Brit. Mus., cited, 6 *n.*, 39 *n.*, 161 *n.*
Ad eundem degrees, 195
Advanced students, 229, 241
Aegrotat degree, 188, 188 *n.*
Age of students, 217 *n.*-218 *n.*
Agriculture, professorship of, 190
studies, board of, 238
Alban's Abbey, S., 172 *n.*
Ale, Cambridge, 221
Alexander (text book), 170
All Souls', Oxford, 176 *n.*, 218 *n.*
Almanacks, printing of, 100 *n.*
Almshouses, 18 *n.*, 117 *n.*
Almum Collegium, 230
America and Cambridge, 61, 146
colonisation of, 262, 263
American fellows at Cambridge, 246 *n.*
independence, 268
professor, 192
Anatomy, 98 *n.*, 180, 180 *n.*, 181
Andrew's (S.), parish of, 117
Street, 50
university, 284

Angers, 150
Angles, 3
Anglesey, Prior of, 24 *n.*, 43 *n.*
Priory, 24, 24 *n.*
Anglo-Saxon burial ground, 318
Chronicle, 5, 6 *n.*, 84
schools, *see Saxon schools*
Anjou, 151
Anne, S., hermitage of, 23
Antipuritanism in Cambridge, 60, 60 *n.*
Arabic professorship, 190
Archidiaconal jurisdiction, 28, 28 *n.*, 55 *n.*
Aristotle, 153, 165, 166, 170, 170 *n.*, 171 *n.*, 178 *n.*, 290
Aristotle's logic, 15, 159 *n.*, 165
Armiger bedell, *see bedell*
Art and universities, 251-2
'Artist,' the, 162 *n.*
Arts, faculty, 119, 153, 166, 168, 170
schools, 98 *n.*
the seven, 153
Ash Wednesday, ceremonies of, 160
Assembly of Ladies, cited, 57
Association of Assistant Mistresses, 335 *n.*
Astronomy, 180, 180 *n.*
Athanasian creed, 274
Audley-End, 129, 130
Augustinians, 18 *n.*, 40, 91 *n.*, 127, 127 *n.*, 272, 293
canons, 143, 292
habit, 91 *n.*
Hospitallers, 22 *n.*
Romites, *see Austinfriars*
rule of, 17, 18, 19 *n.*, 23 *n.*

General Index

Aula, 44, 63, 115 *n.*
  scholarium, 63, 71, 71 *n.*
Austinfriars, 22, 89, 91
  in Cambridge, **22**, 22 *n.*, 23, 97, 98 *n.*,
    107, 174 *n.*, 272, 293 *n.*
  London, 151
Austin's hostel, 25 *n.*, 49, 50, 50 *n.*, 101,
    102 *n.*
  Lane, 89
Avignon, 72, 79, 150

B.A., 104, 158, 168, 168 *n.*, 184
Bachelor, the, 159-160, 160 *n.*, 161
  of arts, 206, 208 *n.*, 217 *n.*, 228, 231 *n.*,
    235
  number of resident, 246 *n.*
Bachelors' school, 98
'Backs,' the, 65, 324, 348
Bailiffs of the town, 16 *n.*, 33, 37 *n.*,
    222 *n.*
Baker, Thos., cited, 122-123
Bale, cited, 20 *n.*
Ball, W. W. Rouse, cited, 95 *n.*
Balliol College, Oxford, 45 *n.*, 174 *n.*
Balsham's Judgment, cited, 28 *n.*, 165 *n.*,
    203, 208 *n.*
Balsham, village, 55 *n.*, 60, 191
Bannockburn, 64 *n.*
Barnwell, 31, 64
  canons, 17, 18, 22 *n.*, 49, 91
  Chartulary, 6 *n.*, 19, 20, 23, 325
  fair, 215 *n.*
  prior of, 40
  priory, 17, 28, 113, 130, 227
  Process, 59
Barons' wars, 260
Bartholomew's the Great (S.), London,
    151
  hospital, Oxford, 18 *n.*
Barton, advowson of, 44 *n.*
  farm, 155
Basingstoke, 44 *n.*
"*Bataille des Sept Arts*," 15 *n.*
Bath, road to, 6
Bathing, 222
B.C., 158, 168 *n.*
B.C.L., 167
B.D., 158, 169
Beata Maria de Gratia, 58
Beaufort, House of, 262
Bede, cited, 3 *n.*-4 *n.*, 5 *n.*, 10, 10 *n.*
Bedell, 8, 50, 160, 164 *n.*, **207-8**, 208 *n.*

Bedford College, 353
Bedfordshire, 19 *n.*, 150
Bedmaker, 234
Begging friars, 22 *n.*, 23 *n.*
Belfry, 72, 313
  East Anglian, 66 *n.*
Benedict (S.), rule of, cited, 29 *n.*
Benedict XII., constitution of, 127, 144 *n.*
Benedictine hostels, 26, 49, 127, 128,
    128 *n.*, 129, 143
  nuns in Cambridge, 16, 23, 25, 115,
    116 *n.*, 312 *n.*
Benedictines, 17, 25, 127, 127 *n*, 128 *n.*,
    143
  'black,' in the fen, 12 *n.*
  in Cambridge, 12, 25 *n.*, 27, 29, 128,
    128 *n.*, 143, 143 *n.*, 311 *n.*
  prior of, at universities, 127, 128, 128 *n.*
Benet College, 78, 83, 176 *n.*
  House, 149
Benet's (S.) church, 78, 80, 83, 85, 89
  parish of, 81
  tower of, 96
Bernard, S., 109, 112 *n.*
Bernard's (S.) Hostel, 49, 50, 83, 109
Berwick, 8 *n.*
Bethlemite friars, 23, 23 *n.*, 91
Beverley, 150, 152
Bible, the English, 84, 100 *n.*, 179,
    272-273
  clerks, 62 *n.*, 153, 217 *n.*
Bibliotistae, 62 *n.*
Biology, chair of, *see Quick professorship*
Birmingham, 341, 346 *n.*
Bishop's Hostel, 138
  Mill, 11, 11 *n.*, 97 *n.*
Black book, the, 20 *n.*
Black death, 86 *n.*, 165 *n.*
  in East Anglia, 79, 80, 86, 88, 117
Blackfriars, *see Dominicans*
Bletsoe, 150, 299, 305 *n.*
Boccaccio, 182
Bodleian, 99 *n.*
Bologna, 35, 166
Botanical gardens, 22, 98 *n.*
  laboratory, 181
Botany, 180 *n.*, 181
Botolph's (S.) church, 83, 89
  parish, 81
Bourne, barony of, 292 *n.*, 303
Bowling green, 66, 70
Bridge, the great, 85, 90

Bridge "of Sighs," 124, 125
Street, 90
British Museum, 99 *n.*
remains, 5
Brownists, the, 262, **277-8**
Buckingham, earls and dukes of, 296, 297 *n.*, 299, 300
College, 128, 129, 176 *n.*
'Bull-dogs,' 223, 237
Bulls, papal, at Cambridge, 276 *n.*
Burleigh's 8 learned men, 274 *n.*
Burnet, bishop, cited, 284 *n.*
Bursar, 210, 210 *n.*, 211
Burwell Rectory, 155
Bury-St.-Edmund's, 8 *n.*, 11, 12, 12 *n.*, 15, 16, 16 *n.*, 19, 143, 165 *n.*, 166, 261, 293, 293 *n.*
patron saint, 15 *n.*
school, 15 *n.*, 106 *n.*
Butley, 143
Butteries, 110, 137

Cair-Graunth, 5, 5 *n.*, 6, 20 *n.*
Caius College, 100, 106 *n.*, 107, 151, 153, 154, 229, 231, 246, 329 *n.*
statutes, 142
Caius, Dr. John, cited, 7 *n.*, 48 *n.*, 62, 99, 207 *n.*, 217 *n.*, 246 *n.*, 326 *n.*
Calvinism, 145
Calvinists, anti-, at Cambridge, 281
Cam, the, 6, 7, 7 *n.*, 9 *n.* (*and see the river*)
Camboricum or *Camboritum*, 5
Cambridge, aldermen, 37, 222 *n.*
bailiffs, 16 *n.*, 33, 37 *n.*, 222 *n.*
bedells or beadles, 8
a British town, 5, 6
burgesses, 18, 18 *n.*, 21, 34, 37, 261
castle, 5, 5 *n.*, 11, 39, 90, 113
castle mound, 5, 6, 7 *n.*
charters, 9, 34, 298
and the Conqueror, 5, 8, 8 *n.*, 11
and the Danes, 8, 8 *n.*
and Domesday survey, 5, 8 *n.*
earldom of, 6 *n.*, 36 *n.*
early landlords in, 23, 24, 24 *n.*, 25, 25 *n.*, 39, 41, 42 *n.*, 43 *n.*, 44, 97 *n.*, 116 *n.*, 132, 292, 292 *n.*
and Ely, 8, 11, 12, 14, 17
fair, *see Stourbridge.*
fire at, 14
a fish market, 10-11
floods, 47

Cambridge, guilds, *see guilds*
and Henry I., 8, 13, 36, 36 *n.*
hospitals and almshouses, 18, 23, 32
Hundred Rolls, 43, 43 *n.*, 44, 292, 294
in 1353, 88
and the Jews, 9, 9 *n.*, 13, 22
under John, 11, 32, 36, 260, 261
jury, 35, 42
Lancastrian, 261
legends of its origin, 4, 20 *n.*
martyrs, 275
mayor, 33, 34, 37 *n.*, 38 *n.*, 222 *n.*
men, groups of, 291-7, 302-8
'mind,' the, 134, 273, 280, 288, 289
a royal mint, 8 *n.*
the name, 5, 6, 6 *n.*, 7 *n.*
the Norman town, 90, 91, 96
oldest academic site in, 122
'oyer and terminer' at, 261
place-names, 294 *n.*
pre-university history, 1
Roman roads in, 6
a Roman town, 4, 5, 6, 10 *n.*
the Saxon town, 5, 83, 89, 91, 96
schools, 14, 16, 16 *n.*, 27, 33
"   first glimpse of the, 33
sheriff of, 17, 34, 36 *n.*
shire, 7, 8, 11, 12 *n.*, 152
town, 5, 7 *n.*, 8, 10, 10 *n.*, 11, 13, 36, 326 *n.*, 341
university jurisdiction in, 222, 222 *n.*, 223
Camden, cited, 7 *n.*, 9 *n.*
Camus, 7, 7 *n.*
Cancellarius scholasticus, 203 *n.*
Candle rents, 84, 84 *n.*
Canon Law, new schools of, 24
Canonical Houses, 17
Canons, 227, 228
in Cambridge, 16, 17, 19, 24, 318
of S. Giles, *see Barnwell*
of S. John, *see S. John's Canons*
in Norfolk, 77
of Sempringham, *see Gilbertines*
Cantaber, 4, 20 *n.*
Cante, 7 *n.*
Cantebrigge etc., *see Cambridge, the name*
Canterbury, 2, 4, 8 *n.*
archbishops of, 259 *n.*
"   and degrees, 193

General Index

Canterbury, psalter, 138
school, 176 *n.*
Cap and gown, **226-231**
when worn, 231
Capitation fees, 154
Cappa, bachelor's, 227, 228, 230, 231, 231 *n.*
Cardinal College, Oxford, colonised from Cambridge, 174, 272, 282
Carmelites at Cambridge, 16 *n.*, **19-20**, 26, 38, 89, 91, 102 *n.*, 109, 292, 294, 325, 326
cloak of, 91
first to take degree, 20, 22
Carter, cited, 99, 104, 130 *n.*, 203 *n.*
Carthusians, the London, 276
Castle, the Conqueror's, *see Cambridge*
Castle Inn, 50
Cathedral officers, 203 *n.*, 209
Catherine's (S.) College, 100, 110, **114**, 150, 153, 154, 156 *n.*
Catholic Emancipation, 269
martyrs, xvi c., 276, 294
Cavendish College, 148
laboratory, *see laboratories*
professorship, 192
Cavaliers in Cambridge, 60, 263, 264
Celar, 66 *n.*
Celts, 3
Chancellor, 14, 26, 35, 38 *n.*, 53, **203-5**, 206, 207, 209, 222 *n.*
and masters, 14, 35, 53, 203
Chancellors, in the xiv c., 203-4, 203 *n.*, 295
list of, in Carter, 203 *n.*
Chapel of S. Lucy, 108 *n.*
of the university, 97, 98 *n.*
"Chapels," 224
Chapels, College, 56, 70, **107**, 176, 313
list of, 108
ritual and services in, 58, 145, 213, 223 *n.*, 240 *n.*
Chaplains, 210, 213, 213 *n.*
Charterhouse, 55 *n.*, 246
Chatteris Abbey, 12 *n.*
Chaucer in Cambridge, 88, 93-96
cited, 11, 47 *n.*, 66
Chelmsford, 150, 151, 152
Cherry Hinton, 61, 62 *n.*, 140 *n.*
Cheshunt College, 149
"Chest," 99 *n.*, 155, 156
college, 155

Chest, University, 114, 155, 313
Chesterton, 20, 44 *n.*
hundred, 42 *n.*
vicarage and rectory, 140, 140 *n.*
Chester, 6
Christ's College, 25 *n.*, 70, 101 *n.*, 103 *n.*, **117-120**, 125, 133, 149, 150, 152, 153, 170 *n.*, 176 *n.*, 180, 210 *n.*, 217 *n.*, 235 *n.*, 271, 275 *n.*, 285, 313 *n.*, 329 *n.*
statutes, cited, 210 *n.*, 217 *n.*, 220-221, 235 *n.*
Christ's Pieces, 25
Churchmen, Cambridge, 254 *n.*, 259
Cirencester, 6
Cistercians, 127 *n.*, 128 *n.*
at Cambridge, 19 *n.*, 25, 143
Rule of the, 19 *n.*
City companies and education, 322
Civil law, *see law*
in the courts, 182 *n.*
Regius of, 190, 191
school of, 154
Clare College, 44, 49, **64-66**, 67, 68, 70, 76, 77, 79, 82, 86 *n.*, 87, 89, 95, 95 *n.*, 101 *n.*, 102 *n.*, 114, 147, 153, 176 *n.*, 214, 217 *n.*, 218 *n.*, 240, 293, 303, 312, 338
chapel, 109 *n.*
Clare, county, 293
'Honour of,' 22 *n.*, 293, 298
statutes, cited, 109 *n.*, 226 *n.*
Clarence, the title, 298
Clark, J. W., cited, 31, 44
Clark-Planché, cited, 103 *n.*
Classes of students, 217-219
Classical tripos, 172, 184, 187 *n.*, 238 *n.*, 322 *n.*
Classics at Cambridge, 119
decline of, 176
see Greek
"Cle," the river, 7 *n.*
Clement's (S.) church, 102 *n.*
Clergy and the University, 212, 213, 217 *n.*, 242, 244
Clerk, 34 *n.*
-canon, 38
-friar, 38
and religious, 29, 30
Clerical patronage, 213
Clough Hall, Newnham, 338
Clubs, 214, 239

'Coaching,' 226, 233
Codex Augiensis, 138
Coe fen, 56, 56 *n.,* 57, 57 *n.,* 89, 325, 327
Colchester, 6
Colet's school, 283
College, benefactors, 131 *n.,* 155, 313
 "on the boards of a," 246 *n.*
 building, eras of, 54-55
 chapels, *see chapels*
 cook, the, 234
 court, *see courts*
 expenses, 219-220, 234-5
 gateway, *see gateways*
 hall, *see hall*
 kitchens, 234
 libraries, 138 *n.*
 lodge, *see lodge*
 plan of a, 69-71
 porter, 224, 225
 rooms, 219-220, 232
 scheme of a residential, 53-54
 statutes of, 6 *n.,* 67-68, 222
 visitor of a, 63
 the word, 63, 65 *n.*
 of Physicians, 141, 167, 260
Colleges, built first for adult students, 54, 217 *n.*
 decoration of, 82, 109 *n.*
 early series of, 77
 educational scope of, 153-154
 founders, *see founders*
 the 'large' and 'small,' 123
 list and dates of, 55
 numbers in, in xvi c., 246 *n.*
 popularity of, 246, 246 *n.*
 the first Protestant, 22, 55, 307 *n.*
 rebuilt since their foundation, 114
 related to different counties, 152
 scope of foundations, 153
 and the University, 52-53
 wealth of, 155-156
Collegiate *domus,* 44, 63, 70
 officers, 208-212
 system, 53
Collegium, 64, 115 *n.,* 122
Colonies, the, and Cambridge, 245
Combination room, 56, 69, 135, 135 *n.,* 214
Commencement, Great, 160
'Commencements,' 107, 160

Commissary, 206
Commission documents, cited, 123
Common Prayer, book of, 100 *n.,* 273, 274, 274 *n.*
'Commons,' 235
 early allowance for, 235 *n.*
Commonwealth committee, 176 *n.*
 marauders, 58
Congregation of the Senate, 205, 206
Congregationalists, 278
Connaught, Earls of, 293
Connecticut, 262
Consistory Court, 97
"Constitutionalize," 215 *n.*
Constitutions of Honorius III., 25
Convivae of Christ's College, 217 *n.*
Convocation, 194
Copyright libraries, 99
Cornhythe, the, *see hythes*
Corpus Christi College, 22, 24 *n.,* 49, 67, 77, 78, 81-86, 87, 89, 89 *n.,* 95 *n.,* 100, 102 *n.,* 106 *n.,* 107, 110 *n.,* 147, 150, 153, 153 *n.,* 154, 156 *n.,* 276, 282, 318, 325, 325 *n.*
 antiquaries at, 85
 arms of, 85
 guild of, 23, 81 *n.,* 87 *n.*
 hall, 81 *n.,* 130
 library, 85
 old court of, 209, 217 *n.,* 232 *n.,* 240
Corpus Christi, feast of, 84, 85
 Oxford, 174 *n.,* 283
 procession in Cambridge, 85
Cosyn's Place, 71 *n.*
Cottenham, 12, 12 *n.*
Council of Constance, 59
 of Lyons, 23, 23 *n.*
Countesses, the four Cambridge, 151, 313
County College Association, 148
Court of the Vice-Chancellor, 223, 223 *n.*
Courts, College, 69, 70, 109 *n.,* 142, 143 *n.,* 240
 arrangement of, 69-70
 bonfires in, 227
 cloistered, 110, 116
 early, 79, 81-82, 132
 grass-plots in, 240
 oldest example of a, 32, 89
 size of, 82, 102 *n.*
Covenant, the, refused at Cambridge, 263, 306 *n.*

General Index

Cross (S.), *see Crouched Hostel*
Crowland Abbey, 11, 12, 12 *n.*, 13, 16, 24, 127, 128, 128 *n.*, 129, 143
Croydon, Cambridgeshire, 151
'Curtain,' 230
Curteys' Register, cited, 165 *n.*

Damietta, 69
Dandies at Cambridge, 66
Danelagh, 8
Danes, 4, 8, 8 *n.*, 10, 12 *n.*
David's (S.) cathedral, 103
D.C.L., 107
D.D., 158, 169
Dean, the college, 210, 213, 223, 223 *n.*, 224
Declamations, 107, 163, 176
Decoration of college rooms, 232 *n.*
Degree, conditions for the, 185, 186
Degrees, kinds of, 158
  meaning of, 157
  by royal mandate, 194, 265, 309
  titular, 195
  and women, 357
Deists, 279
Denney Abbey, 24, 25, 73, 73 *n.*, 150
  monks at, 25 *n.*
'Determiner,' 160
Deva, 62
Dialectic, 159 *n.*, 185 *n.*
Diplomatists and the university, 243, 260
Discipline, college, 221, 223
  early, 221, 223
  present, 221, 223
  university, 221, 223
Disce docendo, 161
Disputations, 97, 107, 159, 171, 182 *n.*
Diversoria Literarum, 63
Divinity, in Cambridge, 166, 192 *n.*
  regius of, 190, 191
  school of, ancient, 97, 98 *n.*
    ,, modern, 98 *n.*
Divorce, question of the, 240, 271
Doctorate, the, 169
Doctores legentes, 161 *n.*
Doctors' gowns, 158, 160, 210 *n.*, 226, 229
Domesday, 5, 6 *n.*, 8 *n.*
Dominicans, 21, 22, 26, 91 *n.*, 92
  in Cambridge, 21, 38, 78, 91, 145, 146, 273, 292, 292 *n.*
  priory of, 21 *n.*

Dominus, 160 *n.*
Domus scholarium, 44, 63, 65 *n.*, 71, 71 *n.*
  universitatis, 65 *n.*
'Dons,' 214, 215, 216, 231, 246, 248
  married, 248-9
  number of, 246 *n.*
'Double-first,' 184
Double monasteries, 311
Downing College, 65, 147, 151, 153, 154, 156 *n.*
  professorships, 147, 192
Dramatists, 255, 256
  list of the, 257
Dublin University, 160, 267, 278, 309, 344, 357
  degrees for women, 344, 357
Dugdale, cited, 21 *n.*, 116 *n.*, 129, 293
Duns Scotus, 170
Dunwich, 3
Durham, 146
  University, 360 *n.*
Dyer, cited, 28 *n.*, 117 *n.*, 163 *n.*

East Anglia and East Anglians, 3, 3 *n.*, 4, 9, 12 *n.*, 21, 44 *n.*, 77, 78, 98, 150, 151, 152, 292, 311 *n.*
  dialect of, 91, 93
Economics tripos, 179
Edinburgh University, 259
Edmund's (S.) chapel, 58
  house, 149
  priory, 19
Educationalists, 251, 254 *n.*, 312
Edward III. and his house, their connection with Cambridge, 36 *n.*, 37, 37 *n.*-38 *n.*, 87, 88, 89, 94, 95, 95 *n.*, 103 *n.*, 104 *n.*, 131, 222 *n.*, 295 *n.*, 297, 297 *n.*
  letters of, cited, 95 *n.*
Edward VI.'s commissioners, 308
Edward (S.), church of, 65, 79
Ee or Ea, 7 *n.*
Egbert's, Abp., *Penitentiale*, 84
Eirenicum of Stillingfleet, 279
Ejections of masters and fellows, 264, 276, 306 *n.*
Electoral roll, 205
Elizabeth, age of, 21, 215, 219 *n.*, 233 *n.*, 274, 274 *n.*
Elizabeth's visit to the university in 1564, 73, 107, 108, 113

383

Ely, 6, 7, 10, 11, 11 *n.*, 12, 12 *n.*, 17, 25, 77, 140, 150, 311
  Abbey, 11, 12 *n.*, 25 *n.*, 31, 49, 337
  archdeacon of, 14, 55 *n.*, 165 *n.*
  bishops of, 14, 28, 28 *n.*, 38, 54, 55 *n.*, 117, 122, 164, 203, 204, 205 *n.*, 235 *n.*
  chartulary, cited, 122 *n.*
  hostel, *see hostel*
  Isle of, 8, 11, 12 *n.*, 19, 36 *n.*, 307 *n.*
  jurisdiction of see of, 28, 55 *n.*
  monks, 10, 91, 127, 128, 128 *n.*
  register, cited, 164 *n.*
  scholars, 37, 38, 45 *n.*, 55, 56, 61, 122, 123, 326
  school at, 12, 311
  see of, 12 *n.*, 16 *n.*, 28, 55 *n.*
  turbulence of men of, 11
Emmanuel College, 76, 107 *n.*, **144-146**, 151, 153, 154, 245, 246, 265, 285, 307, 307 *n.*
"*Enchiridion*" of Henry More, 287
Endowed colleges, 38, 44, 45 *n.*, 217 *n.*
  intention in, 54, 219 *n.*
Endowed foundations, 31, 52, 54
  scholars, 38, 45 *n.*
Endowments vested in religious houses, 40
Engineering, electrical, 192
English philosophical temper, 289-290
Episcopal schools, 2, 12, 30, 30 *n.*
Episcopia, 30
Erasmus, cited, 170
  Holbein's picture of, 111
  his "Three Colleges," 313 *n.*
"Esperanto," 182
Esquire bedell, *see bedell*
Essex, 100, 151, 152, 261
Ethics lecture, 210 *n.*
Ethnology, 192
Eton, 101, 101 *n.*, 105 *n.*, 106 *n.*, 152, 164 *n.*, 210, 221, 239, 246, 283, 354 *n.*
  Provost of, 101 *n.*, 105
Etonians, 101 *n.*, 105, 221 *n.*
Euclid at Cambridge, 171, 185 *n.*
Evangelical movements, 145, 280
"*Evidences of Christianity*" of Paley, 178 *n.*, 185 *n.*
Examinations, 107, 154, 189, 231
  changing value of, 183
  growth of system of, 163

Examinations, oral, 163, 164, 189
  written, 162, 190.
Exclusion, bill of, 265
Exercise, necessity for, 233
"Exercises," scholastic, 107
Exeter, 341
  College, Oxford, 176 *n.*
Exhibitions, 38 *n.*, 107 *n.*, 192 *n.*
Expenses, college, 219-220
Experimental Physics, chair of, *see Cavendish professorship*

Faculties, the learned, 166, 217 *n.*, 226
Fairs, 32
"*Fairy Queen*," the, 7 *n.*
'Father,' presiding, 160
Fellow-commoners, 218, 218 *n.*, 220, 221, 230
Fellows, 68 *n.*, 210, **211-213**, 214, 217 *n.*, 218 *n.*, 220, 222, 226 *n.*, 229 *n.*, 235
  clerical, 212, 213
  married, 211-212, 213 *n.*, 216, 249
  number of, 246 *n.*
  proportion of priests among, 68 *n.*
Fellowships, 28 *n.*, 211, 217 *n.*
  Macaulay on, 211
Fen Abbeys, 11, 12 *n.*, 150
Fens, the, 11 *n.*, 13
Ferry, the, 9
Fettes school, 107 *n.*
Fires in college halls, 313
Fisheries, 116 *n.*
Fitzwilliam museum, 57, 136 *n.*
Flavia Caesariensis, 8
Florence, 290
Flying coach, 215
Ford, the, 8
Forty great Englishmen, 252-254
Foundation scholars, *see scholars*
Founders, 76, 117 *n.*, 251, 295 *n.*, 297, 312
  bishops as, 76
  chancellors of England as, 76, 76 *n.*
  kings as, 76
  list of, 150
  nationality of, 150
  what constitutes, 117 *n.*
  women, 76
Franciscan friary, 21
  readers in Divinity, 21

General Index

Franciscans, 21, 25, 26, 27, 38, 91 *n.*, 293
  at Cambridge, 6 *n.*, 21, 25 *n.*, 33, 73, 73 *n.*, 91, 97, 107, 137, 146, 152, 273
  orders of, 23
  of Waterbeach, 25 *n.*
Free school lane, 78
Free trade, 269
French influence in Cambridge, 69, 109, 152
Freshmen, 159
Friars at Cambridge, 19, 205 *n.*, 307 *n.*
  dissensions with university, 26
  gate, 102 *n.*
  rôle of the, 26
Frideswide, S., Oxford, 30 *n.*, 31, 40 *n.*
Fuller, cited, 5 *n.*, 16 *n.*, 47 *n.*, 99, 119 *n.*, 120 *n.*-121 *n.*, 126 *n.*, 130, 130 *n.*, 140, 160 *n.*, 165 *n.*, 167 *n.*, 171 *n.*, 173 *n.*, 177 *n.*, 180 *n.*, 204 *n.*
  Prickett-Wright, cited, 165 *n.*

Galleries, college, 110, 125
  musicians', 130, 130 *n.*
Gamlingay, 43 *n.*, 44 *n.*, 147
Gardens, fellows', 66, 70
  master's, 70
  the, at Oxford, 65
Gateways, college, 70, 109 *n.*, **140-41**
"Gating," 225
General Examination, the, 185, 185 *n.*
  "excused the," 187
Geographical studies, 238
Geology, 180 *n.*, 181
  museum of, 181
George I. and Cambridge, 267-8
Germany, Christianised, 1
Gibbs' buildings, 102 *n.*
Gilbertines, 19, 22, 49, 57, 91, 227, 319 *n.*
  of Chiksand, 19 *n.*
  a double order, 19 *n.*
Giles, S., canons of, *see Barnwell*
  church of, 17, 90, 101 *n.*, 292, 318
  parish of, 130, 247
Girton College, 148, 313, 315, 316, **317-324**, 325 *n.*, 326, 326 *n.*, 327 *n.*, 328, 330, 341, 343, 345, 348, 350, 352, 357 *n.*, 359, 360
  first committees, 317 *n.*, 318 *n.*
Gisborne buildings, 57

Glasgow, 259
Glomerels, 14, 15, 16, 165 *n.*, 218 *n.*
Glomeriae, vicus, 15 *n.*
Glomeriaus, clers, 15
Glomery Lane, 15 *n.*
Glomery, master of, 14, 164 *n.*, 165 *n.*, 207 *n.*, 208
  school of, 14-16, 164, 164 *n.*
God's House, 25 *n.*, 90, 101, 117, 117 *n.*, 119, 150, 153, 154, 165 *n.*
Gogmagogs, 6
Golden ages of the university, 87
Gonville Hall, 24 *n.*, 50, 67, **77-78**, 78 *n.*, 79 *n.*, 86 *n.*, 87, 89, 94 *n.*, 106 *n.*, 141, 143, 144, 150, 152, 154, 176 *n.*, 296, 325
  chapel, 109 *n.*
  court, 143
Gonville and Caius, *see Caius*
"Graces," 205
  the three, in 1881, 347, 350, 354
Graduate, 52, 158, 195, 229 *n.*
Grammar at Cambridge, 14, 15, 119, 153, 164-5, 165 *n.*, 185 *n.*, 217 *n.*, 218 *n.*
  degrees in, 164-165
  schools, 27, 228, 245
Granta, 5, 5 *n.*, 6, 7, 7 *n.*, 9
Grantabrigge, 5, 7
Grantanus, 20 *n.*
Grantchester, 5, 5 *n.*, 6, 7, 8 *n.*, 10, 10 *n.*, 43, 89, 326, 326 *n.*, 337
Gratian banished the schools, 167
Greek, in Cambridge, 170, **173-175**, 175-176, 179, 180, 182, 210 *n.*, 322 *n.*
  College, Rome, 230
  compulsory, 189
  gospel, in examinations, 185 *n.*, 186 *n.*, 194 *n.*
  and Italy, 172, 173, 173 *n.*, 176 *n.*
  and Oxford, 174 *n.*-176 *n.*
  plays, 239
  printing in England, 99
  pronunciation of, 177 *n.*
  regius professorship, 190, 191
  revivers of, 174 *n.*-175 *n.*
  "scholars" at Pembroke, 175 *n.*
Green, J. R., cited, 258, 258 *n.*
Greencroft, 90
Gregory VII., 248
Gregory's (S.) Hospital, Canterbury, 18 *n.*
Greyfriars, *see Franciscans*

Guant, 7, 7 *n.*
Guild of the Annunciation, 79 *n.*
 Blessed Virgin or S. Mary, 81, 85,
  132, 153, 325
 Corpus Christi, 80, 85, 153, 325
 Holy Trinity, 79 *n.*
Guildhall chapel, 103
Guilds, 80, 81, 86 *n.*, 87 *n.*, 150, 207,
 208
"Gyp," the college, 234

Haddon Hall, 70, 110, 110 *n.*, 296
Hall, the college, 59, 69, 70, 71
Hallam, cited, 121 *n.*
"Halls," 221, 224, 234, 235
Harrow school, 106 *n.*, 283
Haslyngfeld, 24 *n.*
Hat fellow-commoners, 230
Hatcher's *Hist. of Salisbury*, cited, 151 *n.*
"Heads" of colleges, 195, 208, 210,
 212, 223 *n.*
 marriage of, 211-12 (*and see Lodge,
  the Master's*)
 powers of, 205, 210
Hebrew, Regius professorship, 190, 191
Helyg, 10
Henney, 24 *n.*
 Lane, 79 *n.*
Henry III.'s rescripts, cited, 33-34, 34 *n.*,
 35, 46 *n.*, 151 *n.*, 203, 222
Henry VI., charter of, cited, 73 *n.*
Henry VIII., portrait of, at Trinity
 Lodge, 136 *n.*
Heraldry at Cambridge, 103 *n.*-104 *n.*,
 125
Hertfordshire, 7
High Commission, 265
High Steward, 206, 206 *n.*
High Street, 64, 66, 78, 89
Higher Education of Women, Associa-
 tion for the, 337
Higher Local Examination, 315, 326,
 328
Hills Road, 148
"Hind and Panther," Dryden's, 305
Historia Croylandensis, 13 *n.*
Historical Tripos, 238, 238 *n.*
Historiola Cantabrigiae, 20
Hitcham building, *see Pembroke*
Hitchin, 19, 317 *n.*, 318, 319 *n.*, 321,
 326, 328
Hobbism, 289

'Hobson's choice,' 215 *n.*
Homer MS. at Corpus, 84
Honorary degrees, *see degrees*
Honours degree, 104, 161, 184, 185
 examination for, 185 *n.*, 187 *n.*, 188 *n.*
Hoods, academic, 158-9, 213, 226, 226 *n.*,
 227 *n.*, 228
Hospitia locanda, 47, 51 *n.*, 63
Hostel, the, 25 *n.*, 47, **48-51**, 63, 148,
 217 *n.*, 227
 Austin's or Augustine's (S.), 25 *n.*,
  49, 50, 50 *n.*, 89, 102 *n.*
 S. Bernard's, 49, 50, 83
 Bolton's, 72
 Borden's, 49
 Crouched, 24, 25 *n.*, 49, 49 *n.*, 63,
  90, 133
 S. Edmund's, 19, 49
 Ely, 26, 49, 79, 127, 128 *n.*
 Garrett's or Gerard's, 90, 95 *n.*, 133,
  138
 S. Gregory's, 63, 133
 Harleston, 49
 Holy Cross, *see Crouched*
 Jesu, 49, 57
 S. John's, 49
 S. Margaret's, 133, 293
 S. Mary's, 49, 50, 81 *n.*, 83, 275 *n.*
 Monks', 49, 127, 128, 128 *n.*, 129,
  143, 144 *n.*
 Newmarket, 49
 S. Nicholas, 25 *n.*
 Physwick, 49, 50, 133, 141
 principal of a, 48, 51 *n.*
 scholar-principal of a, 51 *n.*
 Rud's, 49
 S. Thomas's, 50, 72
 Trinity, 50
 Tyled, 133
 University, 70, 71, 72
Hostels, catholic, 149
 denominational, 148
 jurists', 50, 154
 number of, 50, 90, 148
 Peterhouse, 49, 56, 57, 58, 89
 statutes relating to, 51 *n.*
Hulsean lecture, 192 *n.*
Hundred, 8 *n.*
Hundred Rolls, 6 *n.*, 16 *n.*, 24 *n.*, 25 *n.*,
 35 *n.*, 39 *n.*, 41, 42 *n.*, 43, 43 *n.*, 44,
 44 *n.*, 292, 294, 325
 entries *re* Merton scholars, 41-44

General Index

Hundred Rolls of Oxford, 25 *n.*
Huntingdon, earls of, 36 *n.*, 297 *n.*
   grammar school, 107 *n.*
   Road, 6, 318
Huntingdonshire, 12 *n.*
Hygiene, college, 142-143
Hythe, hythes, 11 *n.*
   Clay, 11 *n.*
   Corn, 11 *n.*, 132
   Dame Nichol's, 11 *n.*
   Flax, 11 *n.*
   Salt, 11 *n.*

Incorporation in Cambridge University,
   193, 193 *n.*, 194
Independence, declaration of, 268
Independents, 277-78
Index Monasticus, 44 *n.*
Indian civil service board, 237
   languages, 182
Indulgence, declaration of, 266, 266 *n.*
"In Memoriam," 139
Inns, 48, 50
"Installation Ode," cited, 56
Ipswich, 93
Ireland and the Irish, 4, 37, 64 *n.*, 150,
   151, 151 *n.*, 298, 301, 319 *n.*
Irish 'Home Rule,' 269
Isis, 9, 9 *n.*
Islands voyage, 282
Italian, early study of, 182

Jacobitism, 267
James II. and the University, 265,
   266
Jerome's four gospels, 84
Jessopp, Dr., cited, 10 *n.*
Jesus College, 115-117, 150, 153, 154,
   176 *n.*, 235 *n.*, 271, 307, 319 *n.*
   chapel, 109, 116, 116 *n.*, 126
Jewish buildings at Cambridge, 15 *n.*,
   21 *n.*
Jews and Jewish quarter, 9, 9 *n.*, 22
Jocelin of Brakelond, Chronicle of,
   cited, 15 *n.*
John XXII., cited, 35
John of Jerusalem (S.), Order of, at
   Cambridge, 18 *n.*, 24, 25, 25 *n.*, 49
   Baptist (or Zachary) (S.), church of,
   24, 65, 79, 101, 109 *n.*
   parish of, 24 *n.*, 326
   Zachary, London, 150

John's (S.) canons, 18, 22 *n.*, 91, 116 *n.*,
   122
   house, 18, 124, 271
John's (S.) College, 18, 55, 70, 76, 103 *n.*,
   107 *n.*, 110, 114, 120, **121-126**,
   133, 141, 145, 150, 152, 156, 176 *n.*,
   215, 235 *n.*, 246, 271, 274 *n.*, 313 *n.*,
   328 *n.*, 329 *n.*, 338, 338 *n.*, 349
   chapel, 109, 126
   Oxford, 115 *n.*, 143 *n.*
   statutes, 126
John's (S.) Hospital, 18 *n.*, 49, 56, 90,
   122, 124, 127, 132
   Street, 24, 96, 98 *n.*

Keeper or warden, 79 *n.*, 210 *n.*
Kenilworth, defenders of, 307 *n.*
Kent, 2, 42, 151
King's Childer's Lane, 19 *n.*
King's College, 5 *n.*, 16 *n.*, 25 *n.*, 49,
   55, 65 *n.*, 67, 74, 89, **100-106**, 109,
   110, 110 *n.*, 111, 112, 113, 114,
   115 *n.*, 116, 117, 117 *n.*, 133 *n.*, 140,
   147, 150, 152, 153, 154, 156, 176 *n.*,
   184, 210, 217 *n.*, 218 *n.*, 271, 283,
   317, 326, 337, 354 *n.*
   chapel, 52, 89, **102-104**, 107, 109,
   137
   old court of, 102 *n.*
   original design for, 101 *n.*, 102 *n.*
   old gate of, 102 *n.*
   provost of, 101 *n.*, 107
   scholars, 37
      „ privileges of, 104 *n.*
   statutes, 101 *n.*, 164 *n.*, 218 *n.*
King's ditch, 143
   Mill, 11 *n.*, 97 *n.*, 326
   scholars, 131
   school, Canterbury, 106 *n.*
King's Hall, 5 *n.*, 6 *n.*, 19 *n.*, 65 *n.*, 67,
   68, 76, 77, 81, 87, 89, 95, 95 *n.*, 106,
   112, 112 *n.*, **131-133**, 131 *n.*, 135 *n.*,
   139, 139 *n.*, 140, 140 *n.*, 141, 150,
   153, 156, 176 *n.*, 217 *n.*, 218 *n.*,
   226 *n.*, 273 *n.*, 293
   chapel, 5 *n.*, 102, 137
   statutes, 95 *n.*, 228 *n.*
   accounts of, cited, 112
Kirk's coffee-house, 215
Knightbridge professorship, 190
Knights of Malta, *see S. John, Order
   of*

Cambridge

Laboratories, scientific, 98 *n.*, 181, 237, 329 *n.*, 338
Lady Margaret professorships, 120, 190, 191
Lambeth degrees, 192-194, 308
"articles," 274
Lancaster, duchy of, 298
dukes and earls of, 89 *n.*, 297 *n.*
house of, 262, 297 *n.*, 299
"*Lancastrian Chronicle*," 59
Lancastrians at Cambridge, 60, 261
Languages, modern, 181-2
oriental, 182
Latimer-Neville scholarships, 106 *n.*
Latin, 176, 181, 182
grace in hall, 176
professorship, 338 *n.*
pronunciation, 176 *n.*-177 *n.*
Latitudinarianism, 278, 284, 284 *n.*, 285, 289
Law, study of, 79, 119, 153, 154, 166, 167, 242
civil and canon, 153, 167, 167 *n.*, 208
„ schools of, 97, 98, 98 *n.*
tripos, 168, 169, 238 *n.*
Lawyers in Cambridge, 80, 242, 260
"*Lay of Horatius*," parodied, 349, 349 *n.*
Lazars, *see S. Anne's Hermitage for*
Lecture, the, 189-190
Lectures, 208, 231, 233, 329 *n.*
Lecturers, college, 210, 211
university, 192
"*Legend of Good Women*," mentioned, 57
Leicester, earls of, 42 *n.*, 297, 297 *n.*
Le Neve, cited, 16 *n.*
Leonard's (S.) of Stratford le Bow, nuns of, 23, 96
Lepers, S. Magdalene's Hospital for, 23
Lewes, 143
Lewis collection, 83
Liberalism, Manchester school of, 269
Libraries, college, 138 *n.*
Library, the 'old' or 'great,' 97, 98 *n.*
chancellor's, 97, 98, 98 *n.*
Bishop Andrewes', 75
Bishop Moore's, 268
university, 97, **98-99**, 98 *n.*, 155, 231
Librarian, college, 211
university, 207
Licensed lodgings, 224, 225
Lichfield, 140
bishop of (1670), 138

Lincoln, 140
bishops of, 101, 101 *n.*, 203
register of bishops of, 68
diocese, 12 *n.*
shire, 12 *n.*
Lists, classification of candidates in, 189
Literature and the university, 255-8
Litlyngton, advowson of, 65 *n.*
Litt.D., 158
"Little-go," 163, 178 *n.*, 183 *n.*, 185 *n.*
Liverpool, 330
Livery stable, the first, 215 *n.*
LL.B., 158, 167, 168
LL.D., 158, 167, 168
LL.M., 158, 167, 168, 169
Local Examinations, University, 314 *n.*, 324 *n.*, 358
Locke's works at the university, 178, 179
Lodge, the primitive master's, 69, 82, 110, 120, 209
evolution of, in the xvi and xix centuries, 110-111, 125, 209
Lodging-house Syndicate, 225 *n.*
Logic, 14 *n.*, 153, 159 *n.*, 165, 178 *n.*, 179, 179 *n.*, 192 *n.*, 210 *n.*
Lollards, 20, 269, 286
'London Gazette,' 214, 258
London university, 360 *n.*
Long Parliament, 277
vacation term, 241
Lowndean, 191
Lucasian, 190, 191
Lucy, S., chapel of, 108
Lurteburgh Lane, 78, 83
Lutheranism, 272, 275, 276
"*Lycidas*," 119
Lydgate, cited, 7 *n.*, 88 *n.*

M.A., 158, 161, 169, 183, 184, 206, 217, 230 *n.*
Macaulay, cited, 243
Mace, bedells', 208 *n.*
Magdalene College, 76, 106 *n.*, **127-131**, 150, 156 *n.*, 296
Magdalen College, Oxford, 156, 266
Magister, 161
scholarium, 15 *n.*, 39
Malden manor, 39, 40, 41, 44, 44 *n.*, 45
Mandate, royal, *see degrees*
Manfield, Wm. de, deed of, cited, 39 *n.*

General Index

Margaret, *see Lady Margaret*
  S., of Montefiascone, 109, 112 *n.*
Market Hill, 237
Marlborough school, 107 *n.*
Marshal, university, 207
Martyrs, the Cambridge, 272, 275 *n.*, 278
Mary, portrait of, 136 *n.*
Mary's, Great S., 15 *n.*, 21, 78, 81, 89,
    107, 140, 140 *n.*, 155, 160, 161 *n.*,
    169, 185 *n.*, 231, 340
  Guild, 80, 81 *n.*, 87 *n.*
  Hall, 81 *n.*
  Hospital, 32
  parish of, 22
Mary's, Little S., 57, 58, 61, 74 *n.*, 348
Massachusetts, 262, 277
Master of Arts, 27, 38 *n.*, 99, 158, **160-
161**, 169, 217, 228, 230 *n.*
Master, the, 203, **208-9**
  election of, 107
Mathematical method, 170-171, 177
  tripos, 167, **170-2**, 184, 238 *n.*
Mathematics, 164 *n.*, 170, 171 *n.*, 177,
  178, 179, 184
Matriculation, 154
'Mayflower,' the, 262, 278
May term, 31, 235, 239
"Mays," the, 183 *n.*
M.B., 158, 168, 168 *n.*
M.C., 158
M.D., 158
Mechanical Sciences tripos, 183, 238 *n.*
Medical degree, 167, 168, 168 *n.*
  jurisprudence, lecturer in, 192
  school, new, 181
Medicine, study of, 119, 153, 154, 166,
  167, 175 *n.*, 180, 237, 242
  school of, 98
Medieval and Modern Languages tripos,
  183, 238 *n.*
Members of the university, number of,
  206, 246 *n.*
Mental philosophy, *see philosophy*
Merchant adventurers, 144, 242, 282,
  330
  Taylors' school, 106 *n.*, 283, 354 *n.*
Mercia, 12 *n.*
Merton, 39, 44 *n.*
  brethren of, 39, 44
  Clerici de, 34 *n.*, 42, 42 *n.*
  College, Oxford, 40, 41, 43, 43 *n.*,
    45 *n.*, 108, 125

Merton estate, 39
  Hall, 90, 327
  house of, 41, 44, 45, 90
  prior of, 44, 44 *n.*
  priory, 40, 44 *n.*
  scholars, 6 *n.*, 34 *n.*, 37, 39, 39 *n.*, 40,
    41, 42, 42 *n.*, 43, 44, 45, 116 *n.*,
    233, 292, 298, 325
  scholars, Oxford, 40, 41, 43, 43 *n.*, 45
  statutes, 44 *n.*, 67, 68
    ,, cited, 40, 68 *n.*
Metaphysics, 170, 259
  at Cambridge, 170 *n.*-171 *n.*, 177,
    178, 179
Michaelhouse, 16 *n.*, 25 *n.*, **63**, 65 *n.*,
  67, 68, 77, 78 *n.*, 89, 120, 133,
  140, 150, 153, 154, 176 *n.*, 217 *n.*,
  235 *n.*
  book, 68
  statutes of, 29
Michael's (S.) church, 140, 150
  rectory house, 24 *n.*
Middle class, effect on university of
  growth of, 242
Migrating students, 130 *n.*
Mildenhall, 15 *n.*, 16 *n.*, 137, 261
Mill Lane, 100
  (Milne) Street, 11 *n.*, 20, 24, 24 *n.*,
    25 *n.*, 49, 89, 100, 101, 101 *n.*,
    133 *n.*, 326
"*Miller's Tale*," 11, 93
Mills, 11 *n.*, 97 *n.*, 326, 327
Mirmaud-at-Welle, Isle of Ely, 19 *n.*
Moderators, 163 *n.*, 183
Modern History, Regius of, 99, 192
Modern subjects at Cambridge, 198, 201,
  238
Monks at Cambridge, 16, 25-6, 27, 29,
  127-8, 143, 144 *n.*
Montfort, de, parliament of, 307 *n.*
Montpellier, 167
Moral Philosophy, professorship, 190
Moral Sciences tripos, 177-179, 187 *n.*-
  189 *n.*, 290, 356-7
Mullinger, *Hist. Univ.*, cited, 51 *n.*, 68,
  235 *n.*
Muniment room (or treasury), 70, 70 *n.*,
  141
Museums, new, 22
Mus.B., 158
Mus.D., 158
Mus.M., 158

Cambridge

Names, Cambridge, 292-5, 302-8
"Nation," 208
"*Nativity*," Milton's "*Hymn to the*," 119
Natural Sciences tripos, 168, 168 *n.*, 179, 181, 182, 238, 238 *n.*
Navigators, early, 282
Neo-Platonism, 290
Nevile's Court, 137
New College, Oxford, 102 *n.*, 104 *n.*, 105 *n.*, 156, 176 *n.*, 240
New England, 224, 263
New learning, the, 133, 270, 281, 282, 313 *n.*
  men of, 270, 273, 281
Newnham, 20, 324, 325, 325 *n.*, 326
  College, 148, 313, 315, 316, 321 *n.*, **324**, 327, 332, 337, 359, 360
  College Association, 337
  Hall, 327, 337, 337 *n.*, 338, 345
  Hall Company, 337, 337 *n.*
  Lane, 326, 326 *n.*
  Mill, 11 *n.*, 326, 327
"*New Sect of Latitude-men*," quoted, 245
Newspapers, 214, 215, 258, 258 *n.*
Newton, statue of, 137
Newton's works at the University, 170, 171, 179
Non-collegiate students, 220, 246
Nonconformists at Cambridge, 149, 247
Nonjurors, 267
Non-Regent, 161, 161 *n.*
Norfolk, 6, 44 *n.*
  and Cambridge, 77, 80, 106 *n.*, 144
  canons, *see Westacre*
  French of, 90
  litigants, 80
Norman houses, 15 *n.*, 90
  town, the, 90, 91, 122
Normans, 17, 150, 152
Norrisian professorship, 191
Northampton, 46, 46 *n.*
  chapter, 128 *n.*
  S. Peter's, 140 *n.*
  shire, 150, 152
  university, 45, 46, 46 *n.*, 160 *n.*
Northern Christianity, 1
North of England Council of Education, 326, 328
Northumbria, 1, 2, 311 *n.*
Norwich, 16 *n.*, 23, 75, 79 *n.*, 91, 140, 141, 150, 151, 152, 341
  monks, 27, 91, 128 *n.*, 143

Norwich priory, 27, 143, 143 *n.*
  school, 26, 106 *n.*, 245

Observatory, 155
Opponencies, 159, 176
Ordinary degree, the, 161, 184, 317
  examinations for, 185 *n.*-186 *n.*
  " allowed the," 186
Organs in college chapels, 109 *n.*
Oriel College, Oxford, 18 *n.*
Orleans, 12, 13, 14, 16, 16 *n.*, 92, 165 *n.*, 166
  school of, 12, 13, 15
Ostia, titular bishop of, 307 *n.*
'Our-Lady' friars, 23, 91
Ouse, the, 7, 7 *n.*, 9, 310
Over-Merton, 44 *n.*
Oving's Inn, 50, 90, 133
Oxford, 9, 10 *n.*, 11, 13 *n.*, 15 *n.*, 27, 30, 31, 34, 35, 36, 38, 39, 40, 41, 43, 44, 45, 46 *n.*, 68 *n.*, 72, 74, 93, 100, 100 *n.*, 101, 106, 108, 115 *n.*, 117 *n.*, 120, 125, 128 *n.*, 136 *n.*, 143 *n.*, 156, 167, 172, 173, 173 *n.*, 174 *n.*, 175 *n.*, 176 *n.*, 183, 194, 207, 207 *n.*, 215, 218 *n.*, 228 *n.*, 236, 237, 238, 240, 245, 247, 252, 256, 259, 263, 264, 265, 266, 267, 268, 269, 271, 272, 275, 279, 280, 282, 283, 284, 288, 322 *n.*, 359, 359 *n.*
  " brethren," 272
  charter, 34 *n.*
  depleted in 1209, 33
  friars at, 26
  " martyrs," 275

Padua, 92, 141, 174 *n.*, 228
Paley's " *Evidences*," 178, 178 *n.*
Papal bulls, 28, 28 *n.*, 29
  forged, 34 *n.*
" *Paradise Lost* " MS., 138
Paris, Matthew, cited, 23 *n.*, 33 *n.*, 55 *n.*
Paris, 16, 92
  students at Cambridge, 33
  university, 35, 38, 166, 176 *n.*, 254, 284
Parish churches and the colleges, 56, 65, 71, 79, 82, 83, 108
Parliament and the Stuarts, 73, 263, 264
  and the university, 145, 264, 264 *n.*
Parliamentary suffrage, 206, 206 *n.*
Parliaments at Cambridge, 8 *n.*, 112 *n.*

General Index

Paston in Norfolk, 25 n.
Pato, moniales de, 25 n.
Patterne, Sir Willoughby, 315
Paul's (S.) Inn, 50
  School, 86, 106 n., 283
Pavia, 92
Peacock, Geo., dean of Ely, cited, 165 n.
Peasants' revolt, 84, 261
Peers, 195, 218, 229, 232 n., 309
Pembrochiana, aula, 69
Pembroke College, 56, 65 n., 67, 69, 70, 76, 77, 81, 84, 87, 95, 95 n., 100, 106 n., 108, 142, 150, 152, 153, 176 n., 189 n., 217 n., 246, 275, 293, 312, 320
  chapel, 72, 109
  fellowships, 152, 152 n.
  Hitcham building, 72
  statutes of, cited, 152 n., 153 n.
Pembroke, earls of, 69, 297, 297 n., 298, 299
Penitentiae Jesu, de, friars, 22
Pensioners, 52, 217 n., 218, 220, 226 n., 229 n., 232 n.
  number of, in 1574, 217 n.
Pepysian library, 130
Perendinant, 217 n.
Pernare, 60
Peter of Blois, cited, 14, 14 n.
Peterborough, 12, 12 n., 140
  bishopric of, 12
  psalter, 84
  see of, 12 n.
Peterhouse, 16 n., 19, 28 n., 45 n., 49, 55, 64, 65 n., 67, 69, 74 n., 76, 77, 89, 90, 107 n., 108 n., 122, 123, 137, 150, 153, 156 n., 167, 176 n., 183 n., 184, 217 n., 218 n., 227, 262, 271, 294, 302, 326, 328
  chapel, 73
  library, 56, 58
  scholars, 62 n.
  statutes, 29
    ,, cited, 235
  stone parlour, 57 n.
Peter Lombard, 167
Peter's (S.) church, 56, 58, 90
  college, *see Peterhouse*
  parish, 23
Petrarch, 182
Pfeiffer buildings, 338
Philanthropy, 269

Philology, 192
Philosophy at Cambridge, 145, 170, 170 n., 177-179, 185, 189, 190, 191, 192 n., 285-290
  school of, 154
Physics, Linacre lecture, 125
Physic, Regius of, 168, 190, 191
Physiology, 180, 181
Pileum, 230 n.
Pilgrim fathers, 262, 278
Pits, John, cited, 20 n.
Pitt Press, the, 99-100
Plague, the, *see Black Death*
Plate, the university, sent to Charles, 263
Plato, 289, 290
Platonists, Cambridge, 145, 277, 284-290
Plumian professorship, 191
Pluralists and the universities, 63
Poets, the, 255
Politics at Cambridge, modern, 268-269
"Poll" degree, 184, 184 n.
Pollard willows, 11 n.
Pope, the, and university degrees, 192, 193, 193 n.
Portraits, college, 136 n.
Preachership, 120
Prelates, great Cambridge, 259
Pre-Reformation Reformers, 120, 270
Presbyterianism in Cambridge, 149, 265, 276-277, 287
President, 210
  of Queen's, 110
Previous Examination, 165 n., 168, 185, 185 n., 189, 316, 321, 339
Principal, 48, 51 n., 210 n., 339 n.
Printing in Cambridge, 99-100
Proctor, 117 n., 210 n.
Proctors, 183, 206, 207 n., 223, 237
  courts, 97
  fines, 154
Professor, 158
Professorships, 179 n., 180 n., 190-192, 192 n.
Pro-proctors, 206
Protestant college, first, 146
Protestantism, 60 n., 144, 146, 270, 272, 275, 285, 287, 288, 290
Provost, 210
Psychology, 177-8, 179
Public orator, 175 n., 207, 207 n.

Public schools, 218, 221, 223, 245
connected with the university, 106 n.
Greek at, 173
Puritan college, first, 145
commissioners, 60 n.
Puritans, 22, 116, 145, 179, 263, 264, 276, 277, 286, 287, 288, 314
Pythagoras, 288
'school of,' 39, 122

Quadrangle, see court and schools
Quadrivium, 153, 164
Queen's College, 49, 64, 70, 74 n., 76, 101, 102 n., 109-112, 113, 114, 115, 123, 125, 140, 150, 152, 153, 156 n., 170 n., 176 n., 210, 221, 262, 263 n., 264, 282, 296, 313, 313 n., 326, 329 n.
statutes, 112 n.
Oxford, 87
Queens, English, and the university, 112 n., 113, 114
Queens' Lane, 100, 102 n.
Questionist, 159
Quick professorship, 192

Ramsey, 12 n., 128, 137, 143
Readers, 192
Reading, Berks., 46, 318 n.
Rector, 101 n., 210 n.
Recruiting grounds of the university, 245-246
Red-brick buildings, 110
"Reeve's Tale," 89, 93, 95
Reform Bill, the, 268, 269
Reformers and Cambridge, 153, 269-271, 272, 274, 274 n., 275
early, 270, 276
later, 271-272
Regent master, 14, 50, 160, 161 n., 162 n., 207 n.
and non-regent houses, 97, 98, 205 n.
'Regicides,' 264, 265
Registrary, university, 100, 207
Registry, university, 155
MSS. cited, 89 n., 94 n.
Religion at Cambridge, 246-247
Religious Orders in Cambridge, 16-27, 29, 91
Renascence, 92, 131, 281-283
Residence obligatory, 185
Responsions and opponencies, 159

Restoration, the, and the university, 265
Revival of learning temp. Ed. IV., 112
Rhadegund, S., nunnery of, 16, 18, 90, 91, 116 n., 151 n.
Rhee, 7 n.
Rhetoric, 166, 210 n.
Rhodes, 176 n.
Ridley Hall, 145, 148
"Ridley's walk," 75
Ritualistic movement at Cambridge, early, 59, 145, 280
River, 6-7, 7 n., 9-10, 11 n., 233
Roman remains, 10 n., 318
Rome, 1, 2, 3, 4, 5, 6, 8, 176 n., 192, 193, 193 n., 205 n.
Romites in Cambridge, 22 n., 325
Roscellinus, 32
Roundheads at Cambridge, 264
Royal Exchange, 144
Injunctions, 151, 167 n., 176 n.
Society, 265, 283-284, 324
supremacy, 121, 167 n., 276
Rugby school, 283, 296
"Rustication," 225
Rutebeuf, the troubadour, cited, 15, 161 n.
Rye House plot, 265

Sack, friars, 22, 23, 49, 109 n.
Saffron Walden, 151
Salisbury, 46, 151
Sanitation, diploma in, 238
Sawston, 5 n.
Saxon nuns, 312
schools, 3, 3 n., 4, 4 n.
town, the, 83, 89, 91, 96
Saxons, 3, 96
Scapular of Mount Carmel, 20
"Scarlet days," 240, 241 n.
Sc.D., 158
Scholar-fellow, 93, 217 n.
Scholar-principal, 5 n.
Scholars, 14, 34 n., 53, 54, 217, 217 n.
age of, 95, 95 n.
dress of, 226-231
early list of, 48, 139 n.
Hall of, 63
house of, 63
Lane, 24
major and minor, of Pembroke, 95, 217 n.
and masters, 46, 53, 233 n.

General Index

Scholars, poor, 39, 40, 47 n., 52, 62 n., 66, 92, 218 n., 220
secular, 30, 38, 122
Scholarships, extra collegiate, 241
tied, 106 n.
School Hall Street, Bury, 15 n.
School Street, 15 n., 24, 96
"Schoolmaster," the, 283
Schoolmasters, famous Cambridge, 283, 354 n.
Schools, 27, 76 n., 89, 97, 98 n.
Anglo-Saxon, 1, 3, 3 n., 4, 4 n., 311
Enquiry Commission, 314 n.
monastic, 30 n.
new, of Philosophy and Law, 97, 154
pre-university, 14, 30, 166
quadrangle, 24, 25, 76 n., 89, 98, 133 n., 154
see civil law and divinity
Science and Cambridge, 14, 153, 154, 179, 180, 192 n., 290-291
revival of, at Restoration, 180
Scientists, eminent, 255, 290-291
S.C.L., 182 n.
Scotch universities, 360 n.
Scotland, 37, 61, 151, 151 n.
Scottish Church, the, 2
Scroope Terrace, 57, 325
Seaham, 3
Sects, growth of, in the xviith c., 286
Selwyn College, 148
Seminaries, clerical, 29
Semitic languages, 182
Senate, the, 194, 205
council of, 205, 205 n., 321 n.
numbers of, 206, 321 n.
Senate House, the, 100, 107, 155, 163, 183, 206, 233, 348, 359
Sepulchre's, S., 90
Seven arts, the, 153
Sex viri, 206
Shakespeare and Cambridge men. 295-6
Shakespeare, cited, 295-6, 297 n., 307
"Shepherd's Calendar," 74
Sheriff of Cambridge, 36 n.
of Huntingdon, 36 n.
Shrewsbury School, 107 n.
Sidney Street, 21
Sidney Sussex College, 76, 146, 151, 152, 307 n.
Sidgwick Hall, 337
Silver St., 326

Singing taught at Clare, 153
Sixtus IV., Bull of, cited, 143 n., 144 n.
Sizar, 62 n., 74 n., 217 n., 218, 219, 219 n.
Skeat, W. W., cited, 7 n., 164
Slave trade and slavery, 269
Solarium, 58, 66 n., 69, 82
Soler, 66 n.
Hall, 66, 95, 95 n.
Sonneteers, 256 n.
Sophister, 159, 160 n., 171 n.
Sophisters' school, 97, 183
Sophistry, 159 n., 217 n.
Soprana, 230
South and North riots, 34 n., 44 n., 45
Special examinations, the, 185, 186 n.
Spelman, cited, 165 n.
Spinning House, the, 222
"Sporting one's oak," 236
Sports, university, 236, 238
Staffordshire, 150, 152
Stamford, 46, 47, 150
Stans in quadragesima, 160
Stars and stripes, 61
Statesmen, 260
Stationers' Company, 100 n.
Status pupillaris, 159, 223 n., 225 n., 231, 231 n.
Statuta antiqua, 28 n.
cited, 228 n.
Statutes, cited, 131 n., 164 n., 207 n.
college, 29, 54, 67-8, 222
of Elizabeth, 28 n., 210
of Victoria, 28 n.
Stoke Clare, 293
Stokys, cited, 164 n.
Stone houses in Cambridge, 15 n., 24 n., 39, 78 n., 89
Stour, the, 31
Stourbridge fair, 10, 31, 32, 207 n.
leper hospital, 23
S.T.P., 158
Stratford-le-Bowe, 25
prioress of, 43 n.
Stubbs' Const. Hist., cited, 8 n., 27, 86 n., 87 n.
Students' chambers, 70
"Students" of Christchurch, Oxford, 218 n.
Students, classes of, 14, 165 n., 217-219
migration of, 45, 46, 47
Studies in colleges, 70, 232 n.

393

Cambridge

Studium generale, 30 *n.*, 31, 32, 35, 37, 38, 68, 68 *n.*
Suffolk, 14, 16 *n.*, 22 *n.*, 293, 304
  earls and dukes of, 78, 106, 296, 297, 301
Sunday in Cambridge, 240
Surgery, degrees in, 168 *n.*
Surplice, wearing of the, 240 *n.*

Tancred studentship, 144
Tanner, cited, 117 *n.*
"Tawdry," 215 *n.*
Taxatores, see taxors
Taxors, 33, 48, 51 *n.*
  Court of, 98
Teachers, training of, 335, 354 *n.*
Templars, 24, 25
Tennis courts, 70
Test act, 149, 212, 213 *n.*
"Tetoighty," 209
Thames, 9
Theology, study of, 119, 153, 166, 208, 213, 242
  tripos, 167, 168, 238 *n.*
Thirty-nine Articles, 60, 84, 274
Thorney, 12 *n.*, 294 *n.*
Titular degrees, on whom conferrable, 195
Titles connected with Cambridge, 297, 297 *n.*
Tobacco, introduction of, 282
Tonsure, clerical, 92
Tories, 267
Tower of London, 126, 277
Town and gown, 14, 37, 221, 222 *n.*, 232, 233 *n.*
  lodgings, 14, 33, 47, 48
Tractarians, 280, 281
Treasury, 70 *n.*
Trinity College, 50, 63, 64, 68, 73, 76, 77, 89, 106, 106 *n.*, 113, 116, 123, 130-140, 141, 145, 146, 147, 151, 153, 156, 213 *n.*, 226 *n.*, 229, 231, 246, 282, 293, 308 *n.*, 315, 329 *n.*, 335 *n.*, 342
  Babington rooms at, 302
  Bishop's hostel at, 138
  chapel, 107, 108, 136-7
    „ memorial brasses in, 137
  Entrance Gateway, 36 *n.*, 103 *n.*, 104 *n.*, 133, 136 *n.*, 141
  great court, 134, 136
  Great Gate (Edward's), 131, 132, 140

Trinity College, library, 137-38
  Queen's Gateway, 135
  sedan coach, 136 *n.*
Trinity Hall, 25 *n.*, 64 *n.*, 65 *n.*, 74 *n.*, 76, 77, 78-80, 82, 86 *n.*, 87, 89, 90, 127, 143, 150, 152, 156 *n.*, 176 *n.*
  chapel, 109 *n.*
  library, 79
Trinity, the, dedication to, 25 *n.*
  church, 25 *n.*
  Holy, monks of, at Cambridge, 25 *n.*
    „ of Norwich, 79 *n.*
    „ guild of, 25 *n.*, 79 *n.*
  Street, 96
Tripos, 162-3, 163 *n.*, 200, 238 *n.*
  double, 184
  results, 238 *n.*
  standard variable, 184
Triposes, divided, 185 *n.*, 189, 231, 238 *n.*
  list of, 182
  not conferring a degree, 179, 184, 185 *n.*
  popularity among the, 238 *n.*, 356
Trivium, 153, 164, 164 *n.*, 165 *n.*, 166
'Trojans,' 173, 349 *n.*
"*True Intellectual System*" of Cudworth, 287 *n.*
Trumpington, 7, 7 *n.*, 8 *n.*, 23 *n.*, 93
  Street, 23, 23 *n.*, 57, 62, 86, 91, 96, 100, 327
Tudor architecture, 102-3, 103 *n.*
Tudors, the, and Cambridge, 74, 87, 102-4, 104 *n.*, 131, 133-4, 135, 136-7, 206 *n.*, 281, 297
Tutor, 210, 211, 224, 225-226, 226 *n.*
Tyltey monks, 25 *n.*
  Priory, 24

Ulster, earls of, 293, 295 *n.*, 298, 298 *n.*, 320 *n.*
Undergraduates, 99, 115, 160 *n.*, 206, 217 *n.*, 219, 223, 225, 231-237
  numbers of the, 246, 246 *n.*, 357 *n.*, 358
  entertainments given by, 224 *n.*
Union Society, 239
Unitarianism, 279
Universitas, 30 *n.*, 53, 68 *n.*, 166
University, the, 30, 30 *n.*, 31, 38, 53, 166, 243, 244
  aristocratic period of, 216, 220, 242-3, 244
  "on the boards of," 246 *n.*

General Index

University buildings, 96-100
Calendar, 192 *n*., 195
careers prepared by, 242-244
a chartered corporation, 30, 30 *n*.
charters, 34-35
chest, 155
church, *see Great S. Mary's*
classes frequenting, 241-245
and the Colleges, 52, 154
diplomatists and, *see diplomatists*
discipline, *see discipline*
earliest existing references to, 33
and the education of women, 310, 354
and great Englishmen, 250-260
Extension lectures, 382
first public buildings in, 97
Hall, 64, 77, 89, 144 *n*., 150, 339
idea of a, 197-200
and intellectual movements, 281-291
jurisdiction, 37 *n*.-38 *n*., 222-223, *see also chancellor*
and the kings, *see Henry III.'s rescript, Edward III. and his relation to the university*; and in the index of names of persons under *John, Hen. III., Edw. I., II., and III., Edw. IV.*, etc.
legends of origin of, 3-4
and national movements, 281-291
officials, 203-208
and the popes, 28-9, 35, 78, 78 *n*., 143, 143 *n*.-144 *n*., 144, 193
licensed preachers at, 78 *n*.
precincts, 185, 185 *n*.
press, 155
and the professions, 197, 198, 242, 259-260
and religious movements, 269-281
secular and religious studies at, 26, 28
settlement, 247, 248
statutes, *see statutes*
a *studium generale*, 30 *n*., 31, 32, 35, 37, 38, 68, 68 *n*.
and technical education, 197-198, 201
and the town, *see town officers and, above, jurisdiction*
wealth of, 154
University College, Oxford, 45 *n*., 150 *n*.
Universities Commission, 189
continental, 35, 53, 227 *n*., 228
Uppingham school, 107 *n*.

Valence-Mary College, 64, 69
Vercelli monastery, 140 *n*.
Via Devana, the, 6, 7, 8, 318
Vice-chancellor, 38 *n*., **204-205**, 206, 207, 223, 223 *n*., 225 *n*., 231, 241 *n*., 254
Vicecomes of Cambridgeshire, *see sheriff*
Victoria University, 360 *n*.
Vineyards, Cambridge, 221
Visitation of 1401, 109 *n*., 217 *n*.
Visits of sovereigns to the university, 112-114
Viva voce examinations, 163, 169
'Volunteers' at King's, 184

Walden Abbey, 128, 129, 143, 150
Wales and the Welsh, 150, 151, 151 *n*., 298, 301, 319 *n*., 330
Walsingham, 114, 293
Warden, 79 *n*., 93, 210 *n*.
Ware, Herts, 150
Wareham, 8 *n*.
Washington arms, the, 61
Waterbeach, *see Franciscans*
Wealth of the university, 154
Wesleyanism, 280
Westacre, Norfolk, 143
Westminster Abbey, 100, 103, 103 *n*., 120, 120 *n*., 150
Assembly, 277
College, 149, 151
Whigs, 267, 268
Whitefriars, *see Carmelites*
White Horse Inn, 272
'White nights,' 240 *n*.
Whittington Hospital, 18 *n*.
Whittlesey mere, 303
Winchester school, 102 *n*., 107 *n*., 221
Windsor, 150
"Wilderness" the, at S. John's, 124
Willis, Prof., cited, 95 *n*.
Willis and Clark, cited, 58 *n*., 102 *n*., 110, 115, 123, 130 *n*., 141
"Wine," the, 238
Wisbech school, 107 *n*.
Women, colleges for, at Cambridge, 310, 313, 314
and convents, 315
and education, 312, 313
   ,, pioneer committee for, 314 *n*.
first Cambridge lecturers to, 328*n*., 329*n*.
and the ordinary degree, 117

Cambridge

Women and the Reformation, 314
  subjects of study chosen by, 355-357
  academic successes, 321, 339-40
  university settlement, 342, 344, 352
  university status of, 359, 360 n.
  and the university, 216
Wranglers, 171, 172 n., 322 n.
  senior, 171, 172 n., 189
Wyclif's bible, 138
Wycliffism, 286 (& see Lollards)

Yeoman bedell, see bedell
York, 1, 2, 3, 4, 8, 140, 150, 151, 152,
  330
  School of, 2, 3, 4, 173, 311
York and Lancaster, 112, 262, 292, 296,
  299
Yorkshire, 66, 91, 94, 141, 152, 311
  dialect, 93

Zachary's Inn (S.), 50

THE END

Printed by R. & R. CLARK, LIMITED, *Edinburgh.*